SHINOBU OHTAKA

Master Koha, it's volume 19!

MAGI

Volume 19
Shonen Sunday Edition

Story and Art by
SHINOBU OHTAKA

MAGI Vol.19
by Shinobu OHTAKA
© 2009 Shinobu OHTAKA
All rights reserved.
Original Japanese edition published by SHOGAKUKAN.
English translation rights in the United States of America, Canada, the United Kingdom,
Ireland, Australia and New Zealand arranged with SHOGAKUKAN.

Translation & English Adaptation ◆ John Werry

Touch-up Art & Lettering ◆ Stephen Dutro

Editor ◆ Mike Montesa

Printed in the U.S.A.

Published by VIZ Media, LLC
P.O. Box 77010
San Francisco, CA 94107

10 9 8 7 6 5 4 3 2 1
First printing, August 2016

www.viz.com

MAGI

The labyrinth of magic

19

Story & Art by
SHINOBU OHTAKA

MAGI

The labyrinth of magic

19

CONTENTS

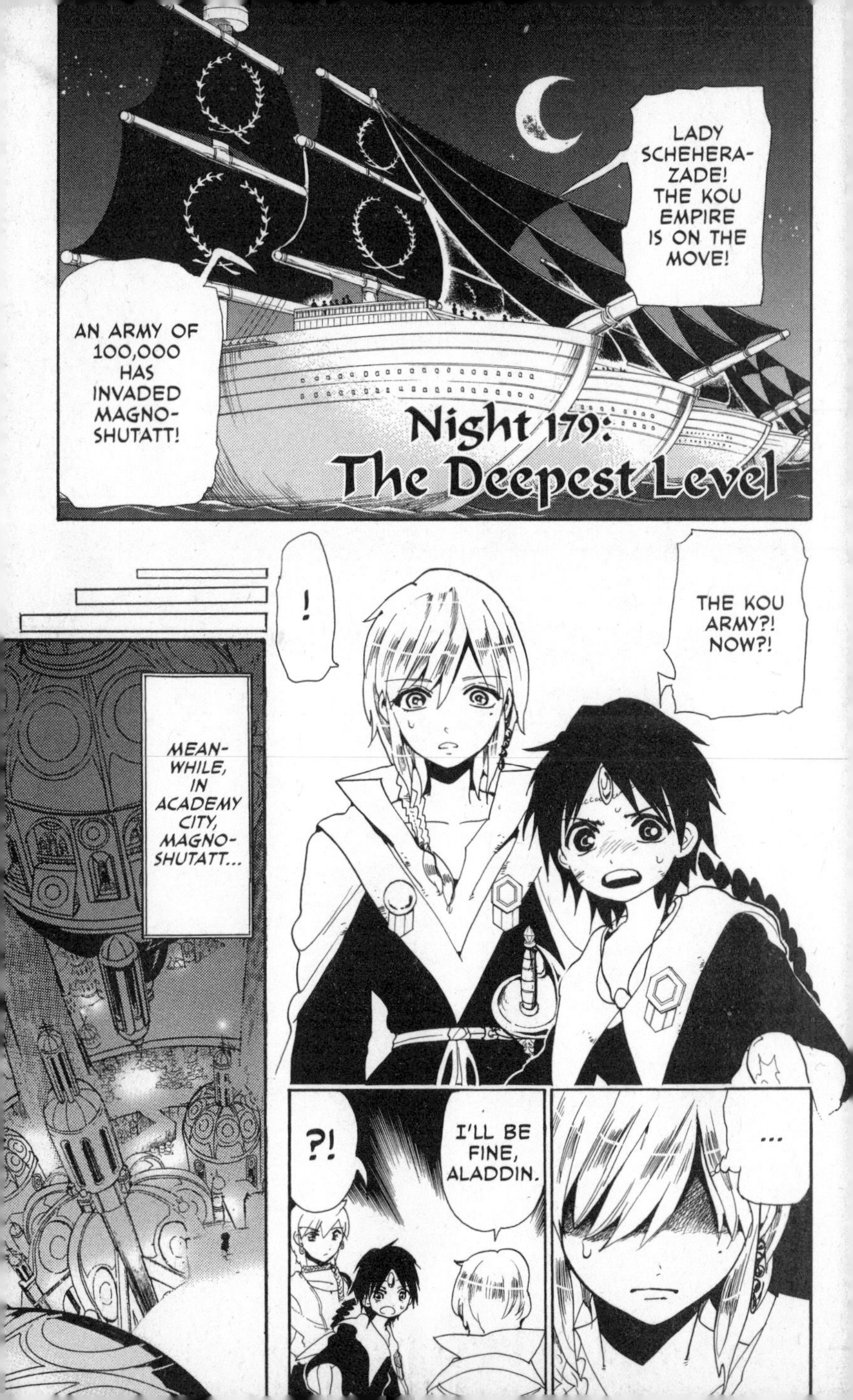
LADY SCHEHERAZADE! THE KOU EMPIRE IS ON THE MOVE!
AN ARMY OF 100,000 HAS INVADED MAGNOSHUTATT!
Night 179: The Deepest Level
THE KOU ARMY?! NOW?!
!
...
I'LL BE FINE, ALADDIN.
?!
MEANWHILE, IN ACADEMY CITY, MAGNOSHUTATT...

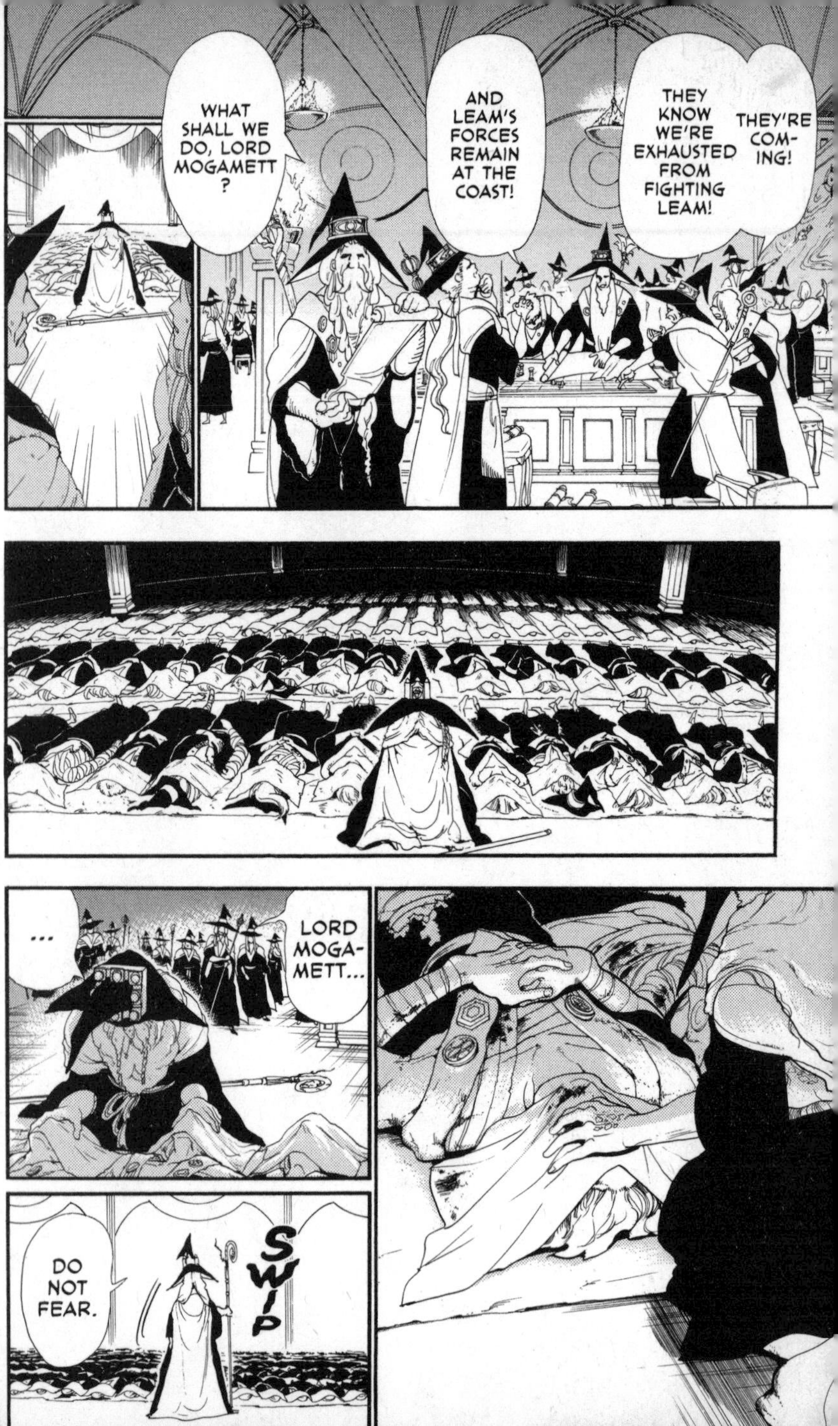
THEY'RE COM-ING!
THEY KNOW WE'RE EXHAUSTED FROM FIGHTING LEAM!
AND LEAM'S FORCES REMAIN AT THE COAST!
WHAT SHALL WE DO, LORD MOGAMETT?
LORD MOGA-METT...
...
SWIP
DO NOT FEAR.

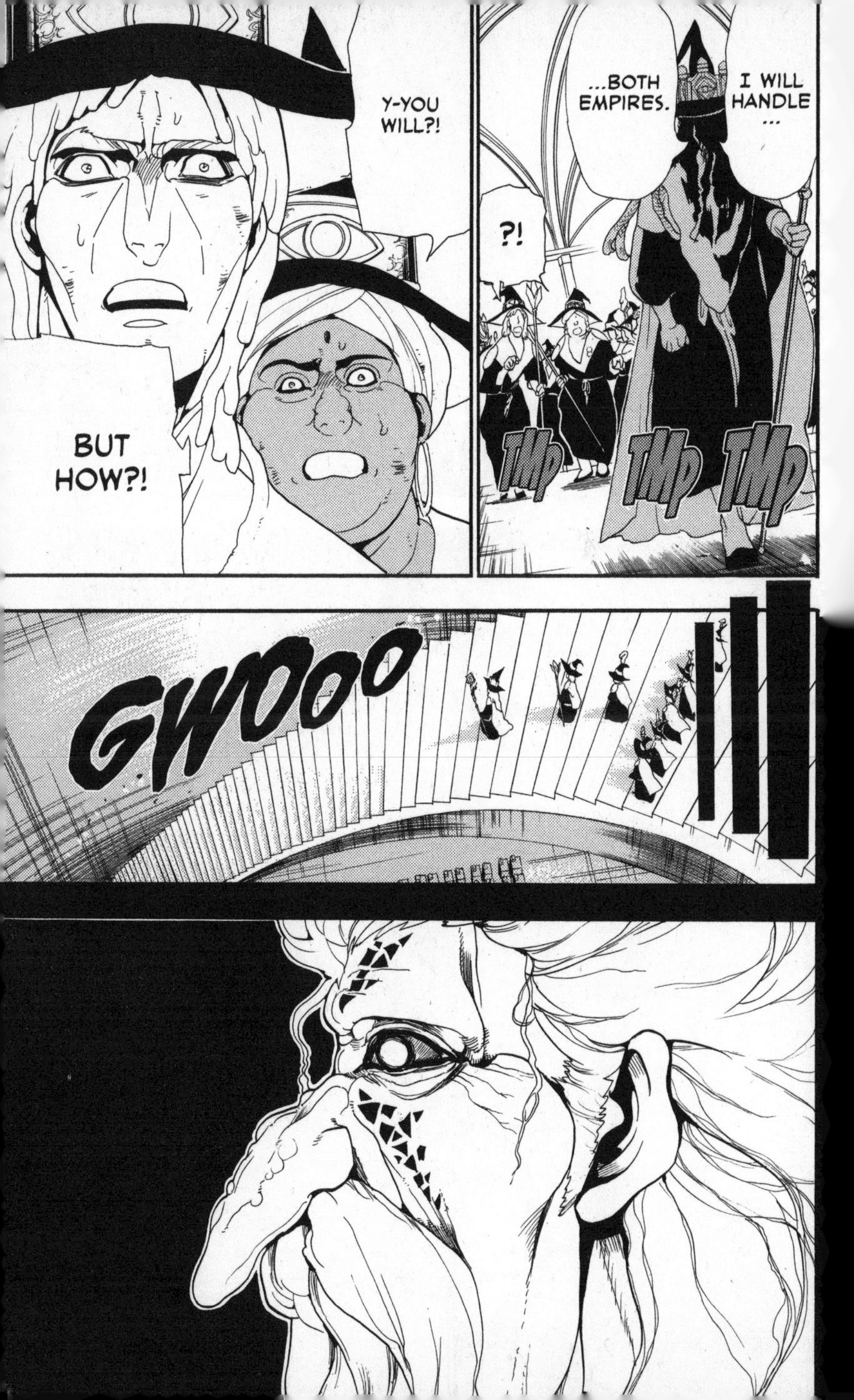
I WILL HANDLE ...
...BOTH EMPIRES.
?!
TMP
TMP
TMP
Y-YOU WILL?!
BUT HOW?!
GWOOO

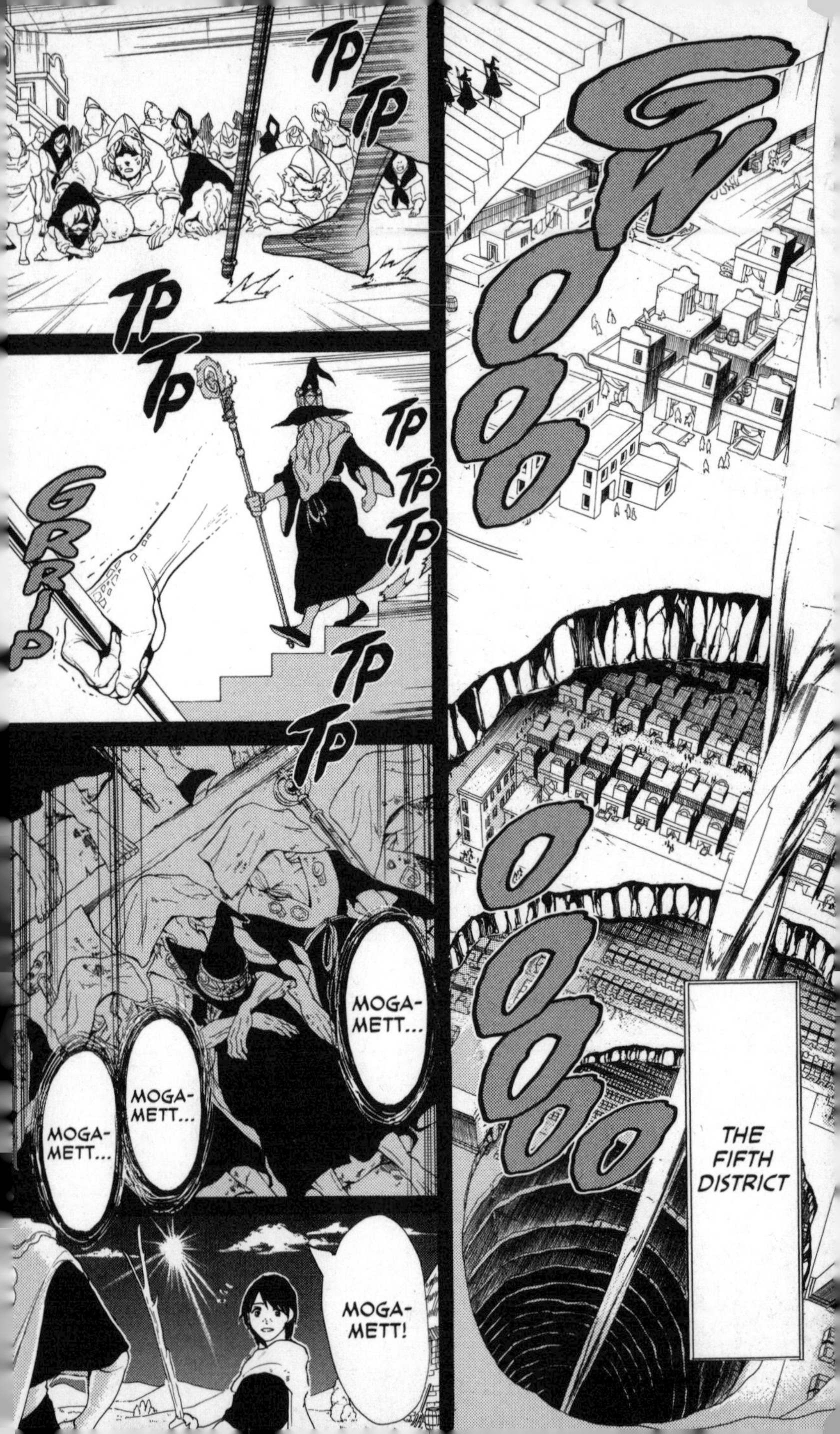
GWOOOOOOOO
THE FIFTH DISTRICT
TP TP
TP TP
TP TP TP
GRRIP
TP TP
MOGA-METT...
MOGA-METT...
MOGA-METT...
MOGA-METT!

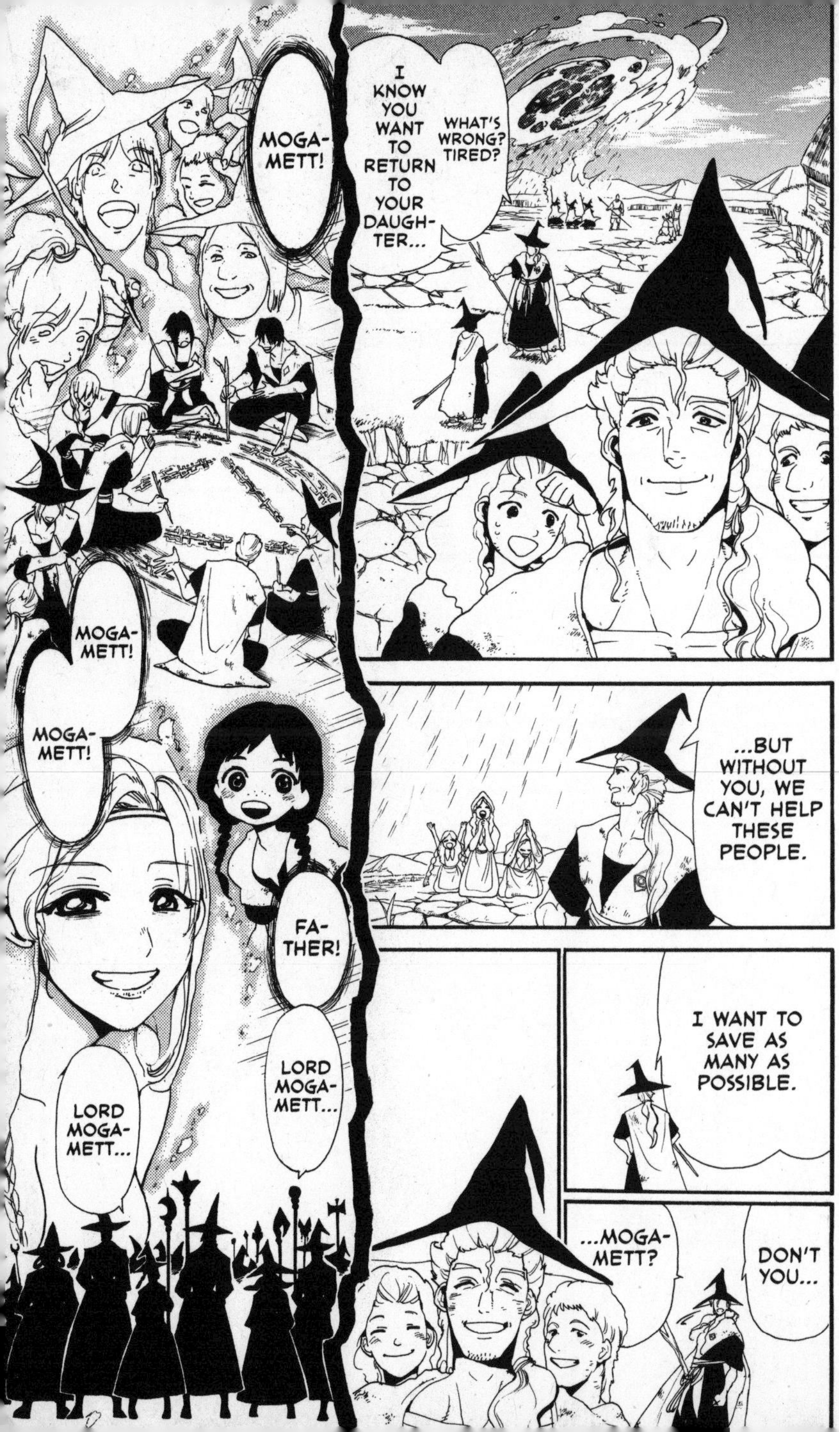
WHAT'S WRONG? TIRED?
I KNOW YOU WANT TO RETURN TO YOUR DAUGHTER...
...BUT WITHOUT YOU, WE CAN'T HELP THESE PEOPLE.
I WANT TO SAVE AS MANY AS POSSIBLE.
DON'T YOU...
...MOGA-METT?
MOGA-METT!
MOGA-METT!
MOGA-METT!
FA-THER!
LORD MOGA-METT...
LORD MOGA-METT...

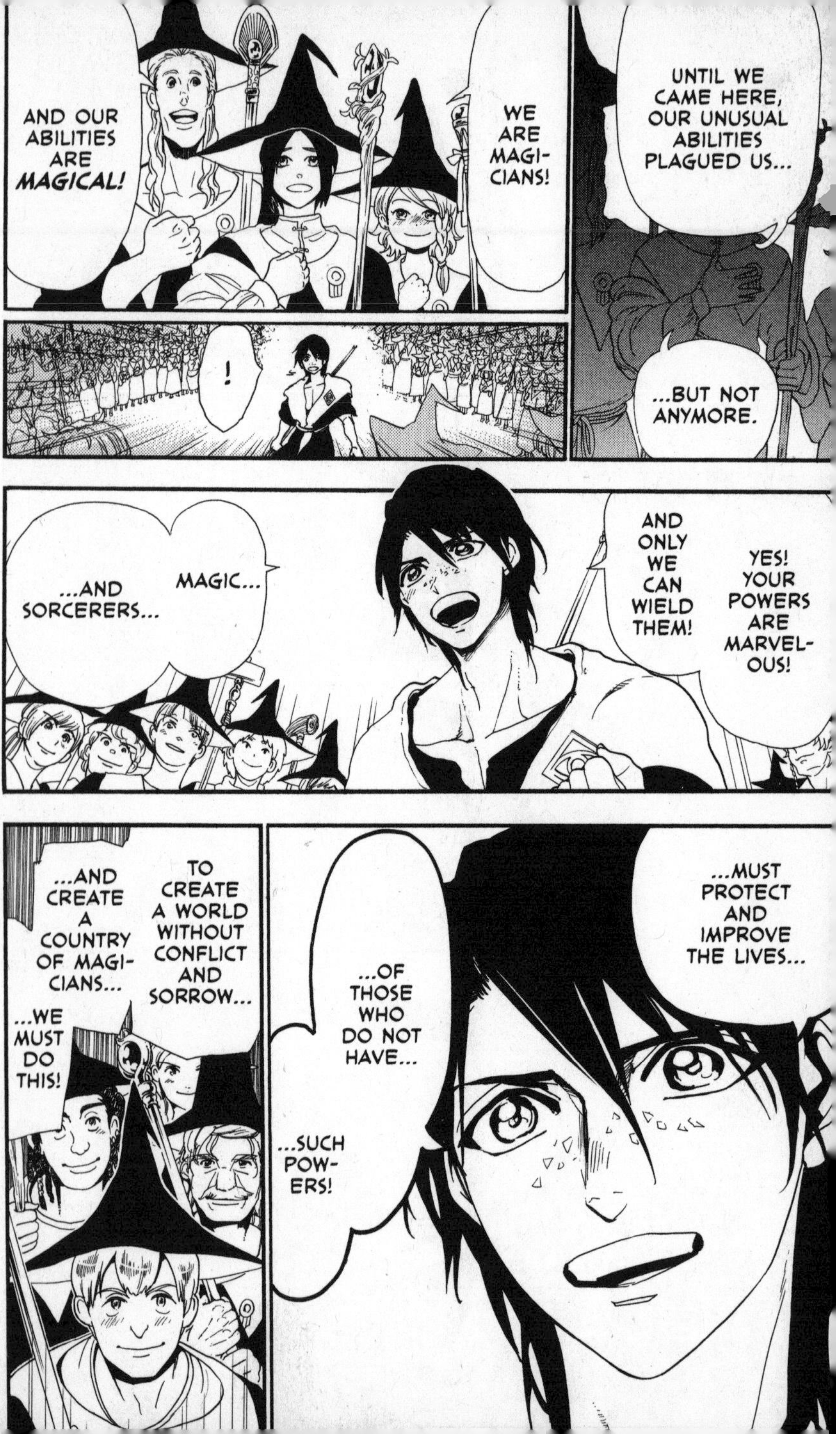
UNTIL WE CAME HERE, OUR UNUSUAL ABILITIES PLAGUED US...
...BUT NOT ANYMORE.
WE ARE MAGI-CIANS!
AND OUR ABILITIES ARE *MAGICAL!*
!
YES! YOUR POWERS ARE MARVEL-OUS!
AND ONLY WE CAN WIELD THEM!
MAGIC...
...AND SORCERERS...
...MUST PROTECT AND IMPROVE THE LIVES...
...OF THOSE WHO DO NOT HAVE...
...SUCH POW-ERS!
TO CREATE A WORLD WITHOUT CONFLICT AND SORROW...
...AND CREATE A COUNTRY OF MAGI-CIANS...
...WE MUST DO THIS!

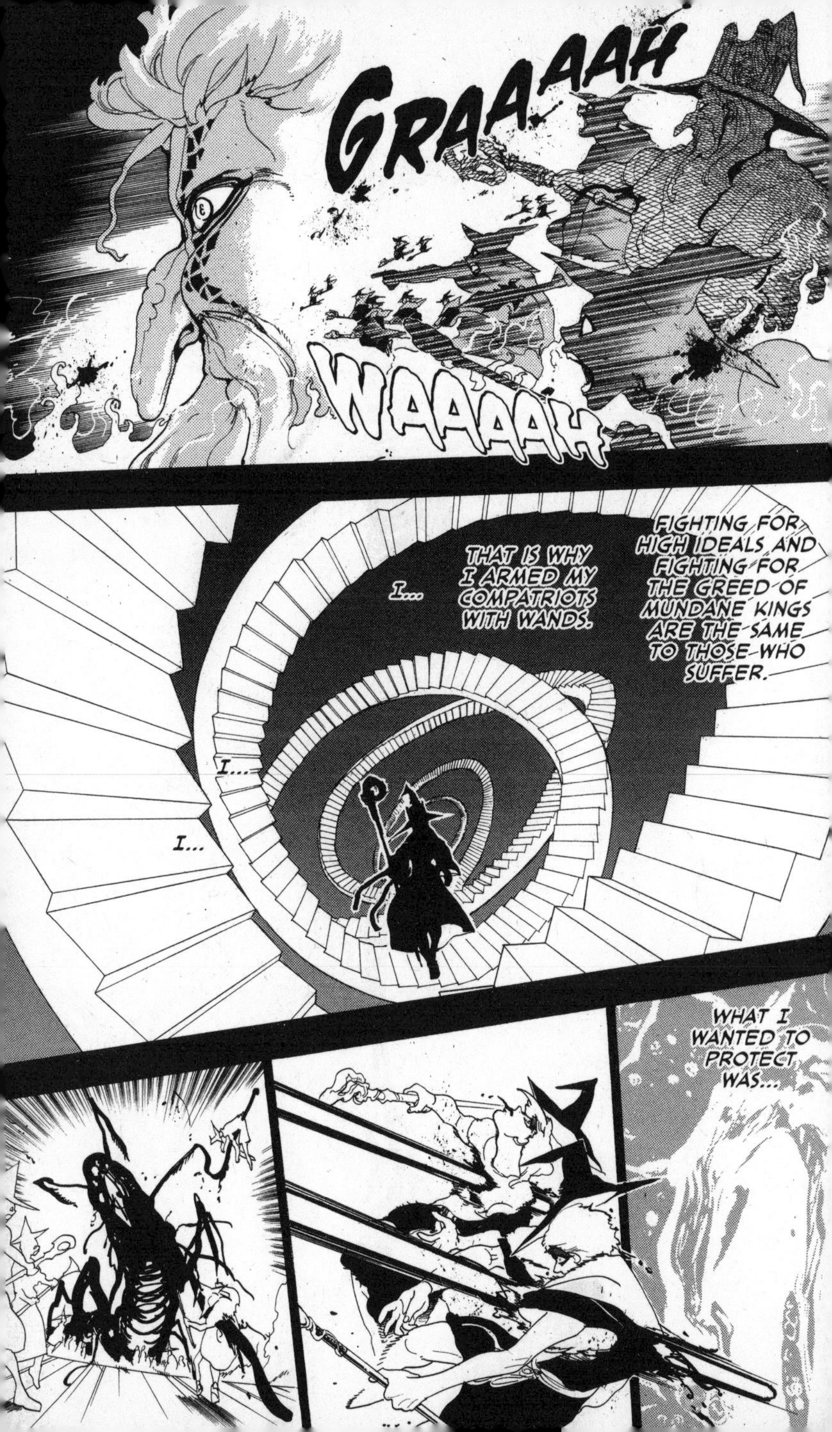
GRAAAAH
WAAAAH
FIGHTING FOR HIGH IDEALS AND FIGHTING FOR THE GREED OF MUNDANE KINGS ARE THE SAME TO THOSE WHO SUFFER.
THAT IS WHY I ARMED MY COMPATRIOTS WITH WANDS.
I...
I...
I...
WHAT I WANTED TO PROTECT WAS...

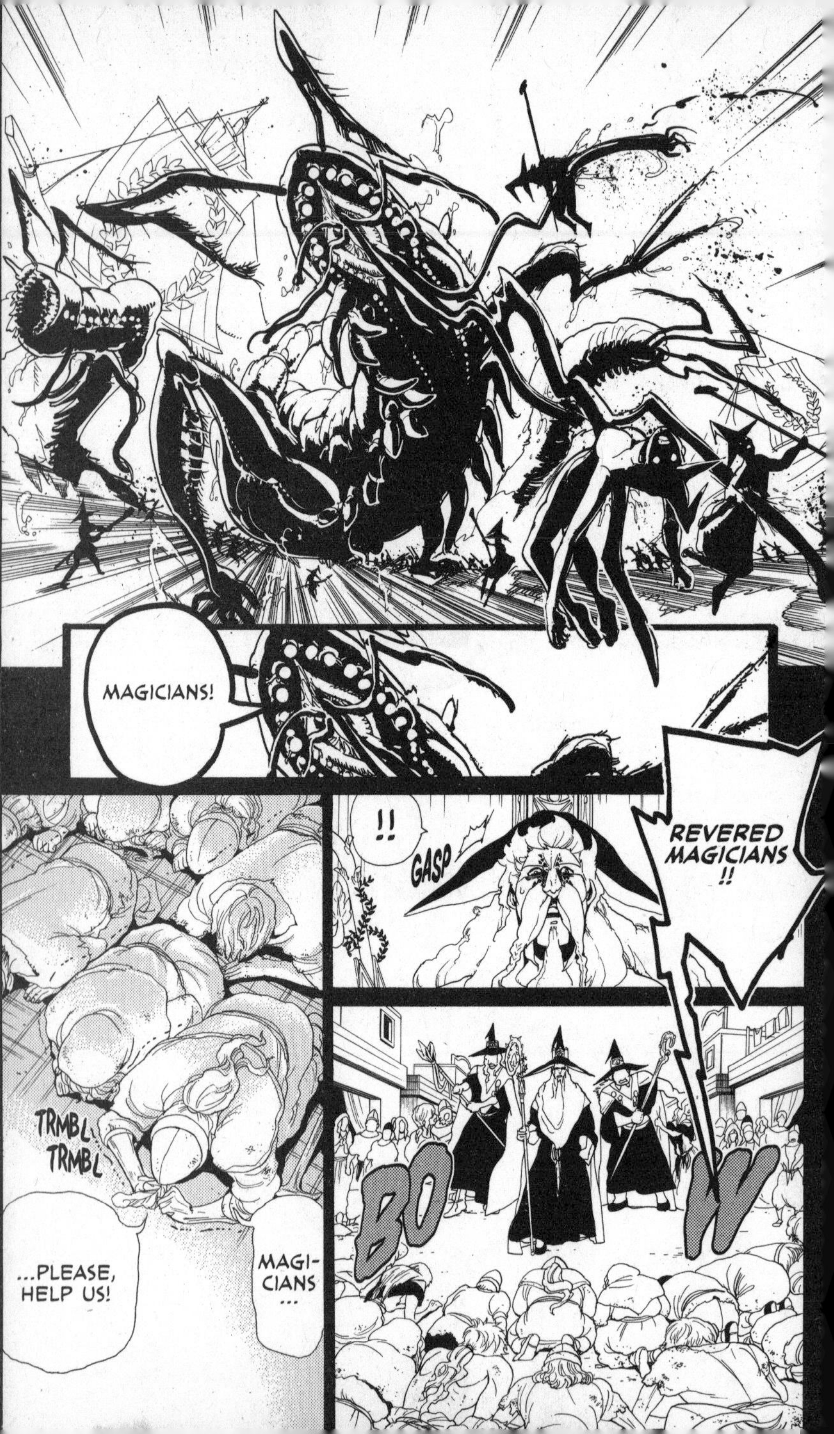
MAGICIANS!
REVERED MAGICIANS !!
!!
GASP
BOW
TRMBL TRMBL
MAGI-CIANS ...
...PLEASE, HELP US!

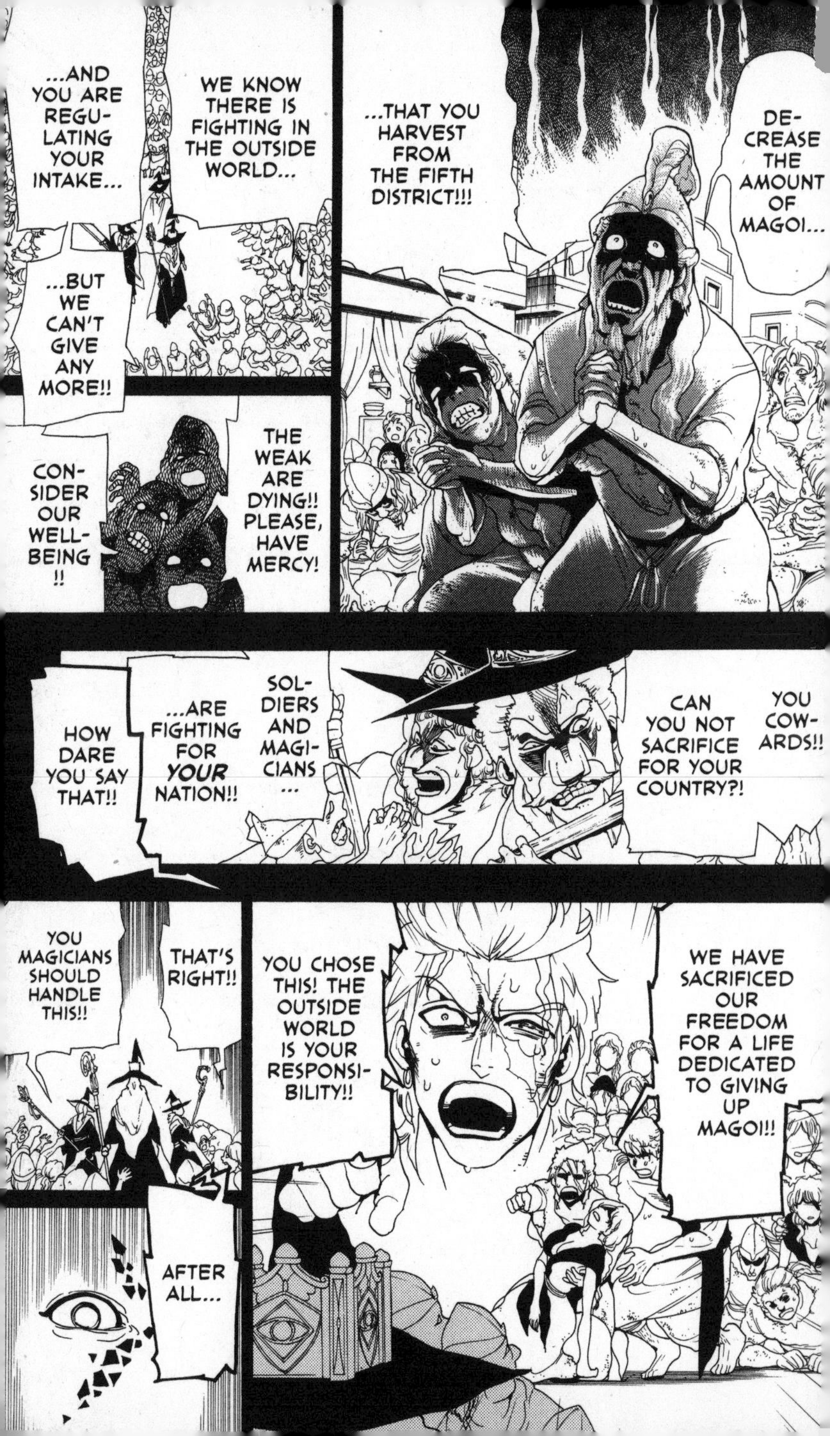
DE-CREASE THE AMOUNT OF MAGOI...
...THAT YOU HARVEST FROM THE FIFTH DISTRICT!!!
WE KNOW THERE IS FIGHTING IN THE OUTSIDE WORLD...
...AND YOU ARE REGULATING YOUR INTAKE...
...BUT WE CAN'T GIVE ANY MORE!!
THE WEAK ARE DYING!! PLEASE, HAVE MERCY!
CONSIDER OUR WELL-BEING!!
YOU COWARDS!!
CAN YOU NOT SACRIFICE FOR YOUR COUNTRY?!
SOLDIERS AND MAGICIANS...
...ARE FIGHTING FOR *YOUR* NATION!!
HOW DARE YOU SAY THAT!!
WE HAVE SACRIFICED OUR FREEDOM FOR A LIFE DEDICATED TO GIVING UP MAGOI!!
YOU CHOSE THIS! THE OUTSIDE WORLD IS YOUR RESPONSIBILITY!!
THAT'S RIGHT!!
YOU MAGICIANS SHOULD HANDLE THIS!!
AFTER ALL...

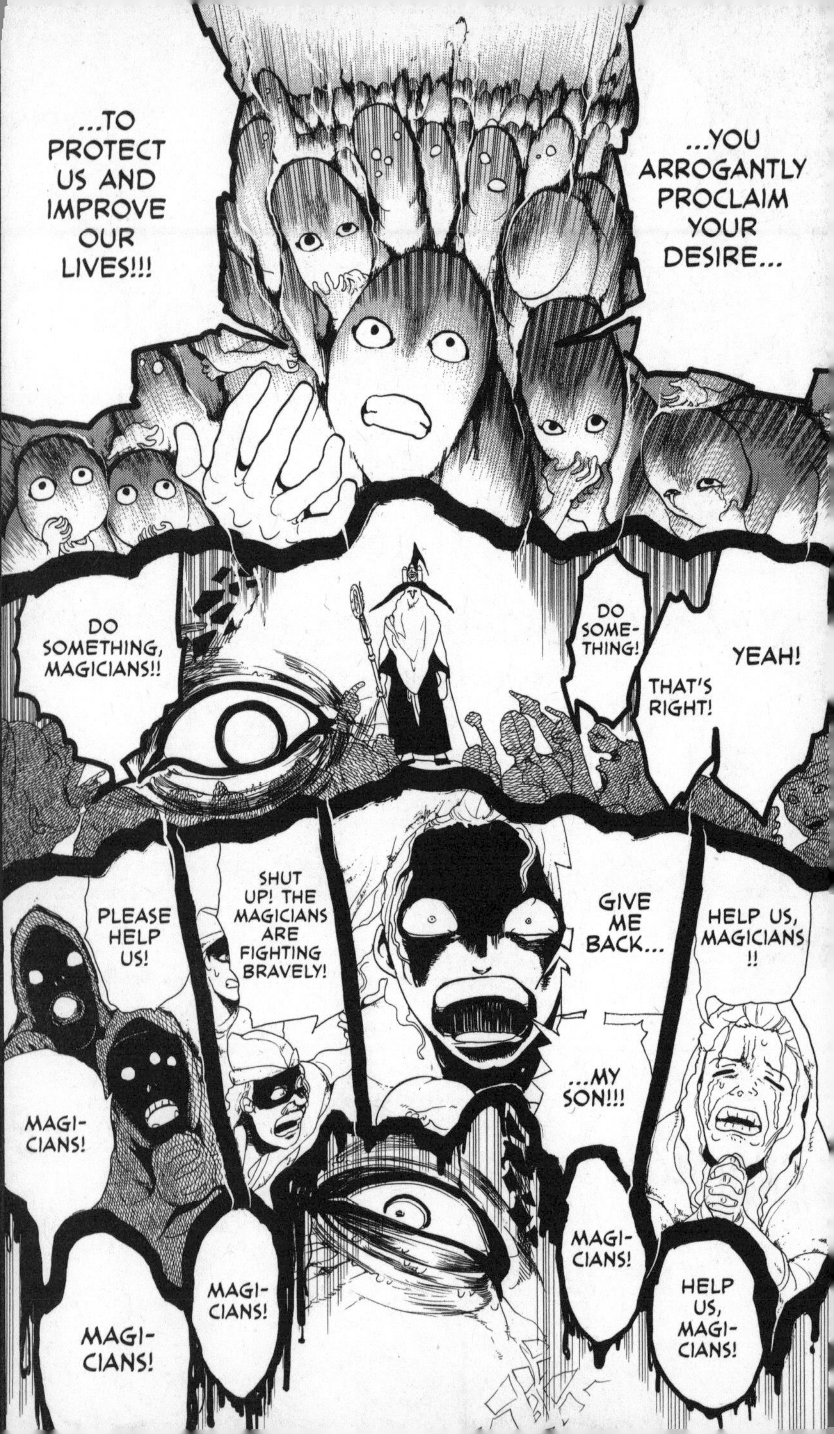
...YOU ARROGANTLY PROCLAIM YOUR DESIRE...
...TO PROTECT US AND IMPROVE OUR LIVES!!!
YEAH!
THAT'S RIGHT!
DO SOME-THING!
DO SOMETHING, MAGICIANS!!
HELP US, MAGICIANS !!
HELP US, MAGI-CIANS!
GIVE ME BACK...
...MY SON!!!
MAGI-CIANS!
SHUT UP! THE MAGICIANS ARE FIGHTING BRAVELY!
MAGI-CIANS!
PLEASE HELP US!
MAGI-CIANS!
MAGI-CIANS!

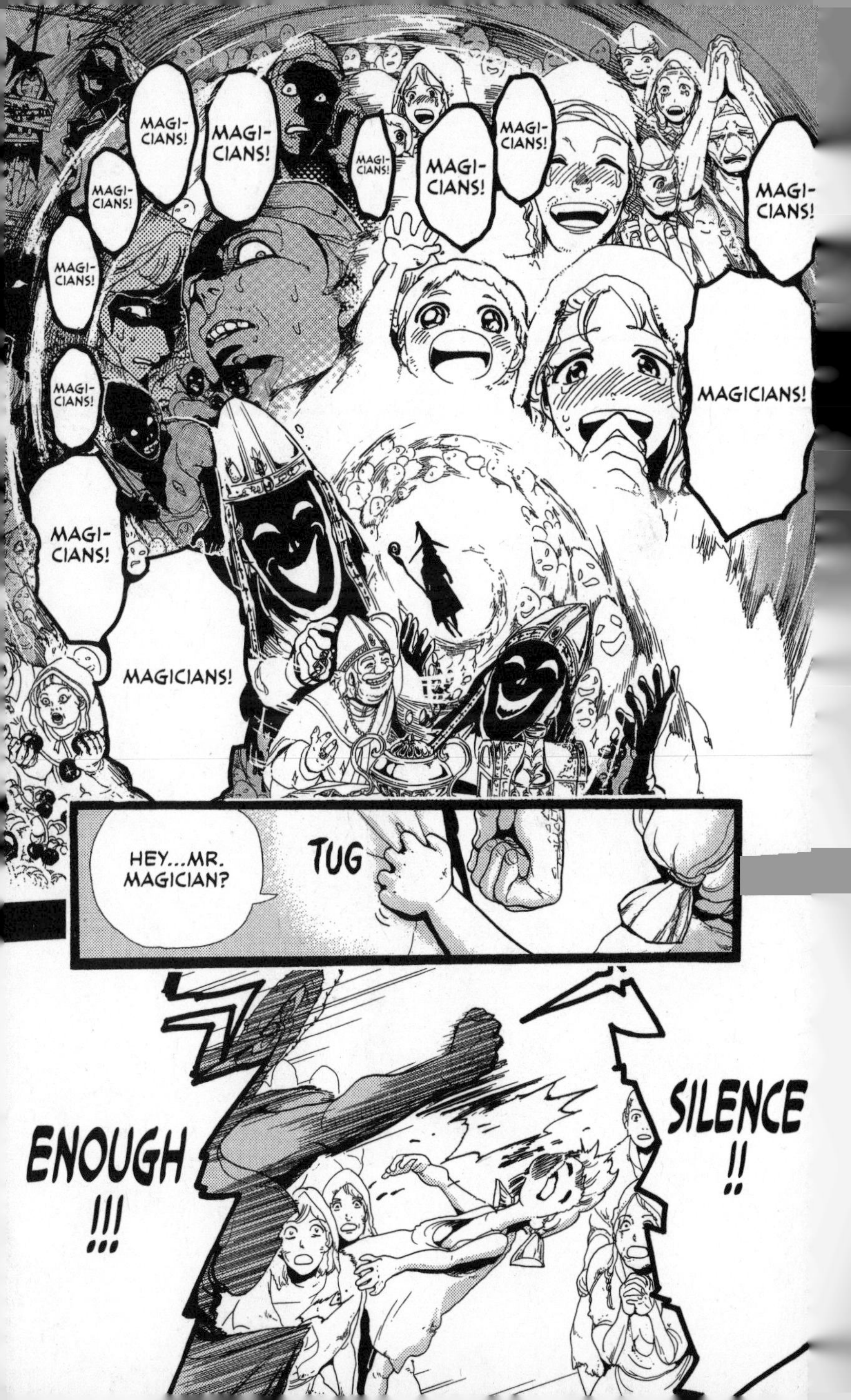
MAGI-
CIANS!
MAGICIANS!
MAGI-
CIANS!
MAGI-
CIANS!
MAGI-
CIANS!
MAGI-
CIANS!
MAGI-
CIANS!
MAGI-
CIANS!
MAGI-
CIANS!
MAGI-
CIANS!
MAGI-
CIANS!
MAGICIANS!
TUG
HEY...MR. MAGICIAN?
SILENCE !!
ENOUGH !!!

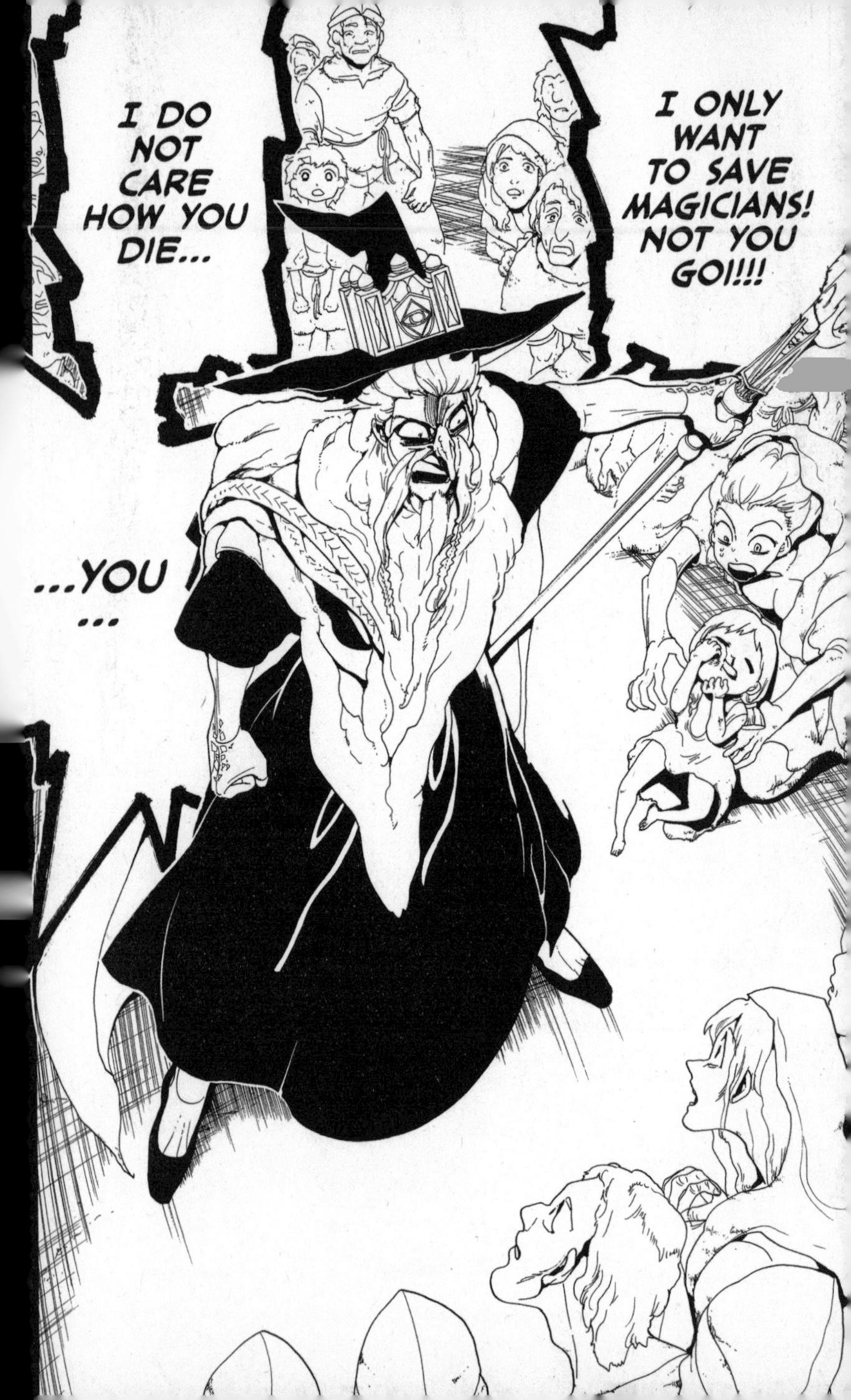
I ONLY WANT TO SAVE MAGICIANS! NOT YOU GOI!!!
I DO NOT CARE HOW YOU DIE...
...YOU ...

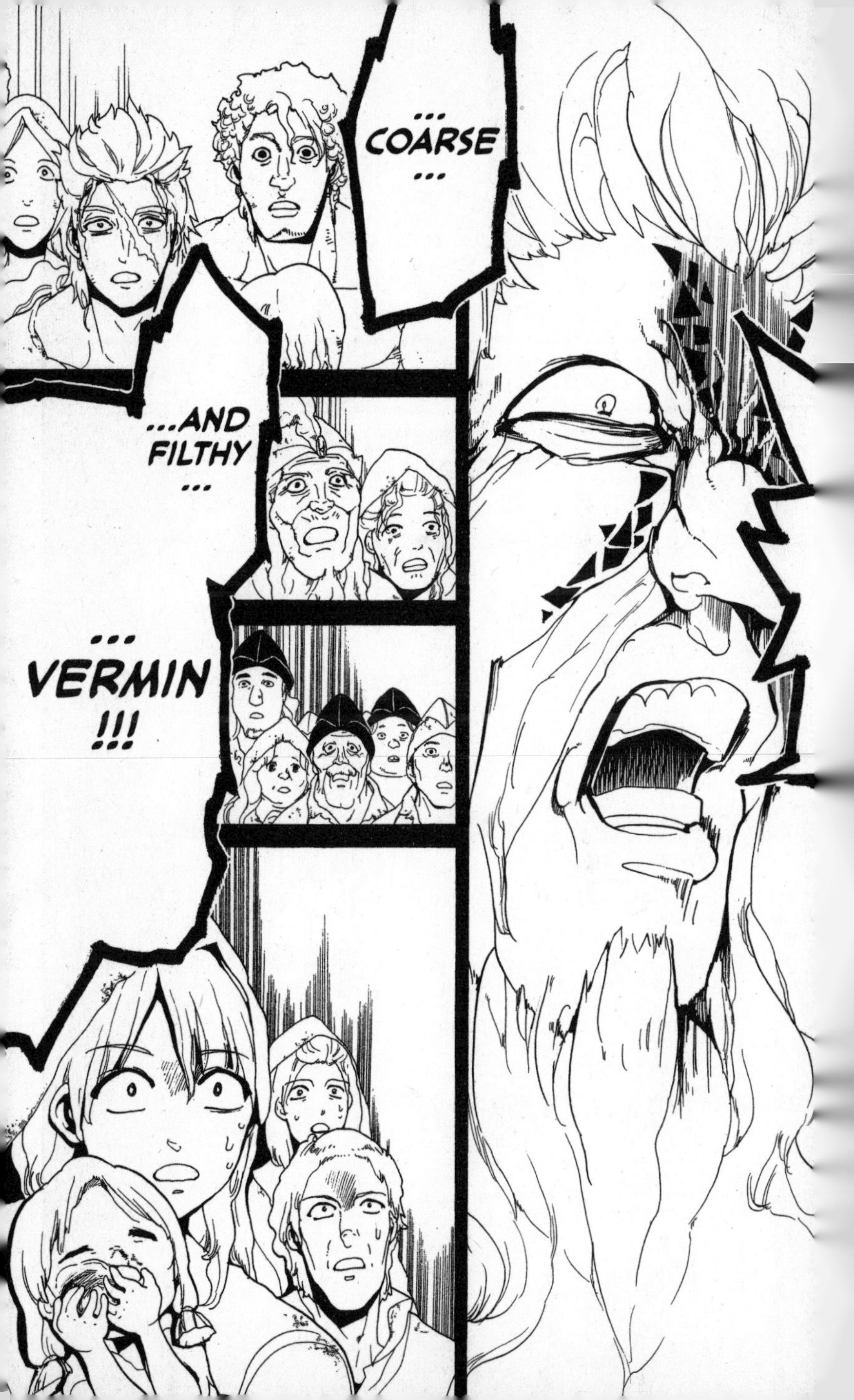
...COARSE...
...AND FILTHY...
...VERMIN!!!

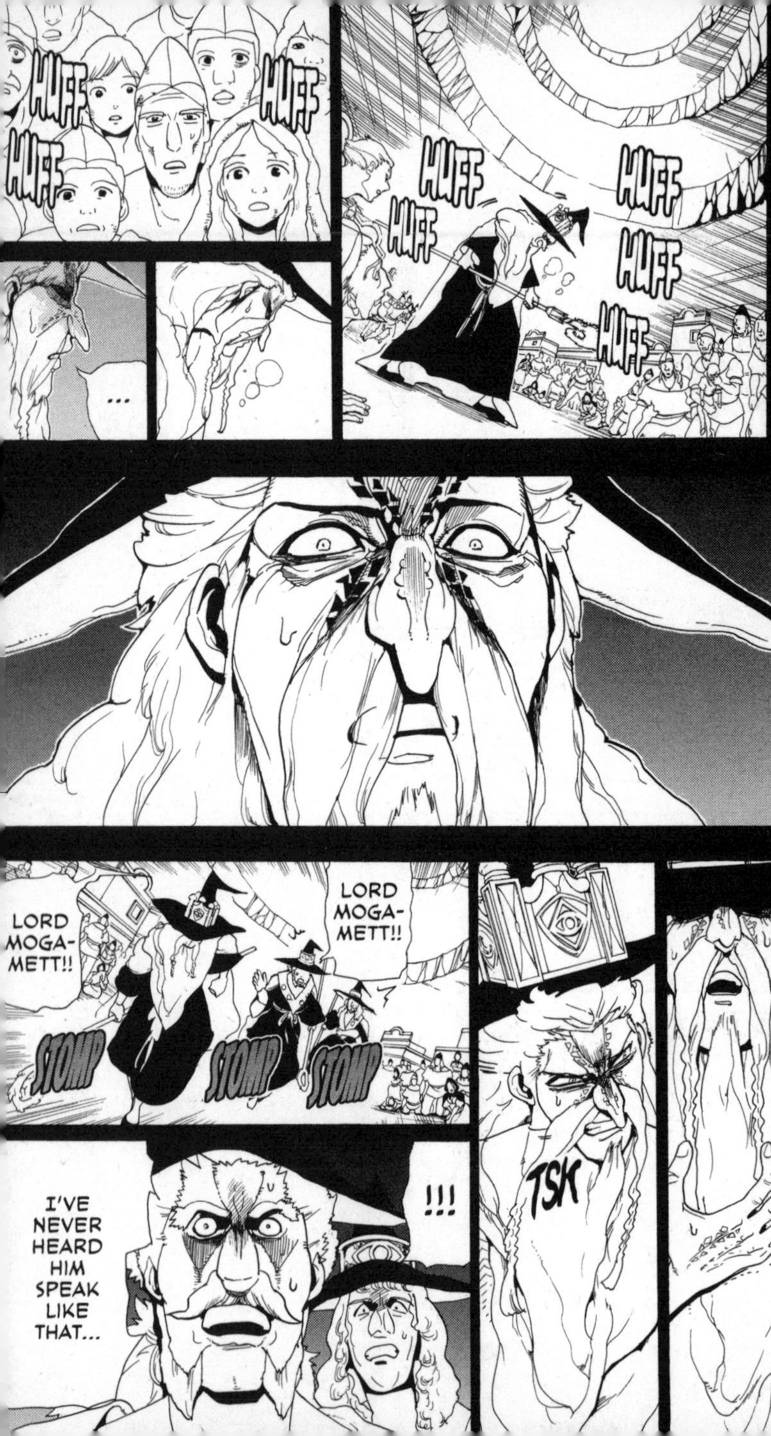
HUFF
HUFF
HUFF
HUFF
HUFF
HUFF
HUFF
HUFF
...
TSK
LORD MOGA-METT!!
LORD MOGA-METT!!
STOMP
STOMP
STOMP
!!!
I'VE NEVER HEARD HIM SPEAK LIKE THAT...

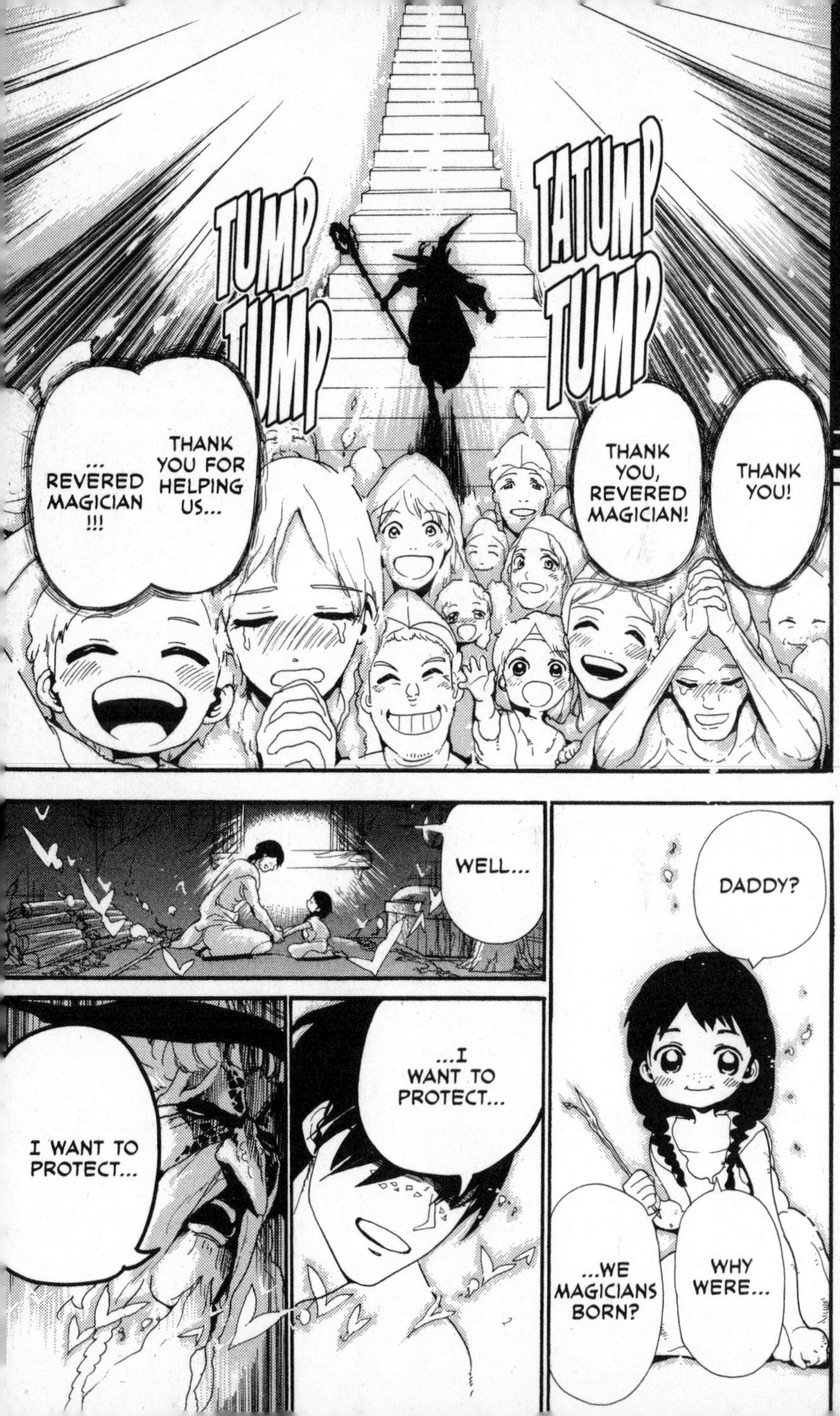
TATUMP TUMP
TUMP TUMP
THANK YOU!
THANK YOU, REVERED MAGICIAN!
THANK YOU FOR HELPING US...
...REVERED MAGICIAN!!!
DADDY?
WHY WERE...
...WE MAGICIANS BORN?
WELL...
...I WANT TO PROTECT...
I WANT TO PROTECT...

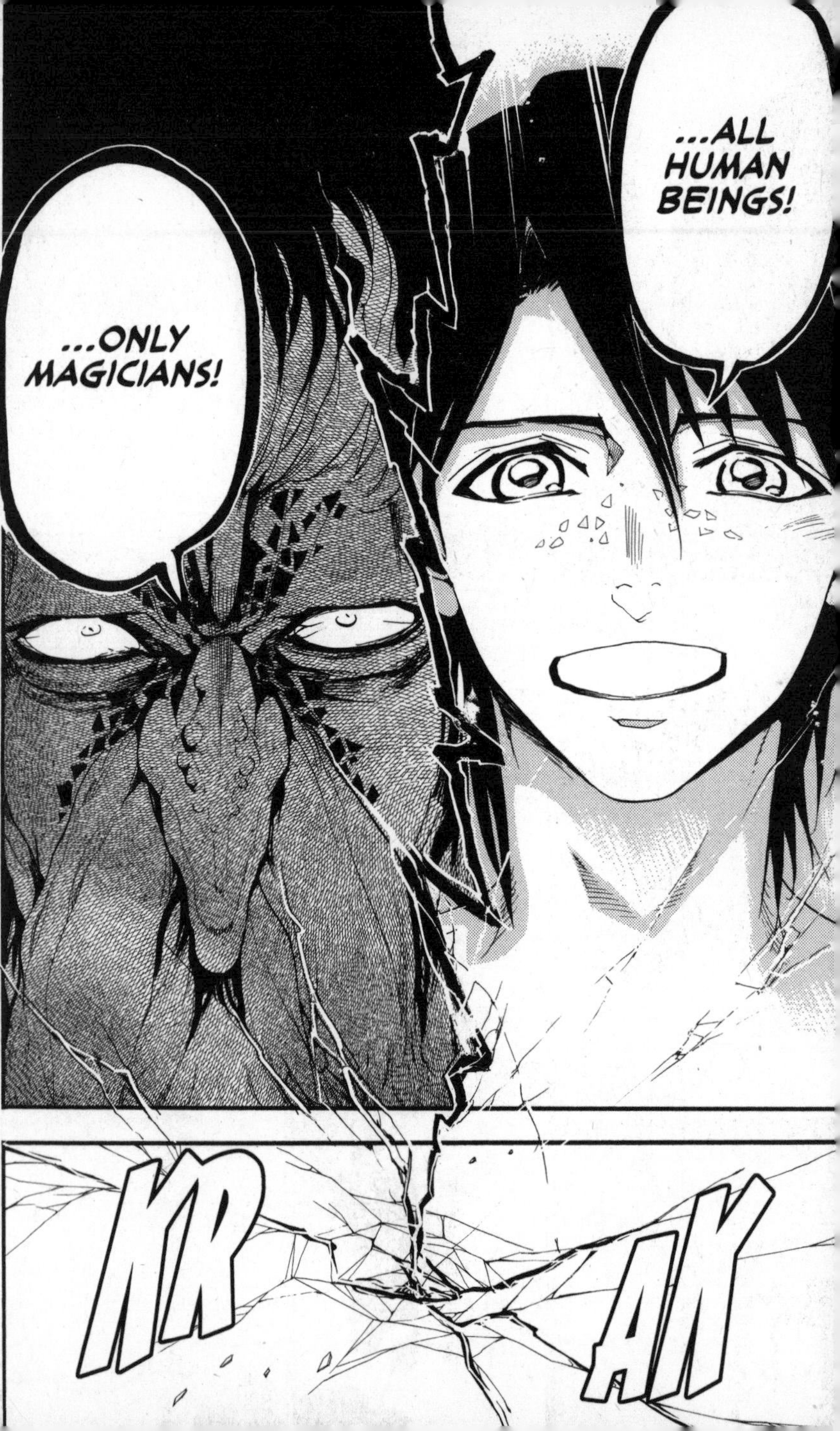
...ALL HUMAN BEINGS!
...ONLY MAGICIANS!
KRAK

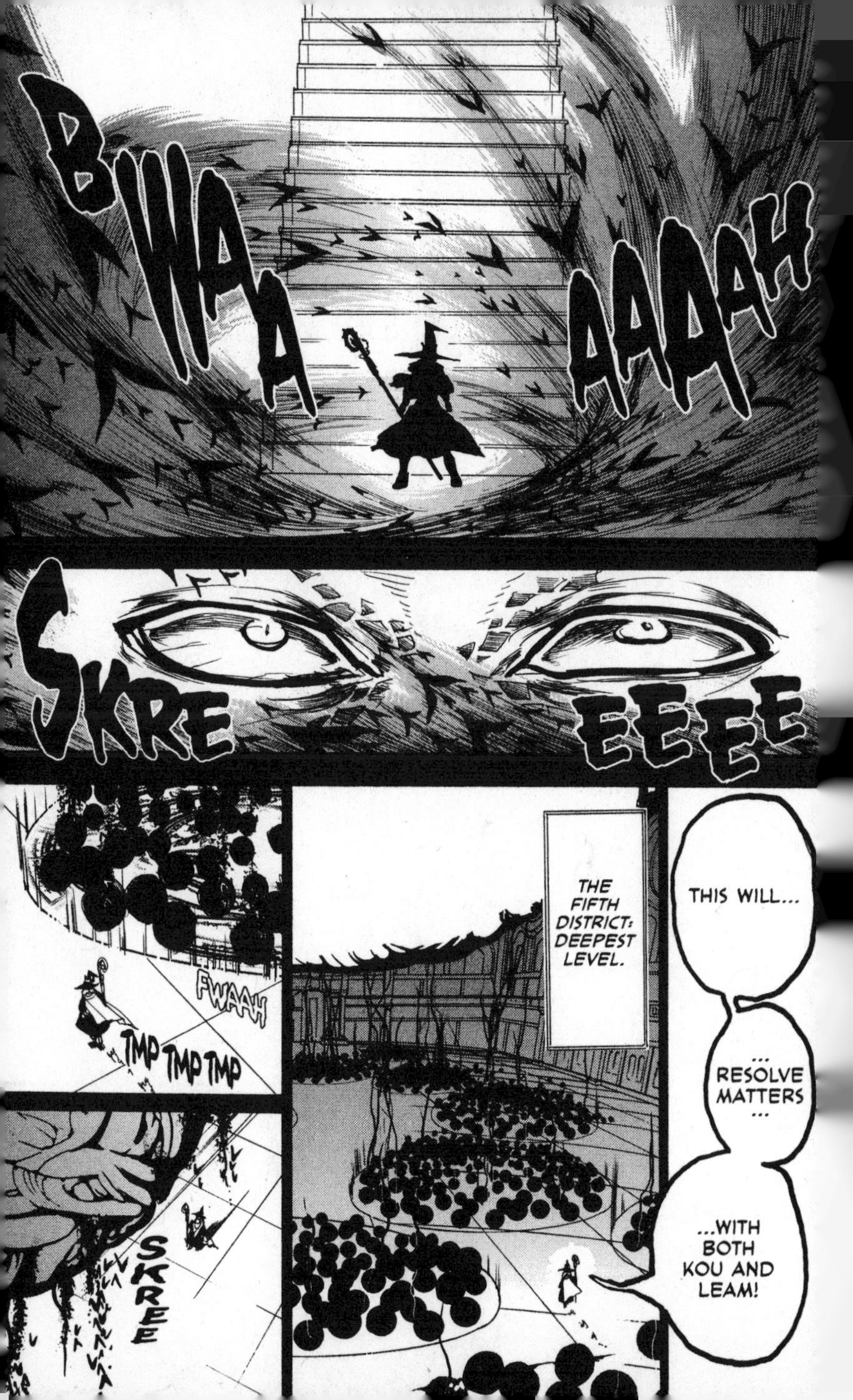
BWAAAAAAH
SKREEEEE
THIS WILL...
...RESOLVE MATTERS...
...WITH BOTH KOU AND LEAM!
THE FIFTH DISTRICT: DEEPEST LEVEL.
FWAAH
TMP TMP TMP
SKREE

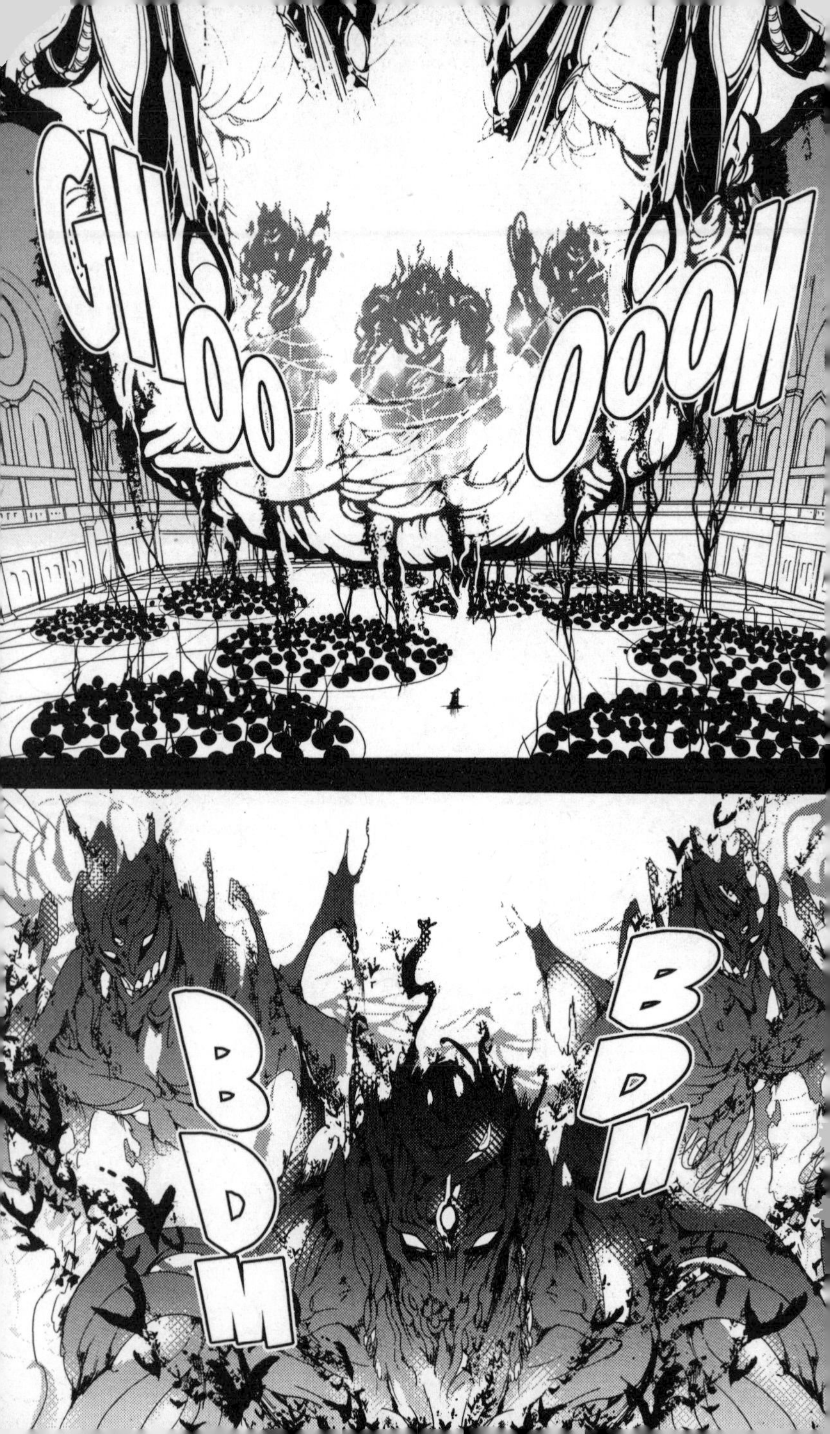
GWOOO OOOOM
BDM
BDM

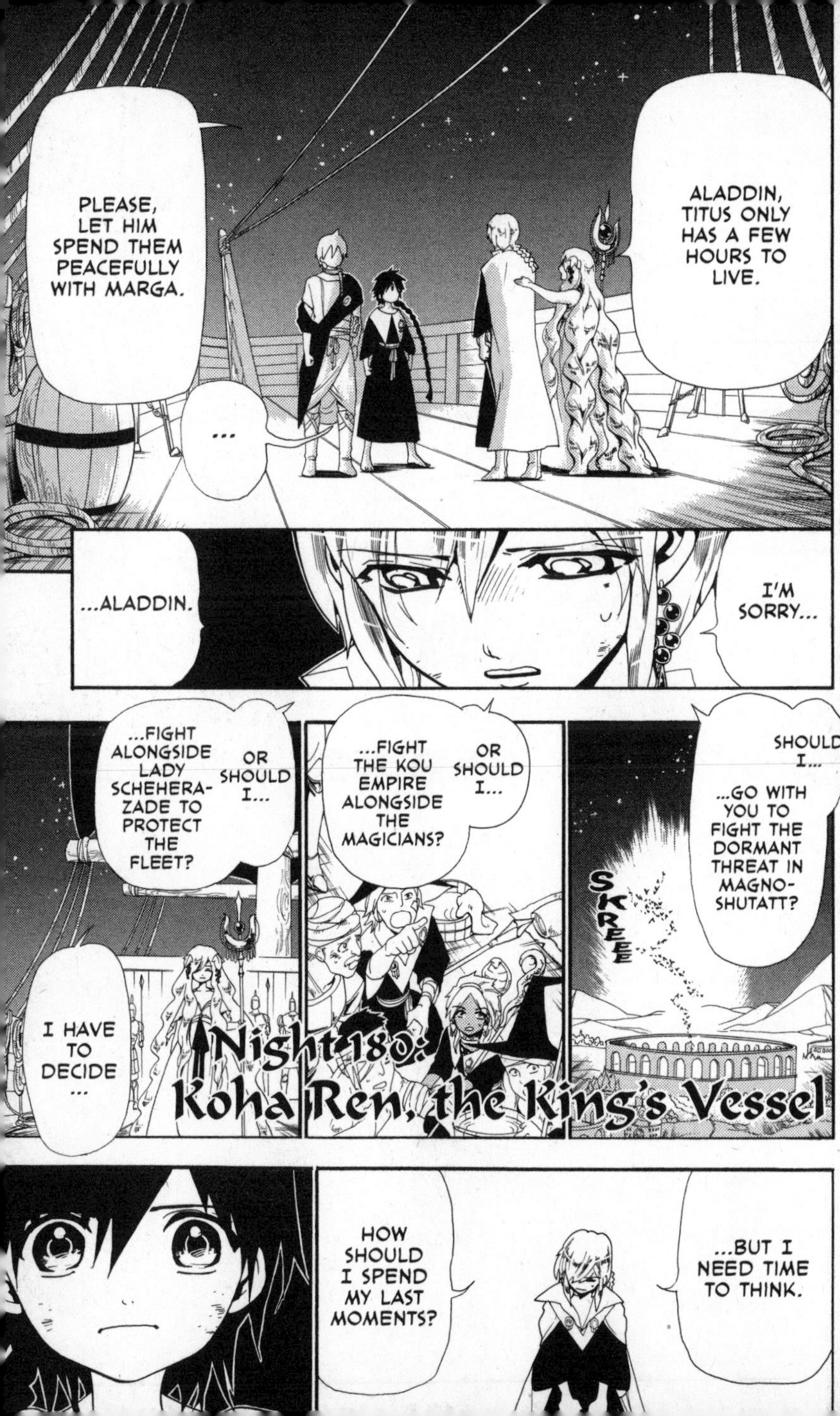
ALADDIN, TITUS ONLY HAS A FEW HOURS TO LIVE.
PLEASE, LET HIM SPEND THEM PEACEFULLY WITH MARGA.
...
I'M SORRY...
...ALADDIN.
SHOULD I...
...GO WITH YOU TO FIGHT THE DORMANT THREAT IN MAGNOSHUTATT?
SKREEE
OR SHOULD I...
...FIGHT THE KOU EMPIRE ALONGSIDE THE MAGICIANS?
OR SHOULD I...
...FIGHT ALONGSIDE LADY SCHEHERAZADE TO PROTECT THE FLEET?
I HAVE TO DECIDE ...
Night 180: Koha Ren, the King's Vessel
...BUT I NEED TIME TO THINK.
HOW SHOULD I SPEND MY LAST MOMENTS?

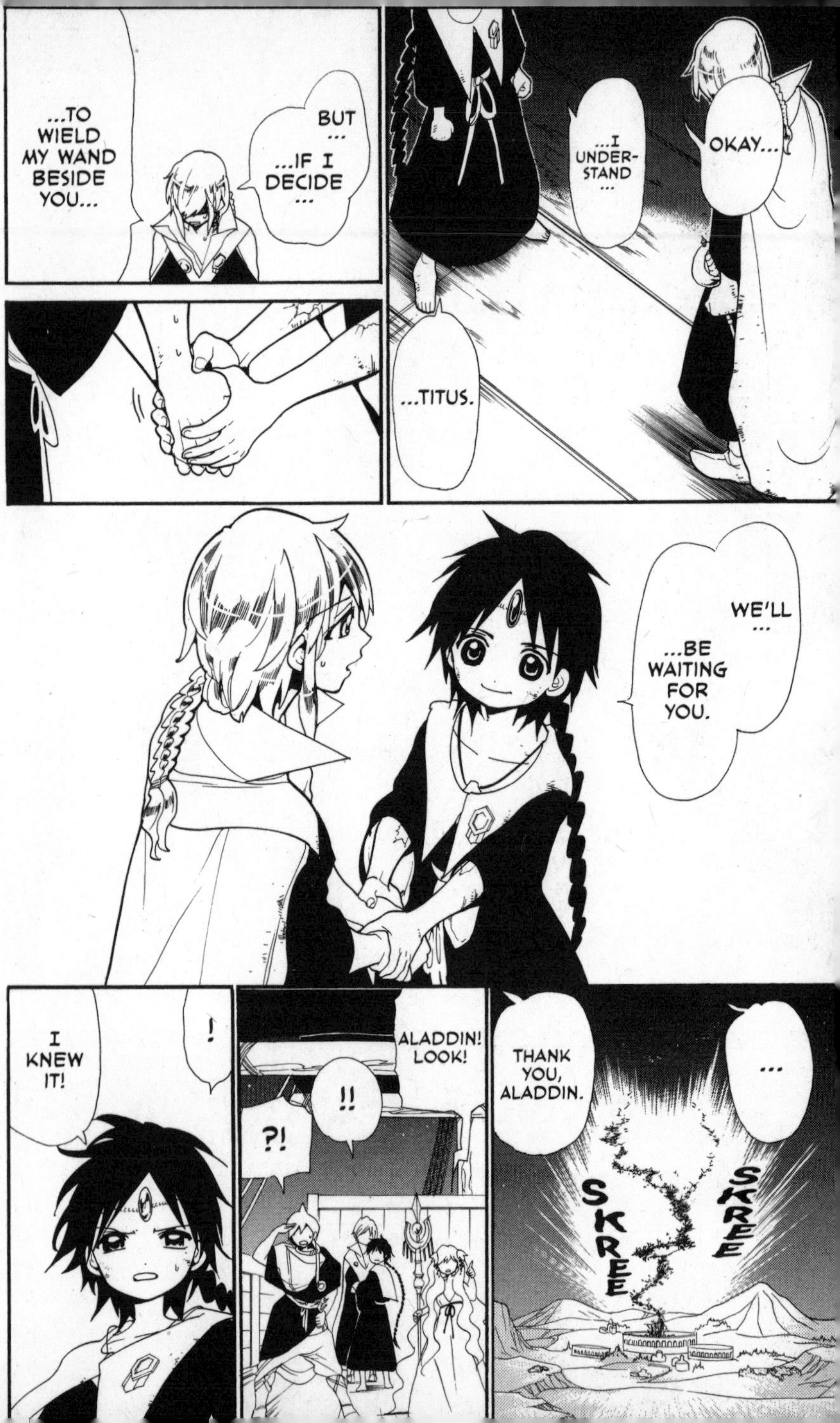
OKAY...
...I UNDER-STAND...
...TITUS.
BUT... ...IF I DECIDE...
...TO WIELD MY WAND BESIDE YOU...
WE'LL... ...BE WAITING FOR YOU.
...
THANK YOU, ALADDIN.
SKREE
SKREE
ALADDIN! LOOK!
!!
?!
!
I KNEW IT!

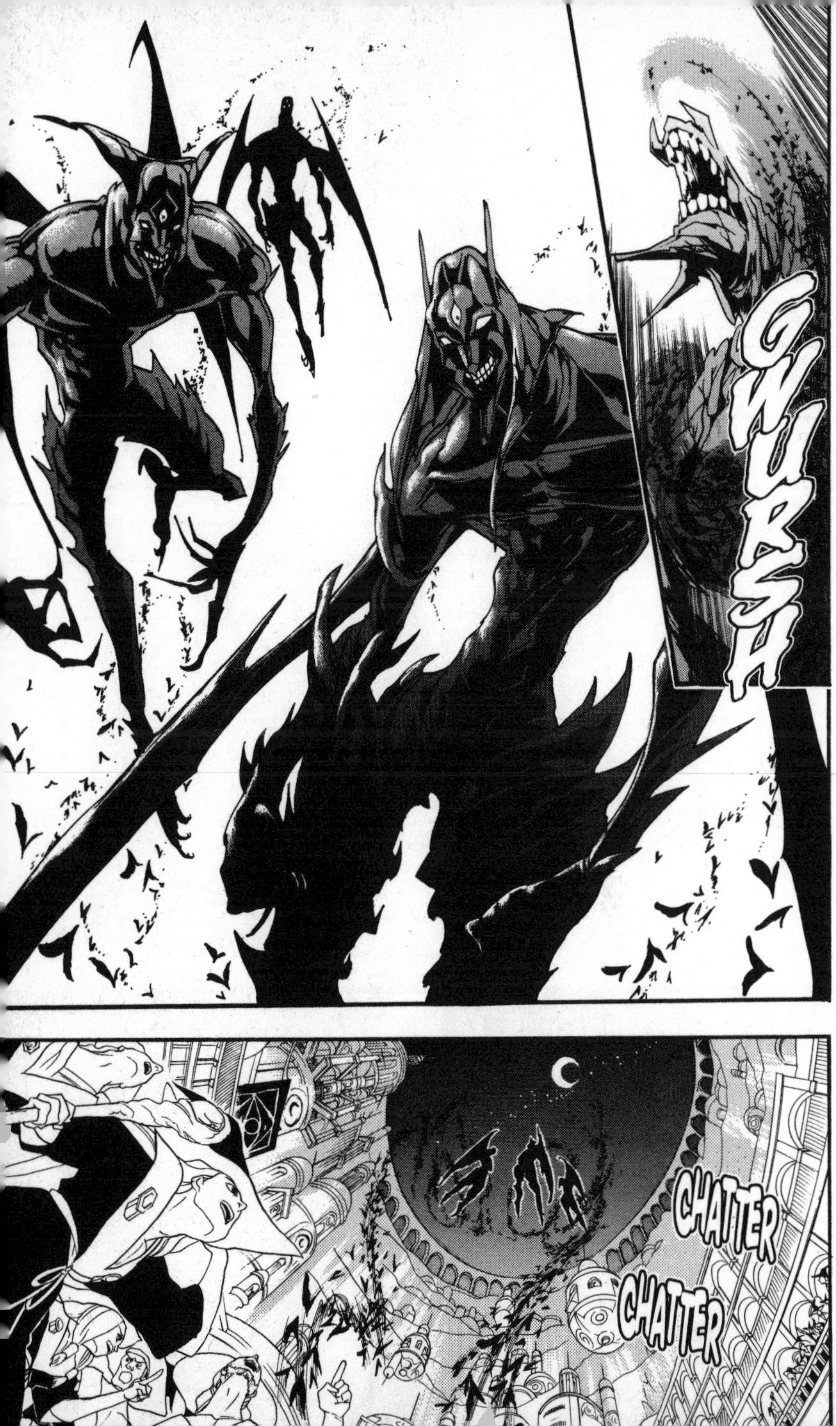
GWURSH
CHATTER
CHATTER

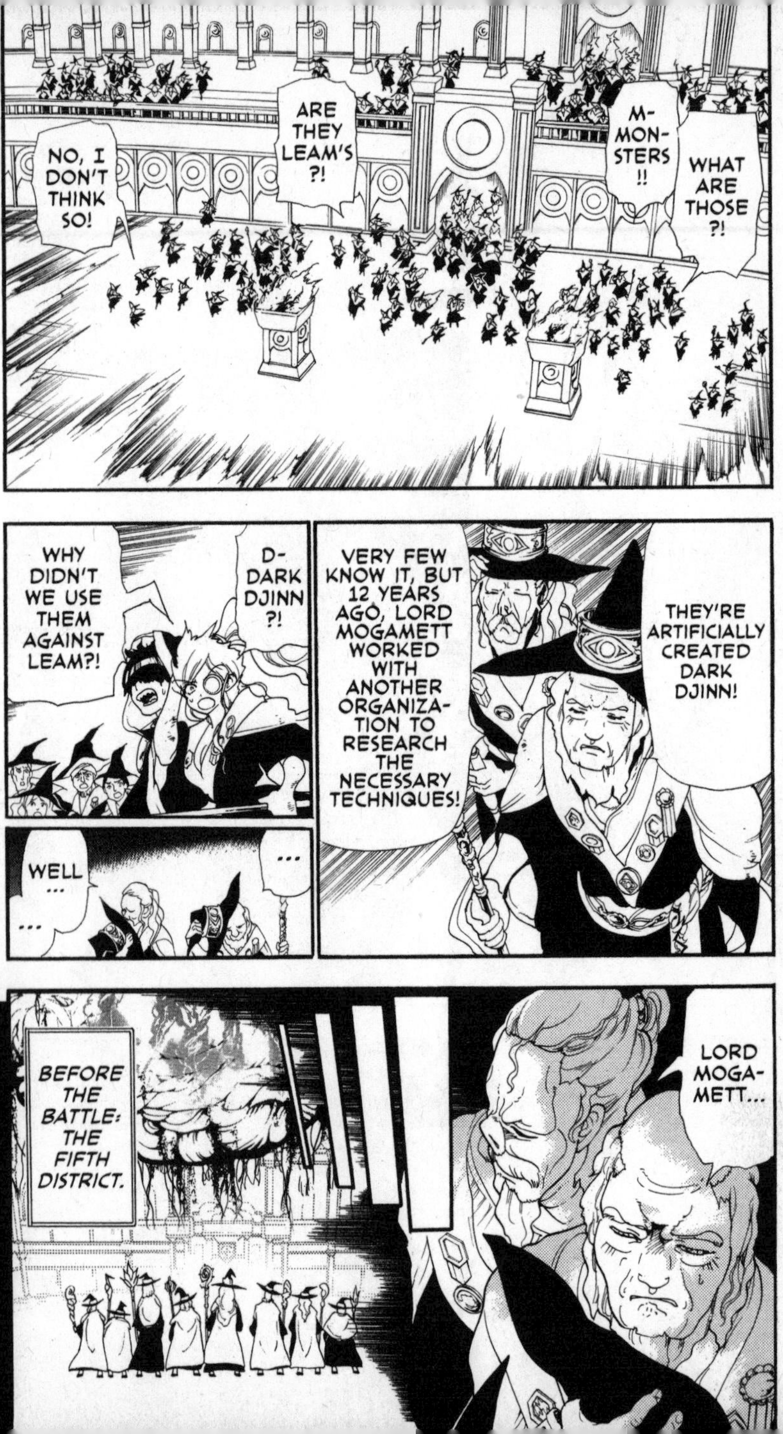
WHAT ARE THOSE?!
M-MONSTERS!!
ARE THEY LEAM'S?!
NO, I DON'T THINK SO!
THEY'RE ARTIFICIALLY CREATED DARK DJINN!
VERY FEW KNOW IT, BUT 12 YEARS AGO, LORD MOGAMETT WORKED WITH ANOTHER ORGANIZATION TO RESEARCH THE NECESSARY TECHNIQUES!
D-DARK DJINN?!
WHY DIDN'T WE USE THEM AGAINST LEAM?!
...
WELL...
...
LORD MOGAMETT...
BEFORE THE BATTLE: THE FIFTH DISTRICT.

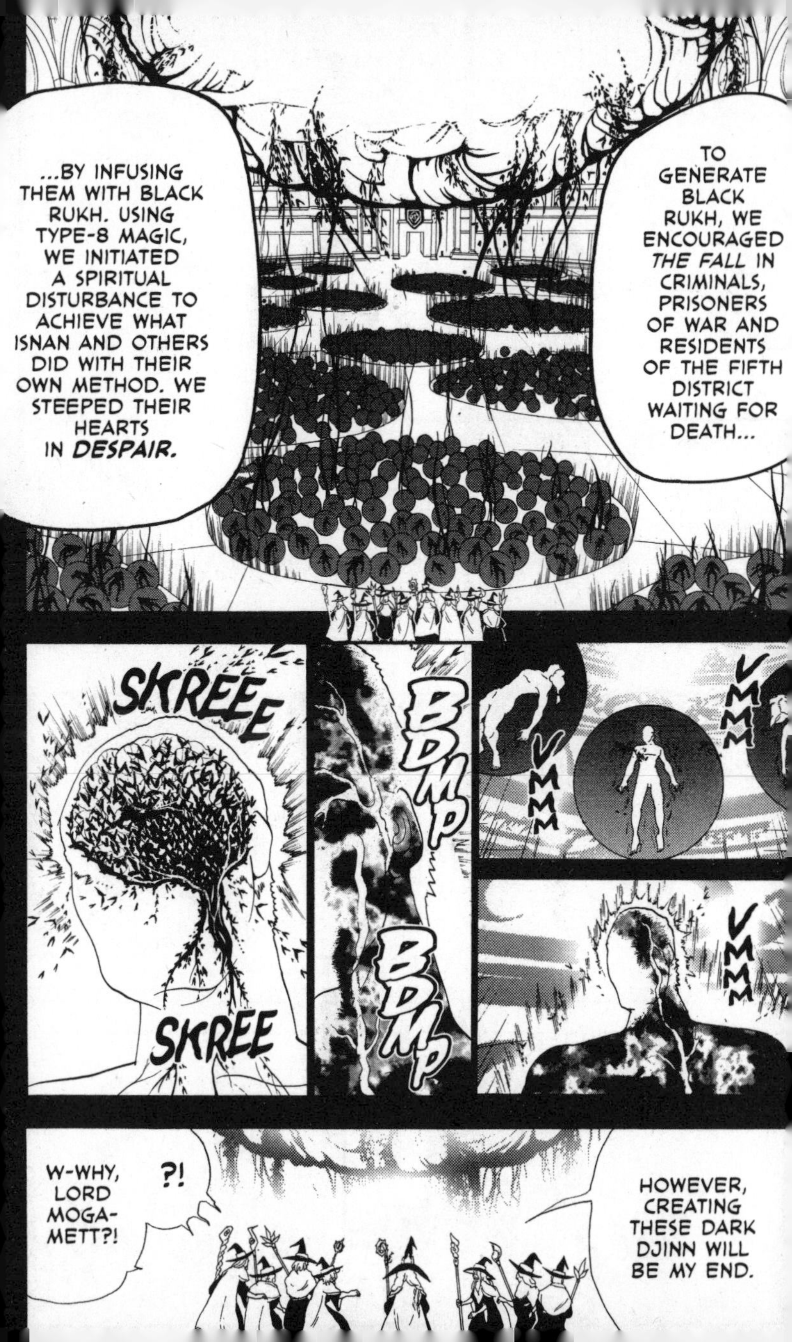
TO GENERATE BLACK RUKH, WE ENCOURAGED *THE FALL* IN CRIMINALS, PRISONERS OF WAR AND RESIDENTS OF THE FIFTH DISTRICT WAITING FOR DEATH...
...BY INFUSING THEM WITH BLACK RUKH. USING TYPE-8 MAGIC, WE INITIATED A SPIRITUAL DISTURBANCE TO ACHIEVE WHAT ISNAN AND OTHERS DID WITH THEIR OWN METHOD. WE STEEPED THEIR HEARTS IN ***DESPAIR.***
VMMM
VMMM
VMMM
BDMP
BDMP
SKREEE
SKREE
HOWEVER, CREATING THESE DARK DJINN WILL BE MY END.
?!
W-WHY, LORD MOGA-METT?!

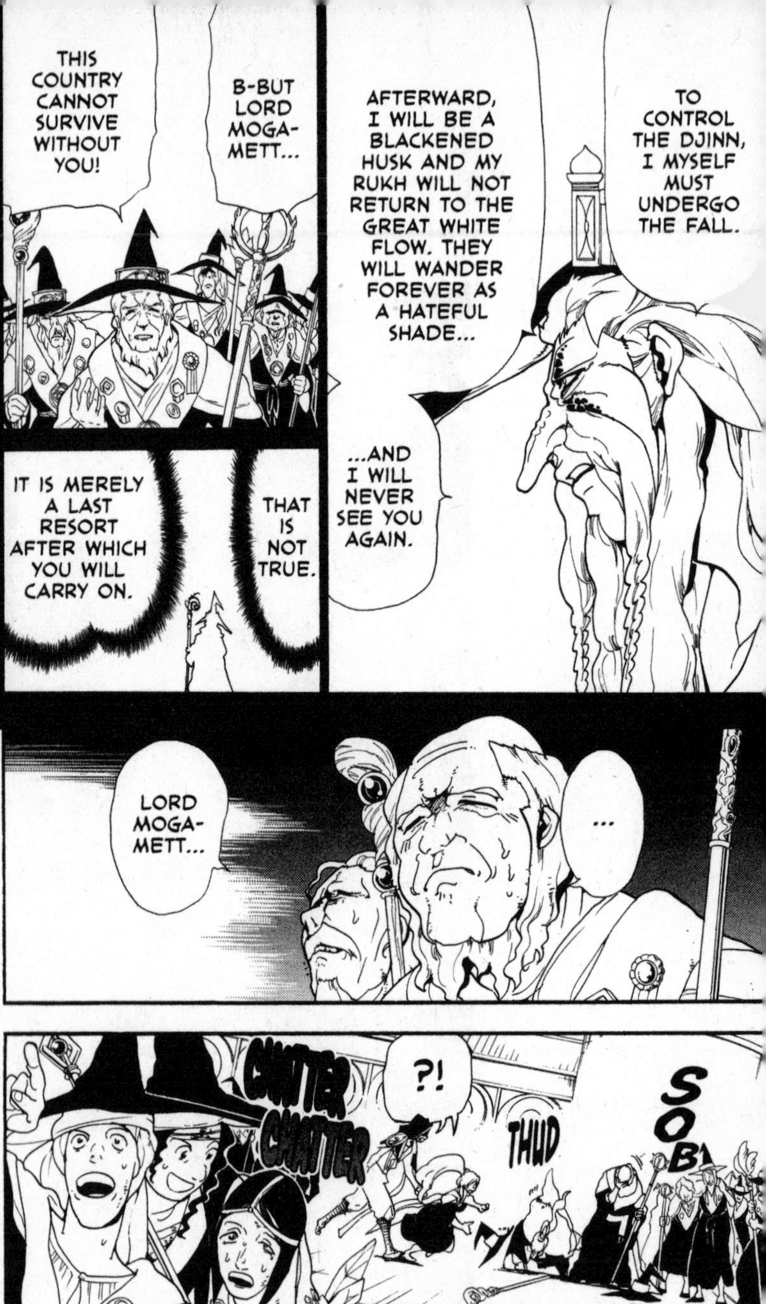

TO CONTROL THE DJINN, I MYSELF MUST UNDERGO THE FALL.
AFTERWARD, I WILL BE A BLACKENED HUSK AND MY RUKH WILL NOT RETURN TO THE GREAT WHITE FLOW. THEY WILL WANDER FOREVER AS A HATEFUL SHADE...
...AND I WILL NEVER SEE YOU AGAIN.
B-BUT LORD MOGA-METT...
THIS COUNTRY CANNOT SURVIVE WITHOUT YOU!
THAT IS NOT TRUE.
IT IS MERELY A LAST RESORT AFTER WHICH YOU WILL CARRY ON.
...
LORD MOGA-METT...
SOB
THUD
?!
CHATTER
CHATTER

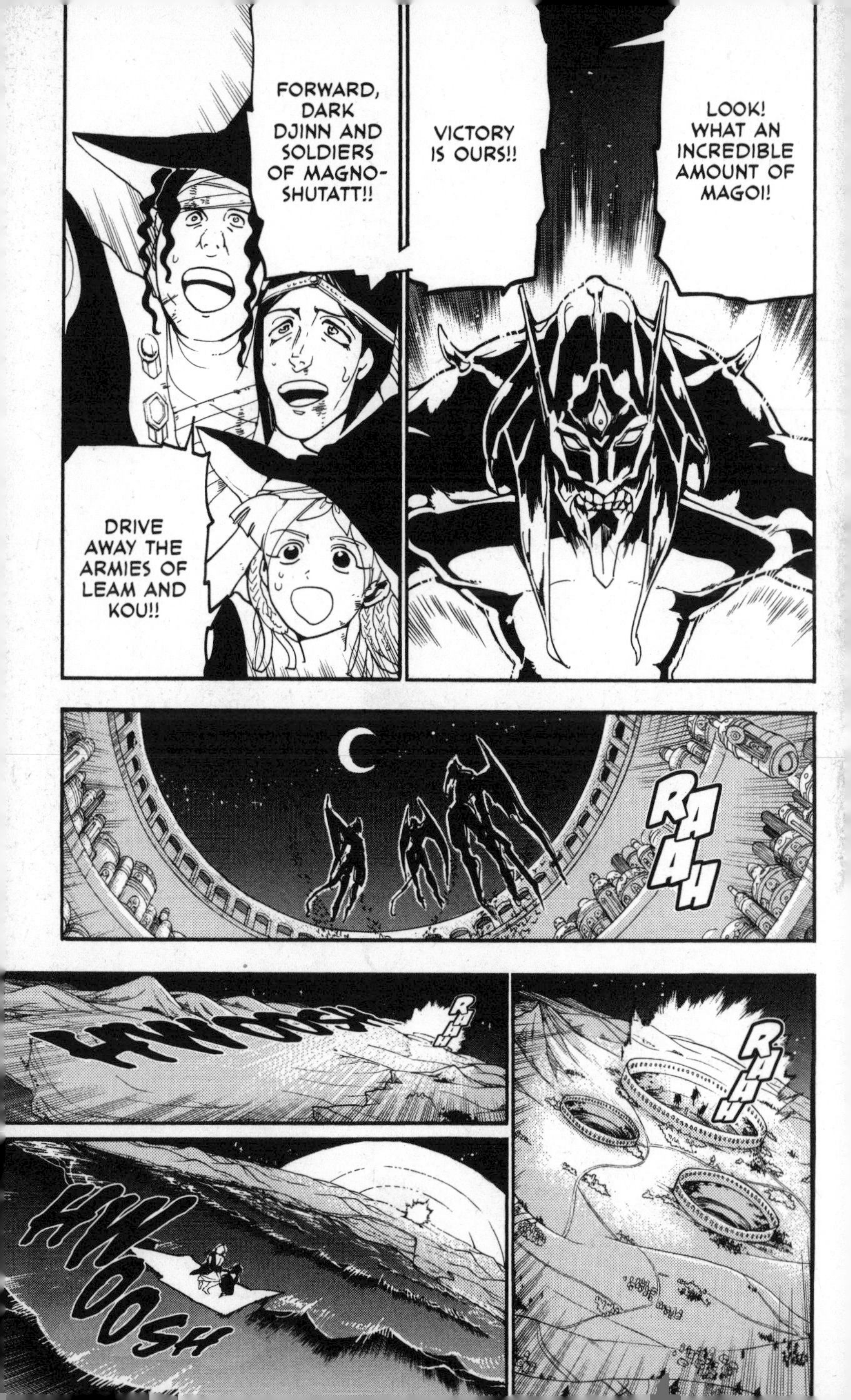
LOOK! WHAT AN INCREDIBLE AMOUNT OF MAGOI!
VICTORY IS OURS!!
FORWARD, DARK DJINN AND SOLDIERS OF MAGNO-SHUTATT!!
DRIVE AWAY THE ARMIES OF LEAM AND KOU!!
RAAAH
RAAAH
HWOOSH
RAHH
HWOOSH

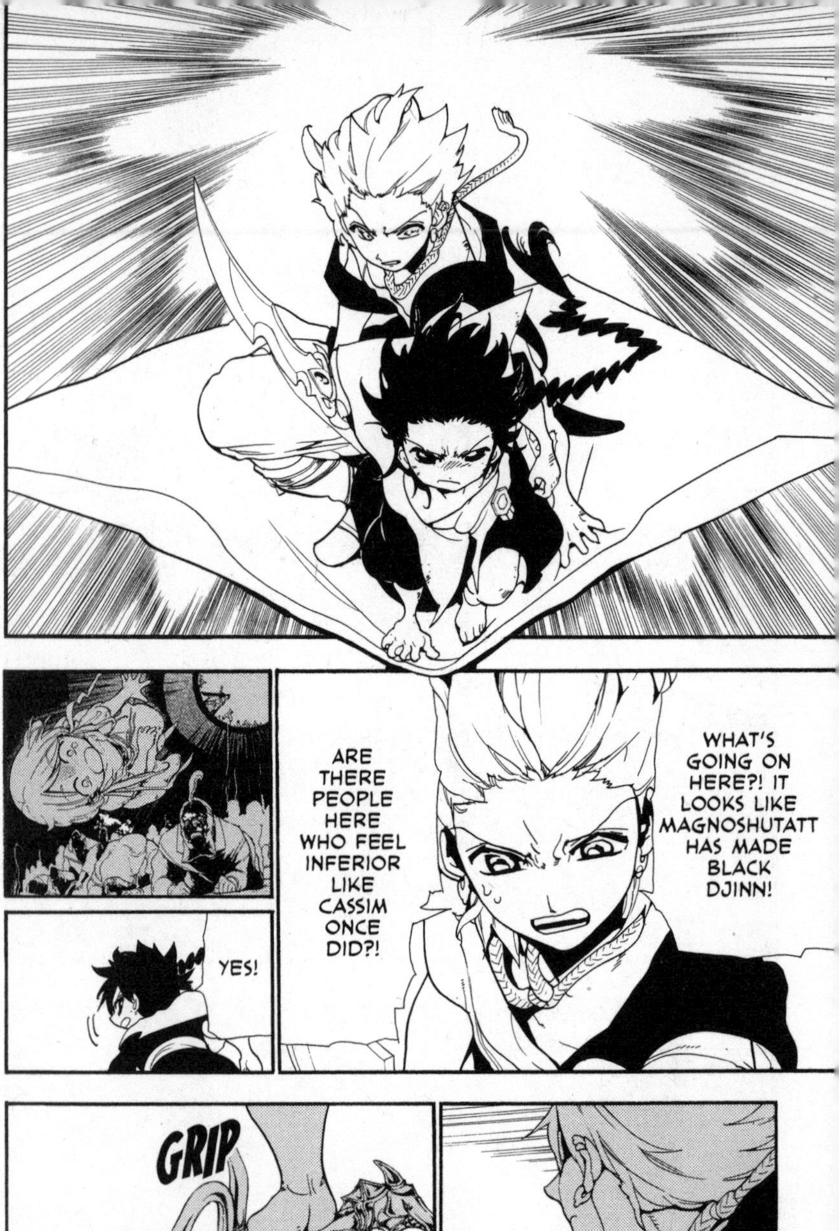
WHAT'S GOING ON HERE?! IT LOOKS LIKE MAGNOSHUTATT HAS MADE BLACK DJINN!
ARE THERE PEOPLE HERE WHO FEEL INFERIOR LIKE CASSIM ONCE DID?!
YES!
GRIP

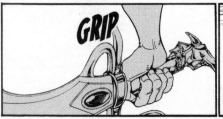

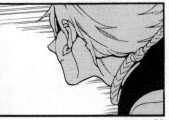

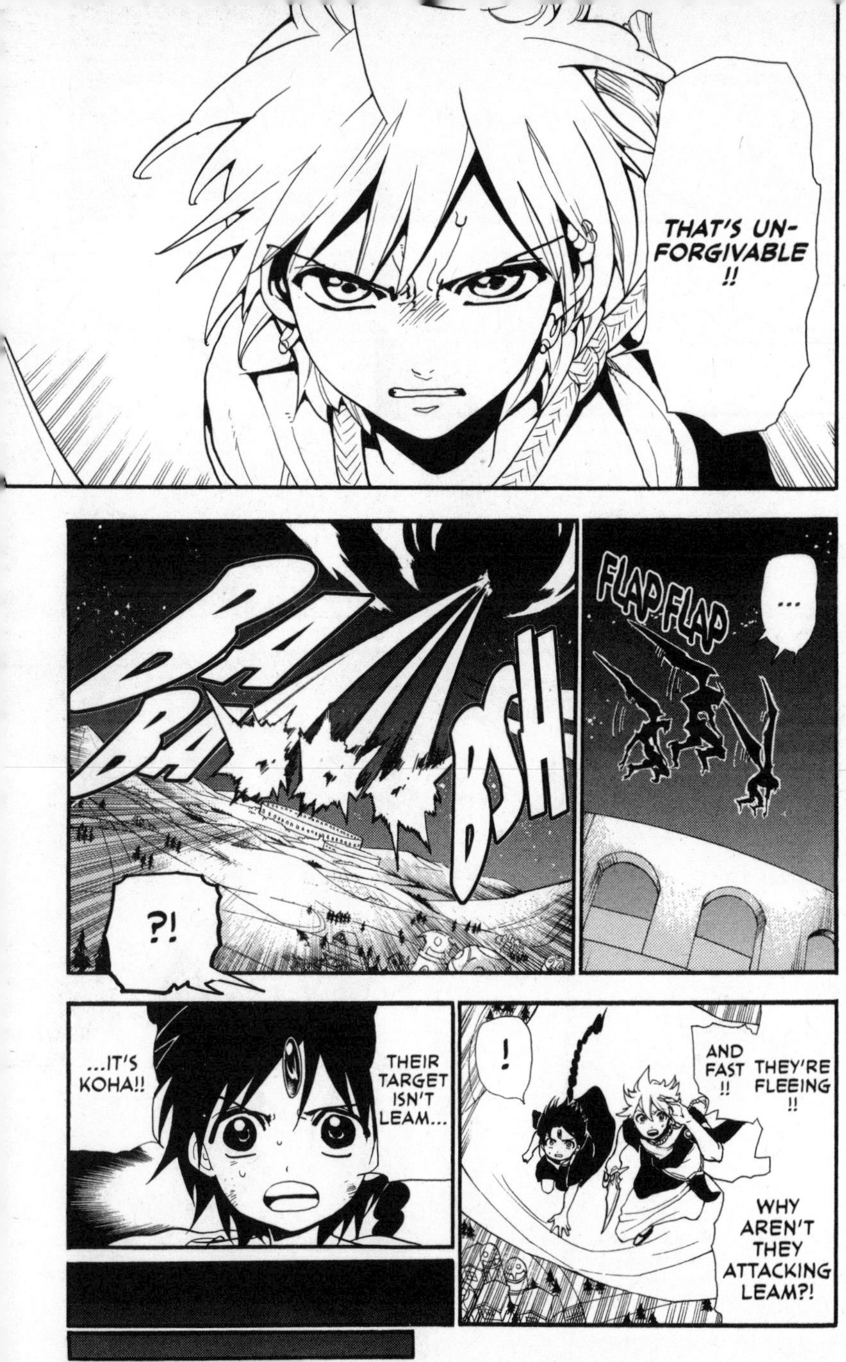
THAT'S UN-FORGIVABLE !!
FLAP FLAP
...
BA BA
BSH
?!
!
THEY'RE FLEEING !!
AND FAST !!
WHY AREN'T THEY ATTACKING LEAM?!
THEIR TARGET ISN'T LEAM...
...IT'S KOHA!!

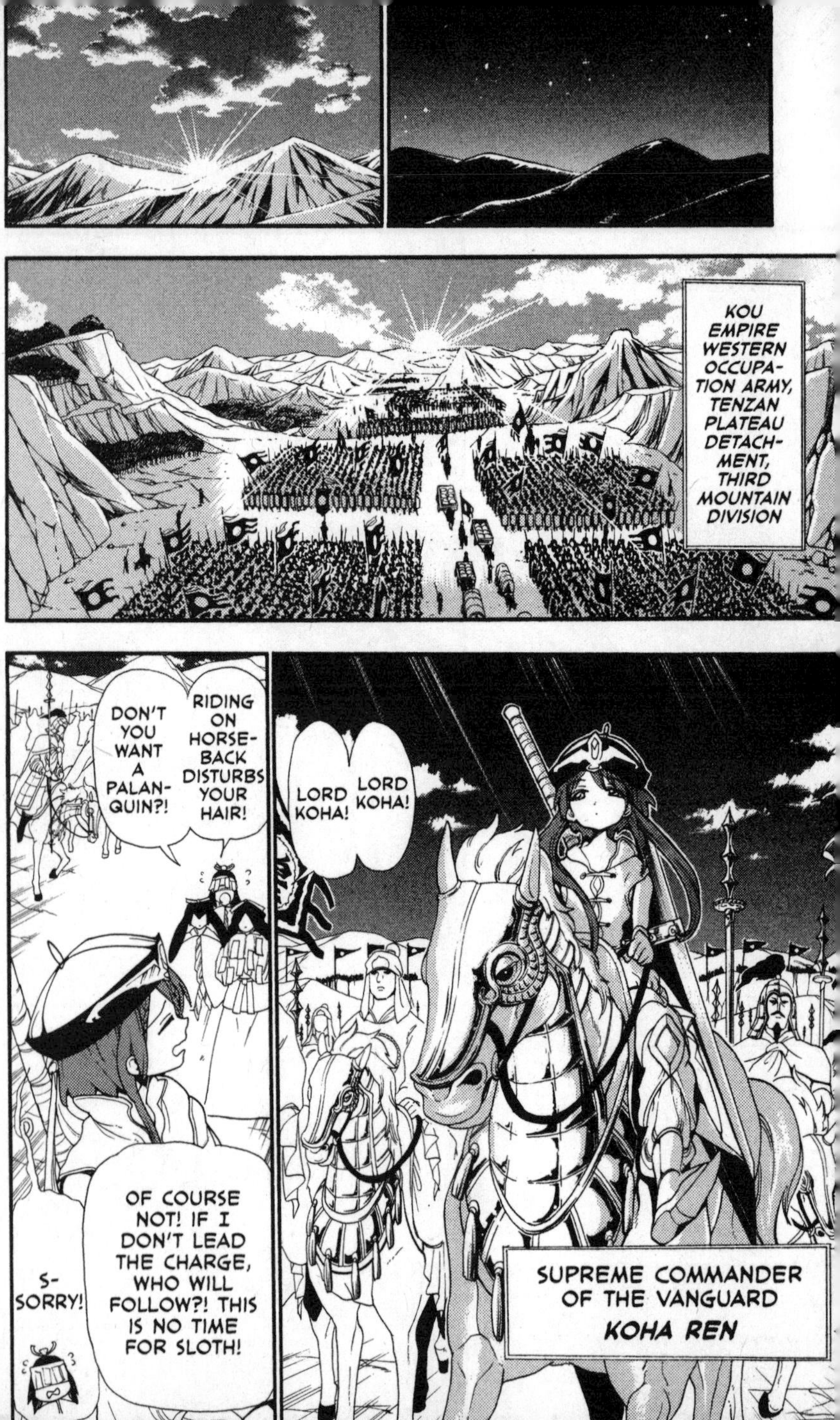
KOU EMPIRE WESTERN OCCUPATION ARMY, TENZAN PLATEAU DETACHMENT, THIRD MOUNTAIN DIVISION
LORD KOHA!
LORD KOHA!
SUPREME COMMANDER OF THE VANGUARD *KOHA REN*
RIDING ON HORSEBACK DISTURBS YOUR HAIR!
DON'T YOU WANT A PALANQUIN?!
OF COURSE NOT! IF I DON'T LEAD THE CHARGE, WHO WILL FOLLOW?! THIS IS NO TIME FOR SLOTH!
S-SORRY!

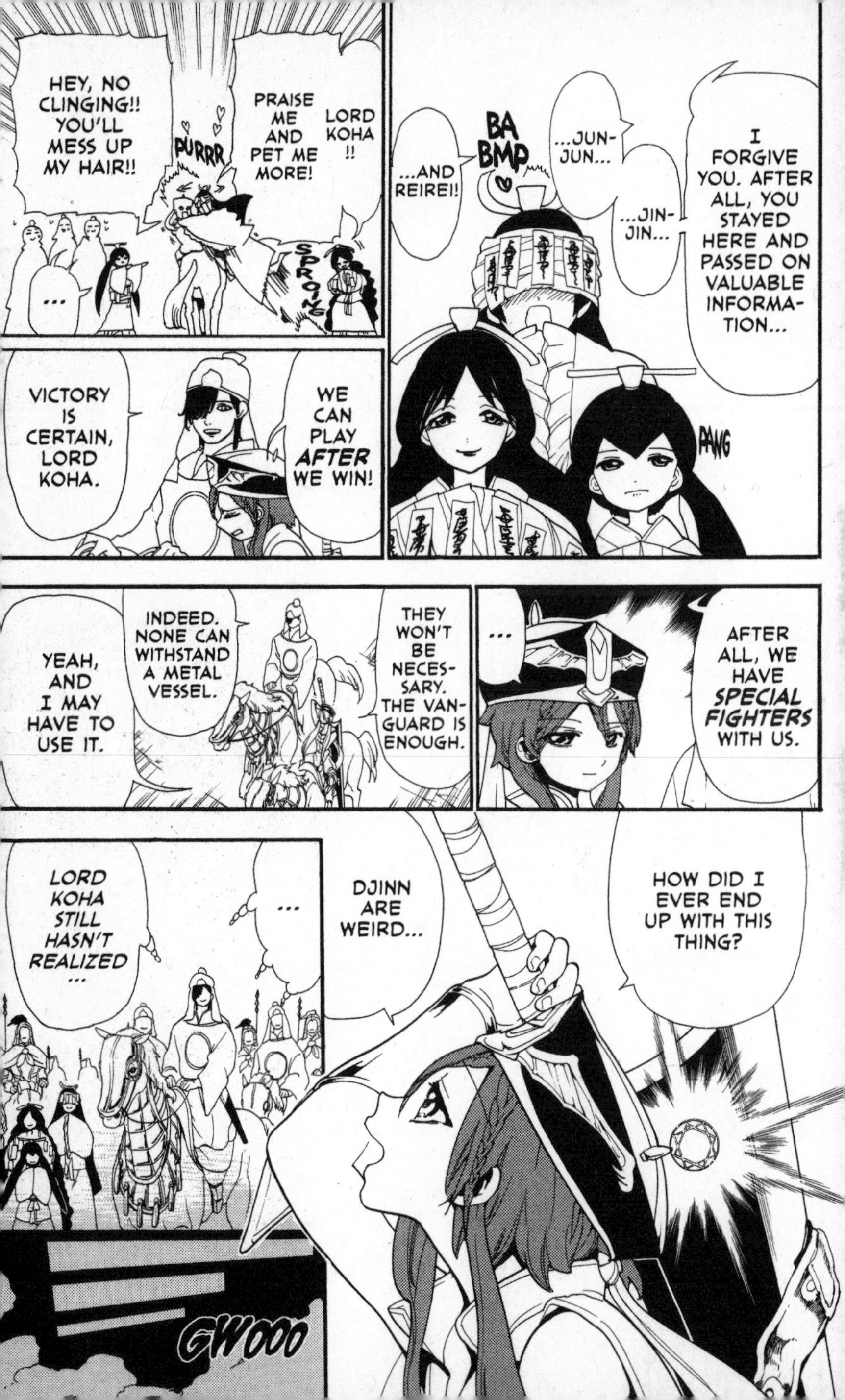

I FORGIVE YOU. AFTER ALL, YOU STAYED HERE AND PASSED ON VALUABLE INFORMA-TION...
...JUN-JUN...
...JIN-JIN...
BA BMP
...AND REIREI!!
PANG
LORD KOHA!!
PRAISE ME AND PET ME MORE!
PURRR
HEY, NO CLINGING!! YOU'LL MESS UP MY HAIR!!
SPROING
...
WE CAN PLAY AFTER WE WIN!
VICTORY IS CERTAIN, LORD KOHA.
AFTER ALL, WE HAVE SPECIAL FIGHTERS WITH US.
...
THEY WON'T BE NECES-SARY. THE VAN-GUARD IS ENOUGH.
INDEED. NONE CAN WITHSTAND A METAL VESSEL.
YEAH, AND I MAY HAVE TO USE IT.
HOW DID I EVER END UP WITH THIS THING?
DJINN ARE WEIRD...
...
LORD KOHA STILL HASN'T REALIZED...
GWOOO

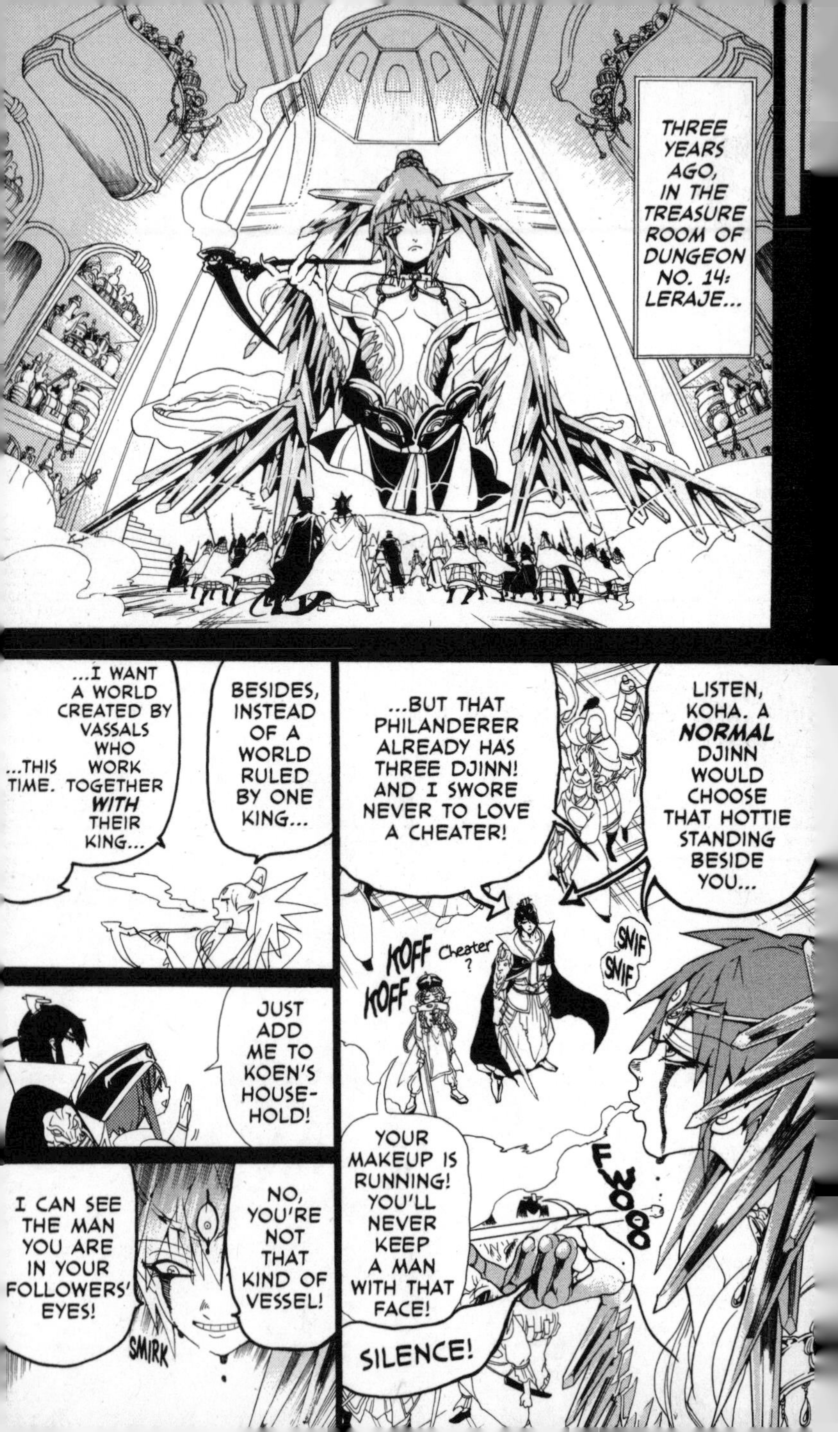
THREE YEARS AGO, IN THE TREASURE ROOM OF DUNGEON NO. 14: LERAJE...
LISTEN, KOHA. A ***NORMAL*** DJINN WOULD CHOOSE THAT HOTTIE STANDING BESIDE YOU...
...BUT THAT PHILANDERER ALREADY HAS THREE DJINN! AND I SWORE NEVER TO LOVE A CHEATER!
SNIF SNIF
Cheater?
KOFF KOFF
FWOOO
YOUR MAKEUP IS RUNNING! YOU'LL NEVER KEEP A MAN WITH THAT FACE!
SILENCE!
BESIDES, INSTEAD OF A WORLD RULED BY ONE KING...
...I WANT A WORLD CREATED BY VASSALS WHO WORK TOGETHER ***WITH*** THEIR KING...
...THIS TIME.
JUST ADD ME TO KOEN'S HOUSE-HOLD!
NO, YOU'RE NOT THAT KIND OF VESSEL!
I CAN SEE THE MAN YOU ARE IN YOUR FOLLOWERS' EYES!
SMIRK

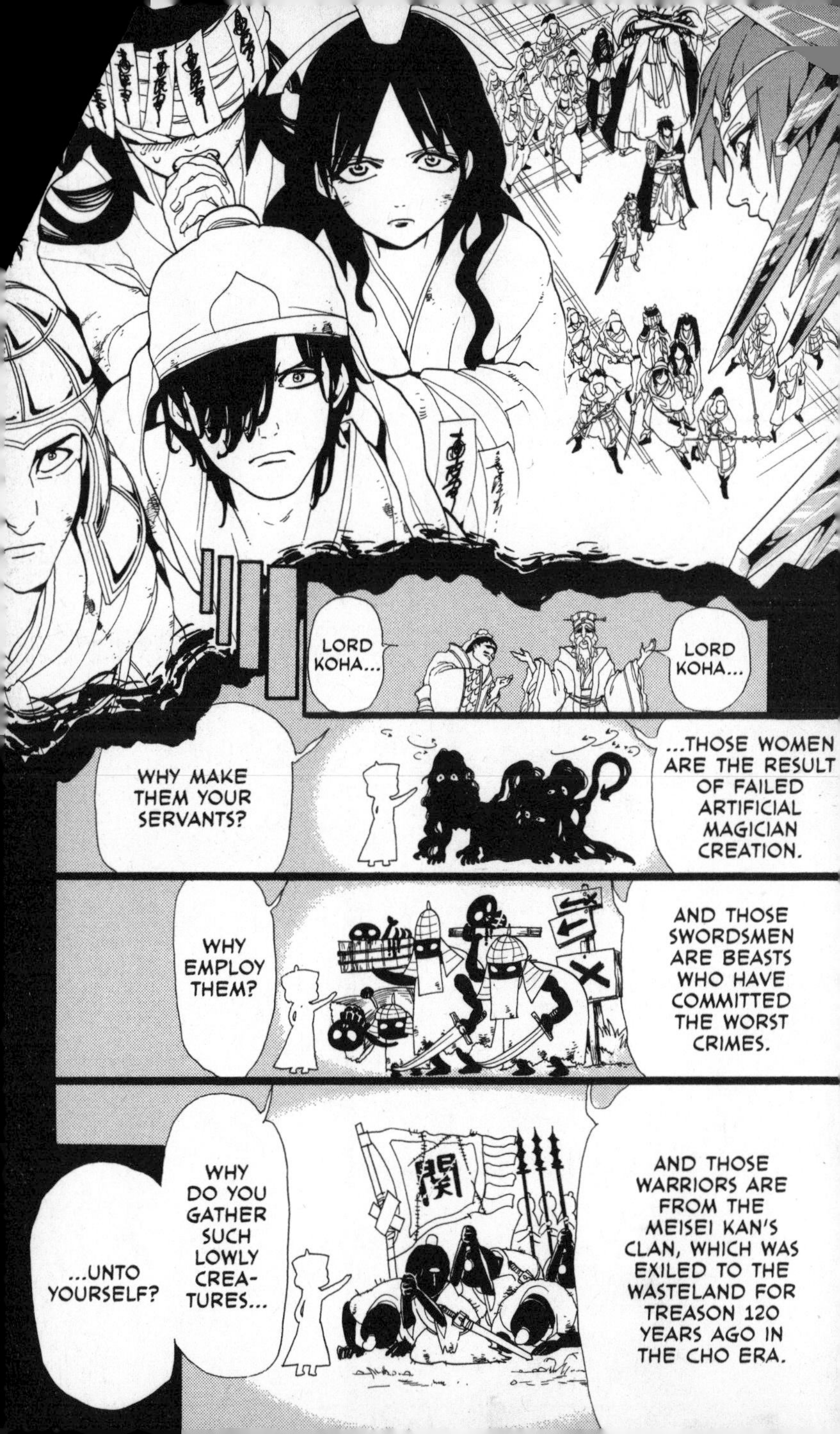
LORD KOHA...
LORD KOHA...
...THOSE WOMEN ARE THE RESULT OF FAILED ARTIFICIAL MAGICIAN CREATION.
WHY MAKE THEM YOUR SERVANTS?
AND THOSE SWORDSMEN ARE BEASTS WHO HAVE COMMITTED THE WORST CRIMES.
WHY EMPLOY THEM?
AND THOSE WARRIORS ARE FROM THE MEISEI KAN'S CLAN, WHICH WAS EXILED TO THE WASTELAND FOR TREASON 120 YEARS AGO IN THE CHO ERA.
WHY DO YOU GATHER SUCH LOWLY CREA-TURES...
...UNTO YOURSELF?

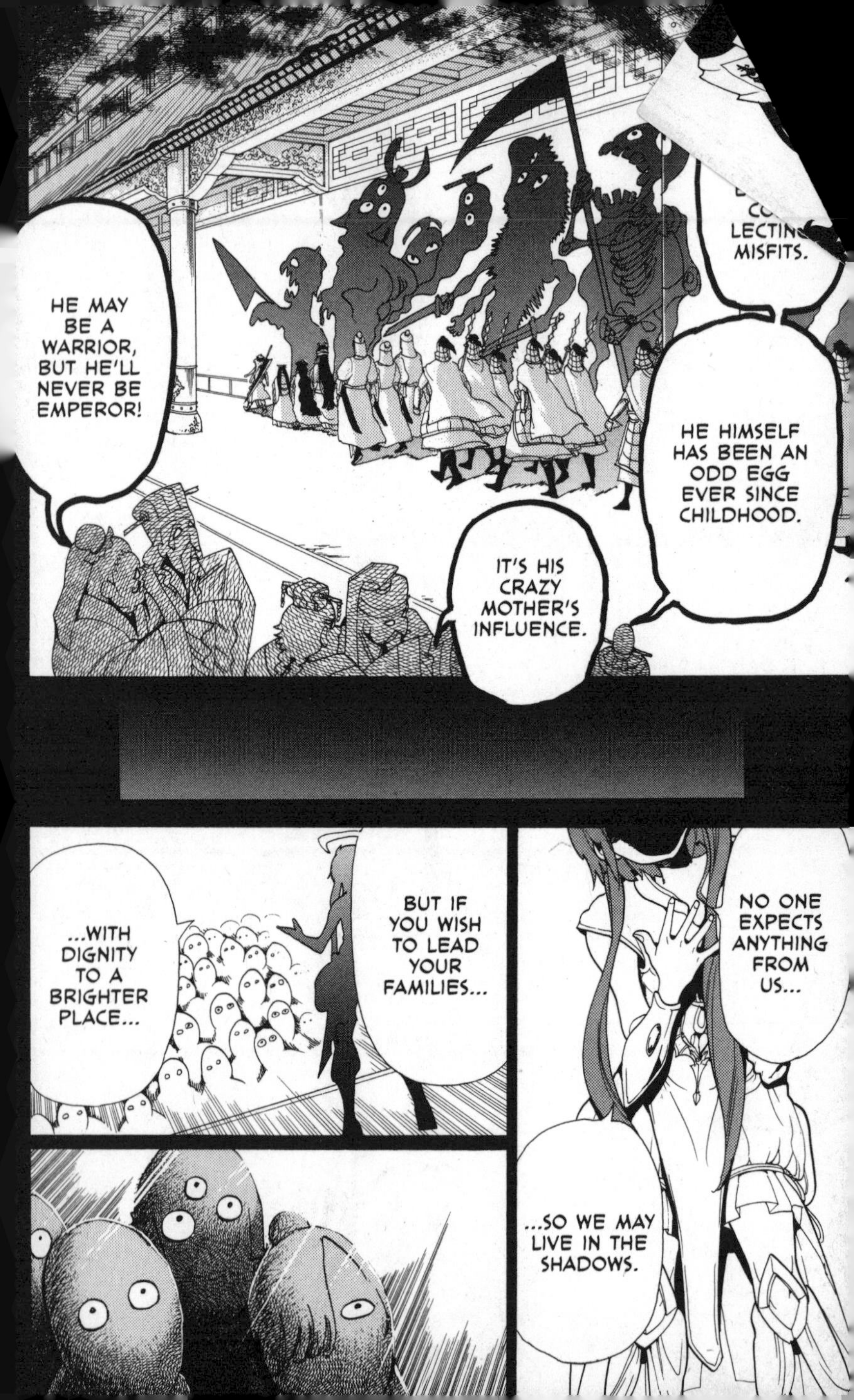
CO
LECTIN
MISFITS.
HE HIMSELF HAS BEEN AN ODD EGG EVER SINCE CHILDHOOD.
IT'S HIS CRAZY MOTHER'S INFLUENCE.
HE MAY BE A WARRIOR, BUT HE'LL NEVER BE EMPEROR!
NO ONE EXPECTS ANYTHING FROM US...
...SO WE MAY LIVE IN THE SHADOWS.
BUT IF YOU WISH TO LEAD YOUR FAMILIES...
...WITH DIGNITY TO A BRIGHTER PLACE...

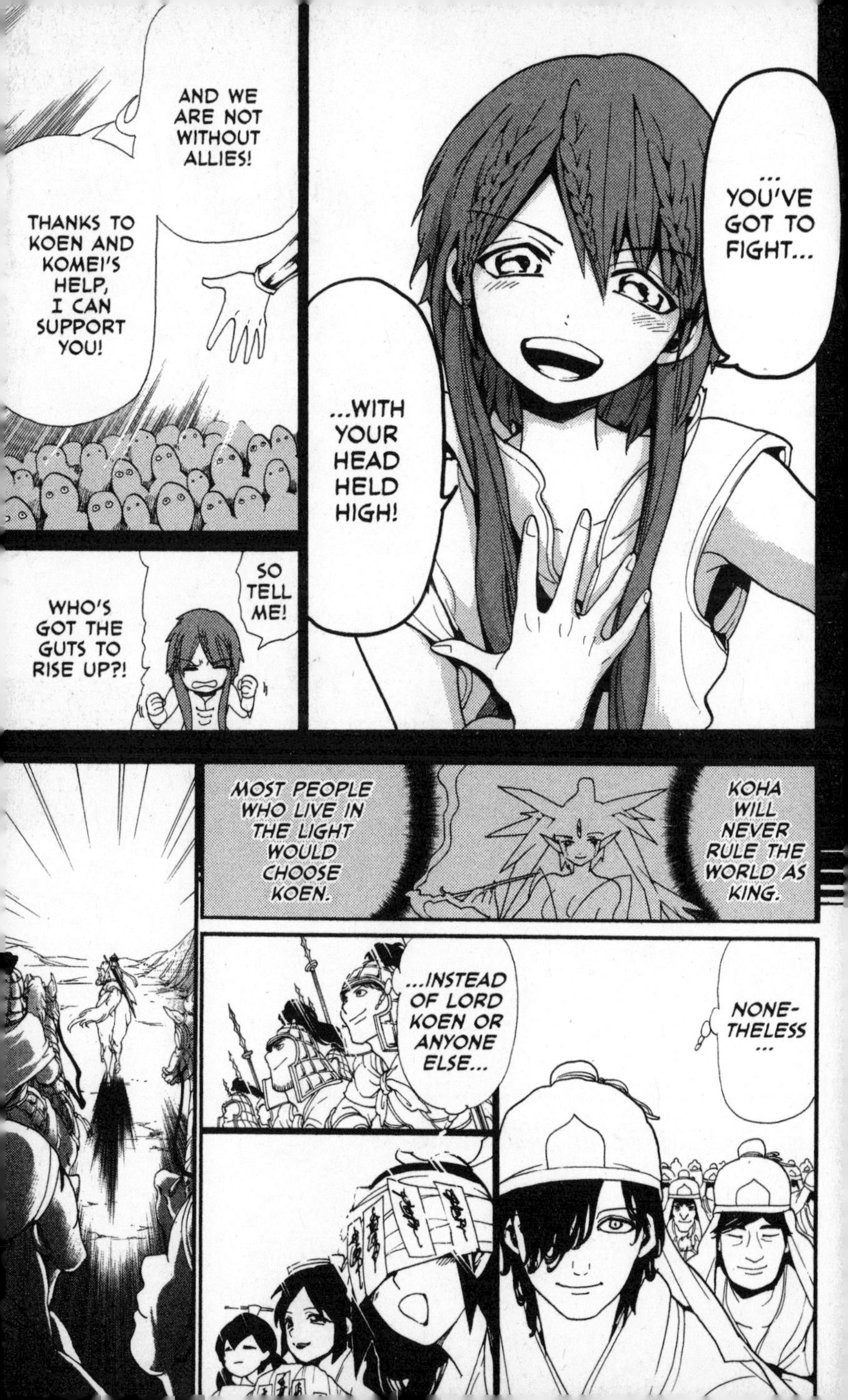

... YOU'VE GOT TO FIGHT...
...WITH YOUR HEAD HELD HIGH!
AND WE ARE NOT WITHOUT ALLIES!
THANKS TO KOEN AND KOMEI'S HELP, I CAN SUPPORT YOU!
SO TELL ME!
WHO'S GOT THE GUTS TO RISE UP?!
KOHA WILL NEVER RULE THE WORLD AS KING.
MOST PEOPLE WHO LIVE IN THE LIGHT WOULD CHOOSE KOEN.
NONE-THELESS ...
...INSTEAD OF LORD KOEN OR ANYONE ELSE...

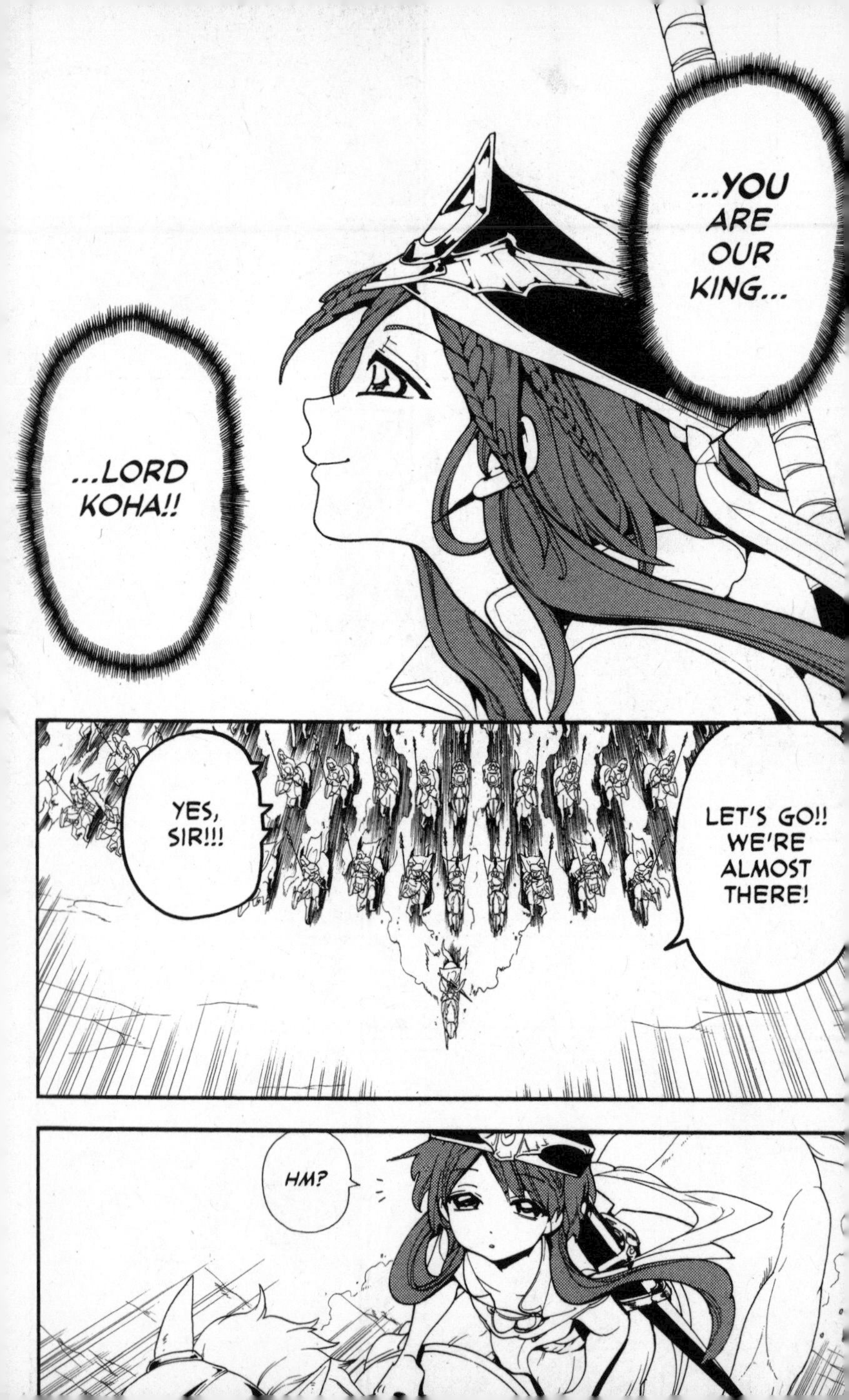
...YOU ARE OUR KING...
...LORD KOHA!!
LET'S GO!! WE'RE ALMOST THERE!
YES, SIR!!!
HM?

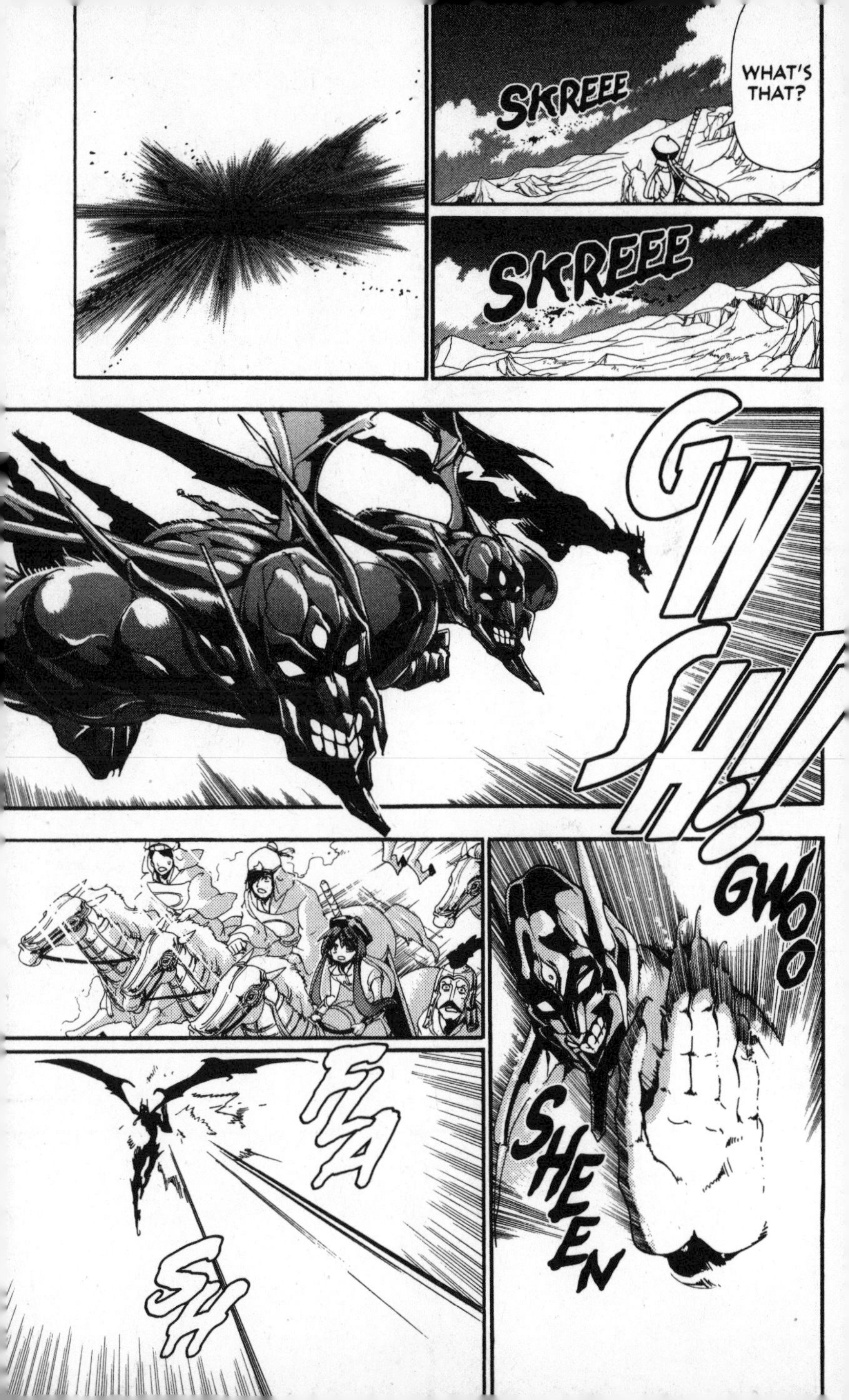
SKREEE
WHAT'S THAT?
SKREEE
GWSHH!!
GWOOO
SHEEEN
FLA
SH

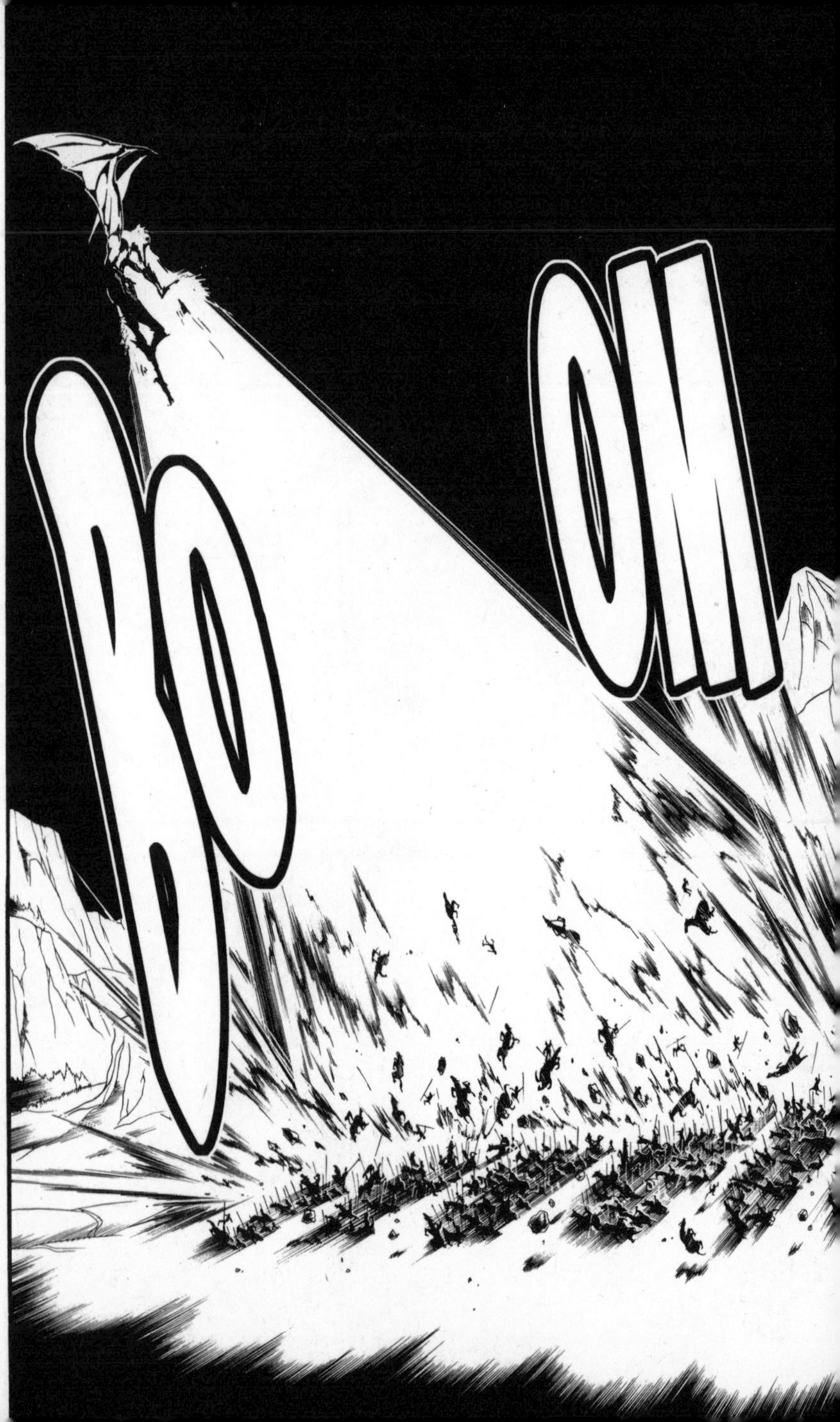
BOOM

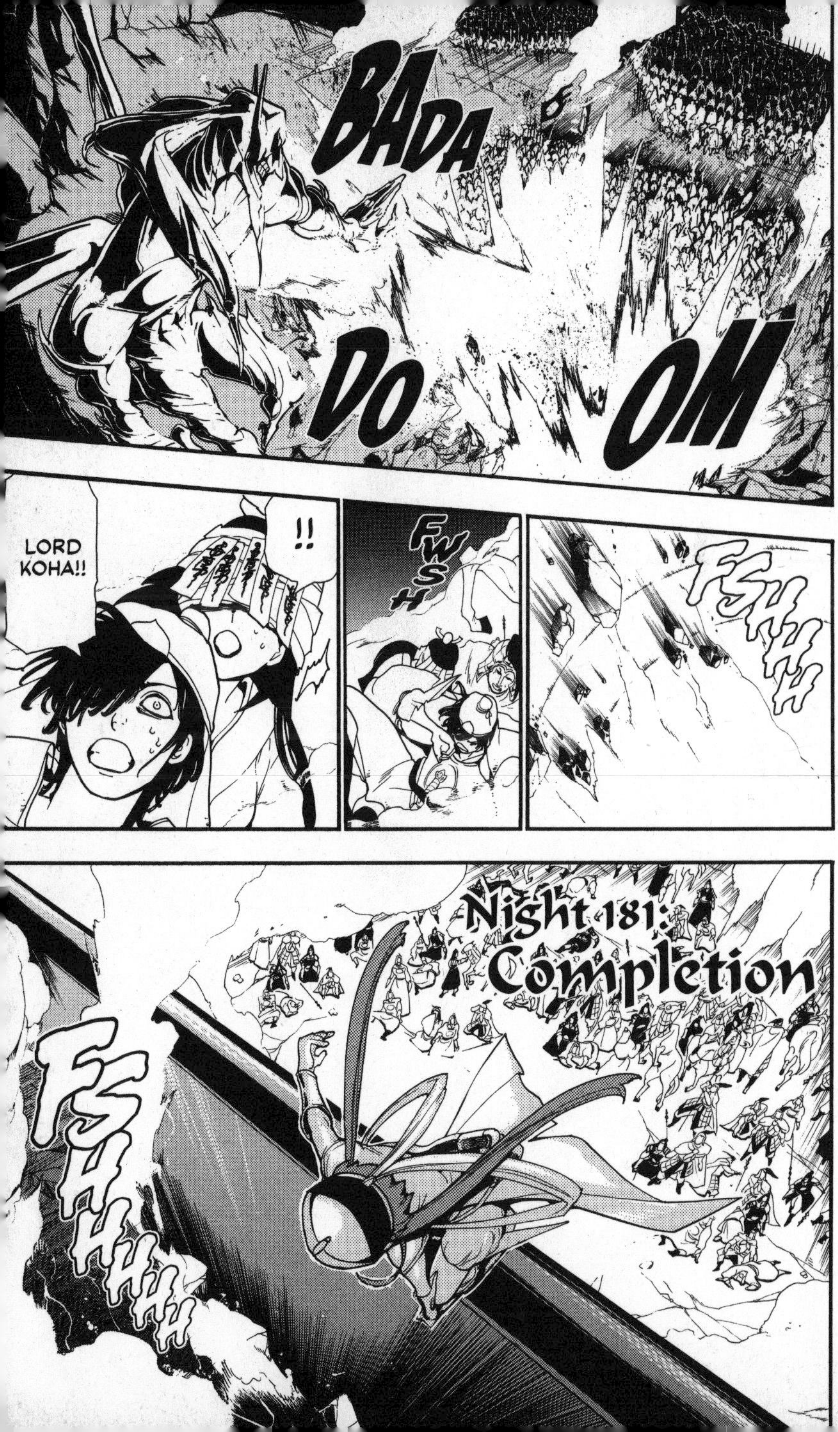
BADA
DO
OM
FSHHHH
FWSH
!!
LORD KOHA!!
Night 181: Completion
FSHHHHH

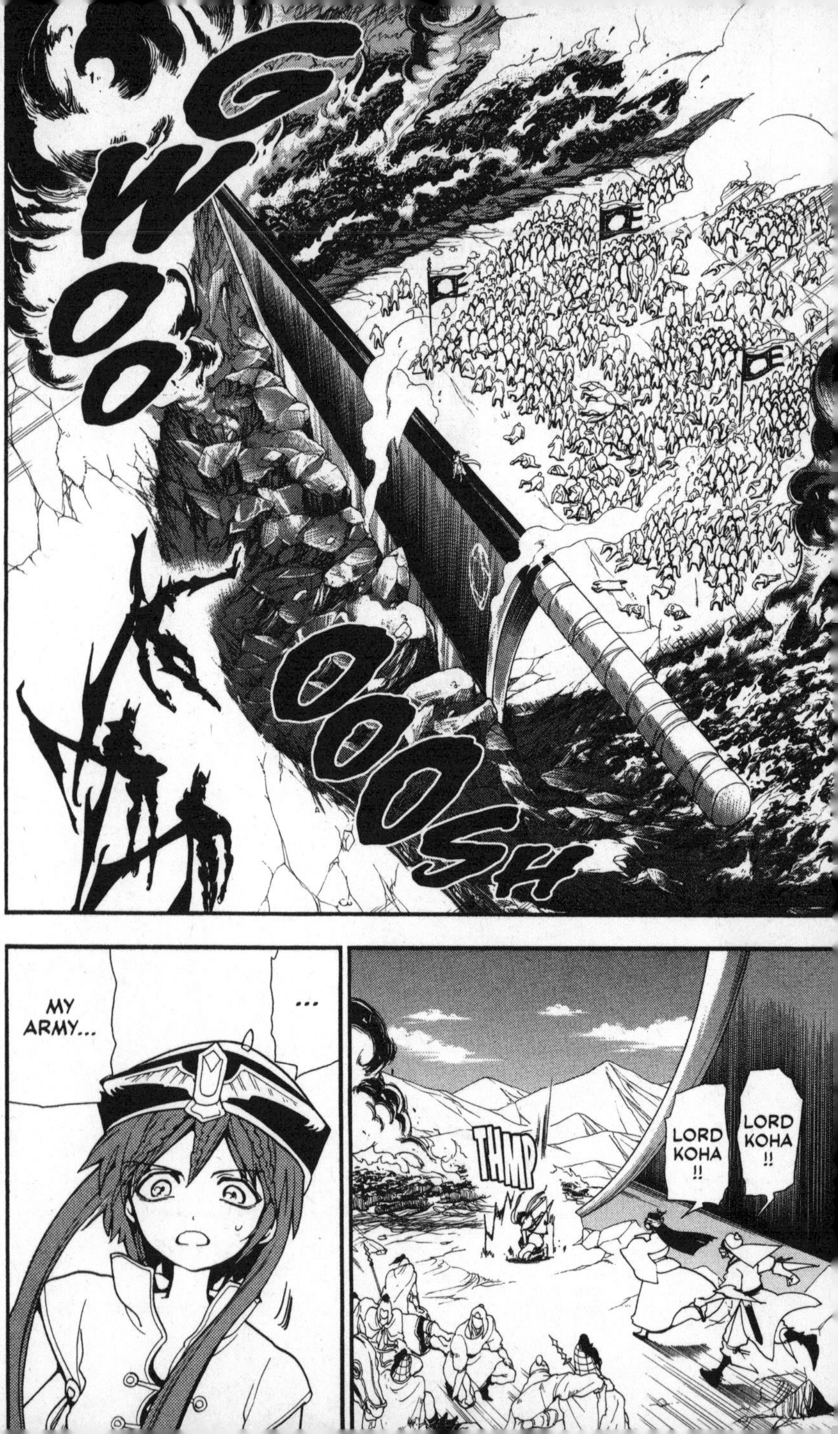
GWOO
OOOOSH
LORD KOHA!!
LORD KOHA!!
THMP
...
MY ARMY...

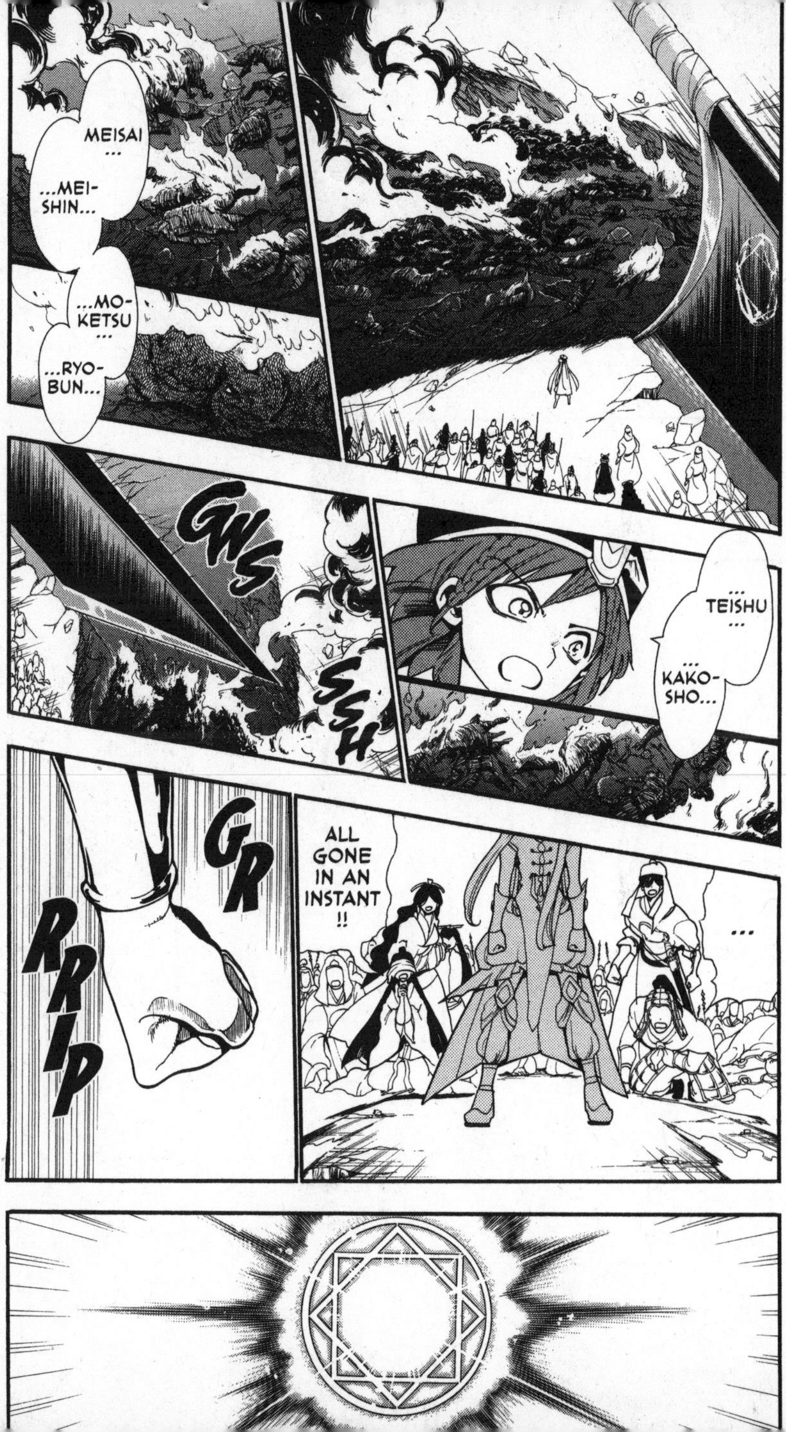
MEISAI ...
...MEI-SHIN...
...MO-KETSU ...
...RYO-BUN...
... TEISHU ...
... KAKO-SHO...
GWS
SSSH
ALL GONE IN AN INSTANT !!
...
GR
RRIP

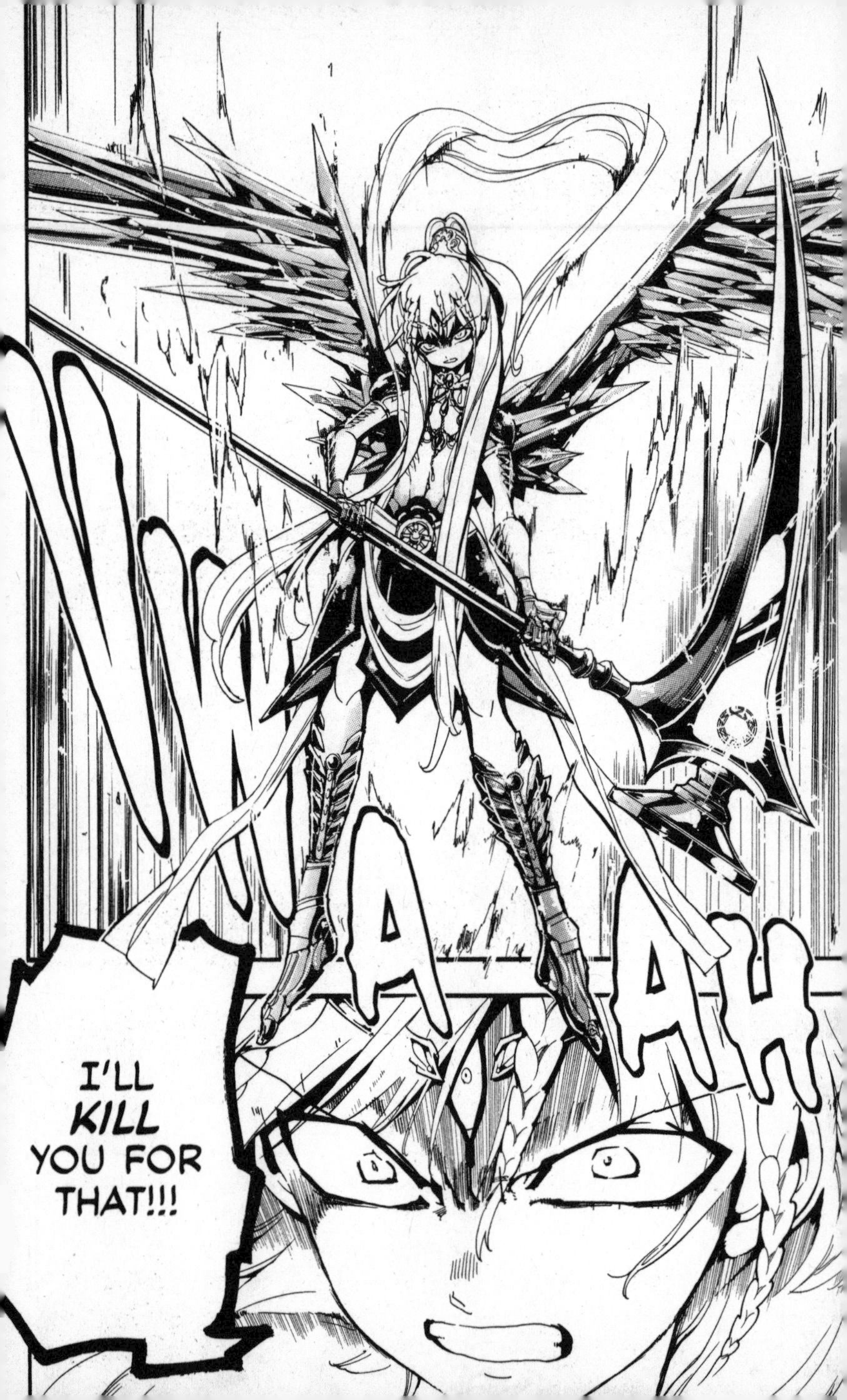
I'LL **KILL** YOU FOR THAT!!!

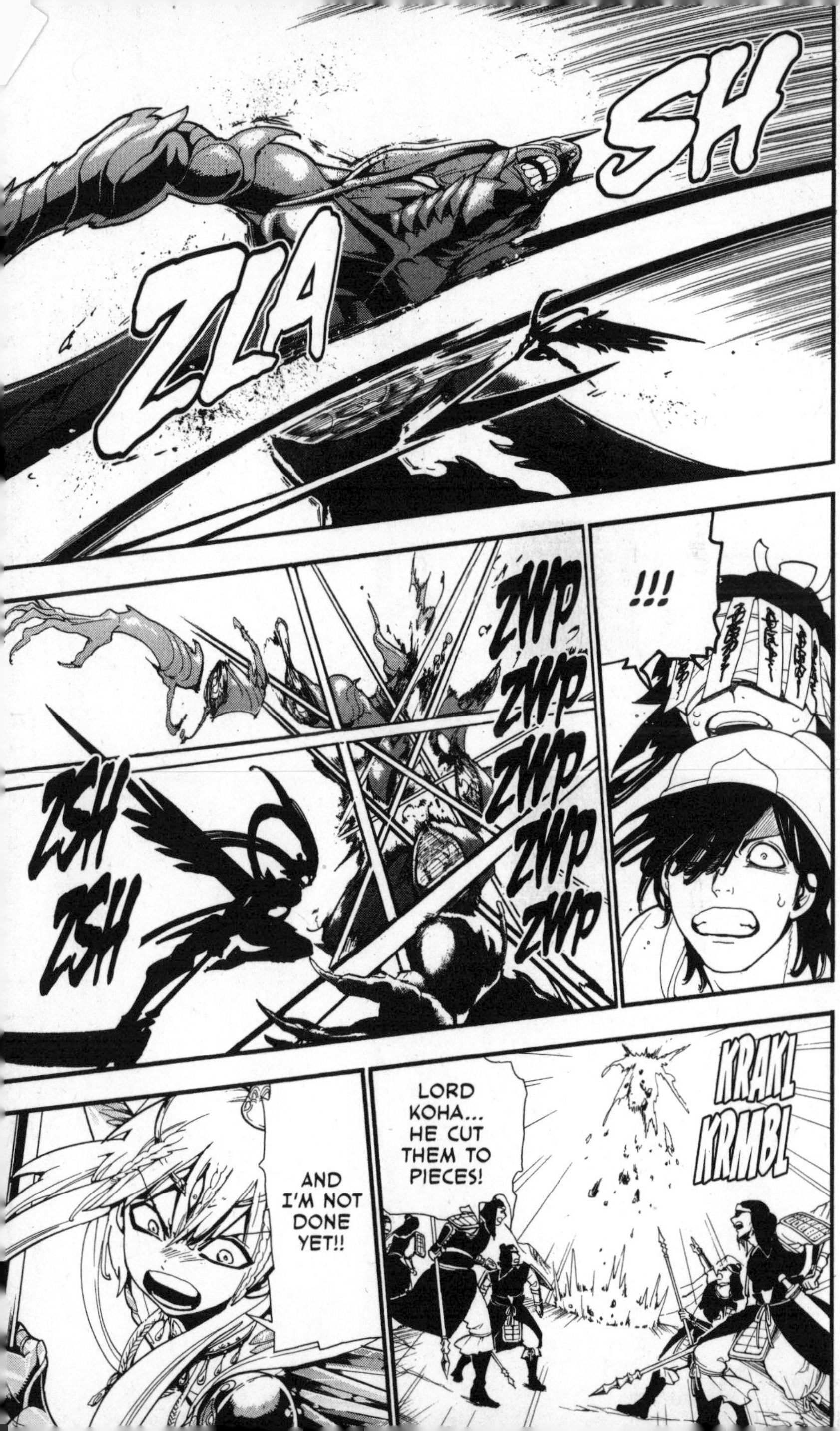
SH
ZLA
!!!
ZWP
ZWP
ZWP
ZWP
ZWP
TSH
TSH
KRAKL
KRMBL
LORD KOHA... HE CUT THEM TO PIECES!
AND I'M NOT DONE YET!!

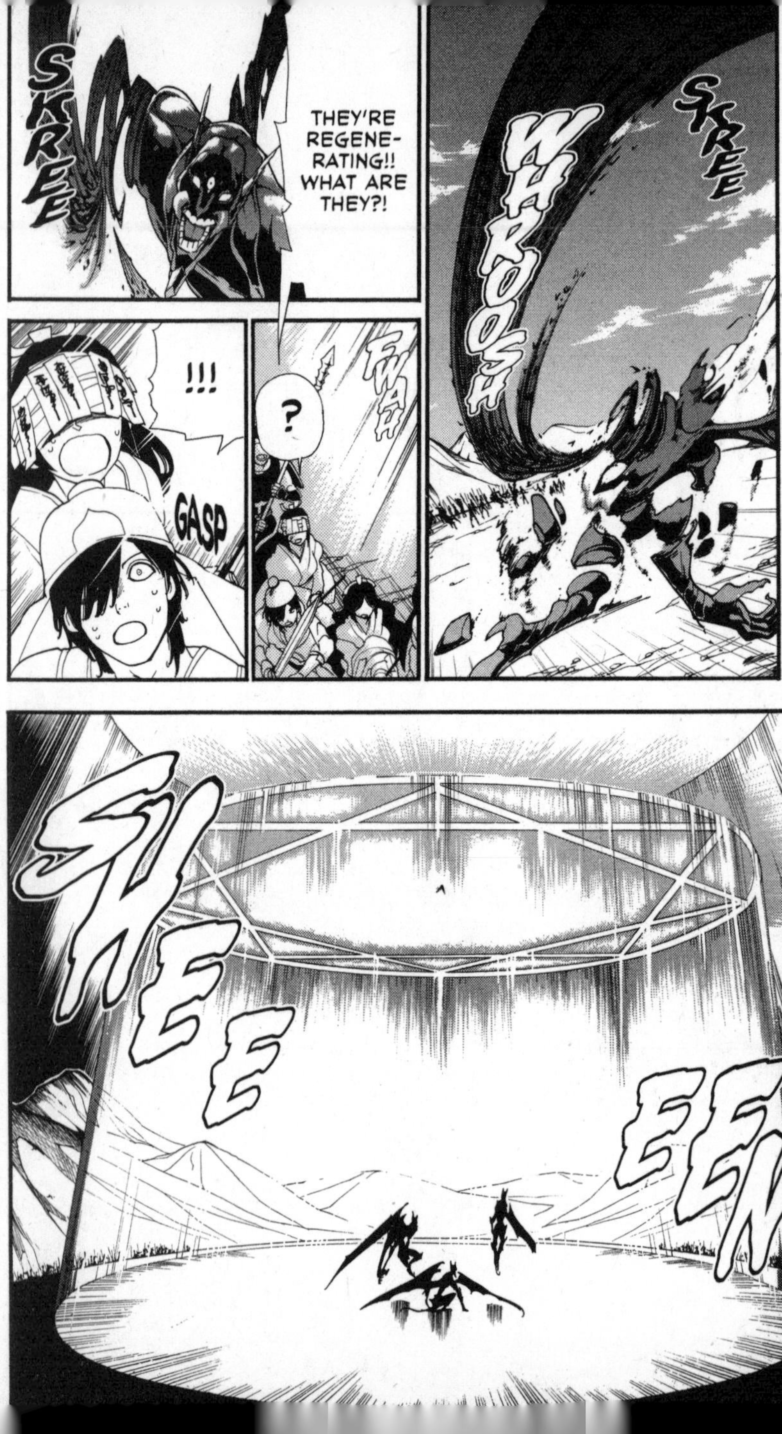
SKREE
WHOOSH
SKREE
THEY'RE REGENE-RATING!! WHAT ARE THEY?!
FWAH
?
!!!
GASP
SHEEEEEN

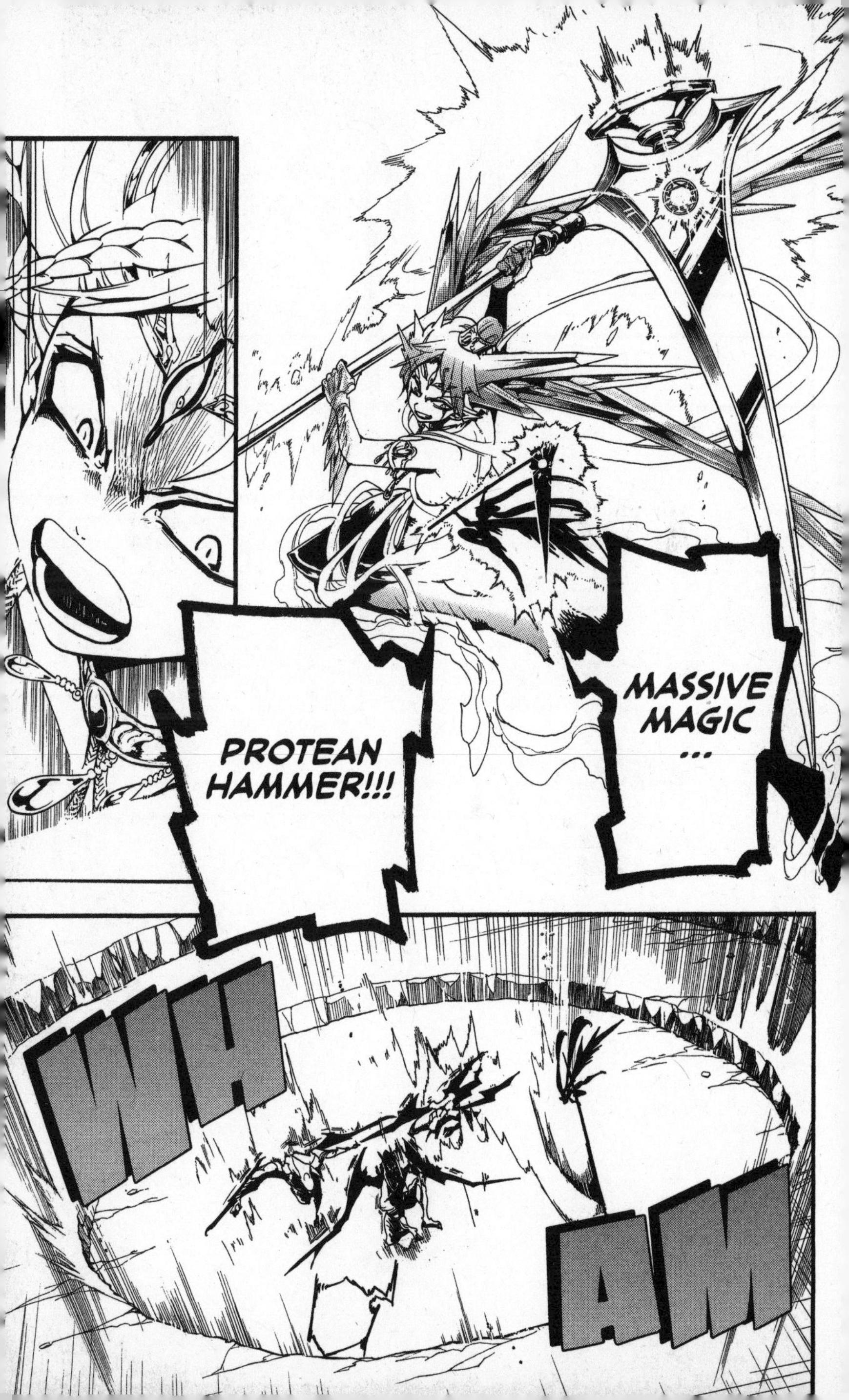
MASSIVE MAGIC ...
PROTEAN HAMMER!!!
WHAM

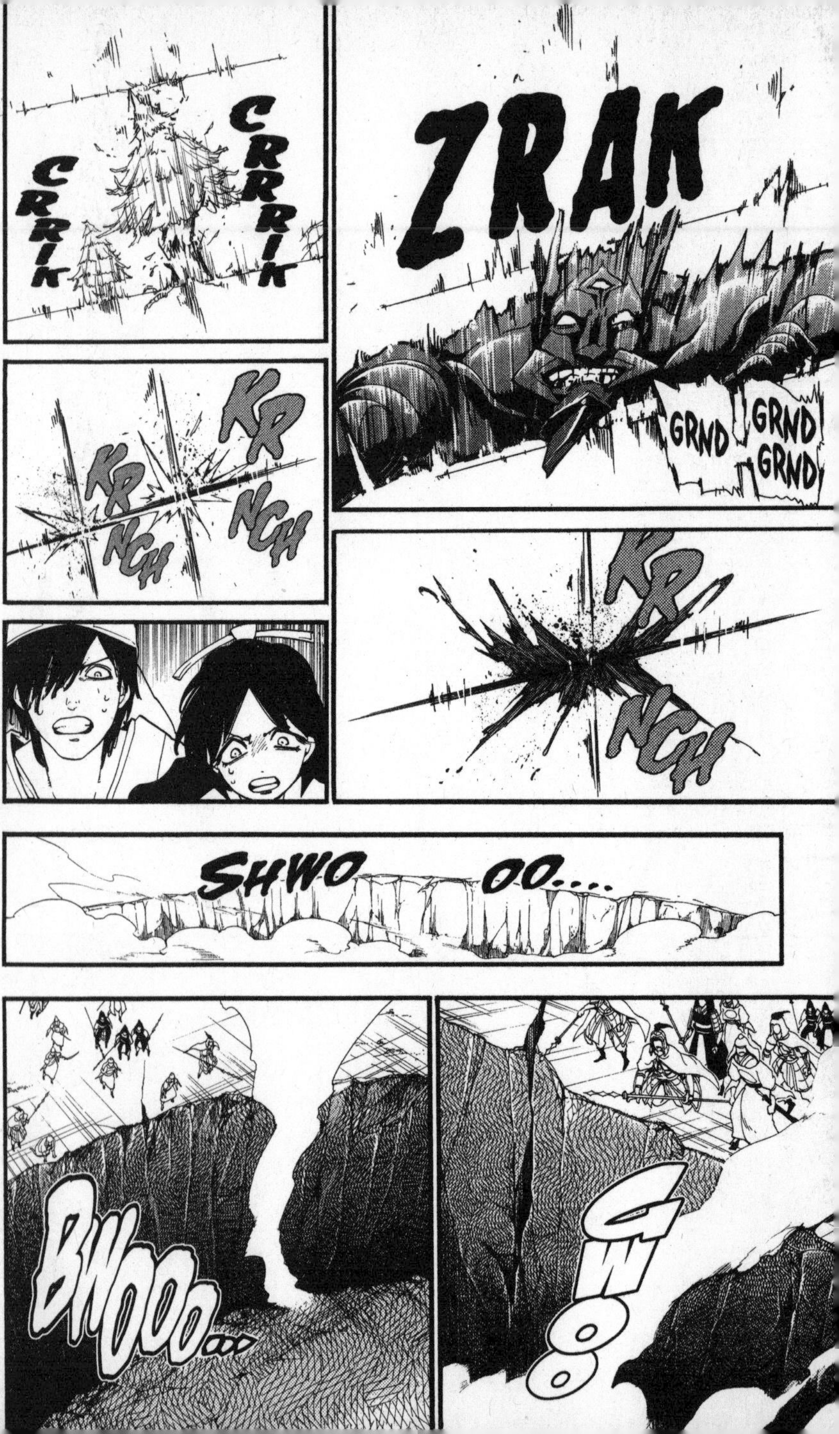
ZRAK
GRND GRND
GRND
GRND
CRRRIK
CRRIK
KR NCH
KR NCH
KR NCH
SHWO OO....
GWOO
BWOOO...

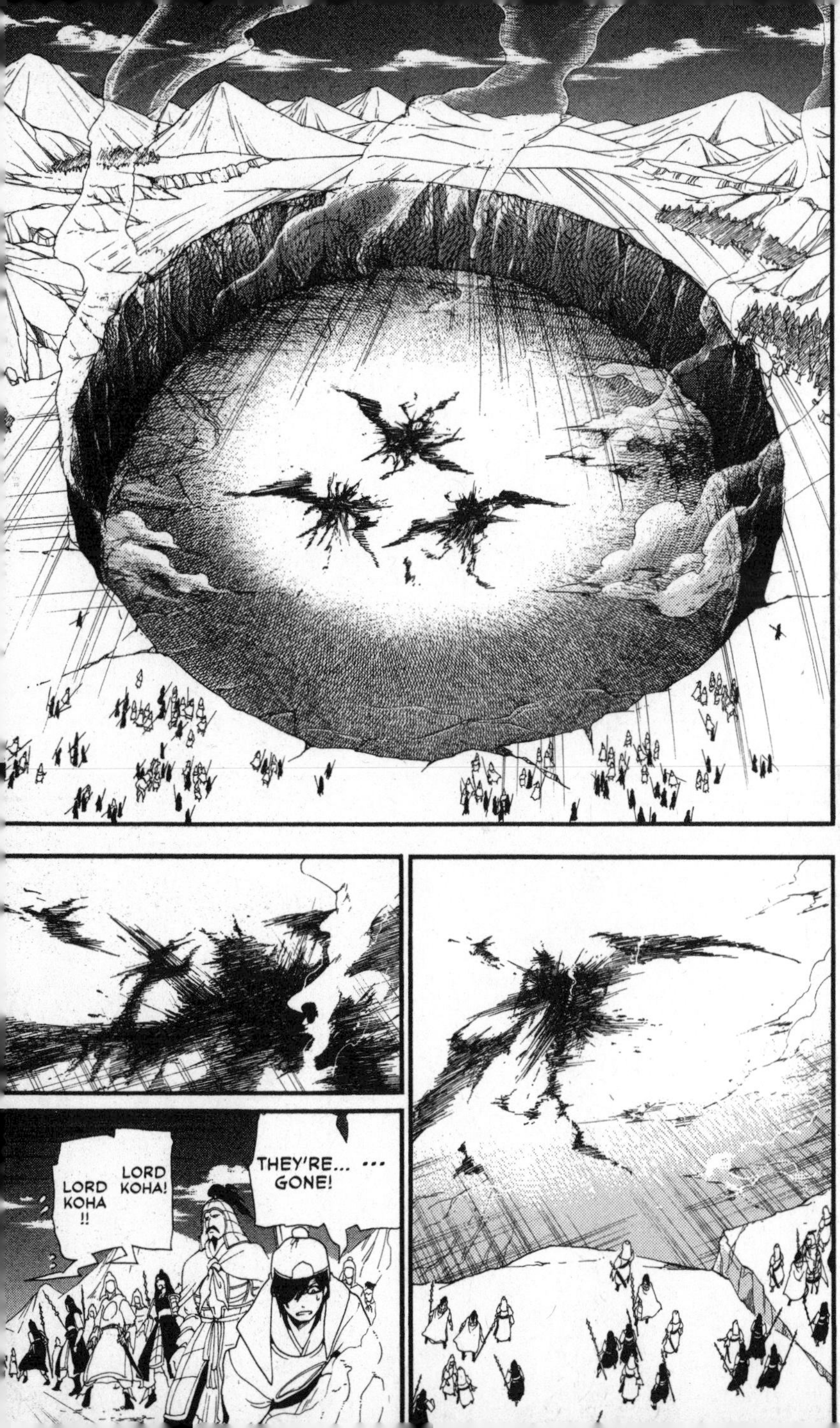
THEY'RE... ...GONE!
LORD KOHA!
LORD KOHA!!

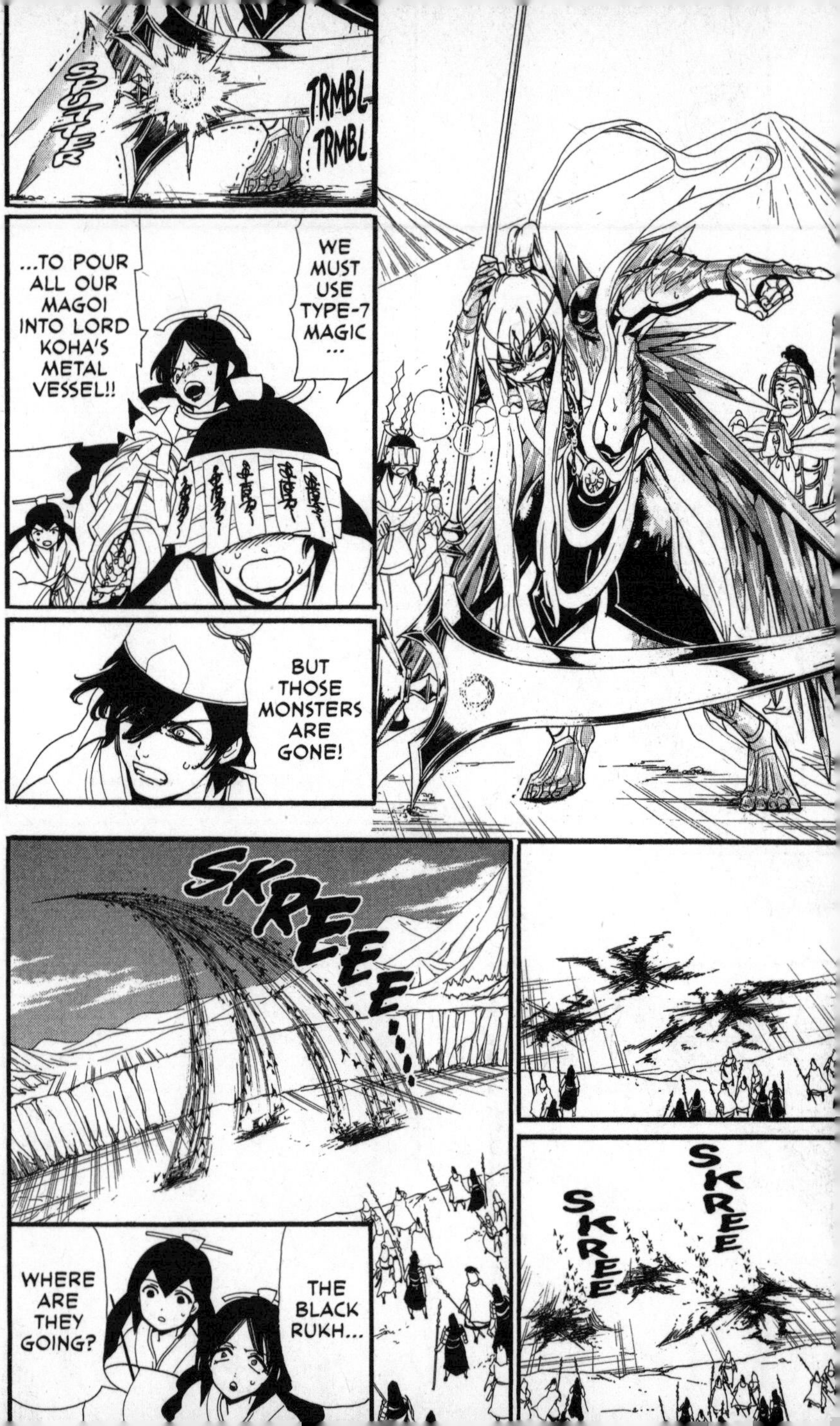
TRMBL TRMBL
SPUTTER
WE MUST USE TYPE-7 MAGIC...
...TO POUR ALL OUR MAGOI INTO LORD KOHA'S METAL VESSEL!!
BUT THOSE MONSTERS ARE GONE!
SKREE
SKREE
SKREEEE...
THE BLACK RUKH...
WHERE ARE THEY GOING?

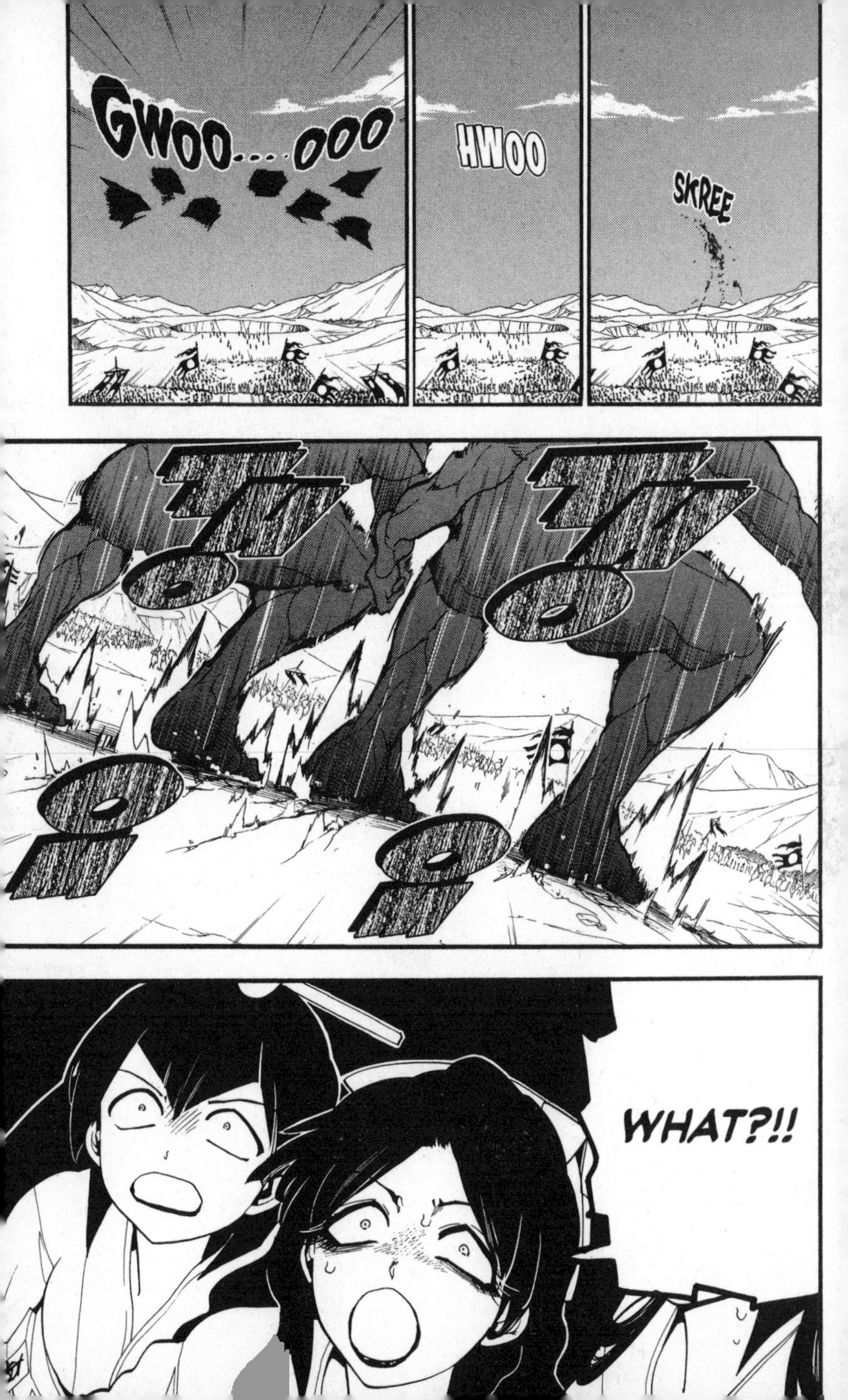
SKREE
HWOO
GWOO....OOO
WHAT?!!

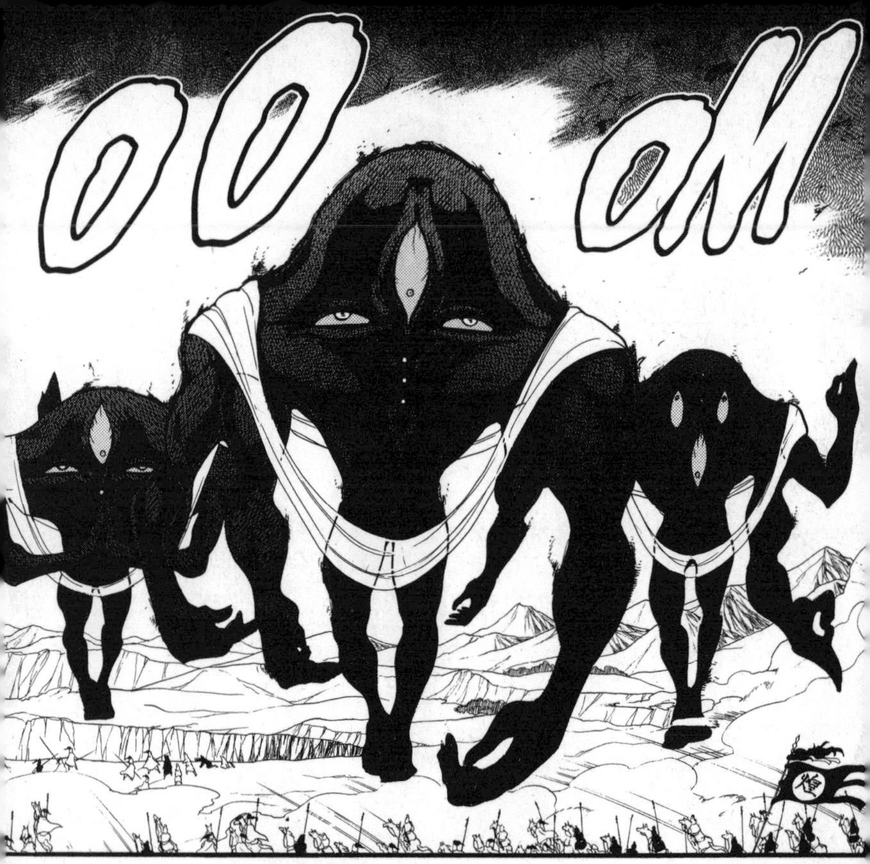
OOAH
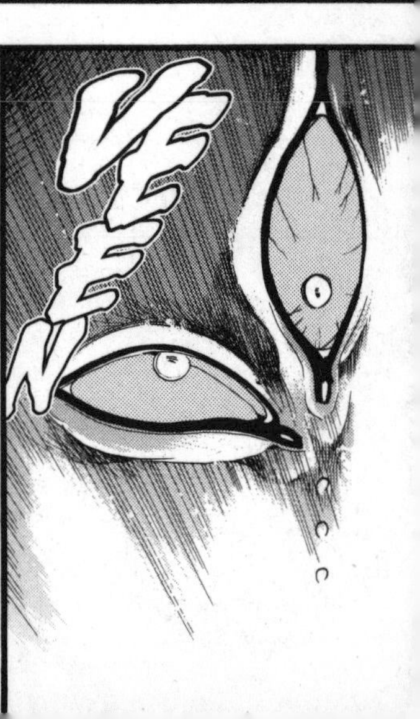
VEEEN
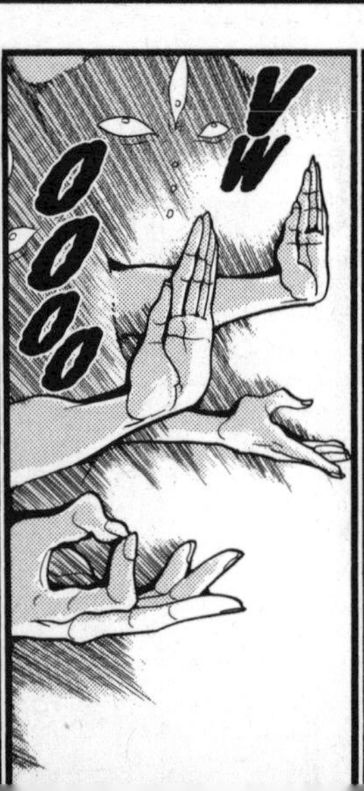
VWOOOOOO
W...
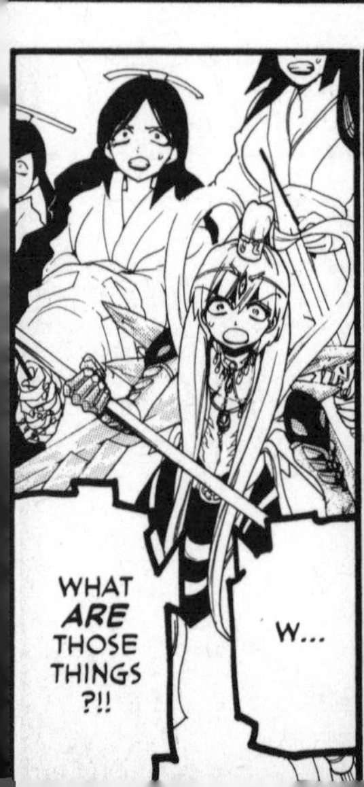
WHAT ARE THOSE THINGS ?!!

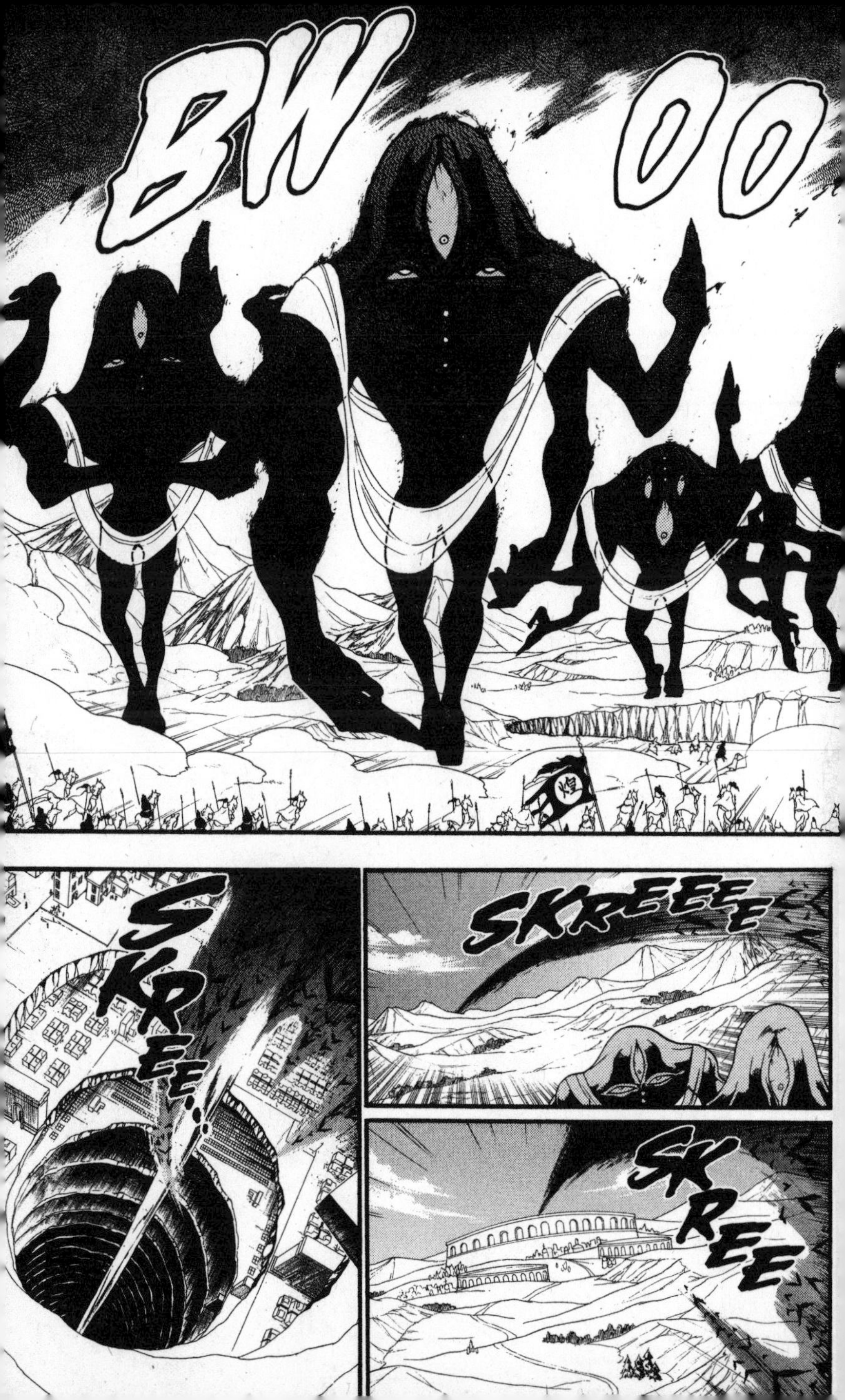
BWOO
煌
SKREEEEE
SKREE
SKREE...

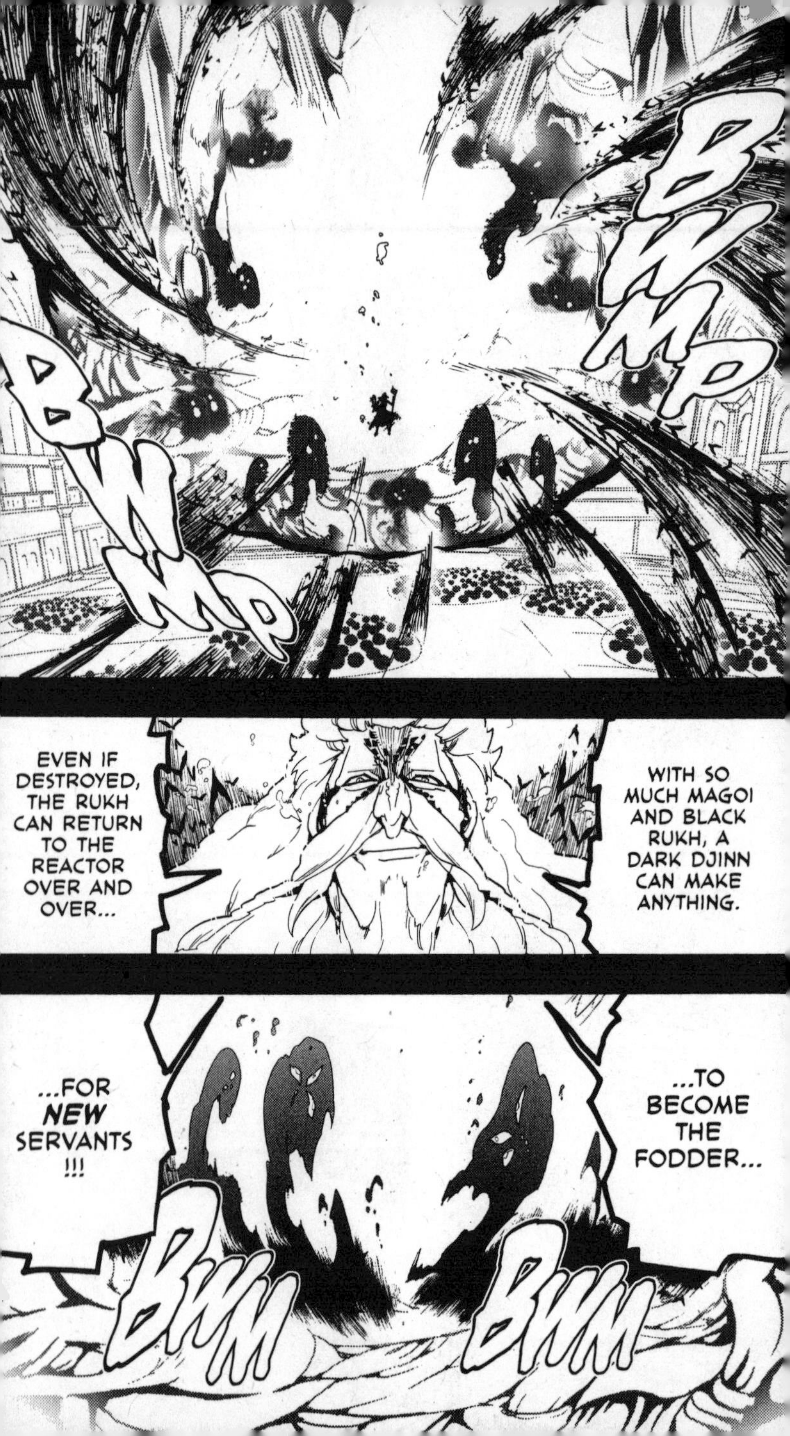
WITH SO MUCH MAGOI AND BLACK RUKH, A DARK DJINN CAN MAKE ANYTHING.
EVEN IF DESTROYED, THE RUKH CAN RETURN TO THE REACTOR OVER AND OVER...
...TO BECOME THE FODDER...
...FOR *NEW* SERVANTS!!!

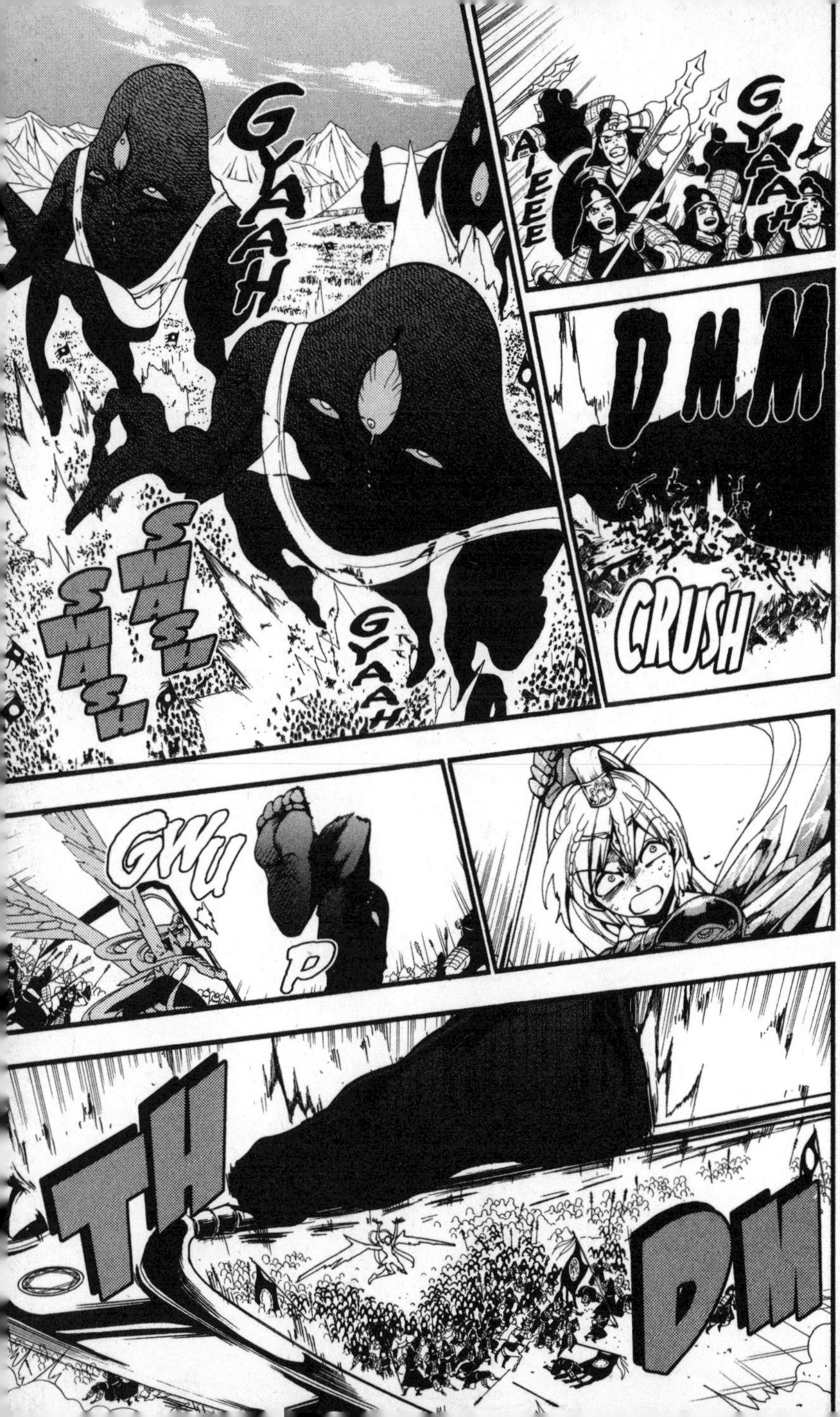

GYAAH
AIEEE
DMM
CRUSH
GYAAH
GYAAH
SMASH
SMASH
GWU
P
TH
DM

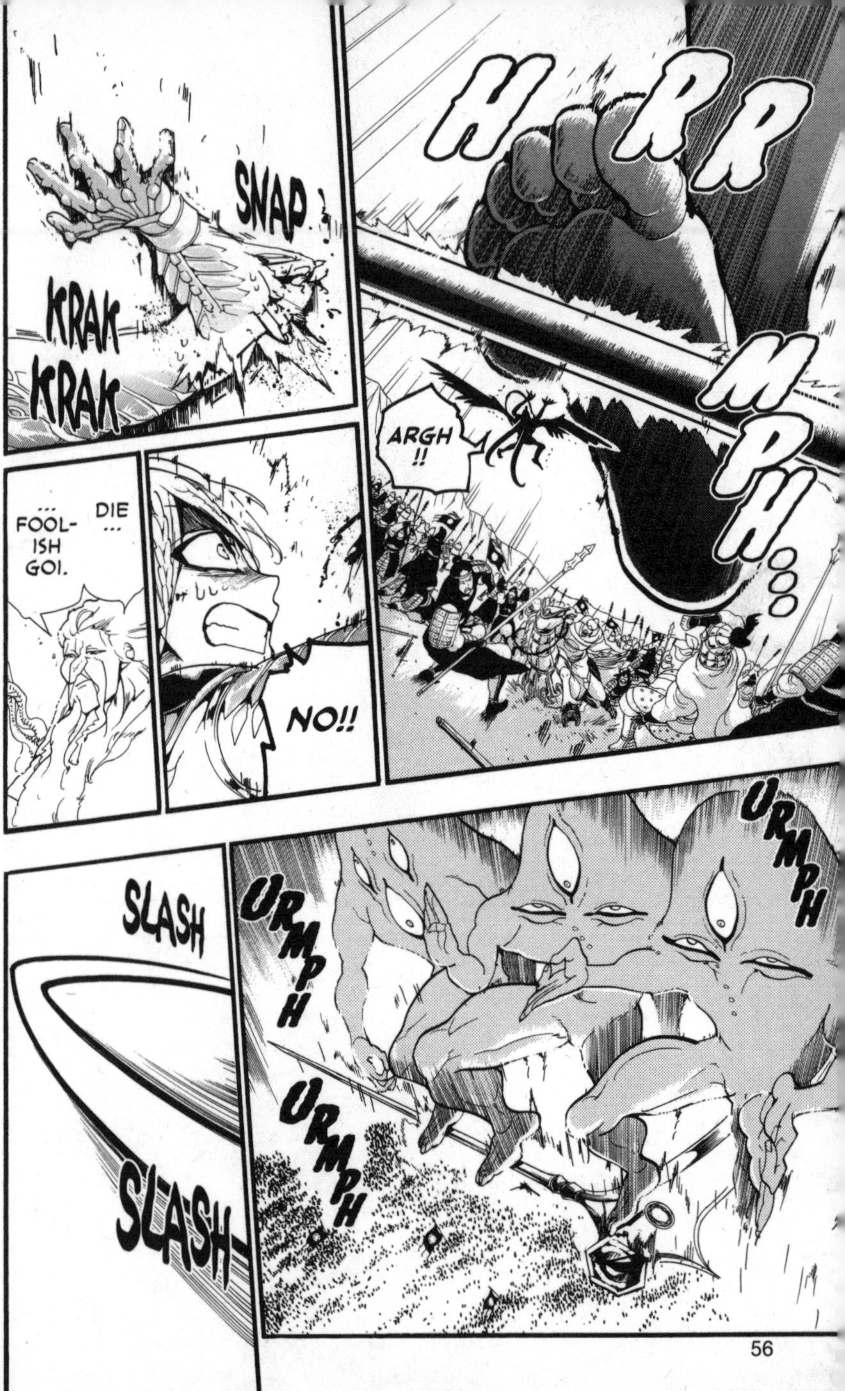
HRR
MPH...
ARGH!!
SNAP
KRAK KRAK
NO!!
DIE ...
... FOOL-ISH GOI.
URMPH
URMPH
URMPH
SLASH
SLASH

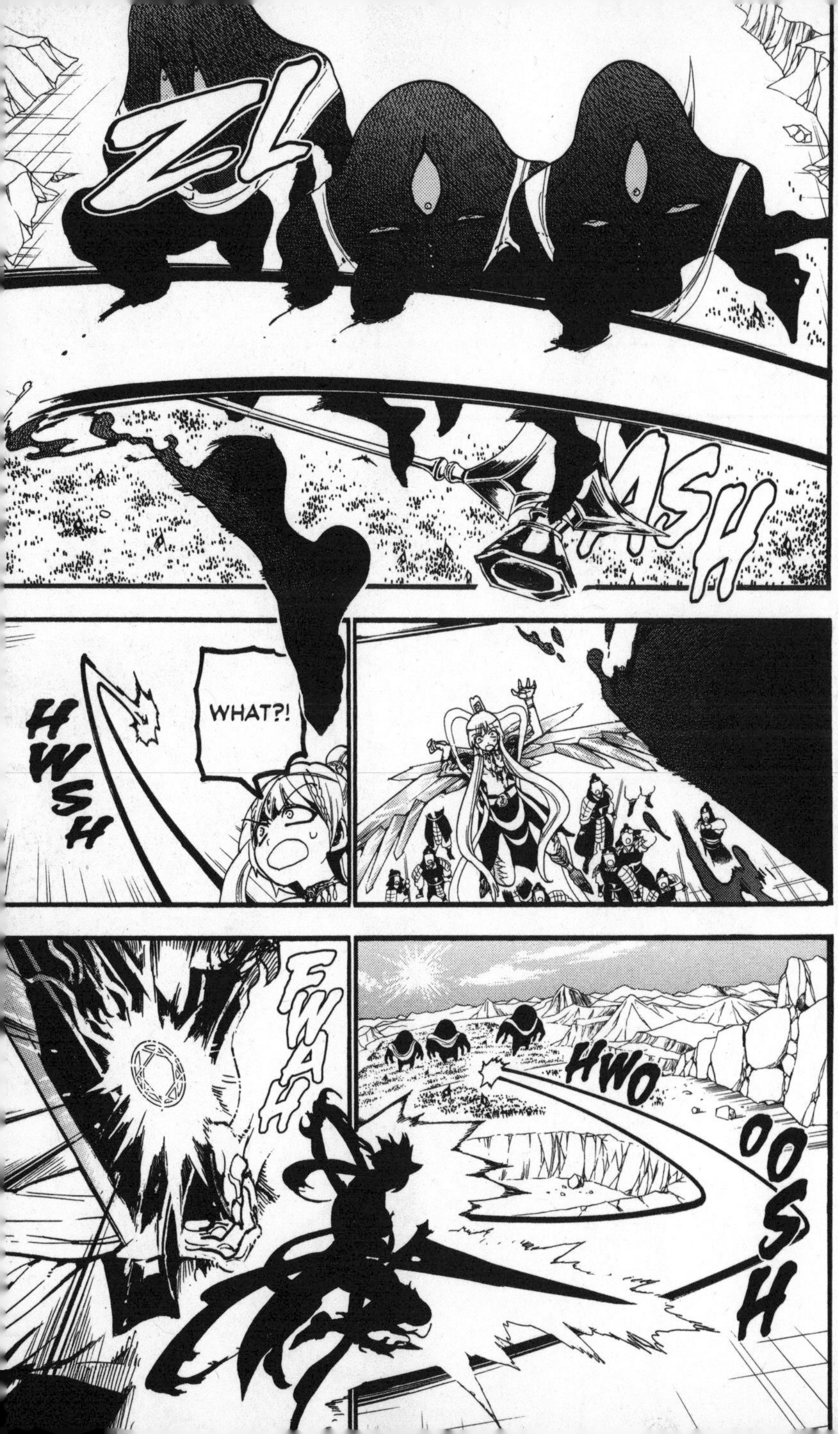
ZH
ASH
WHAT?!
HWSH
HWOOOOSH
FWAH

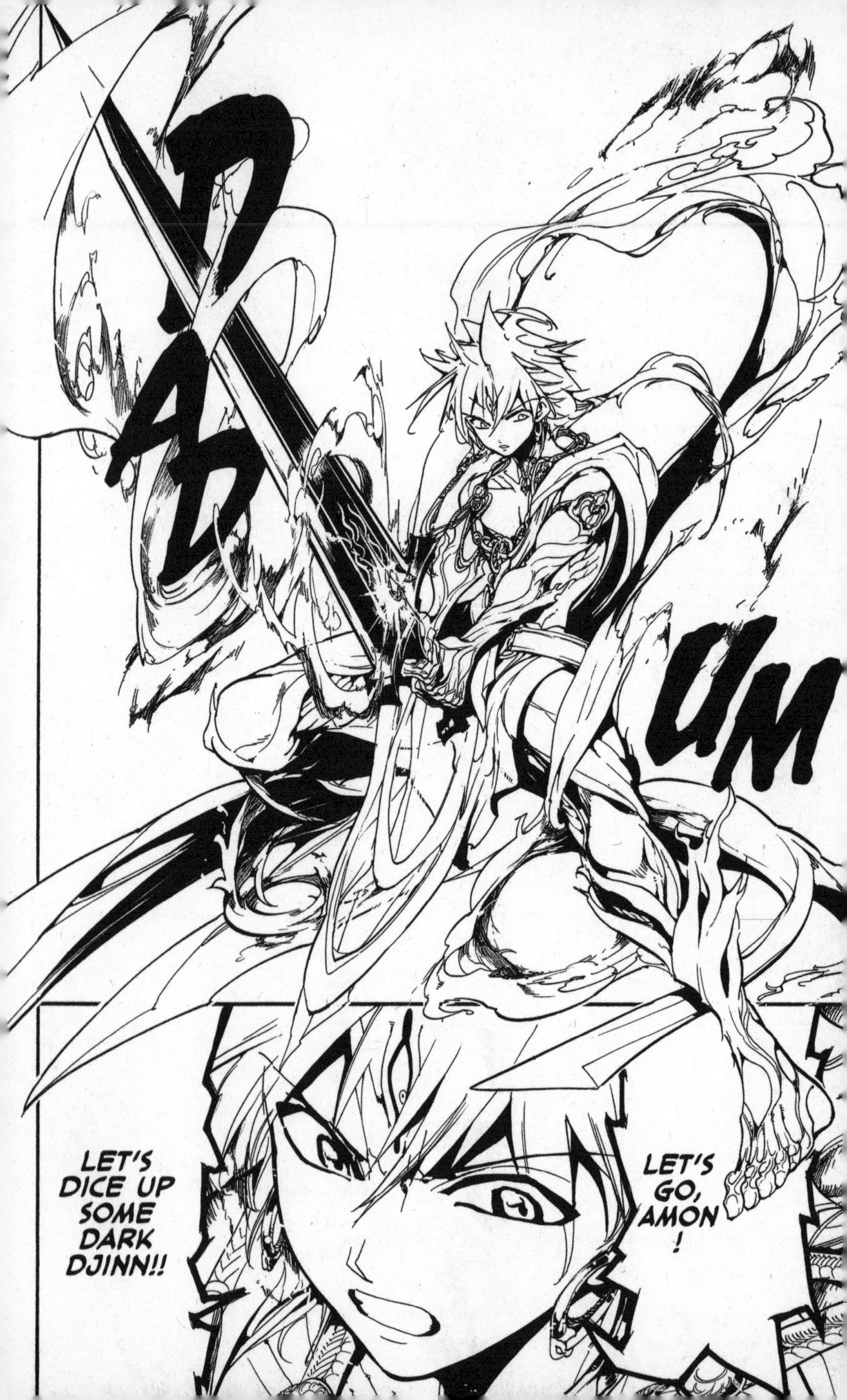
LET'S GO, AMON!
LET'S DICE UP SOME DARK DJINN!!

Night 182: Djinn Equip Amon

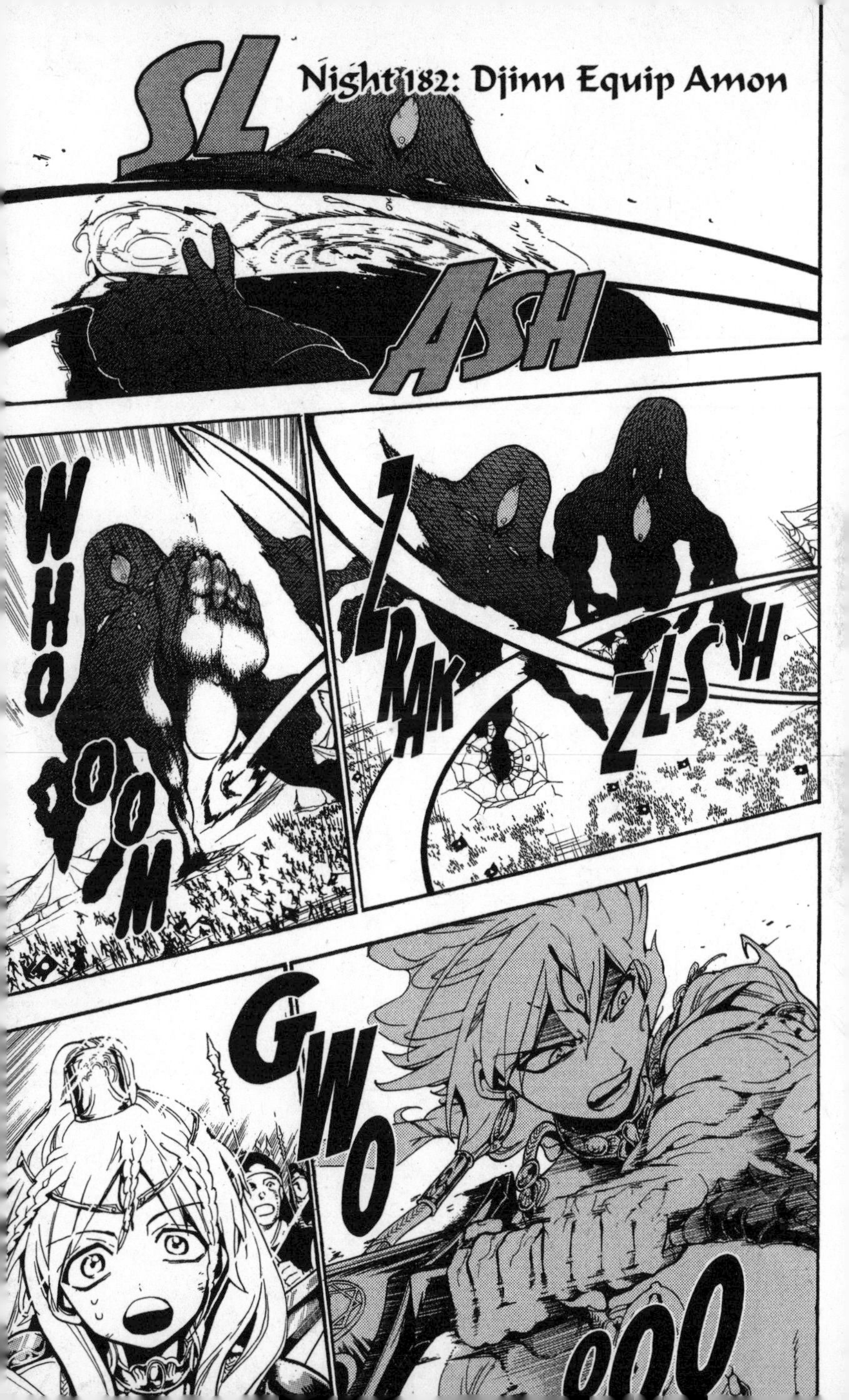
SLASH
ZRAK
ZLSH
WHOOOOM
GWOOOO

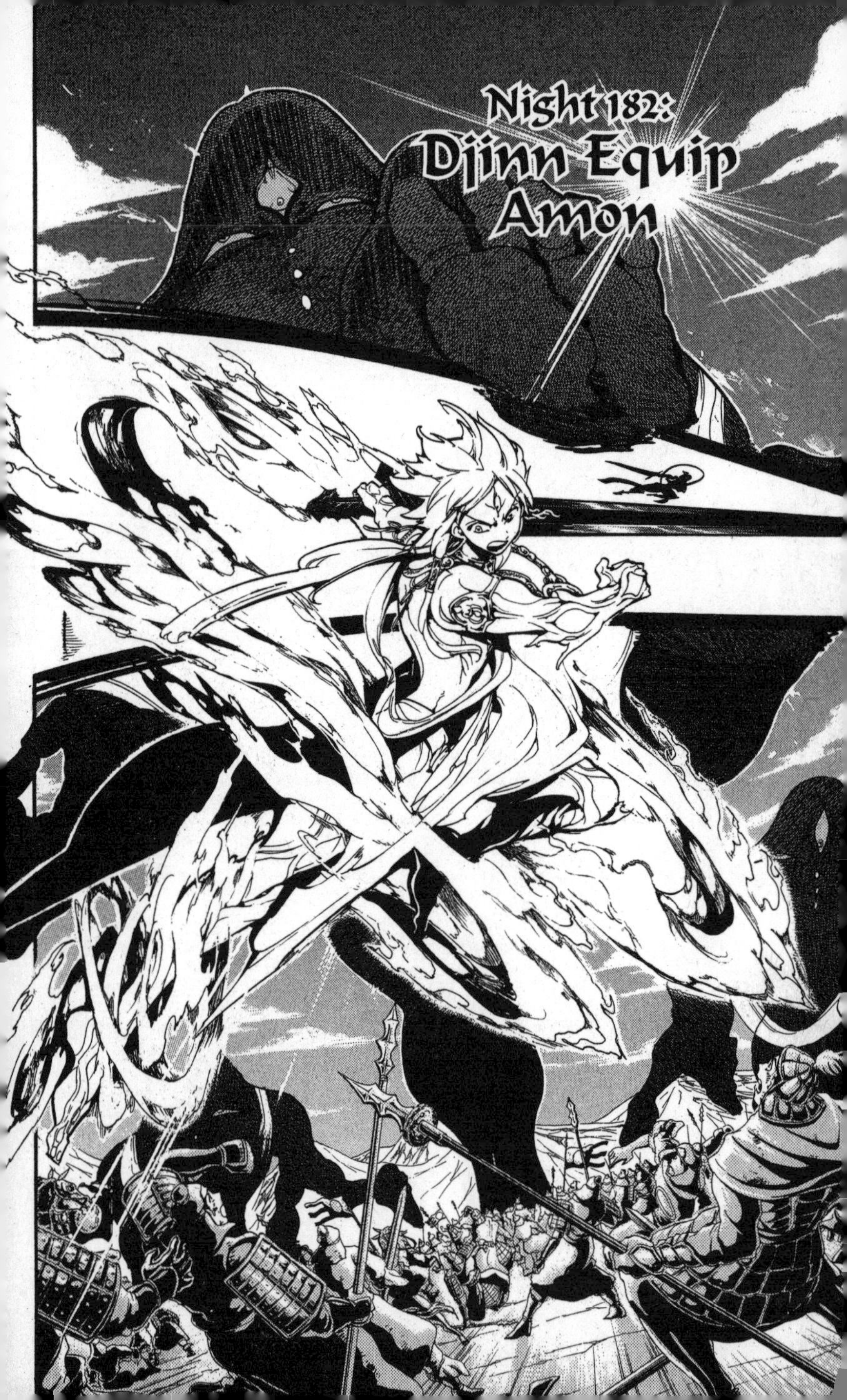
Night 182:
Djinn Equip
Amon

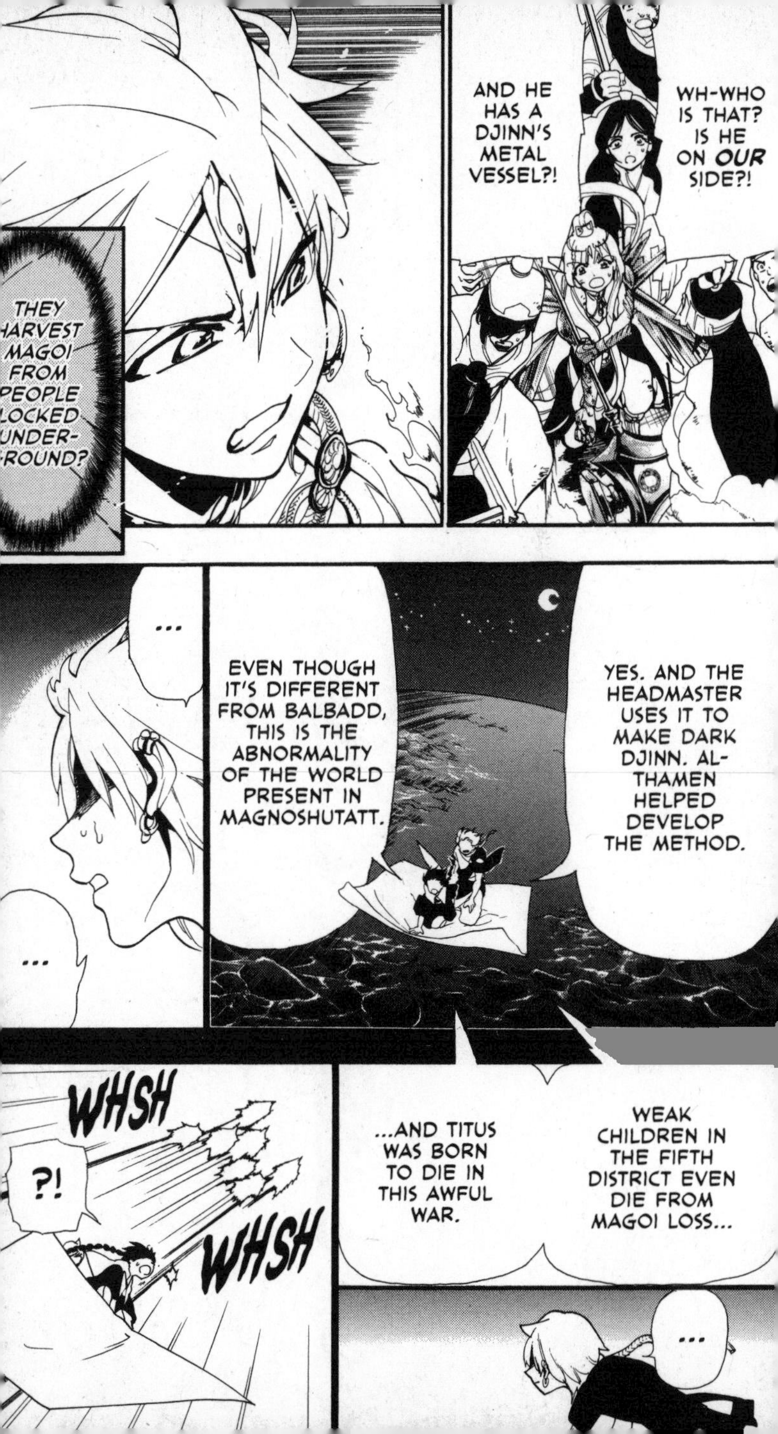
WH-WHO IS THAT? IS HE ON OUR SIDE?!
AND HE HAS A DJINN'S METAL VESSEL?!
THEY HARVEST MAGOI FROM PEOPLE LOCKED UNDER-GROUND?
YES. AND THE HEADMASTER USES IT TO MAKE DARK DJINN. AL-THAMEN HELPED DEVELOP THE METHOD.
EVEN THOUGH IT'S DIFFERENT FROM BALBADD, THIS IS THE ABNORMALITY OF THE WORLD PRESENT IN MAGNOSHUTATT.
...
...
WEAK CHILDREN IN THE FIFTH DISTRICT EVEN DIE FROM MAGOI LOSS...
...AND TITUS WAS BORN TO DIE IN THIS AWFUL WAR.
...
WHSH
?!
WHSH

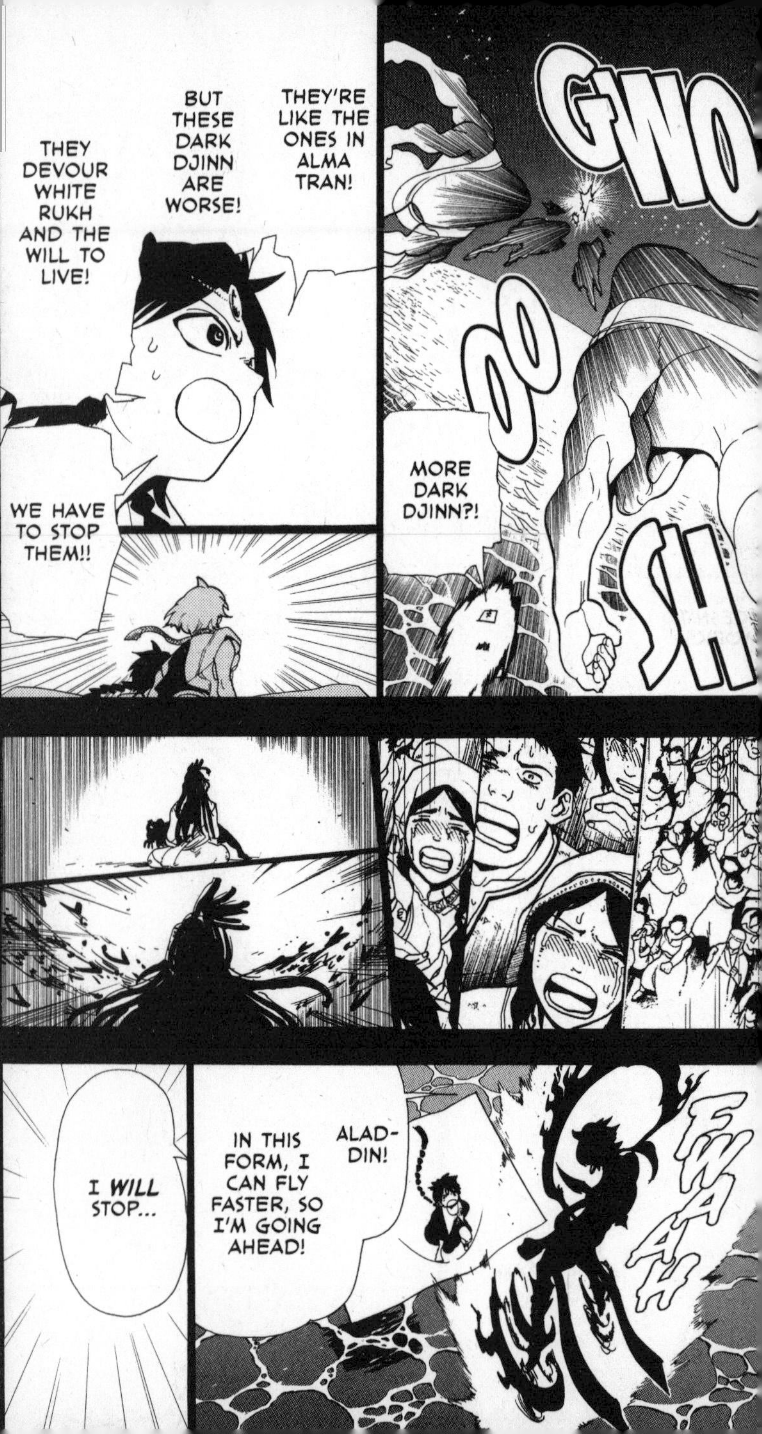
GWOOOO
SH
MORE DARK DJINN?!
THEY'RE LIKE THE ONES IN ALMA TRAN!
BUT THESE DARK DJINN ARE WORSE!
THEY DEVOUR WHITE RUKH AND THE WILL TO LIVE!
WE HAVE TO STOP THEM!!
FWAAH
ALAD-DIN!
IN THIS FORM, I CAN FLY FASTER, SO I'M GOING AHEAD!
I *WILL* STOP...

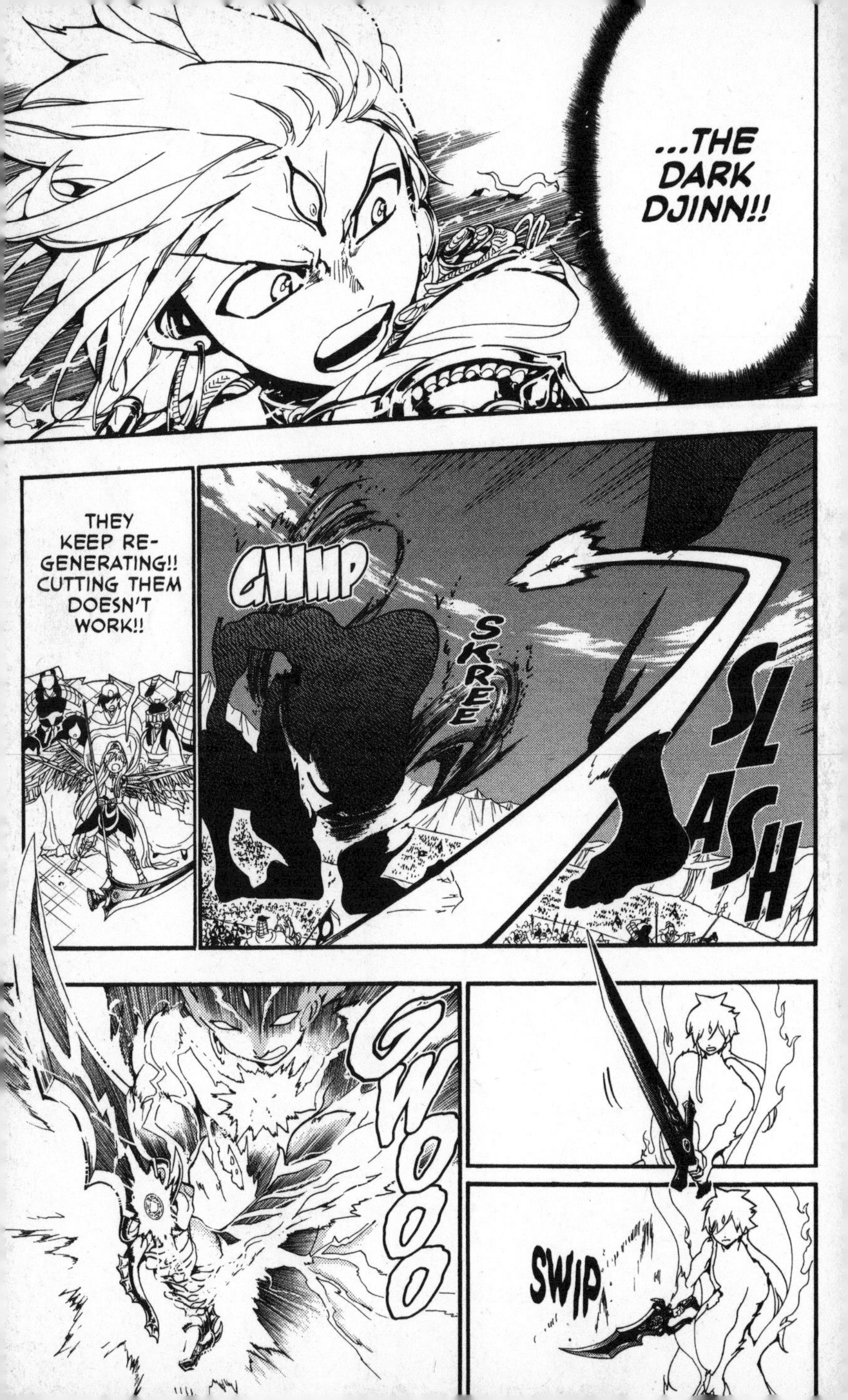
...THE DARK DJINN!!
SLASH
SKREE
GWMP
THEY KEEP RE-GENERATING!! CUTTING THEM DOESN'T WORK!!
GWOOOO
SWIP

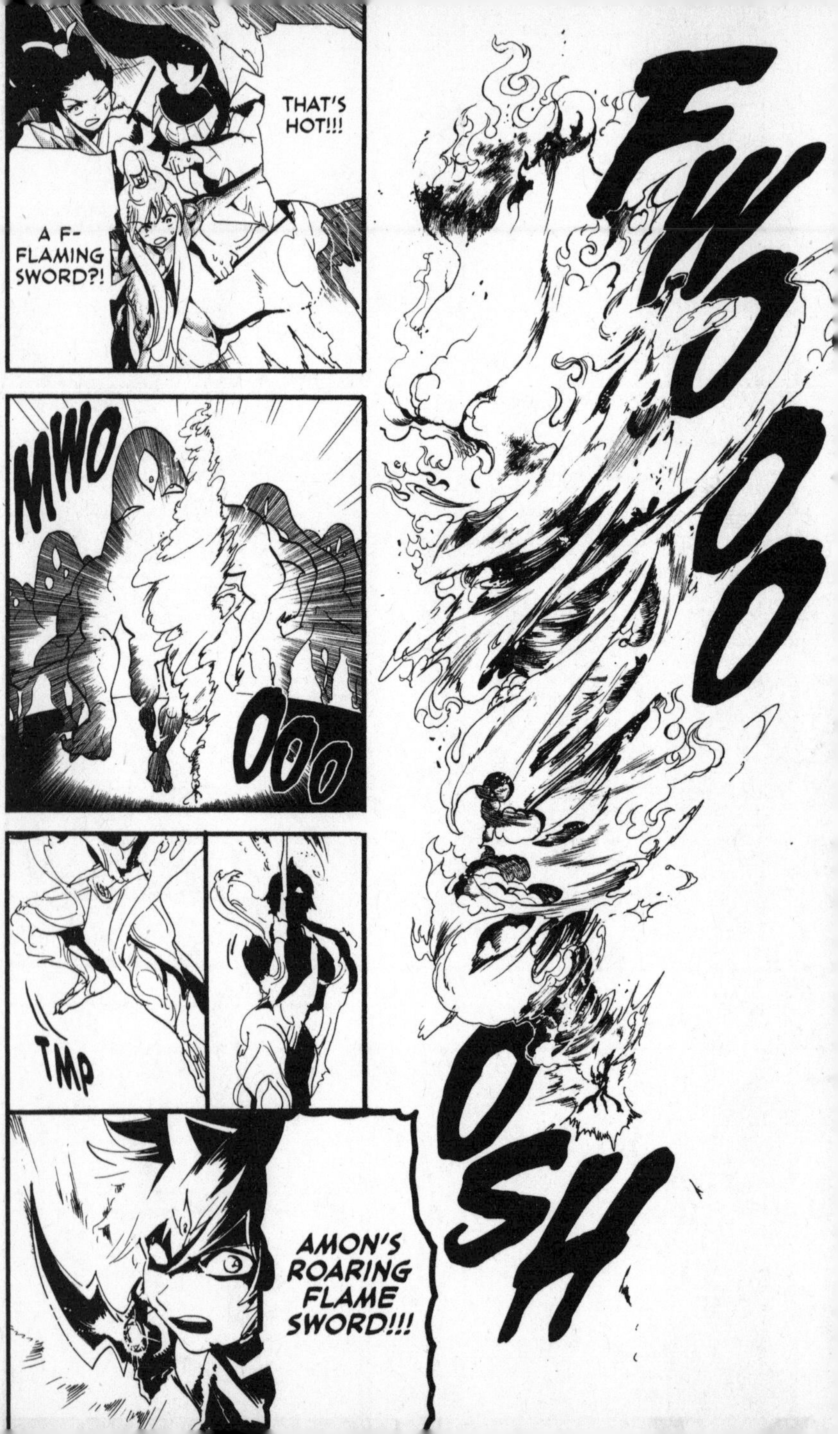
FWOOOOOOSH
THAT'S HOT!!!
A F-FLAMING SWORD?!
MWOOOO
TMP
AMON'S ROARING FLAME SWORD!!!

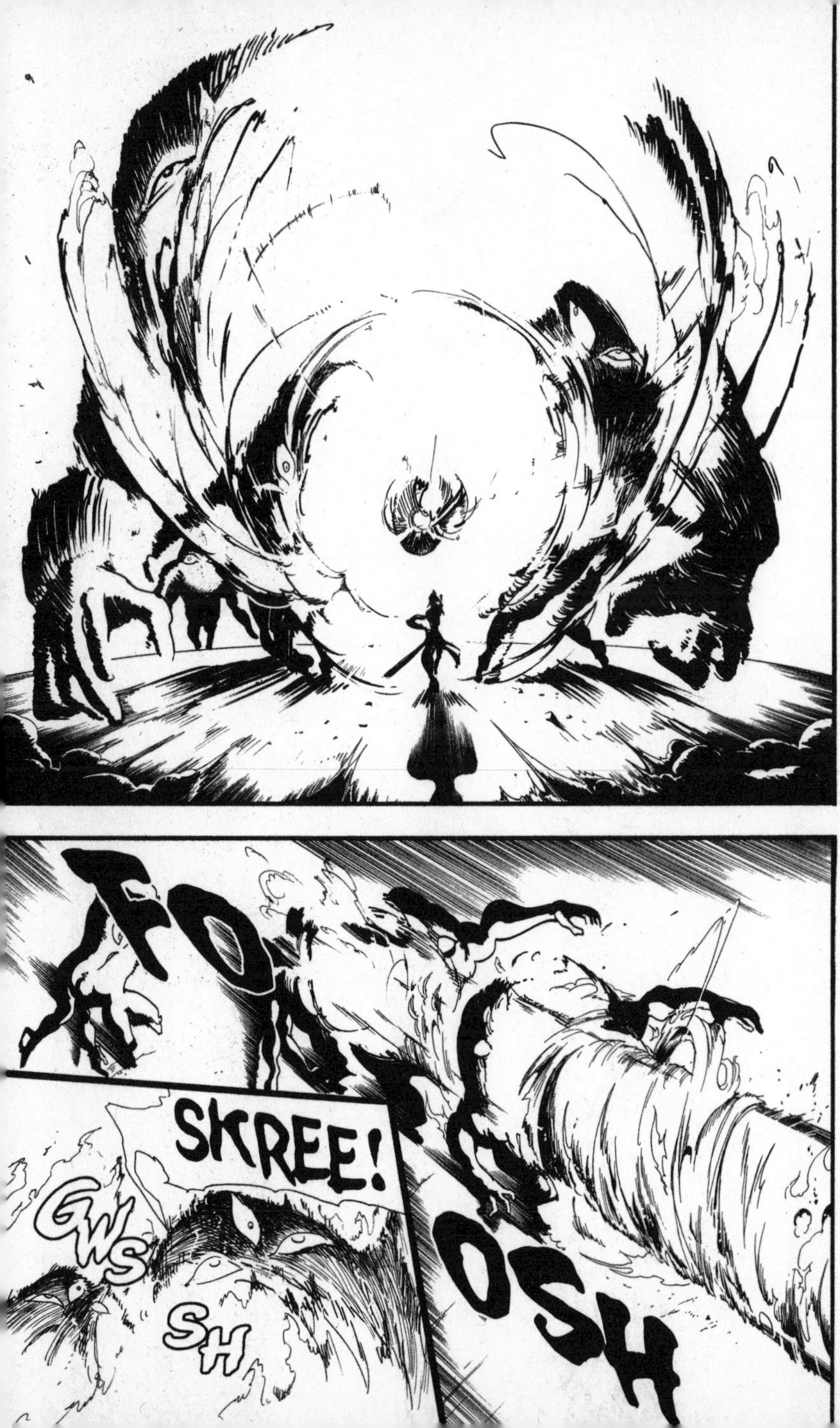
FO
OSH
SKREE!
GWS
SH

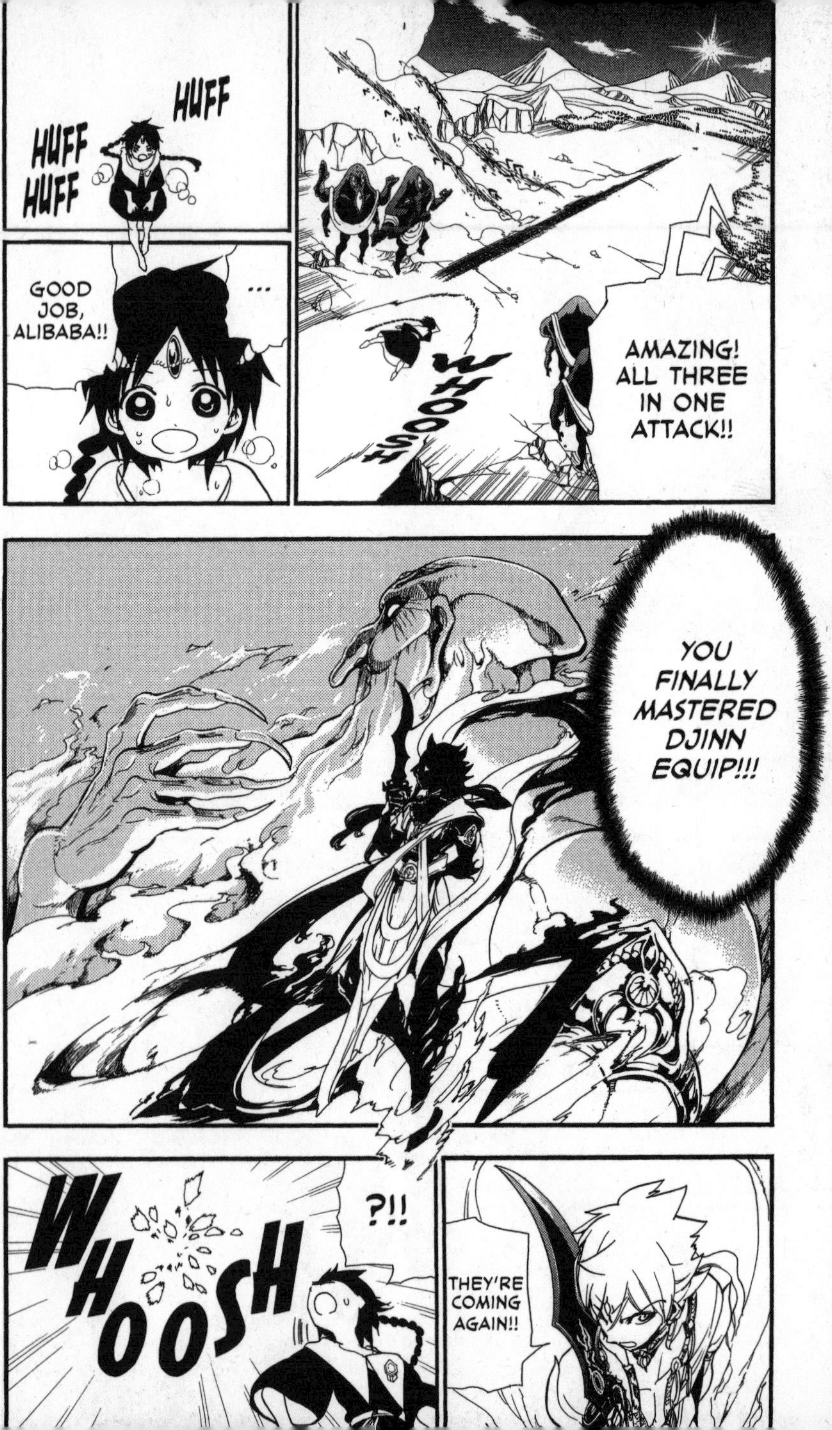
WHOOSH
AMAZING! ALL THREE IN ONE ATTACK!!
HUFF
HUFF HUFF
...
GOOD JOB, ALIBABA!!
YOU FINALLY MASTERED DJINN EQUIP!!!
THEY'RE COMING AGAIN!!
?!!
WHOOSH

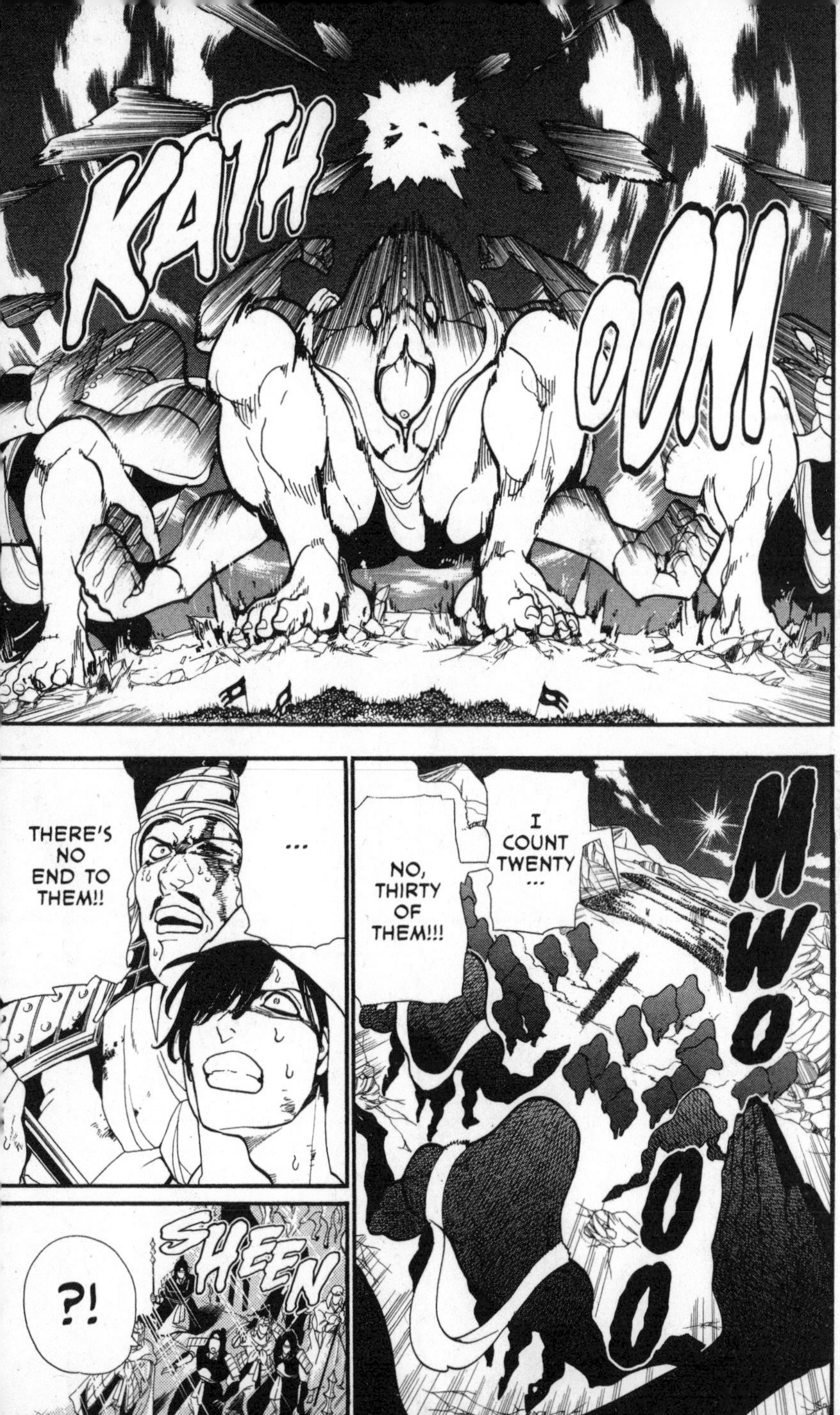
KATH
OOM
I COUNT TWENTY...
NO, THIRTY OF THEM!!!
MWOOOOO
...
THERE'S NO END TO THEM!!
SHEEN
?!

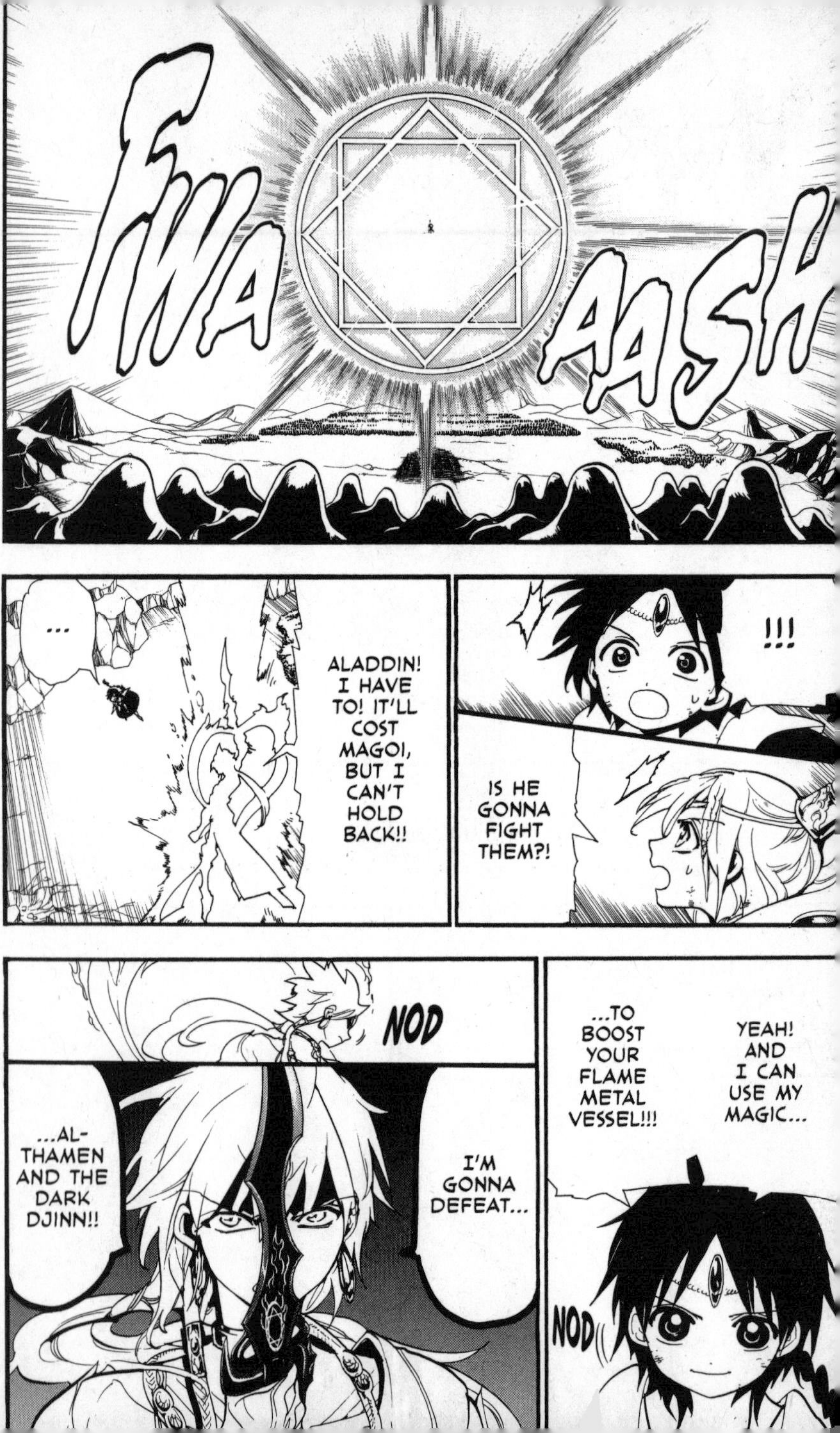
FWAAASH
!!!
IS HE GONNA FIGHT THEM?!
ALADDIN! I HAVE TO! IT'LL COST MAGOI, BUT I CAN'T HOLD BACK!!
...
YEAH! AND I CAN USE MY MAGIC...
...TO BOOST YOUR FLAME METAL VESSEL!!!
NOD
NOD
I'M GONNA DEFEAT...
...AL-THAMEN AND THE DARK DJINN!!

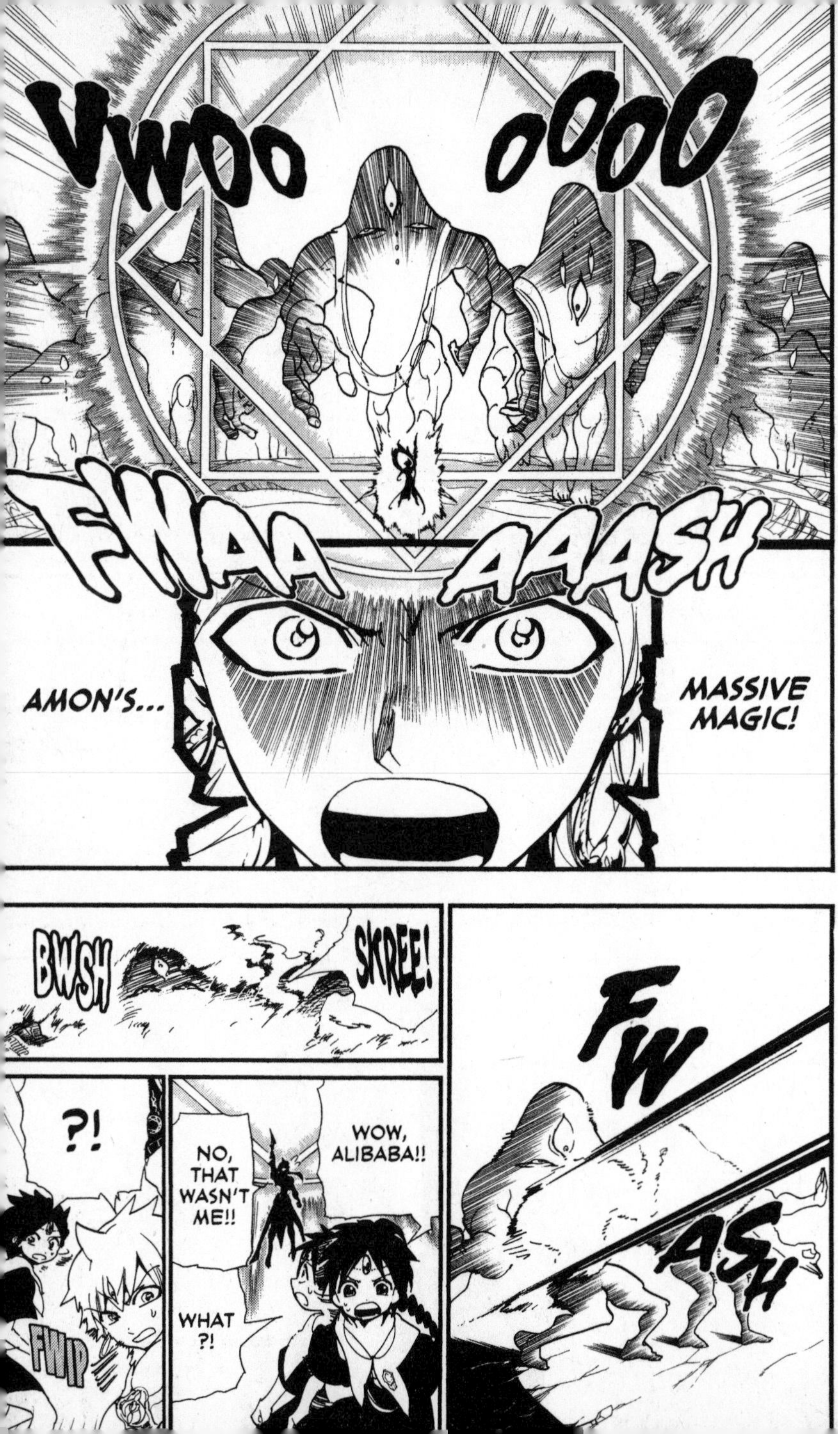
VWOO OOOOO
FWAA AAASH
AMON'S...
MASSIVE MAGIC!
FW ASH
SKREE!
BWSH
WOW, ALIBABA!!
NO, THAT WASN'T ME!!
WHAT ?!
?!
FWIP

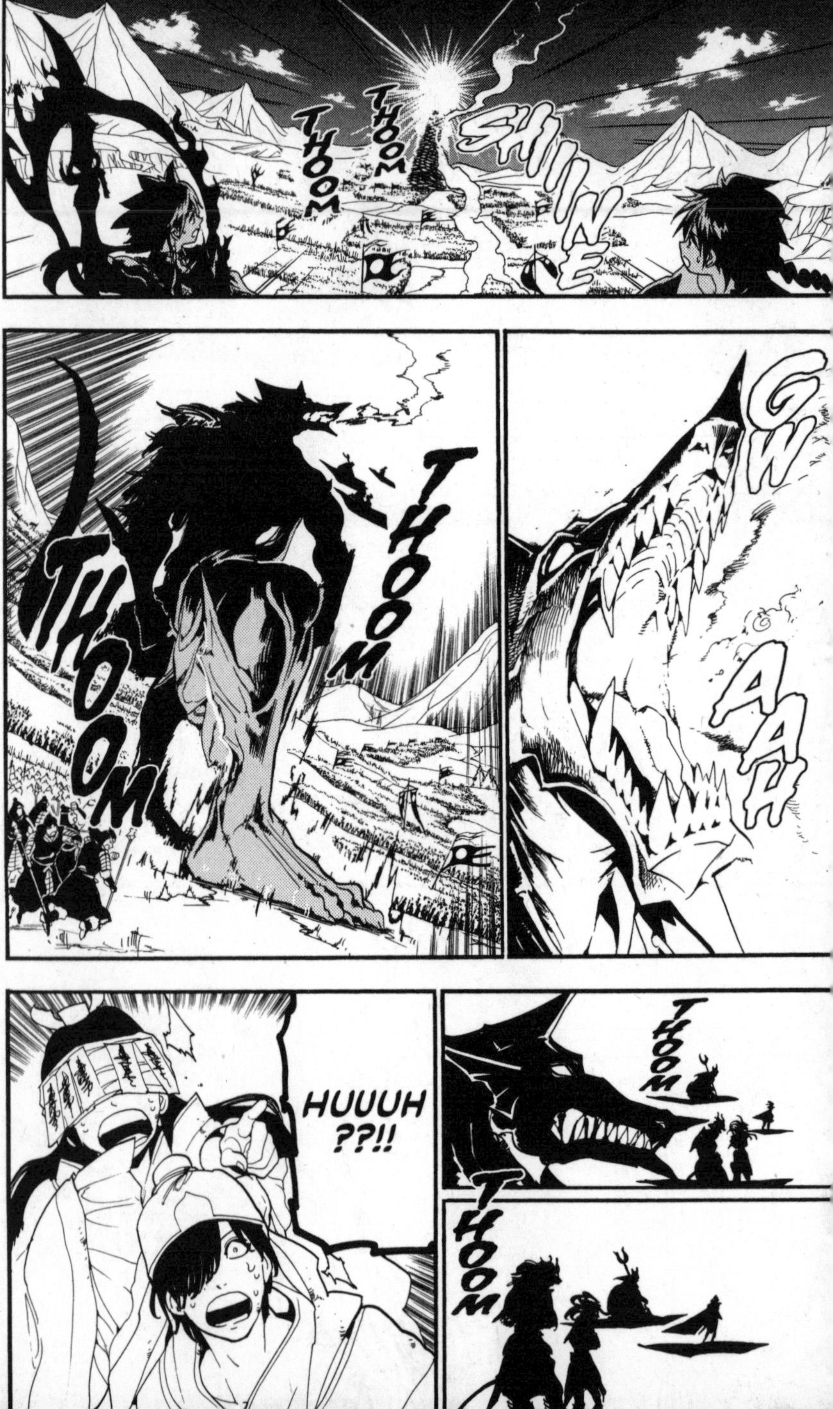
SHIIINE
THOOM
THOOM
GWAAAH
THOOM
THOOM
THOOM
THOOM
HUUUH ??!!

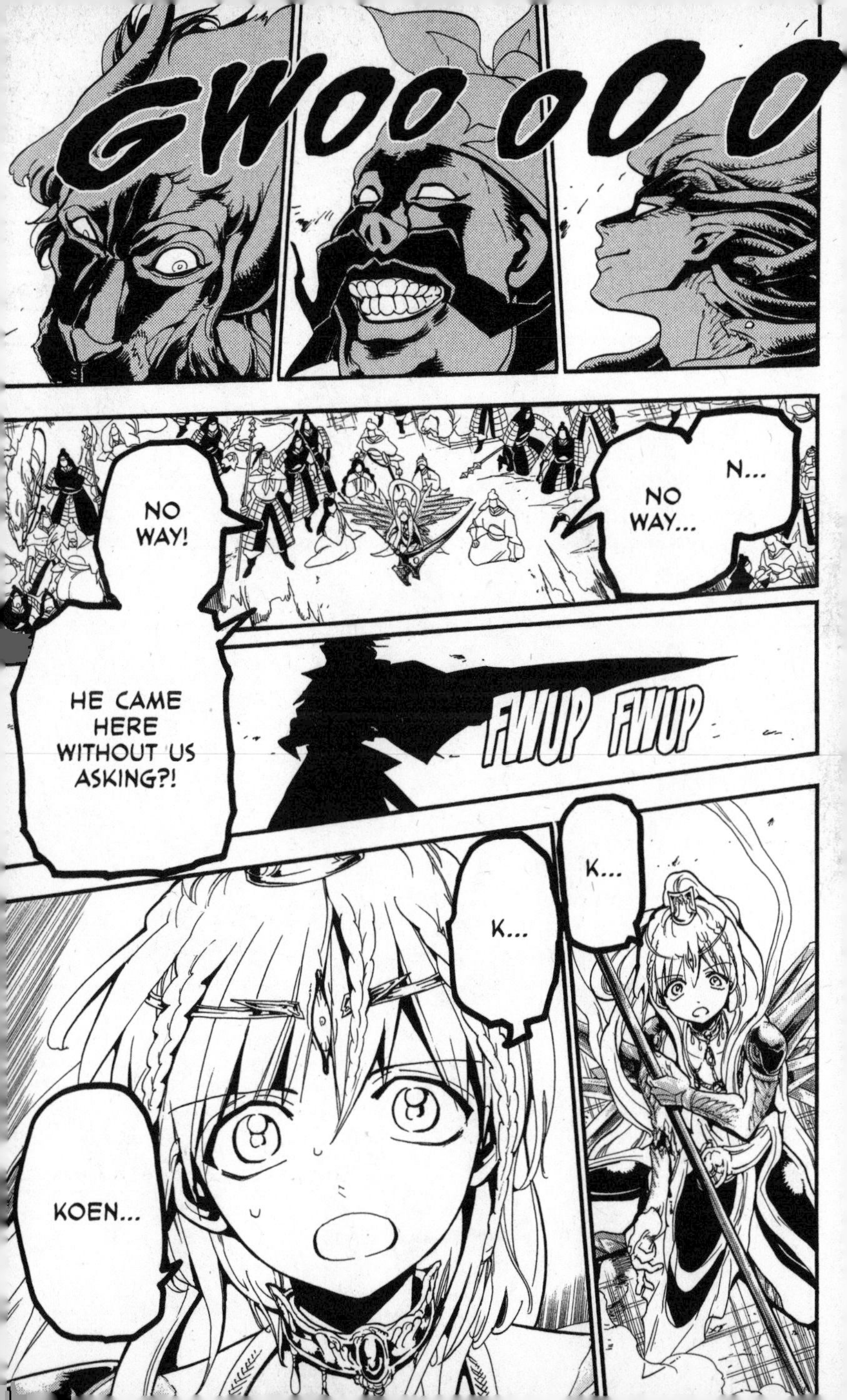

GWOO O O O
N...
NO WAY...
NO WAY!
HE CAME HERE WITHOUT US ASKING?!
FWUP FWUP
K...
K...
KOEN...

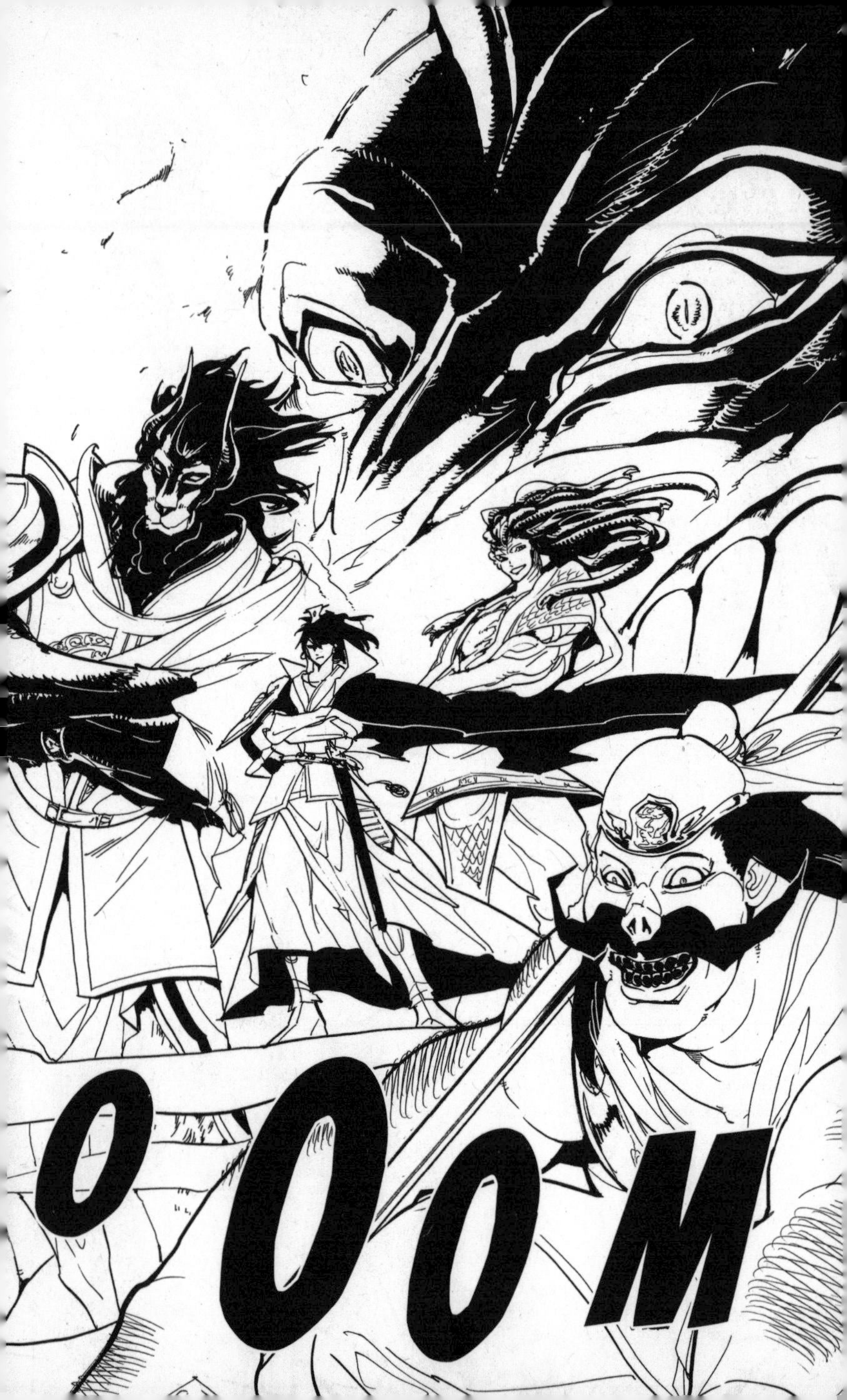
OOOM

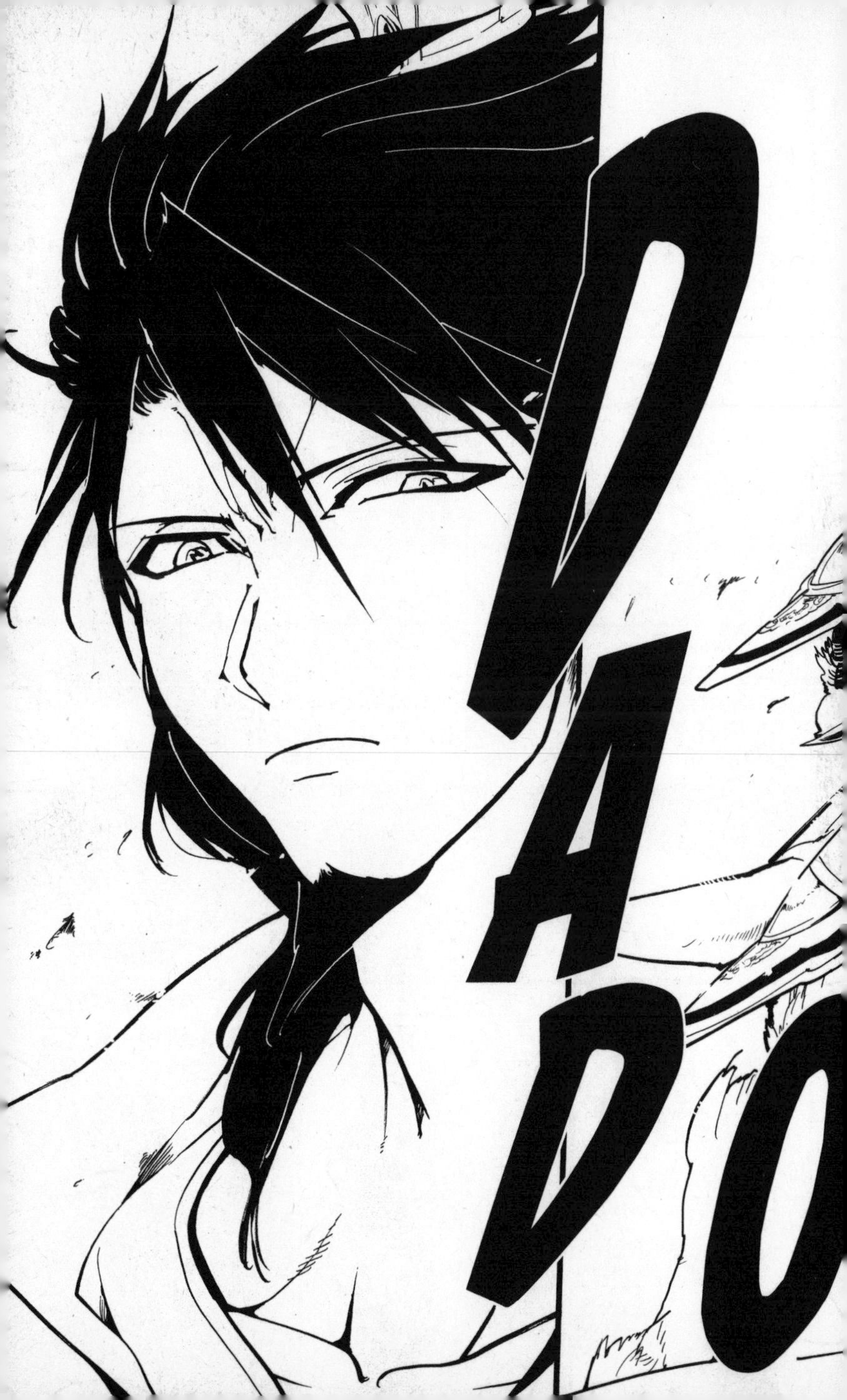
DADO

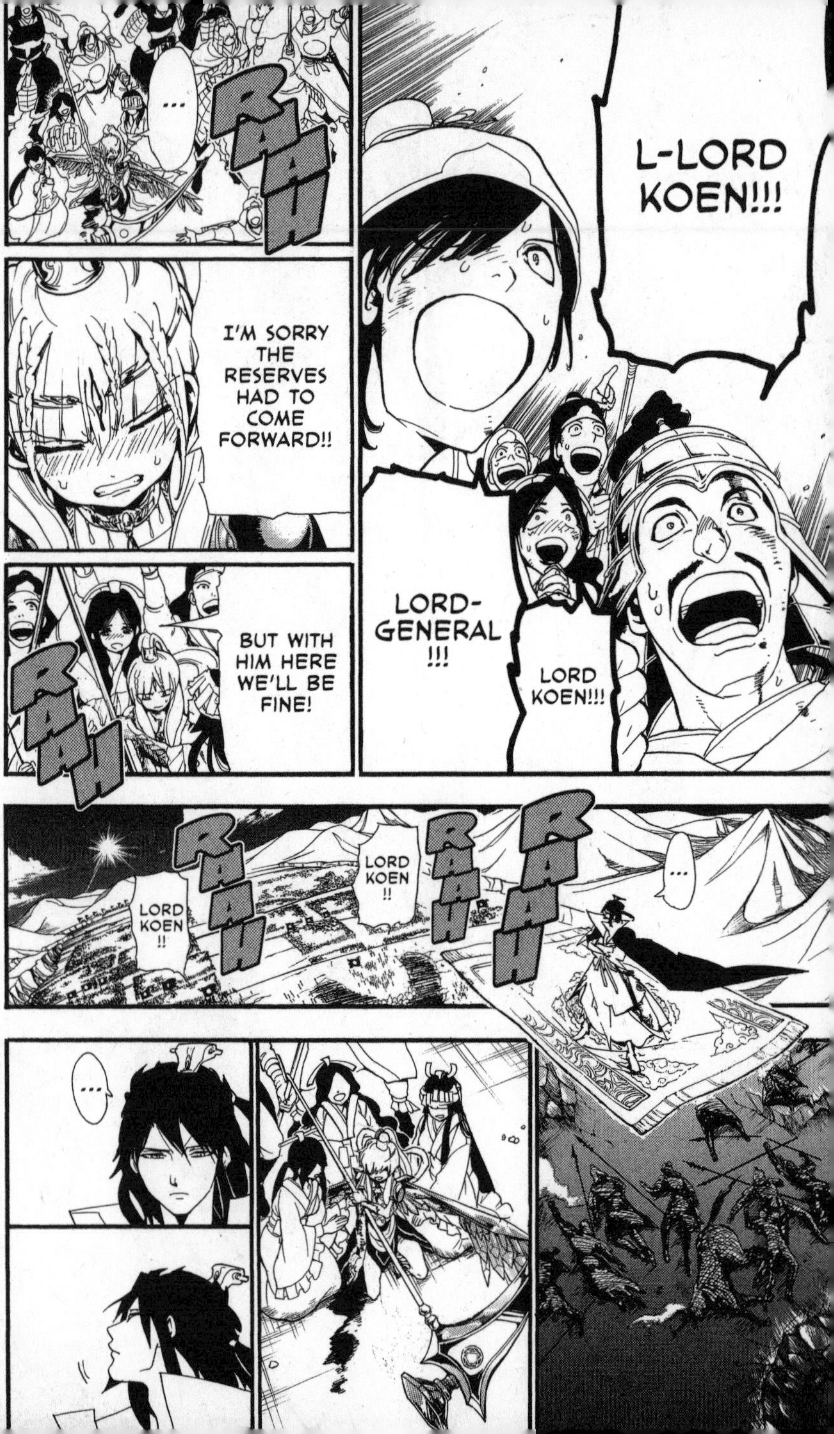
L-LORD KOEN!!!
LORD KOEN!!!
LORD-GENERAL!!!
RAAH
...
I'M SORRY THE RESERVES HAD TO COME FORWARD!!
BUT WITH HIM HERE WE'LL BE FINE!
RAAH
...
RAAH
RAAH
LORD KOEN!!
RAAH
LORD KOEN!!
...

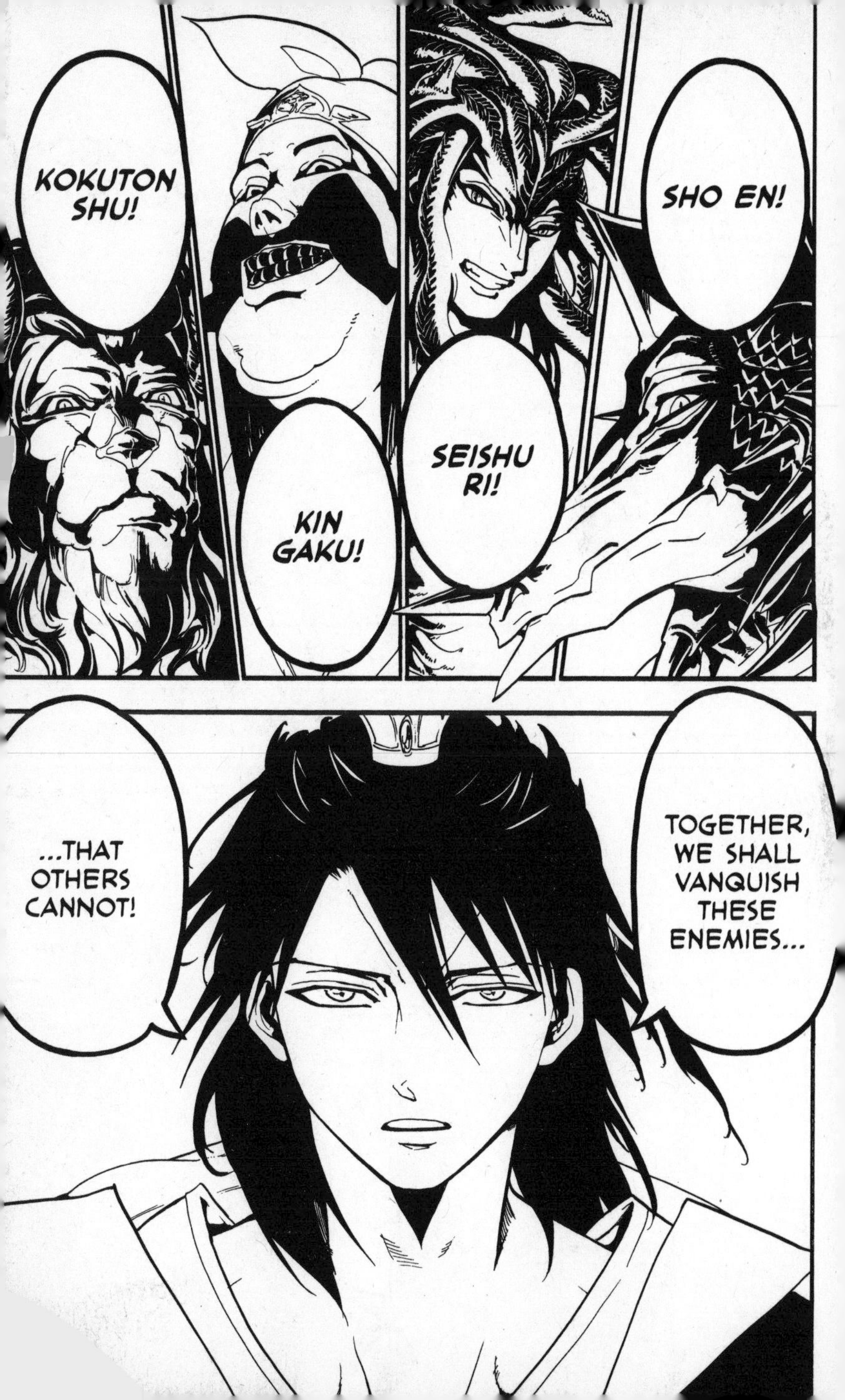
SHO EN!
SEISHU RI!
KIN GAKU!
KOKUTON SHU!
TOGETHER, WE SHALL VANQUISH THESE ENEMIES...
...THAT OTHERS CANNOT!

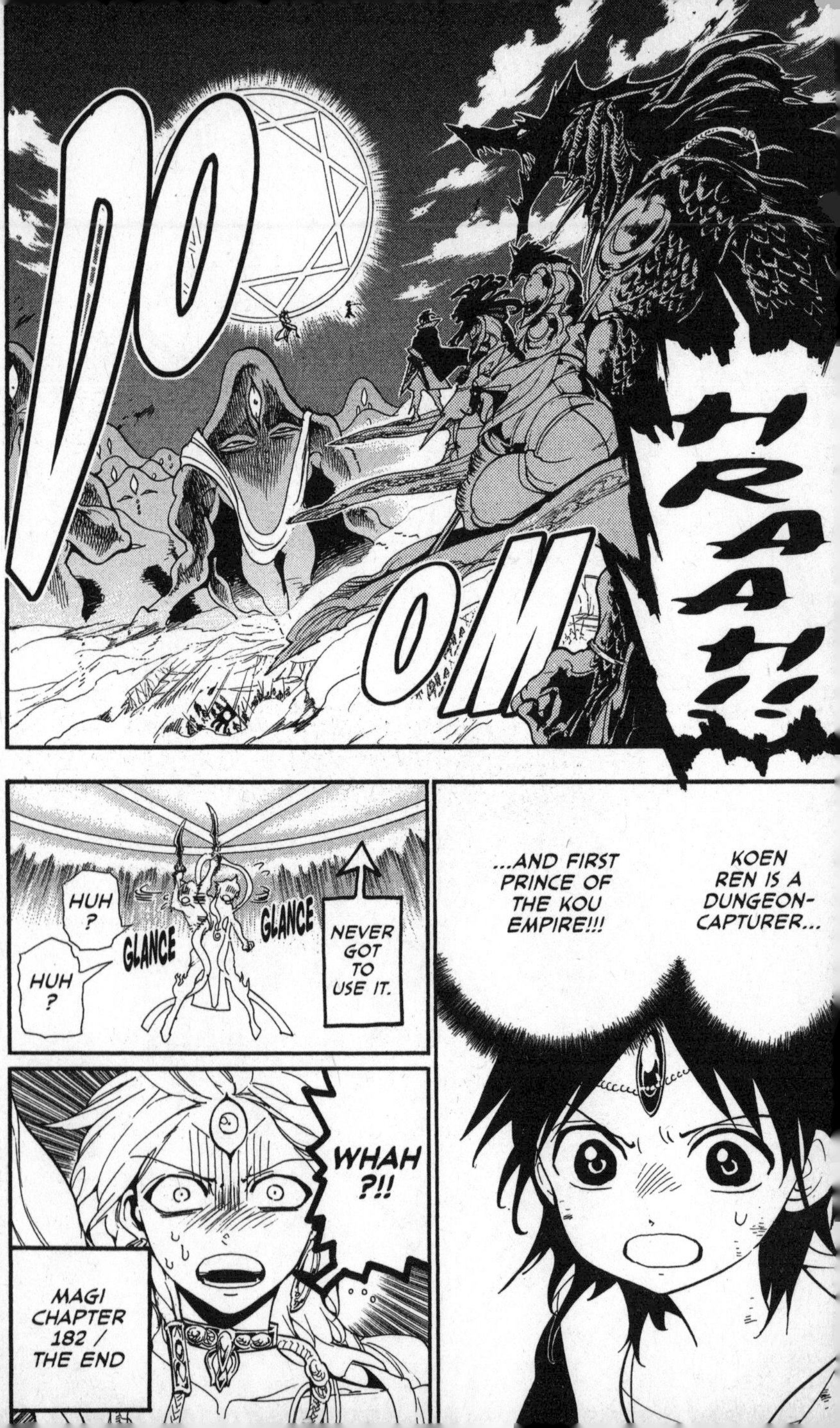
HIRAAH!!
DOOM
KOEN REN IS A DUNGEON-CAPTURER...
...AND FIRST PRINCE OF THE KOU EMPIRE!!!
NEVER GOT TO USE IT.
GLANCE
HUH?
GLANCE
HUH?
WHAH?!!
MAGI CHAPTER 182 / THE END

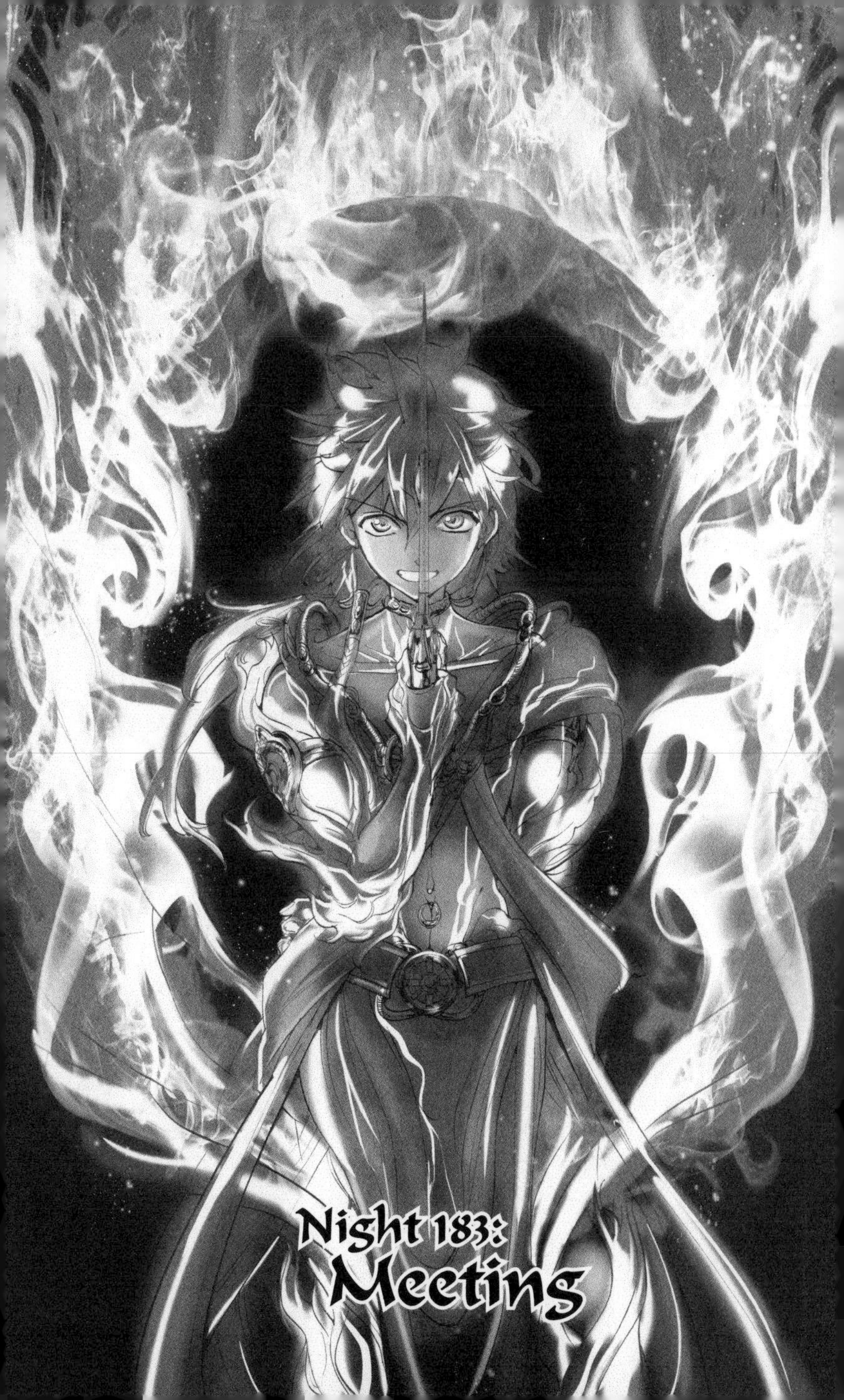
Night 183:
Meeting

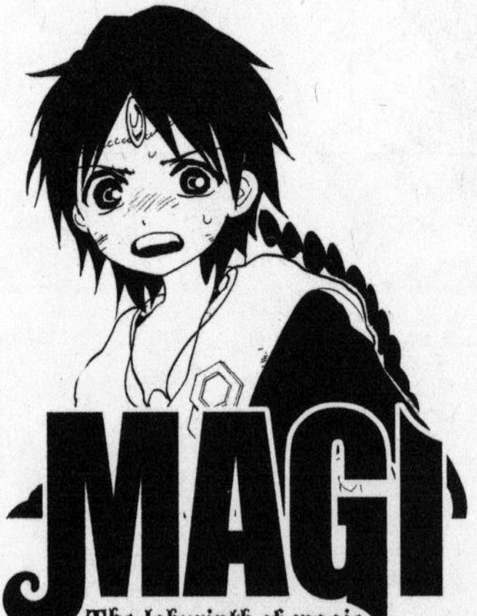
MAGI
The labyrinth of magic

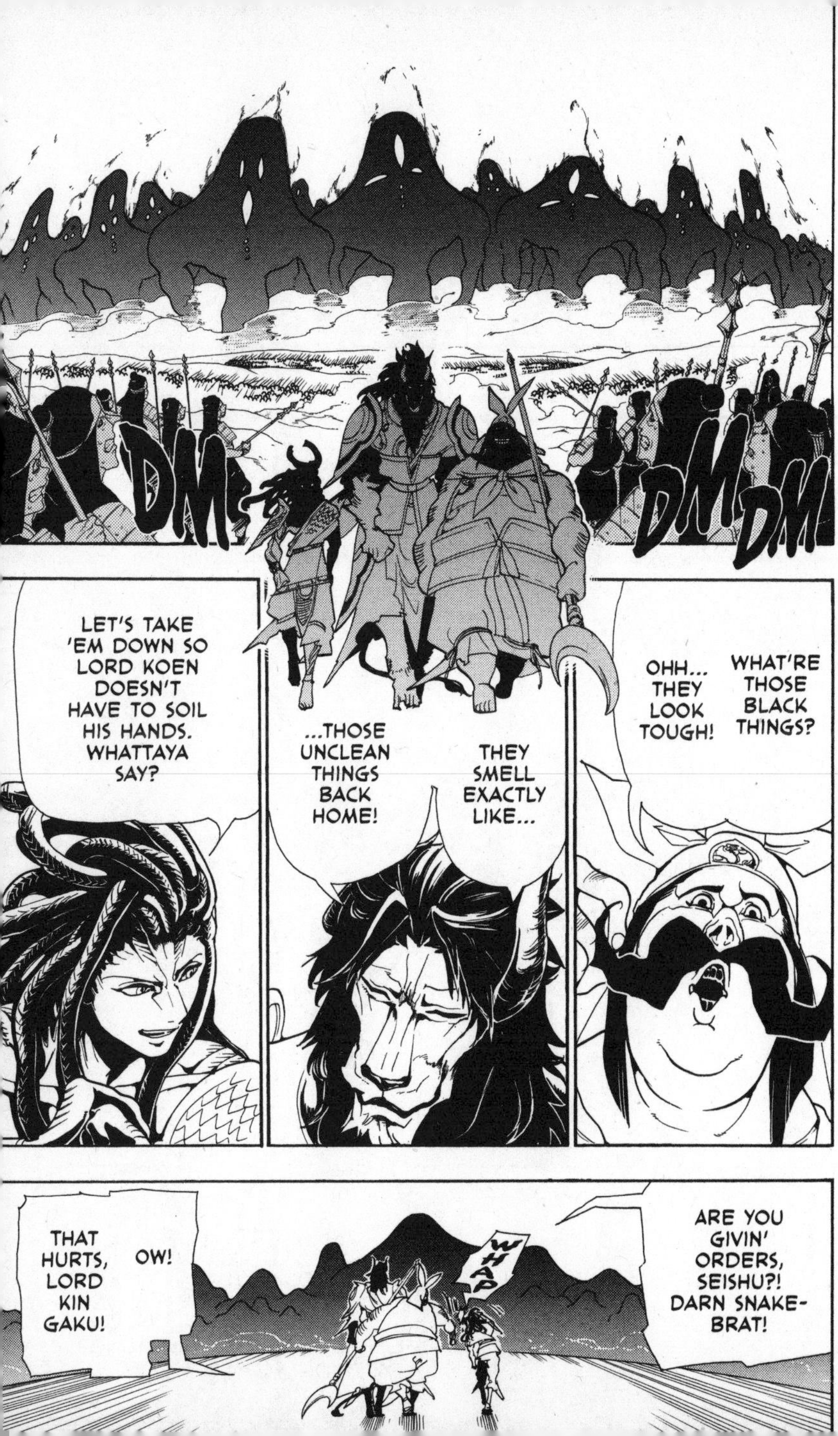
DM DM
DM
WHAT'RE THOSE BLACK THINGS?
OHH... THEY LOOK TOUGH!
THEY SMELL EXACTLY LIKE...
...THOSE UNCLEAN THINGS BACK HOME!
LET'S TAKE 'EM DOWN SO LORD KOEN DOESN'T HAVE TO SOIL HIS HANDS. WHATTAYA SAY?
ARE YOU GIVIN' ORDERS, SEISHU?! DARN SNAKE-BRAT!
WHAP
OW!
THAT HURTS, LORD KIN GAKU!

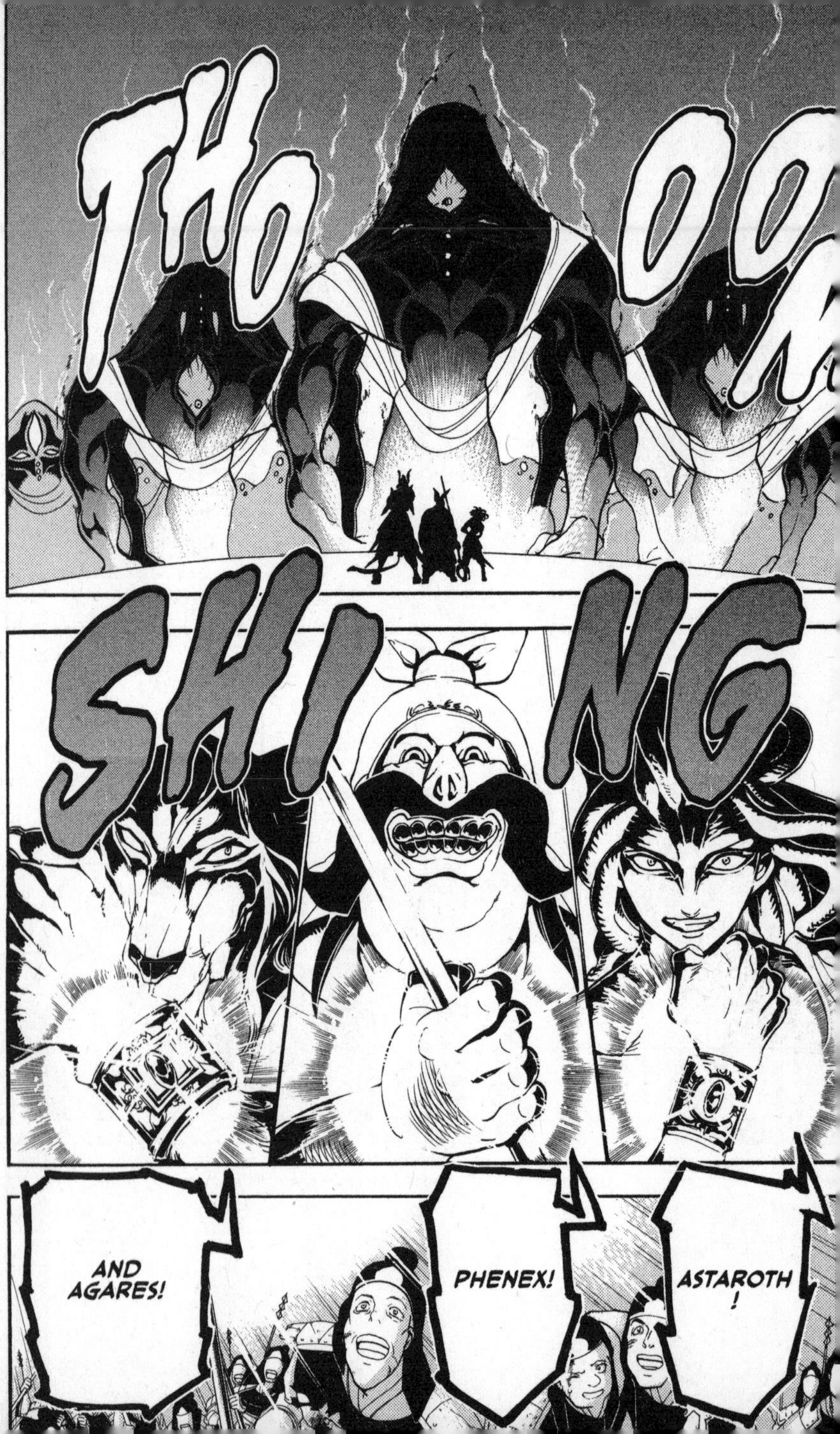
THOOOM
SHING
ASTAROTH!
PHENEX!
AND AGARES!

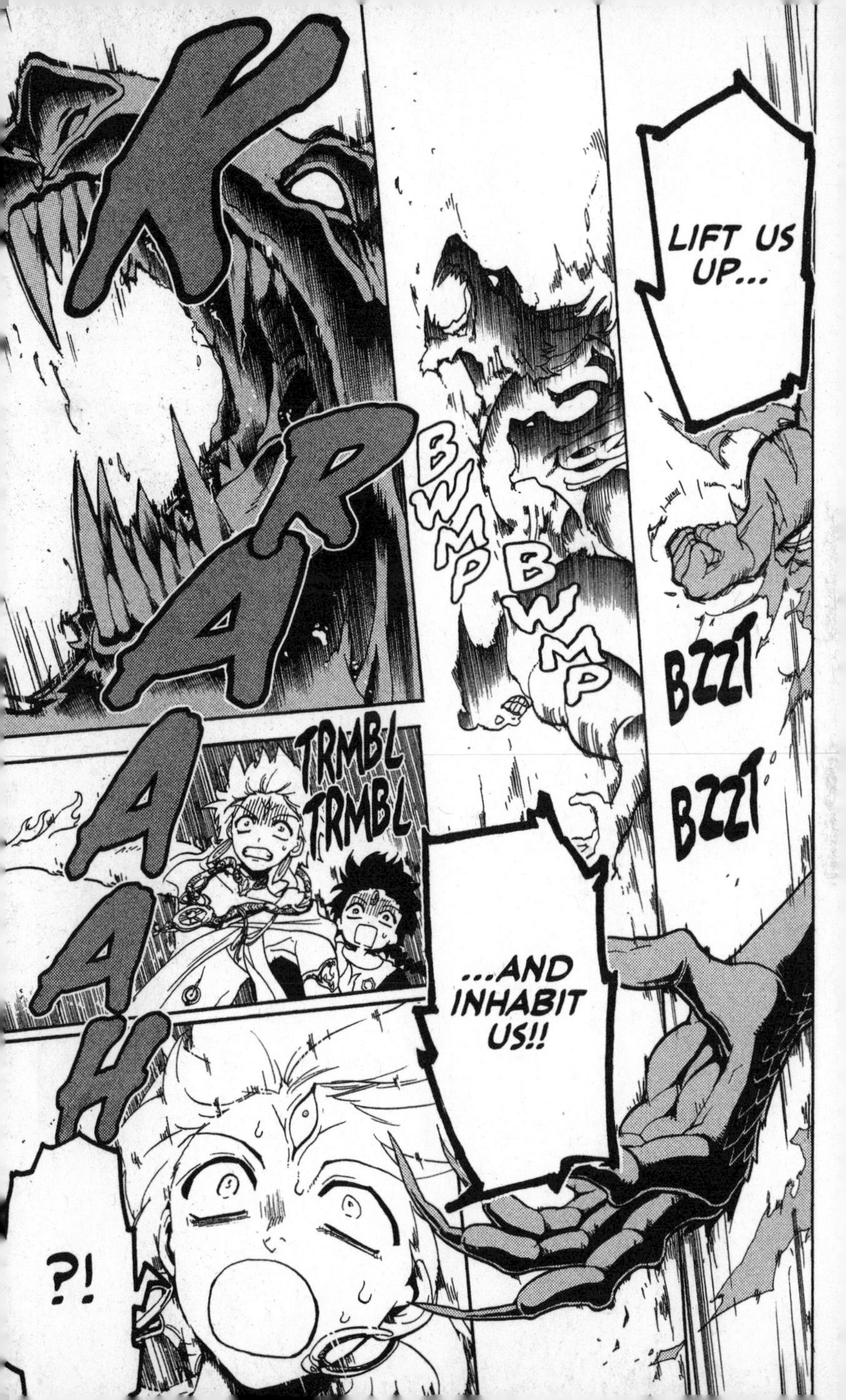
LIFT US UP...
BZZT
BZZT
BWMP
BWMP
...AND INHABIT US!!
KRAAAH
TRMBL TRMBL
?!

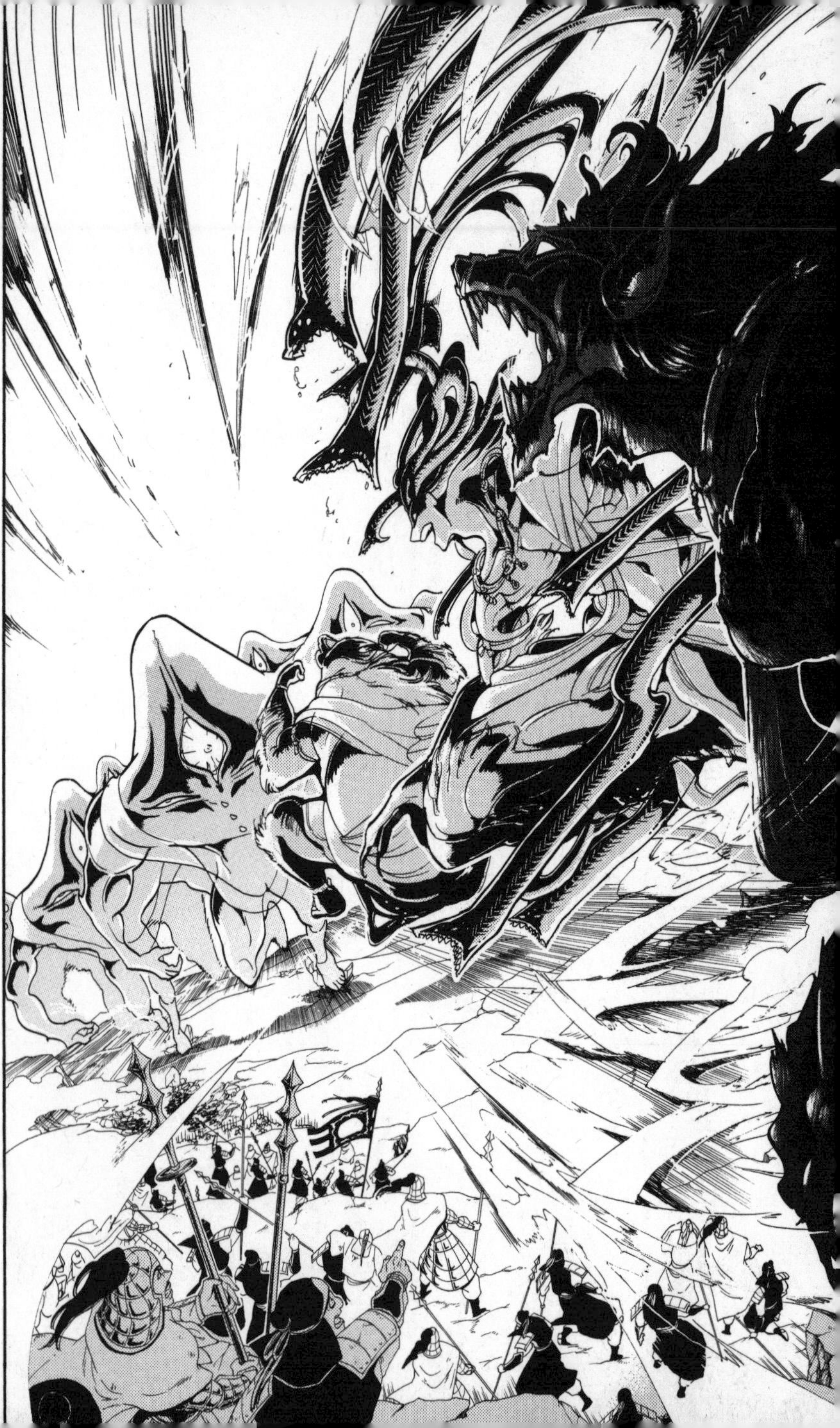

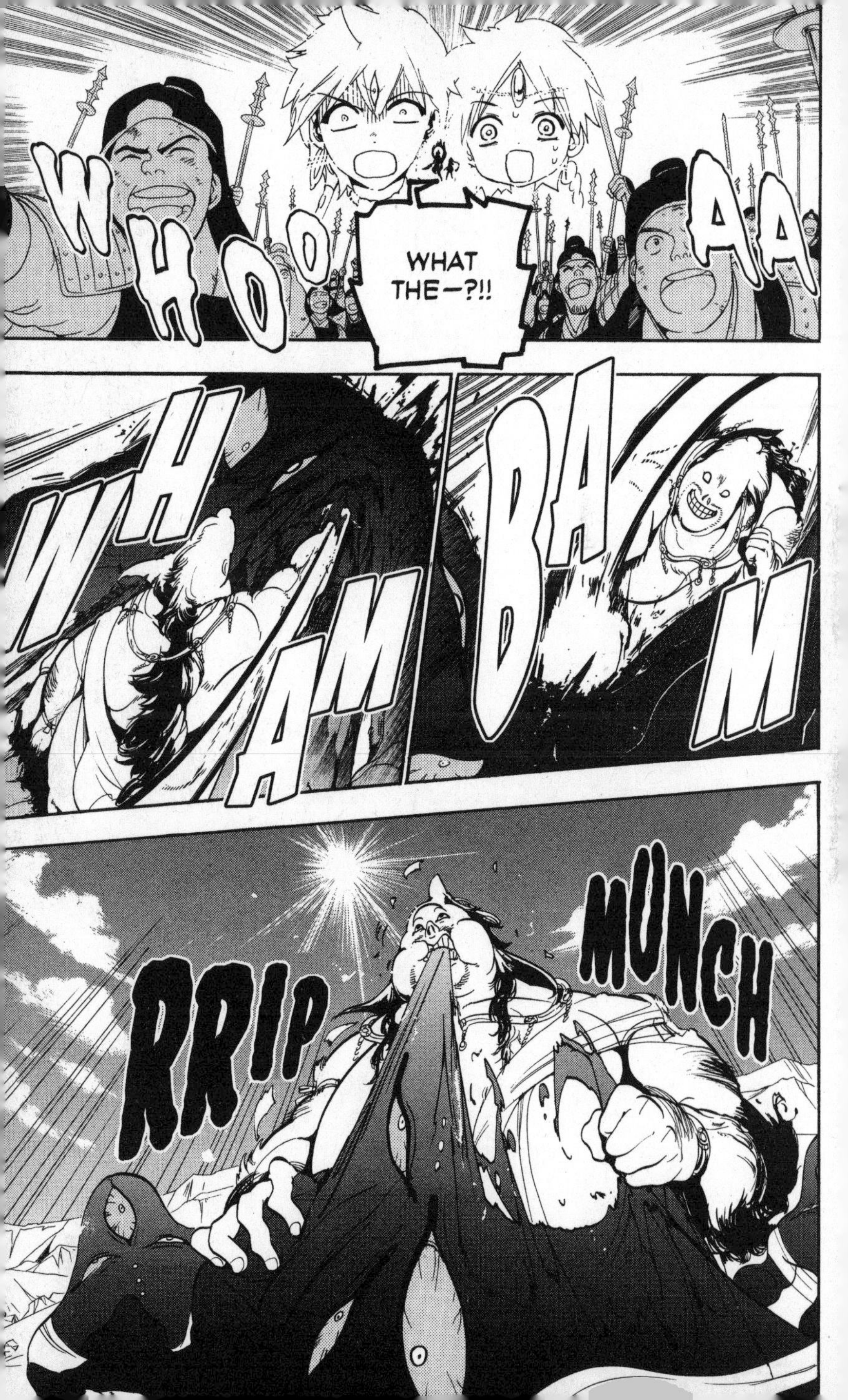
WHAT THE—?!!
WHOOOAA
BAM
WHAM
MUNCH
RRIP

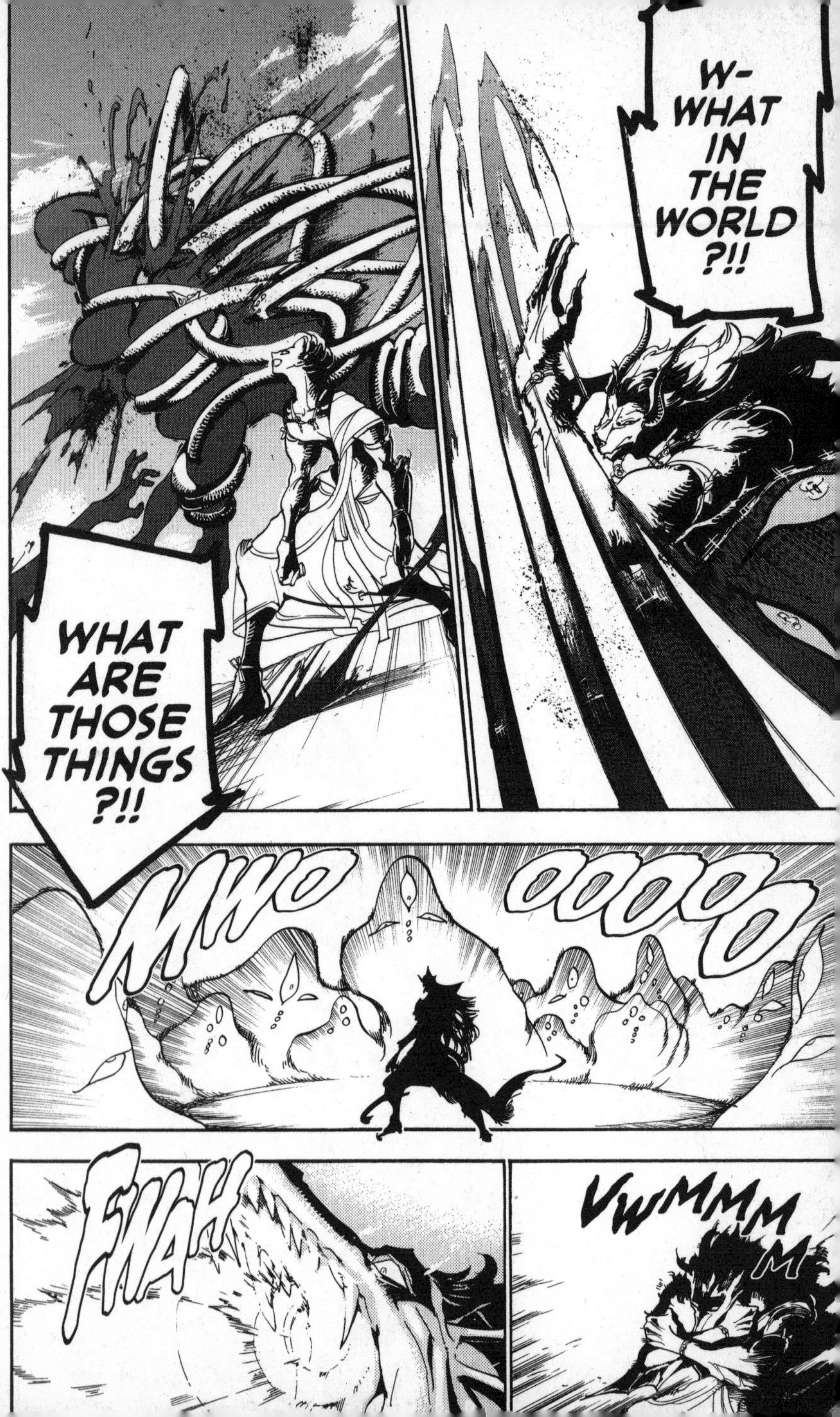
W- WHAT IN THE WORLD ?!!
WHAT ARE THOSE THINGS ?!!
MWOOOOOO
VWMMMM M
FWAH

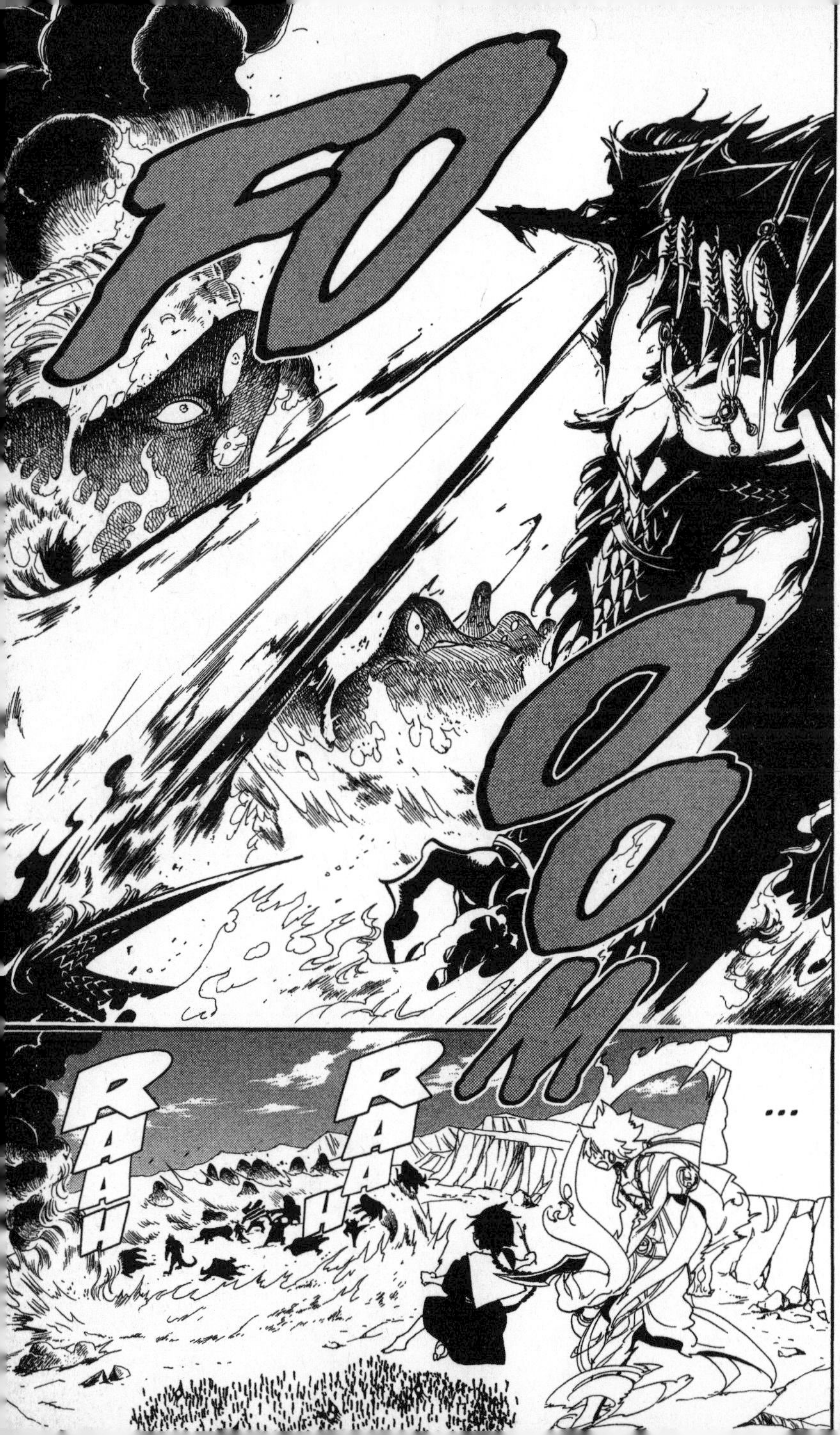

FOOOOM
...
RAAAH
RAAAH

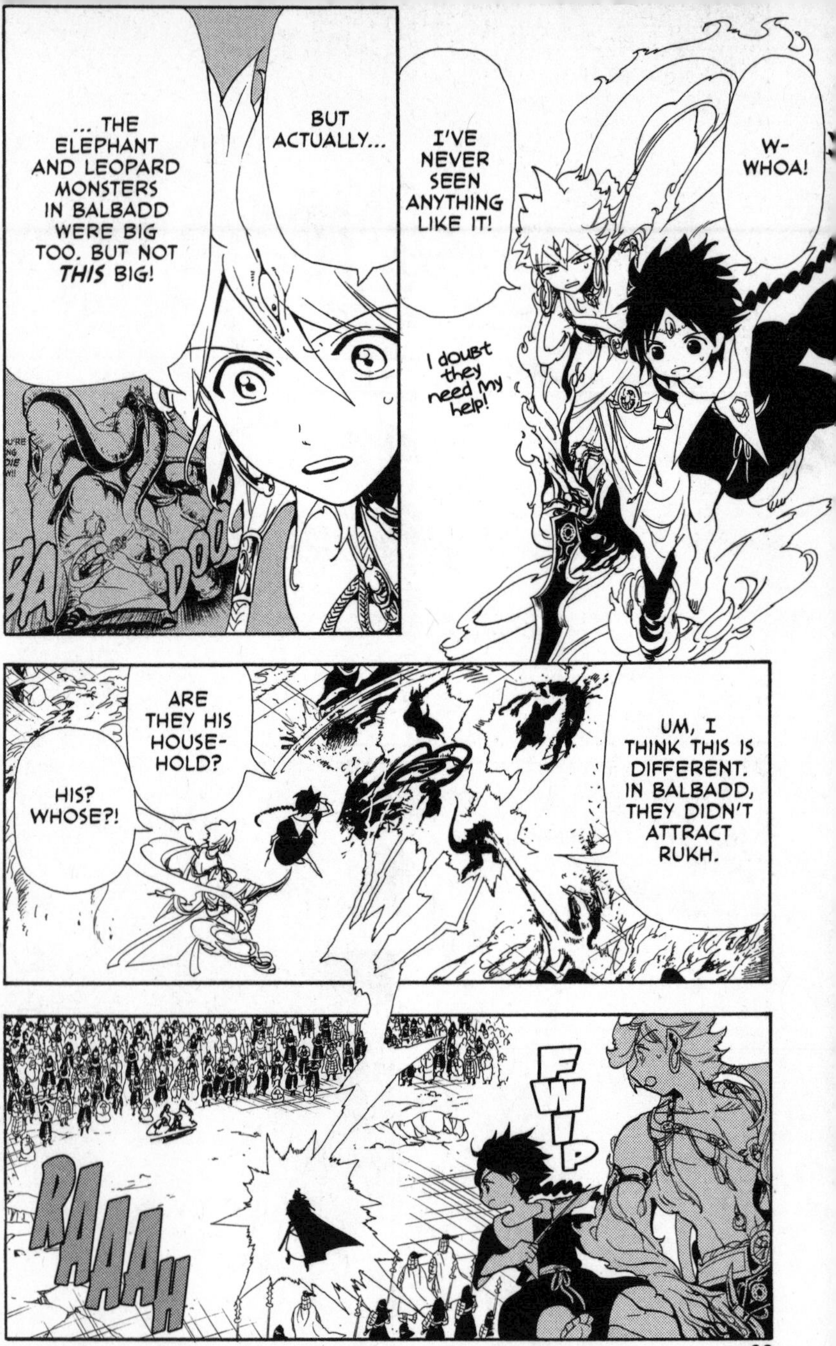
W-
WHOA!
I'VE NEVER SEEN ANYTHING LIKE IT!
I doubt they need my help!
BUT ACTUALLY...
... THE ELEPHANT AND LEOPARD MONSTERS IN BALBADD WERE BIG TOO. BUT NOT *THIS* BIG!
UM, I THINK THIS IS DIFFERENT. IN BALBADD, THEY DIDN'T ATTRACT RUKH.
ARE THEY HIS HOUSE-HOLD?
HIS? WHOSE?!
FWIP
RAAAAH

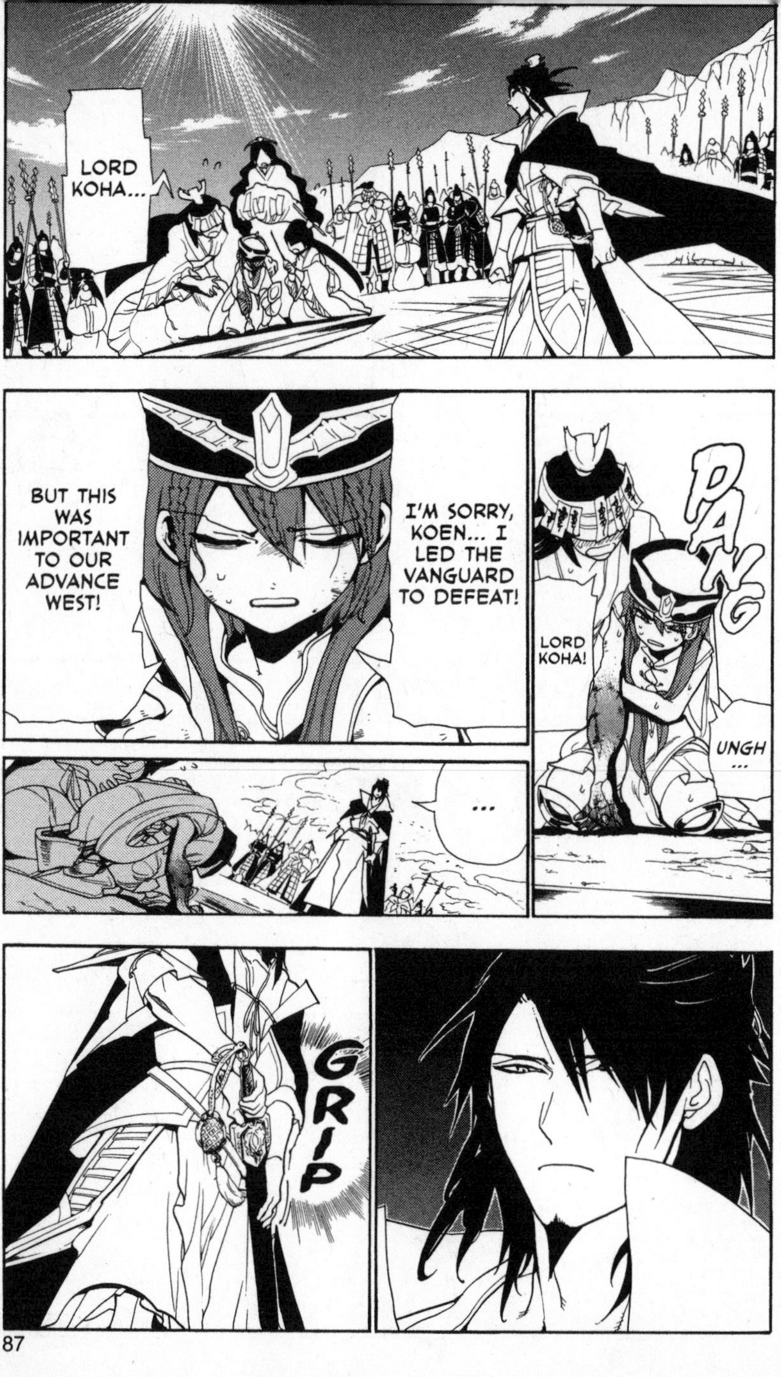
LORD KOHA...
PANG
LORD KOHA!
UNGH...
I'M SORRY, KOEN... I LED THE VANGUARD TO DEFEAT!
BUT THIS WAS IMPORTANT TO OUR ADVANCE WEST!
...
GRIP

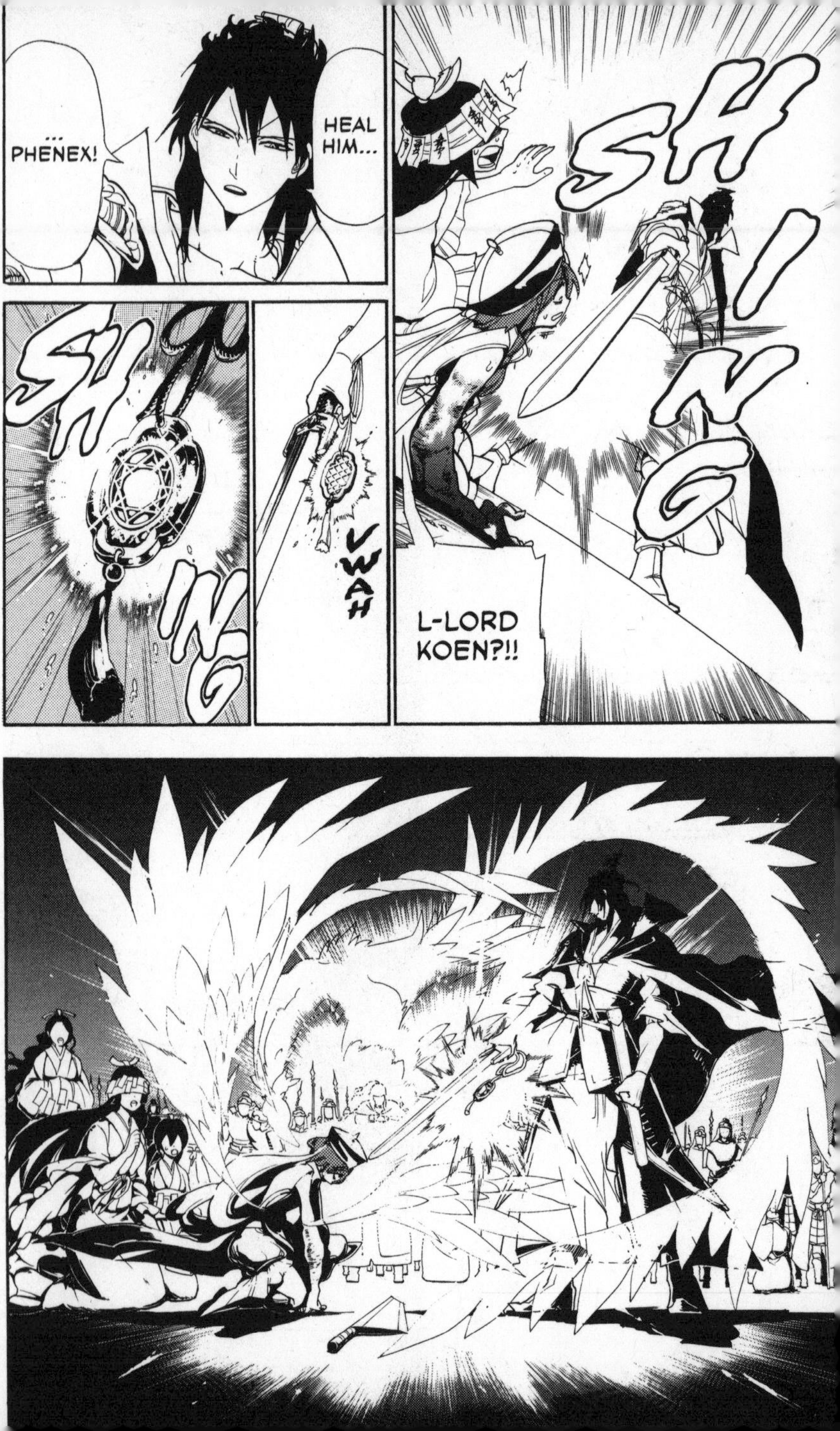
SHING
L-LORD KOEN?!!
HEAL HIM...
...PHENEX!
VWAH
SHING

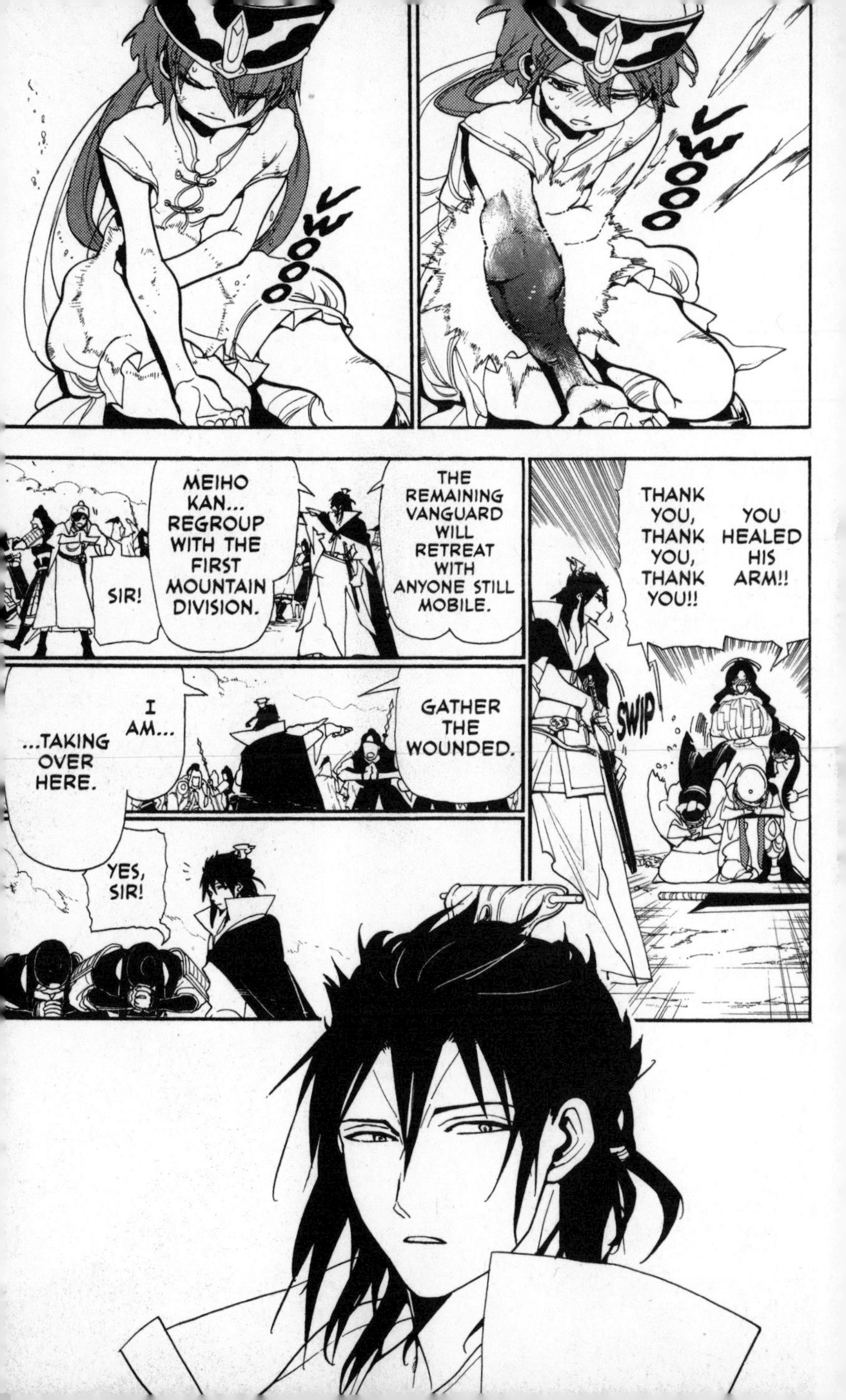
VWOOOO
VWOOOO
YOU HEALED HIS ARM!!
THANK YOU, THANK YOU, THANK YOU!!
SWIP
THE REMAINING VANGUARD WILL RETREAT WITH ANYONE STILL MOBILE.
MEIHO KAN... REGROUP WITH THE FIRST MOUNTAIN DIVISION.
SIR!
GATHER THE WOUNDED.
I AM...
...TAKING OVER HERE.
YES, SIR!

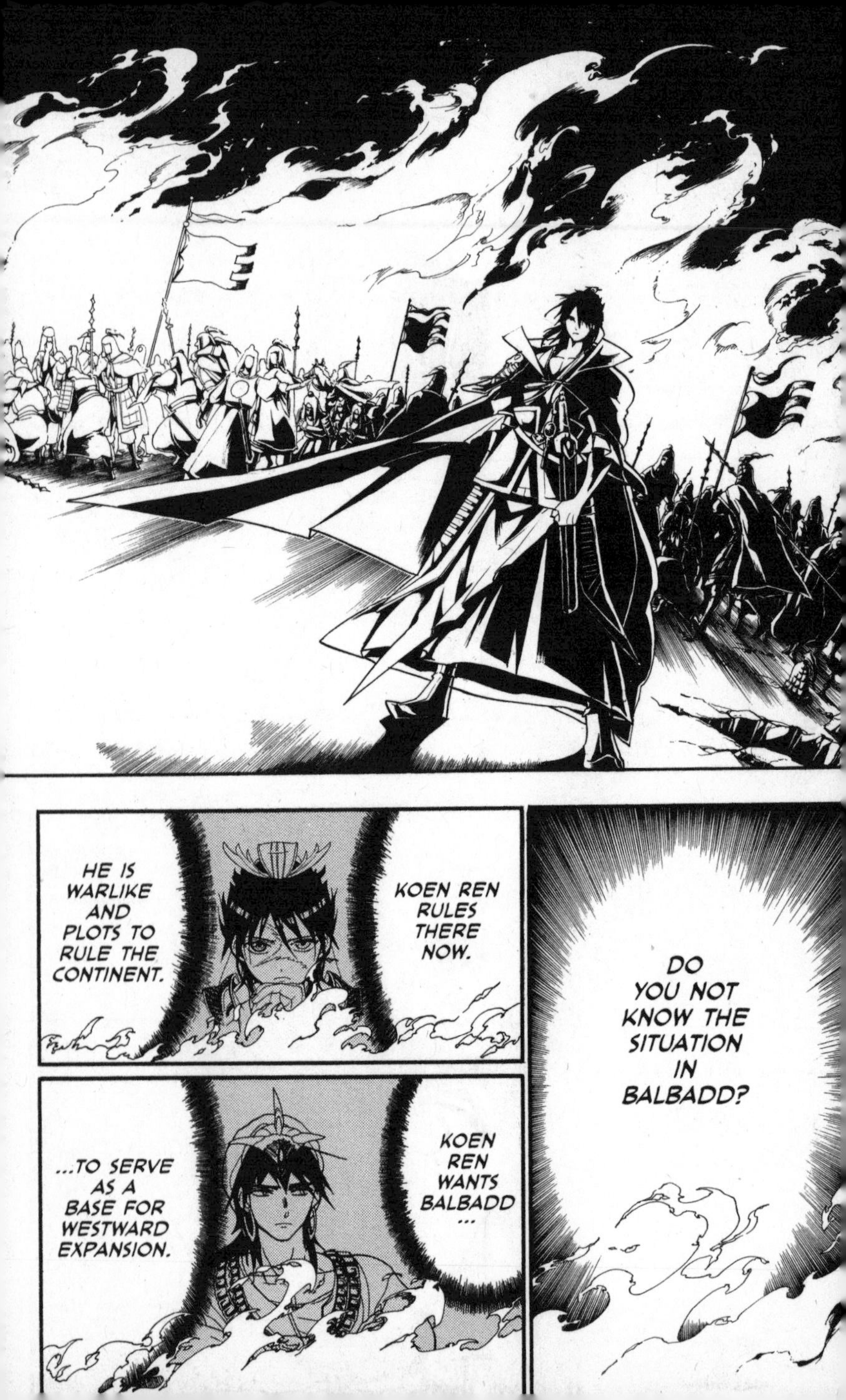
DO YOU NOT KNOW THE SITUATION IN BALBADD?
KOEN REN RULES THERE NOW.
HE IS WARLIKE AND PLOTS TO RULE THE CONTINENT.
KOEN REN WANTS BALBADD...
...TO SERVE AS A BASE FOR WESTWARD EXPANSION.

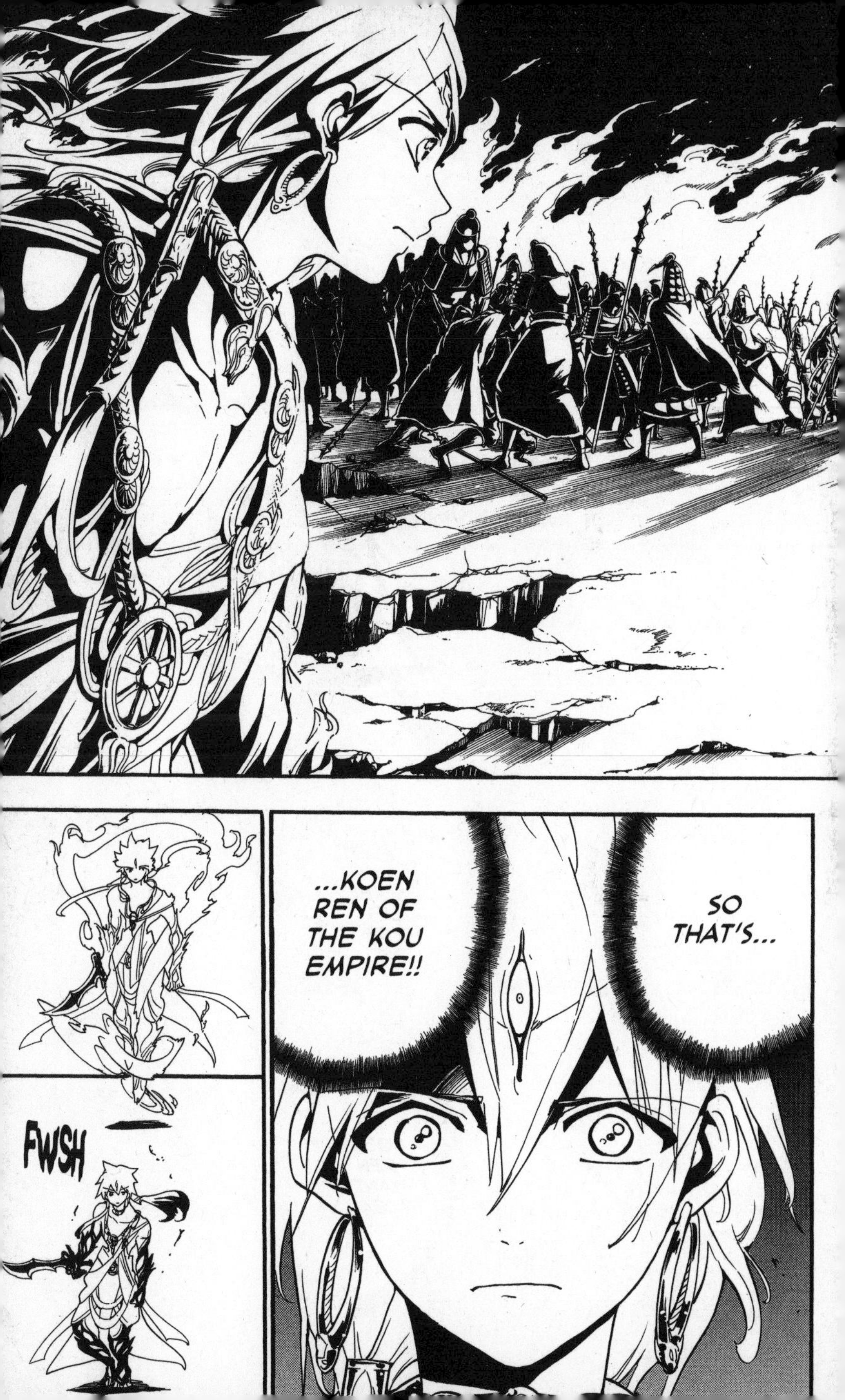
SO THAT'S...
...KOEN REN OF THE KOU EMPIRE!!
FWSH

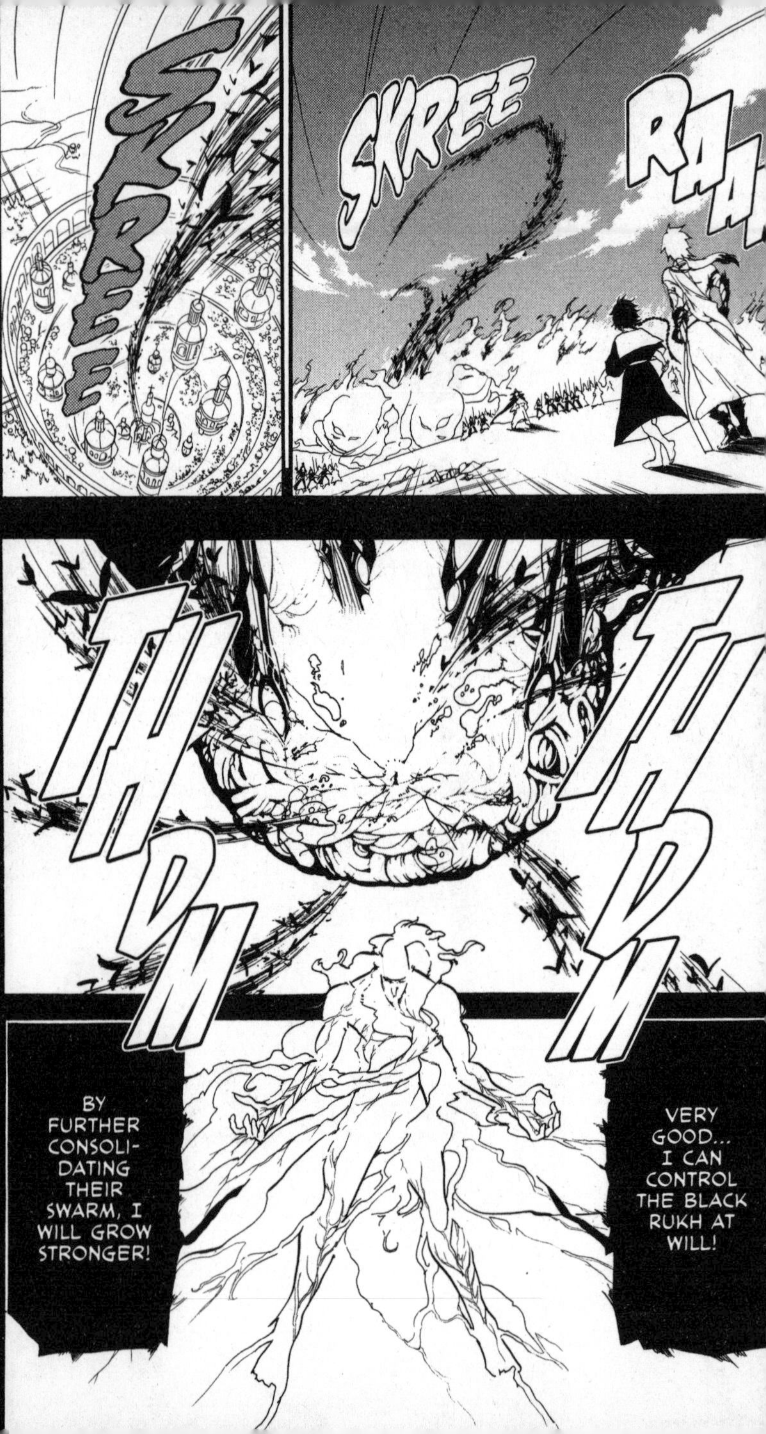
SKREE
RAA
SKREEE
THDUM
THDUM
VERY GOOD... I CAN CONTROL THE BLACK RUKH AT WILL!
BY FURTHER CONSOLI-DATING THEIR SWARM, I WILL GROW STRONGER!

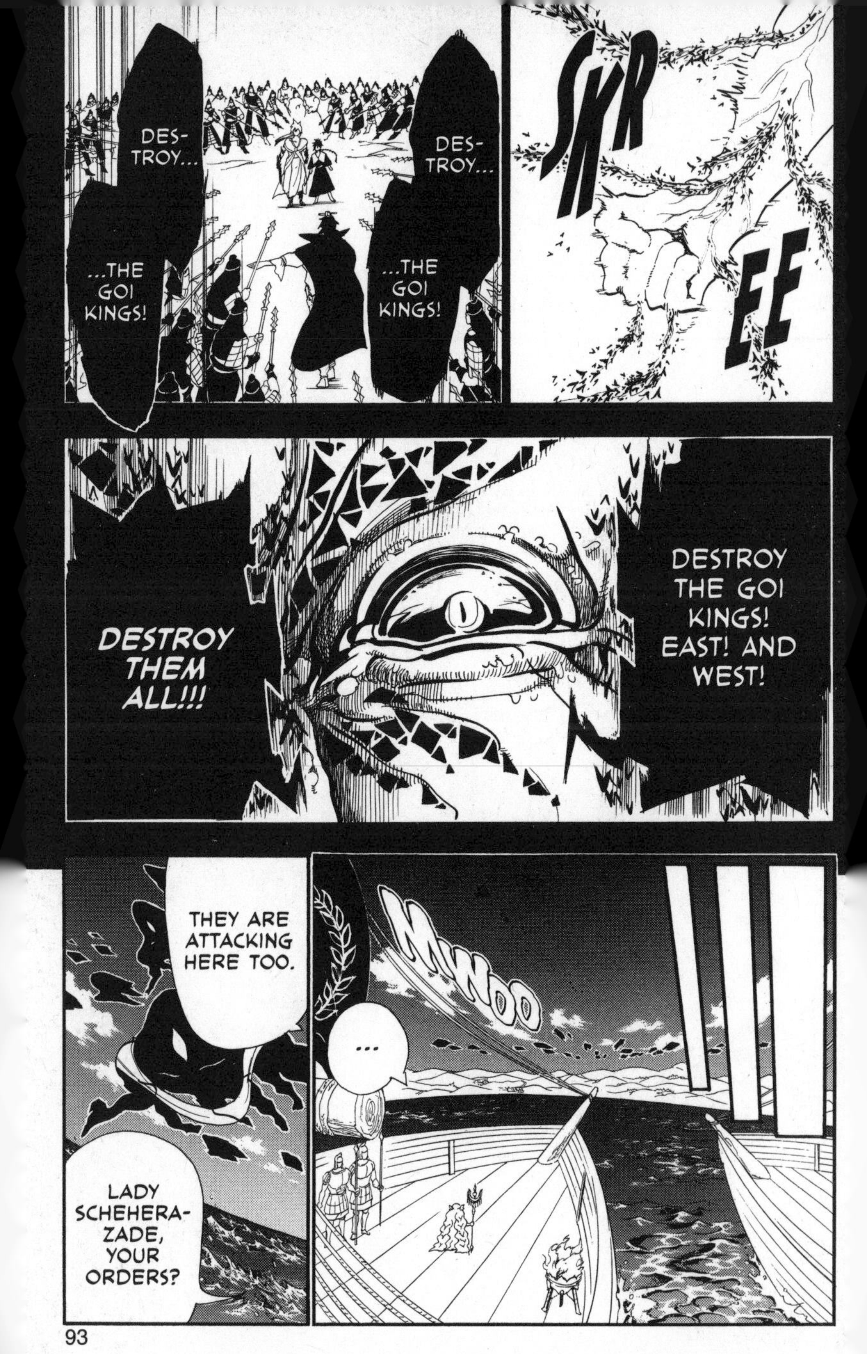
SKREE
DES-TROY...
...THE GOI KINGS!
DES-TROY...
...THE GOI KINGS!
DESTROY THE GOI KINGS! EAST! AND WEST!
DESTROY THEM ALL!!!
MUNOO
...
THEY ARE ATTACKING HERE TOO.
LADY SCHEHERA-ZADE, YOUR ORDERS?

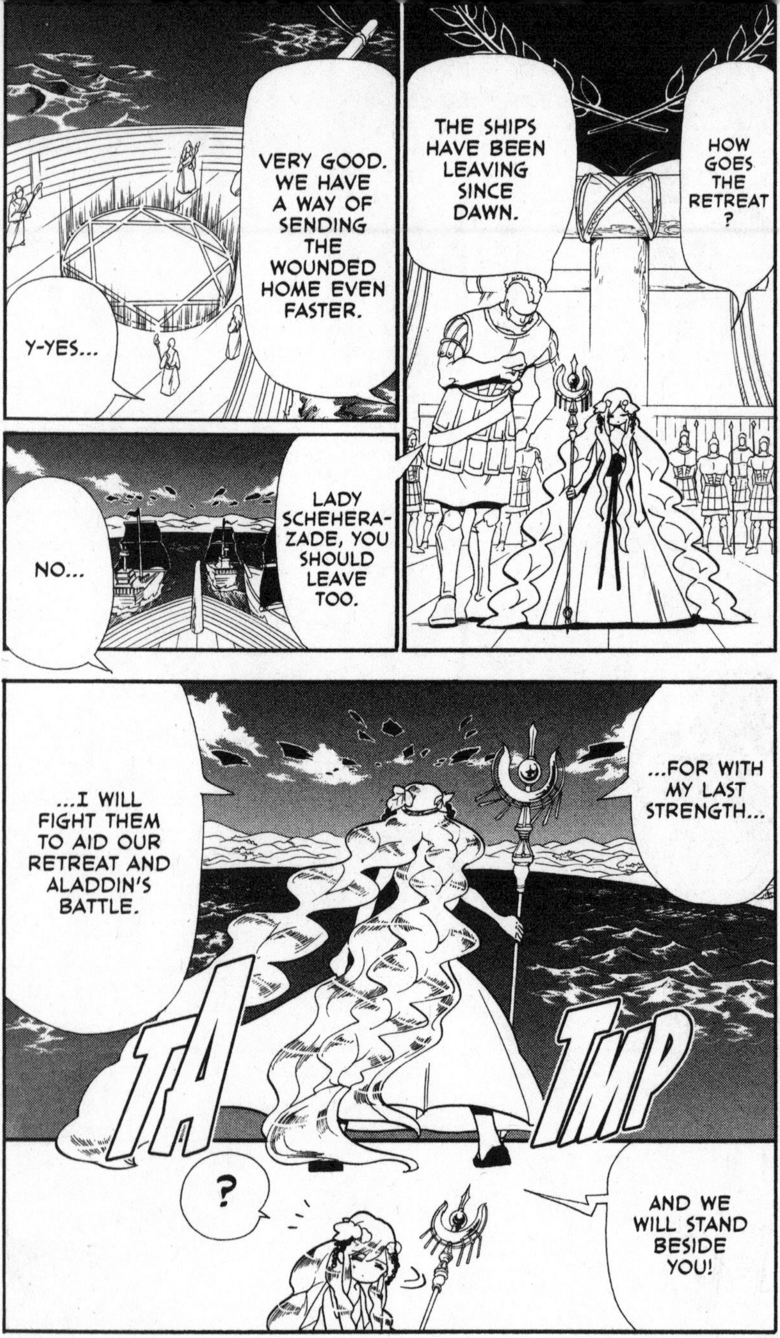
HOW GOES THE RETREAT?
THE SHIPS HAVE BEEN LEAVING SINCE DAWN.
VERY GOOD. WE HAVE A WAY OF SENDING THE WOUNDED HOME EVEN FASTER.
Y-YES...
LADY SCHEHERAZADE, YOU SHOULD LEAVE TOO.
NO...
...FOR WITH MY LAST STRENGTH...
...I WILL FIGHT THEM TO AID OUR RETREAT AND ALADDIN'S BATTLE.
TMP
TA
AND WE WILL STAND BESIDE YOU!
?

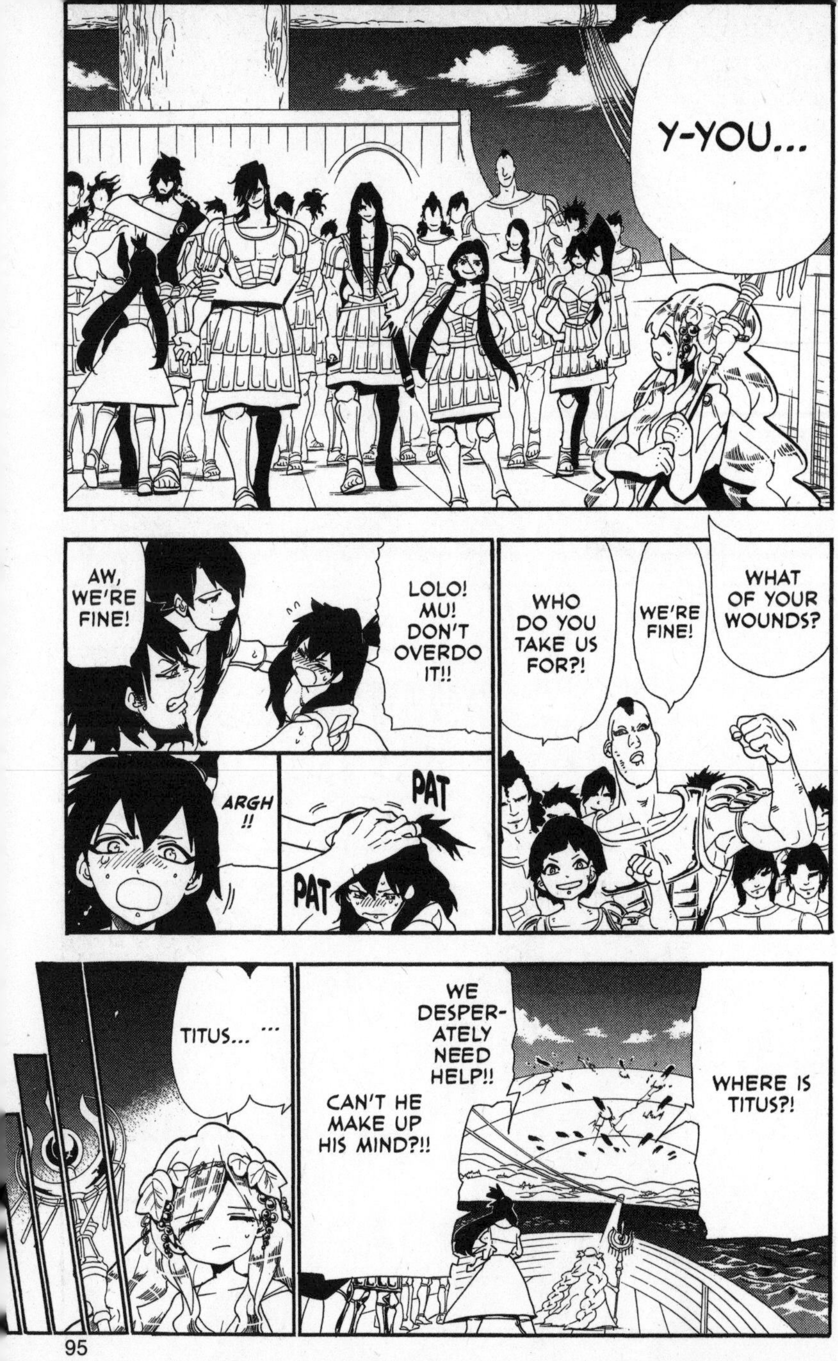
Y-YOU...
WHAT OF YOUR WOUNDS?
WE'RE FINE!
WHO DO YOU TAKE US FOR?!
LOLO! MU! DON'T OVERDO IT!!
AW, WE'RE FINE!
PAT
PAT
ARGH!!
WHERE IS TITUS?!
WE DESPER-ATELY NEED HELP!!
CAN'T HE MAKE UP HIS MIND?!!
TITUS... ...

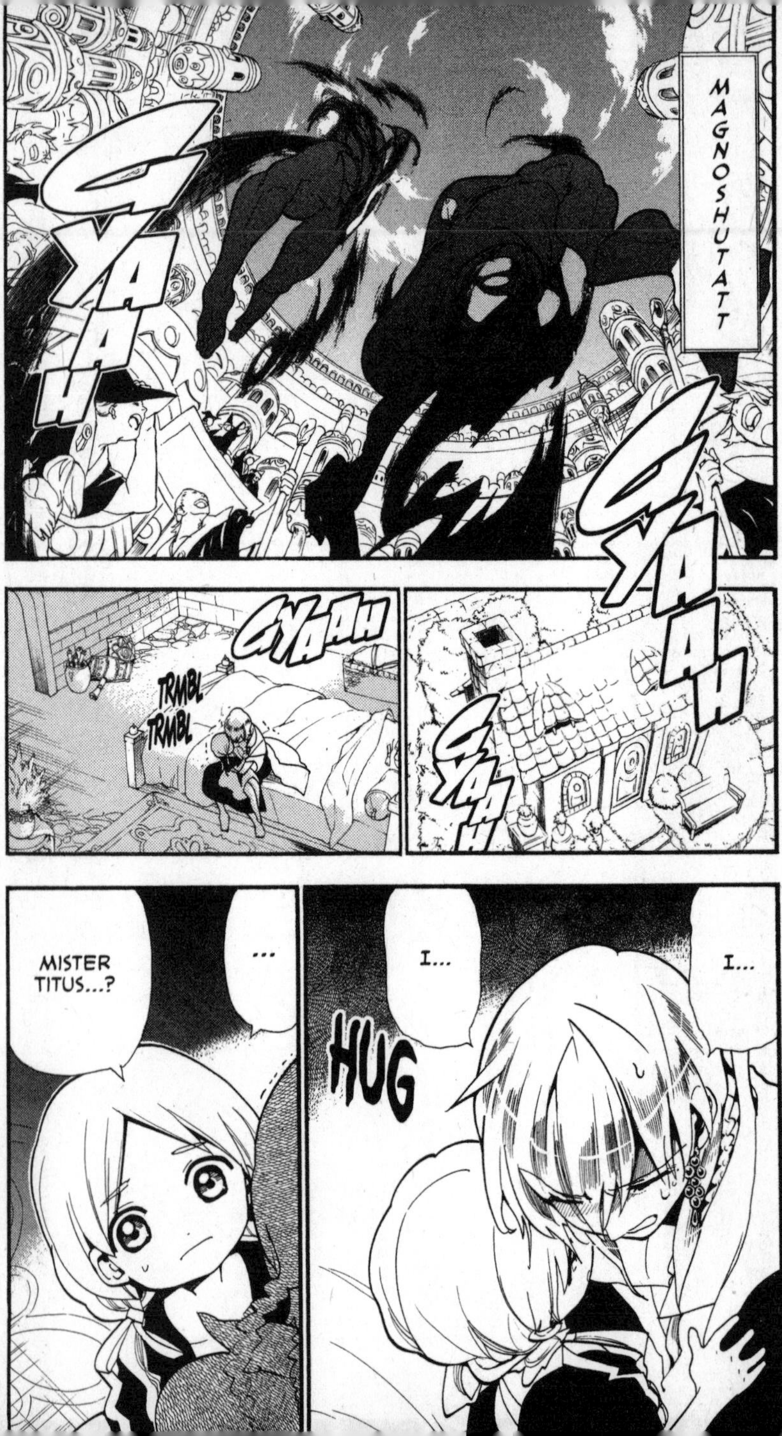
MAGNOSHUTATT
GYAAH
GYAAH
GYAAH
GYAAH
TRMBL TRMBL
I...
I...
HUG
...
MISTER TITUS...?

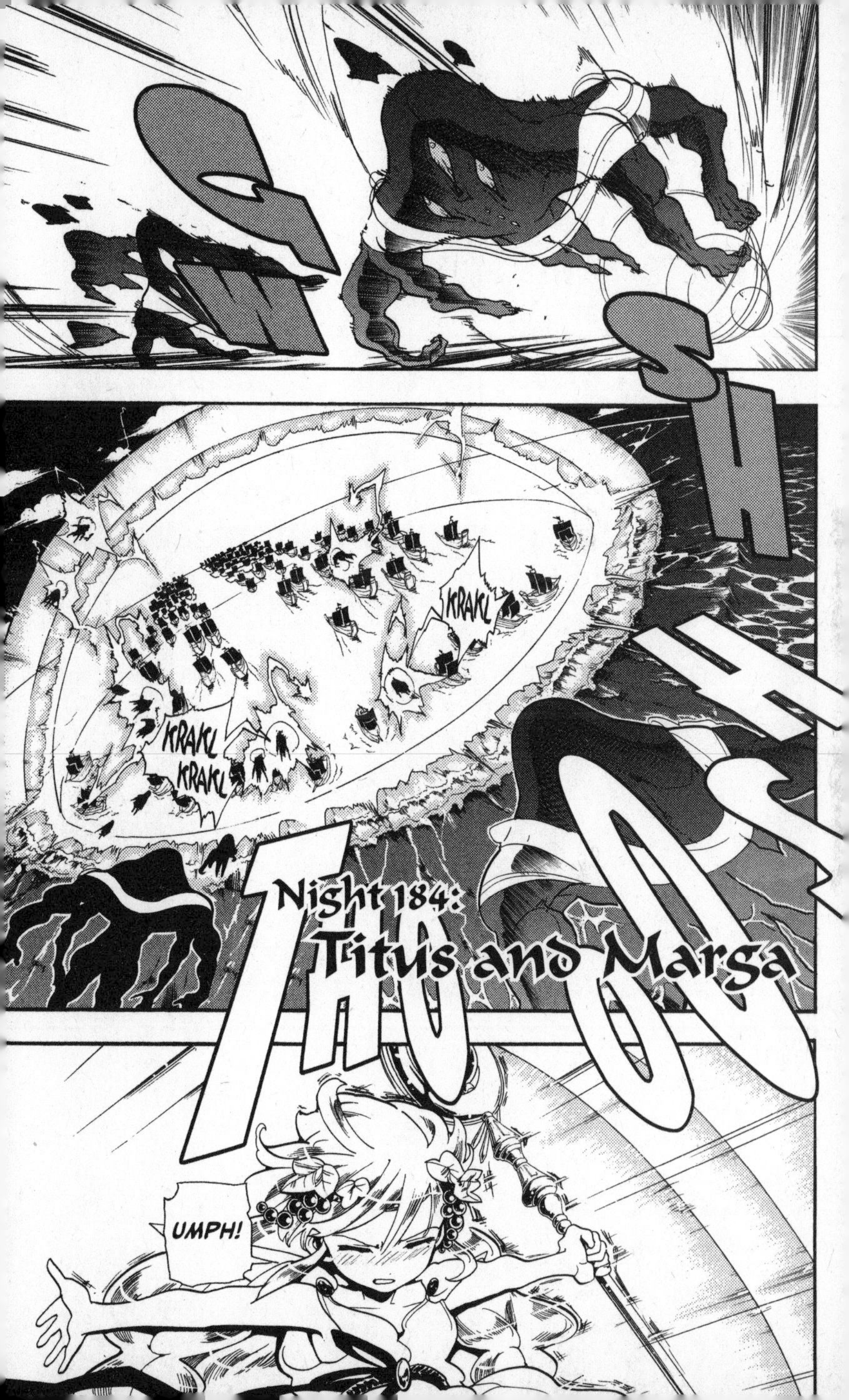
KRAKL
KRAKL
KRAKL
Night 184:
Titus and Marga
UMPH!

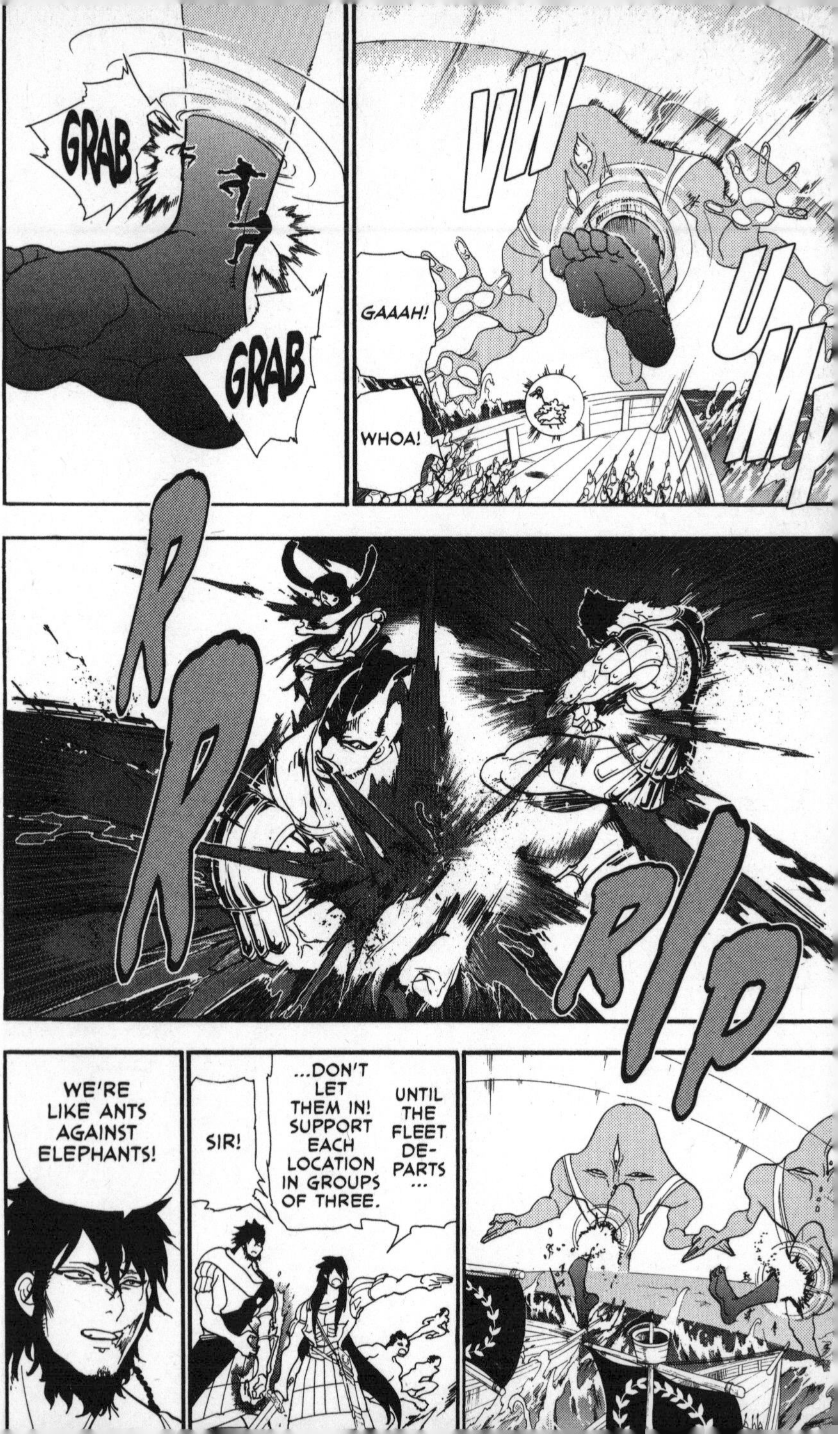
VW
UMP
GAAAH!
WHOA!
GRAB
GRAB
RRRIP
UNTIL THE FLEET DE-PARTS...
...DON'T LET THEM IN! SUPPORT EACH LOCATION IN GROUPS OF THREE.
SIR!
WE'RE LIKE ANTS AGAINST ELEPHANTS!

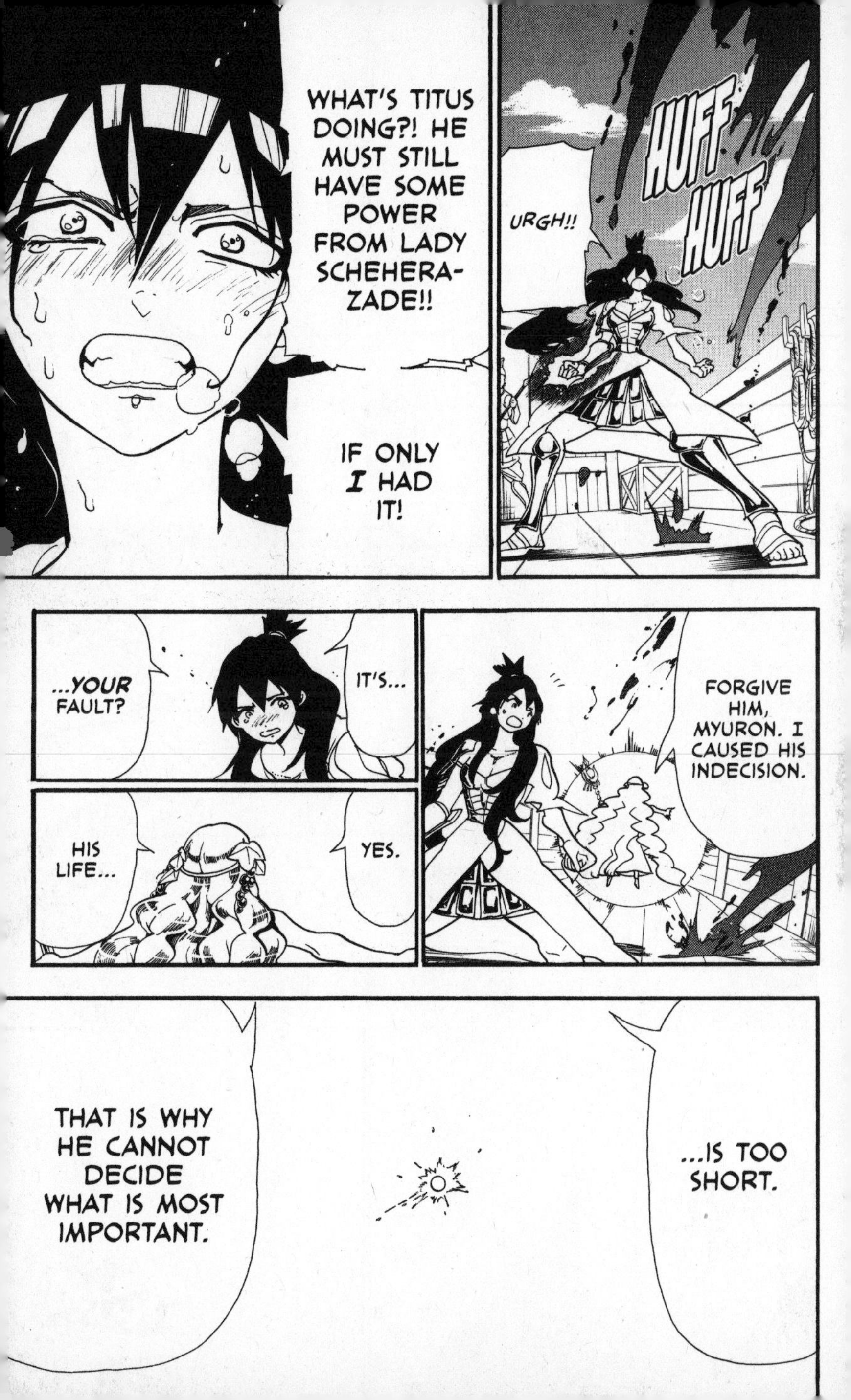
HUFF HUFF
URGH!!
WHAT'S TITUS DOING?! HE MUST STILL HAVE SOME POWER FROM LADY SCHEHERA-ZADE!!
IF ONLY I HAD IT!
FORGIVE HIM, MYURON. I CAUSED HIS INDECISION.
IT'S...
...YOUR FAULT?
YES.
HIS LIFE...
...IS TOO SHORT.
THAT IS WHY HE CANNOT DECIDE WHAT IS MOST IMPORTANT.

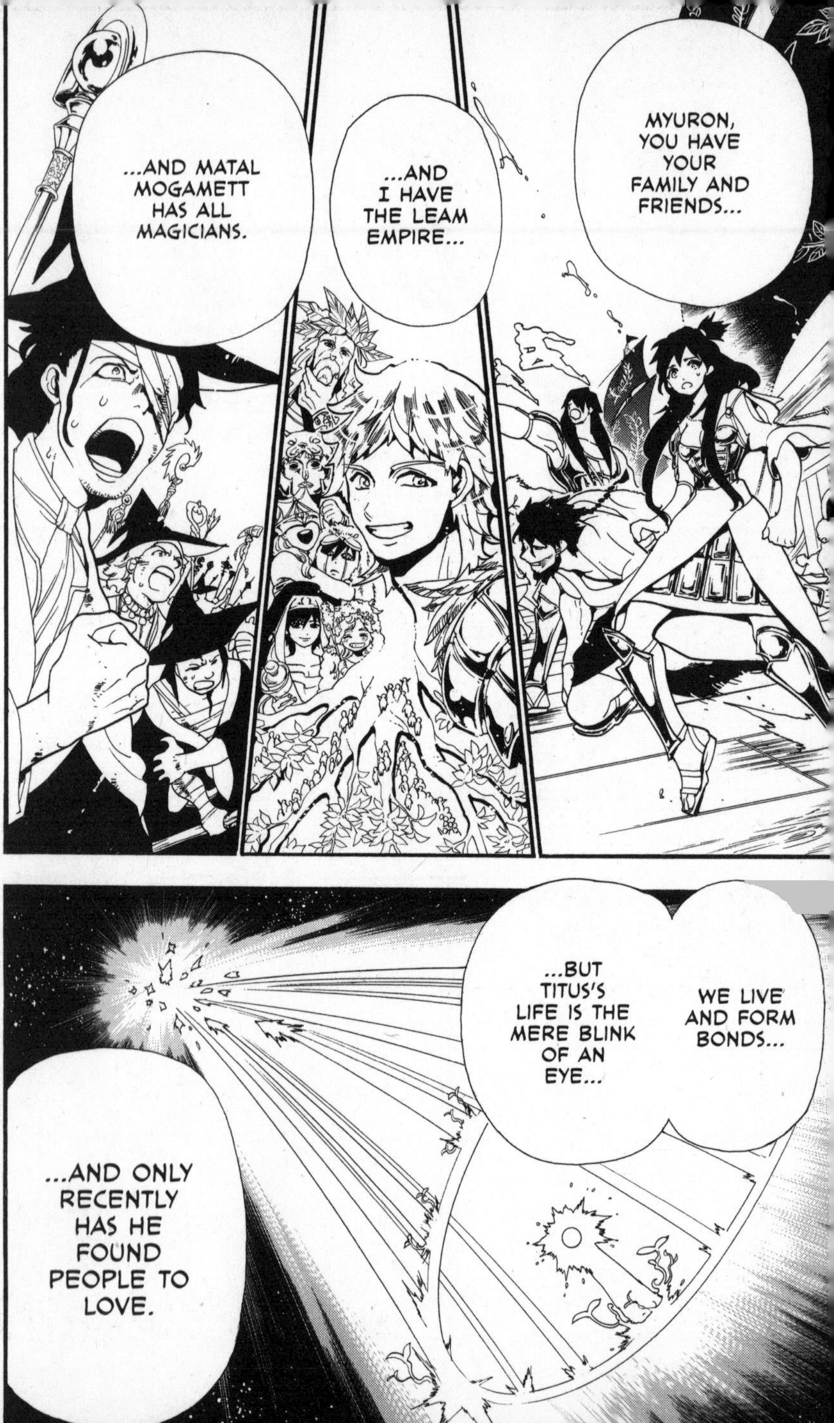
MYURON, YOU HAVE YOUR FAMILY AND FRIENDS...
...AND I HAVE THE LEAM EMPIRE...
...AND MATAL MOGAMETT HAS ALL MAGICIANS.
WE LIVE AND FORM BONDS...
...BUT TITUS'S LIFE IS THE MERE BLINK OF AN EYE...
...AND ONLY RECENTLY HAS HE FOUND PEOPLE TO LOVE.

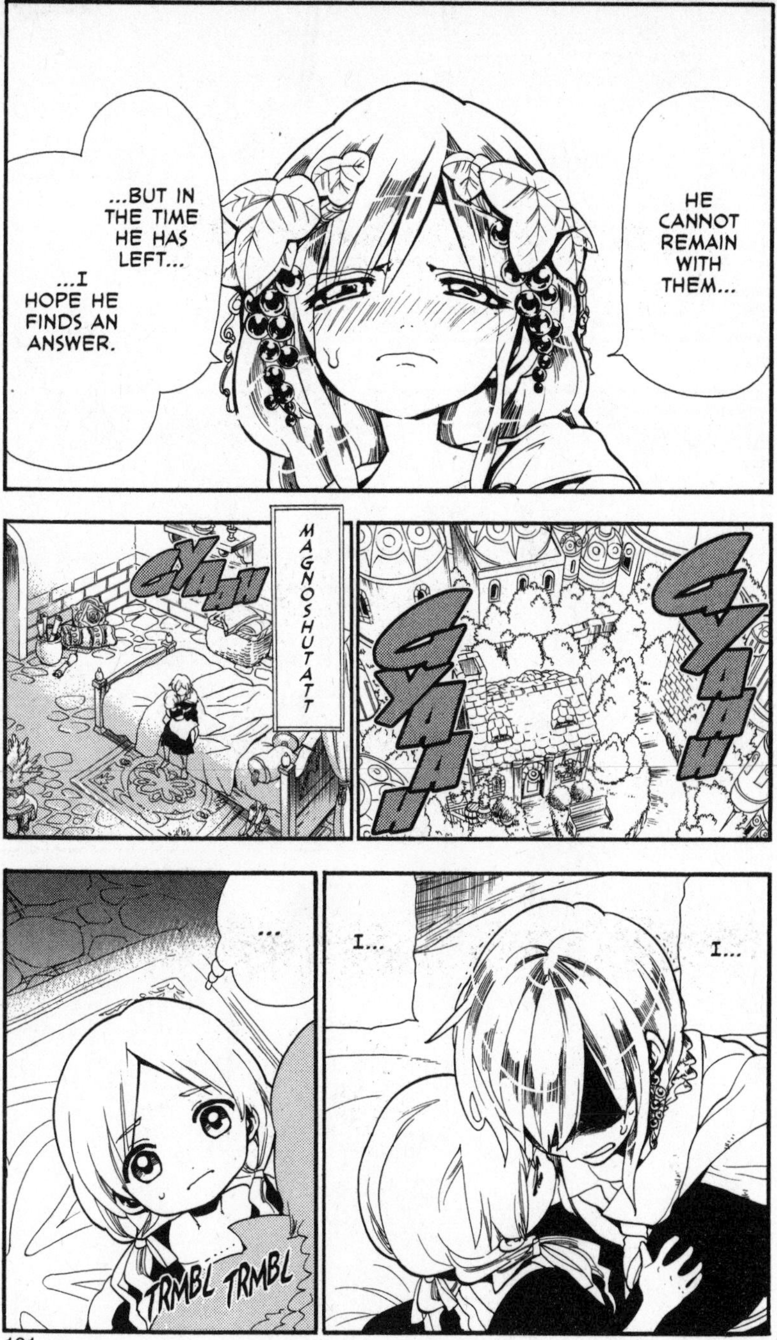
HE CANNOT REMAIN WITH THEM...
...BUT IN THE TIME HE HAS LEFT...
...I HOPE HE FINDS AN ANSWER.
GYAAAH
GYAAAH
MAGNOSHUTATT
GYAAAH
I...
I...
...
TRMBL TRMBL

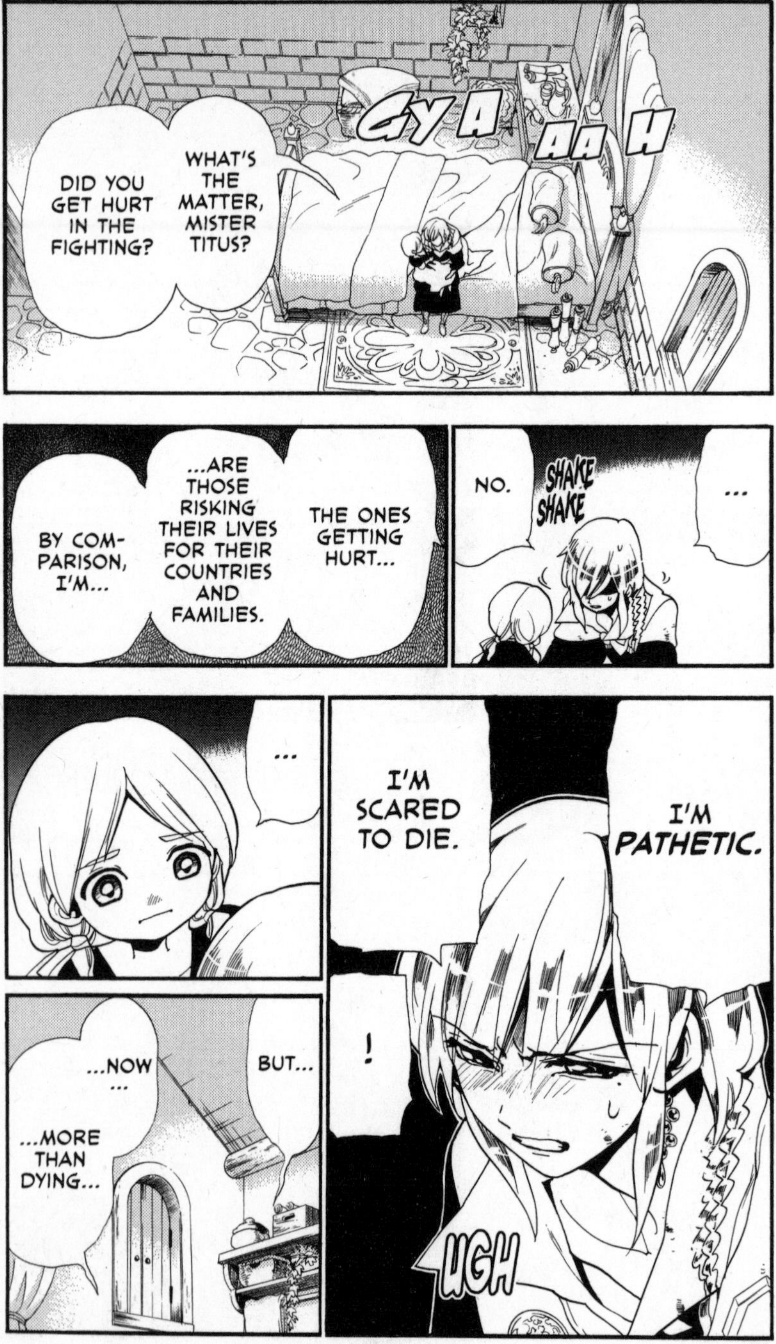
GYAAAH
WHAT'S THE MATTER, MISTER TITUS?
DID YOU GET HURT IN THE FIGHTING?
...
SHAKE SHAKE
NO.
THE ONES GETTING HURT...
...ARE THOSE RISKING THEIR LIVES FOR THEIR COUNTRIES AND FAMILIES.
BY COMPARISON, I'M...
I'M PATHETIC.
I'M SCARED TO DIE.
!
UGH
...
BUT...
...NOW ...
...MORE THAN DYING...

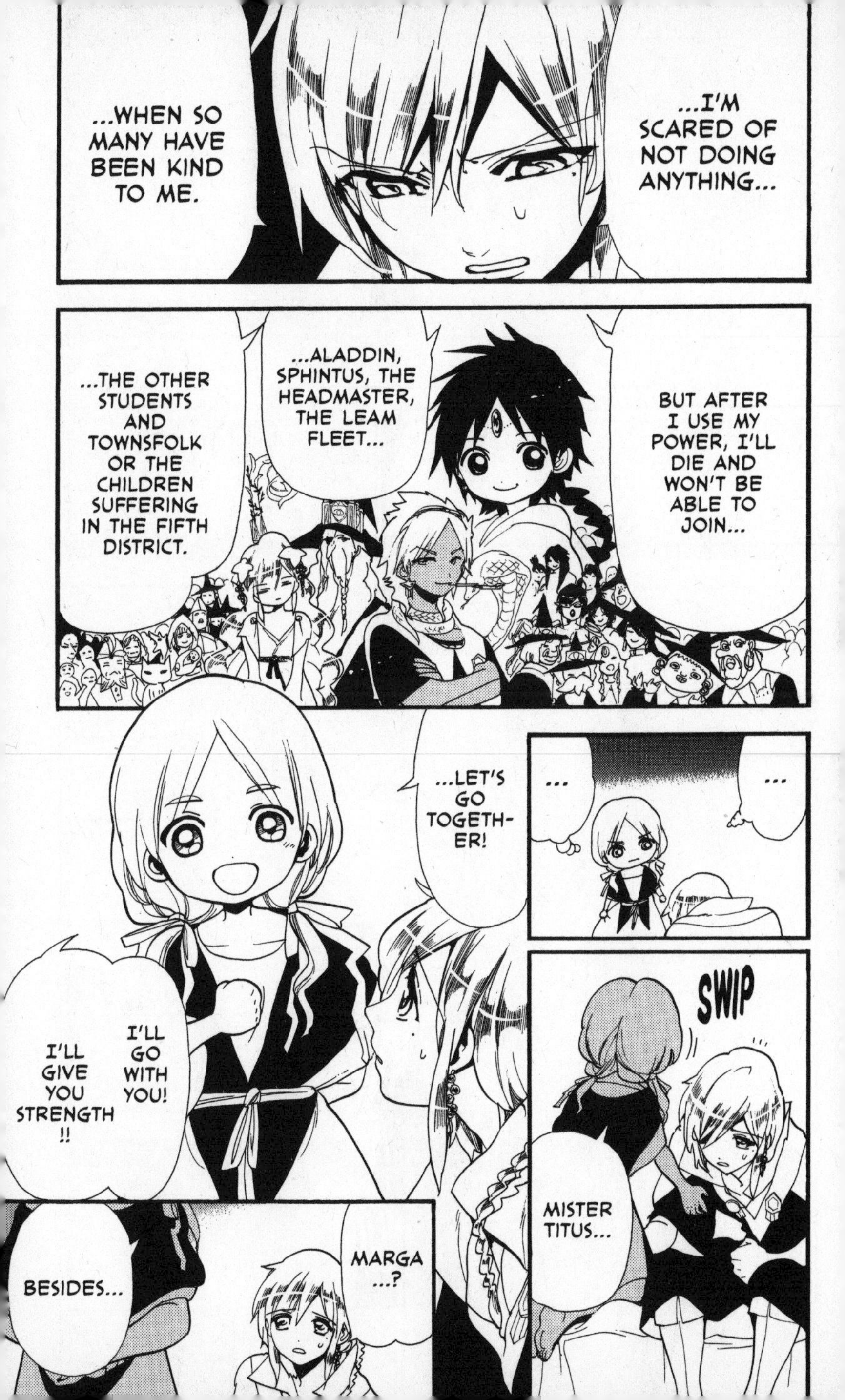

...I'M SCARED OF NOT DOING ANYTHING...
...WHEN SO MANY HAVE BEEN KIND TO ME.
BUT AFTER I USE MY POWER, I'LL DIE AND WON'T BE ABLE TO JOIN...
...ALADDIN, SPHINTUS, THE HEADMASTER, THE LEAM FLEET...
...THE OTHER STUDENTS AND TOWNSFOLK OR THE CHILDREN SUFFERING IN THE FIFTH DISTRICT.
...
...
SWIP
MISTER TITUS...
...LET'S GO TOGETHER!
I'LL GO WITH YOU!
I'LL GIVE YOU STRENGTH!!
MARGA ...?
BESIDES...

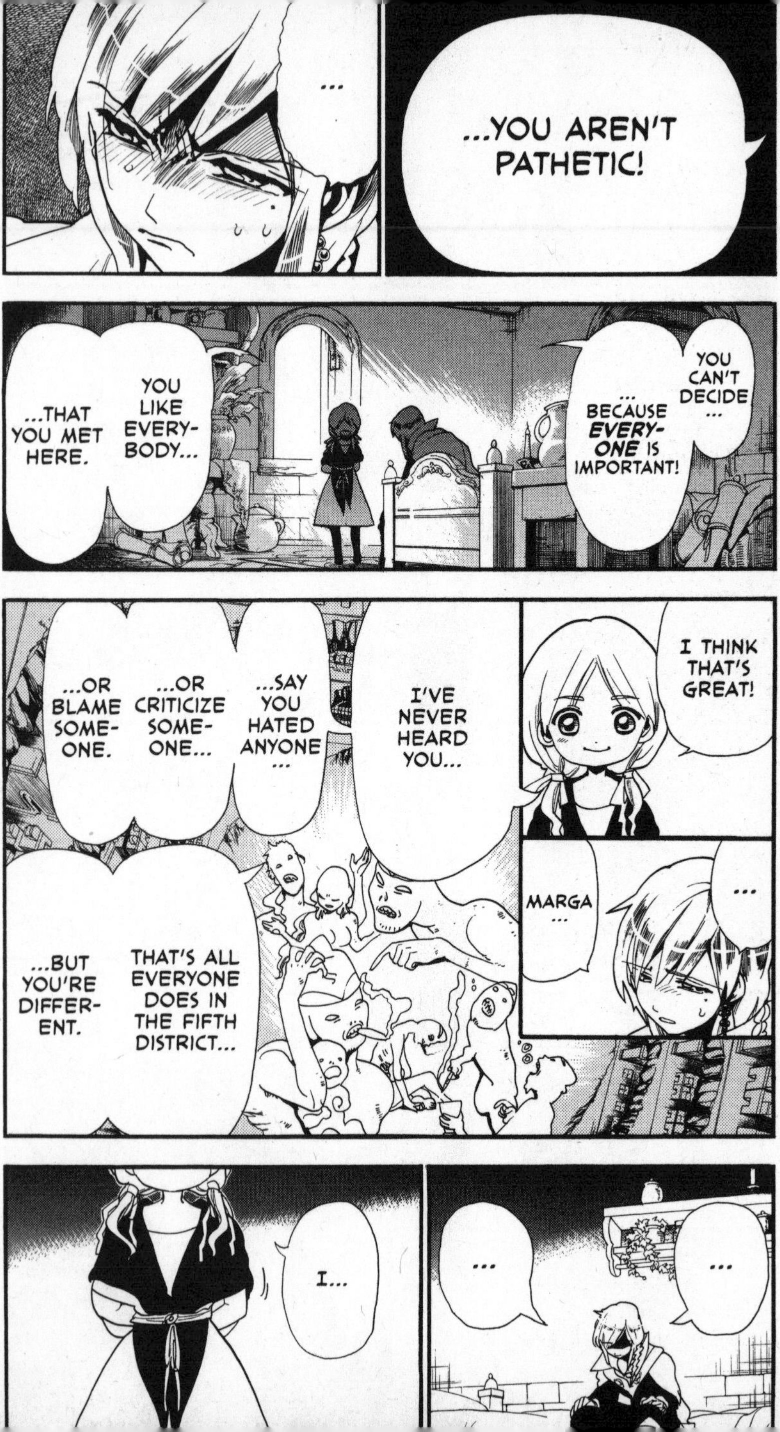
...YOU AREN'T PATHETIC!
...
YOU CAN'T DECIDE...
...BECAUSE EVERY-ONE IS IMPORTANT!
YOU LIKE EVERY-BODY...
...THAT YOU MET HERE.
I THINK THAT'S GREAT!
...
MARGA...
I'VE NEVER HEARD YOU...
...SAY YOU HATED ANYONE...
...OR CRITICIZE SOME-ONE...
...OR BLAME SOME-ONE.
THAT'S ALL EVERYONE DOES IN THE FIFTH DISTRICT...
...BUT YOU'RE DIFFER-ENT.
...
...
I...

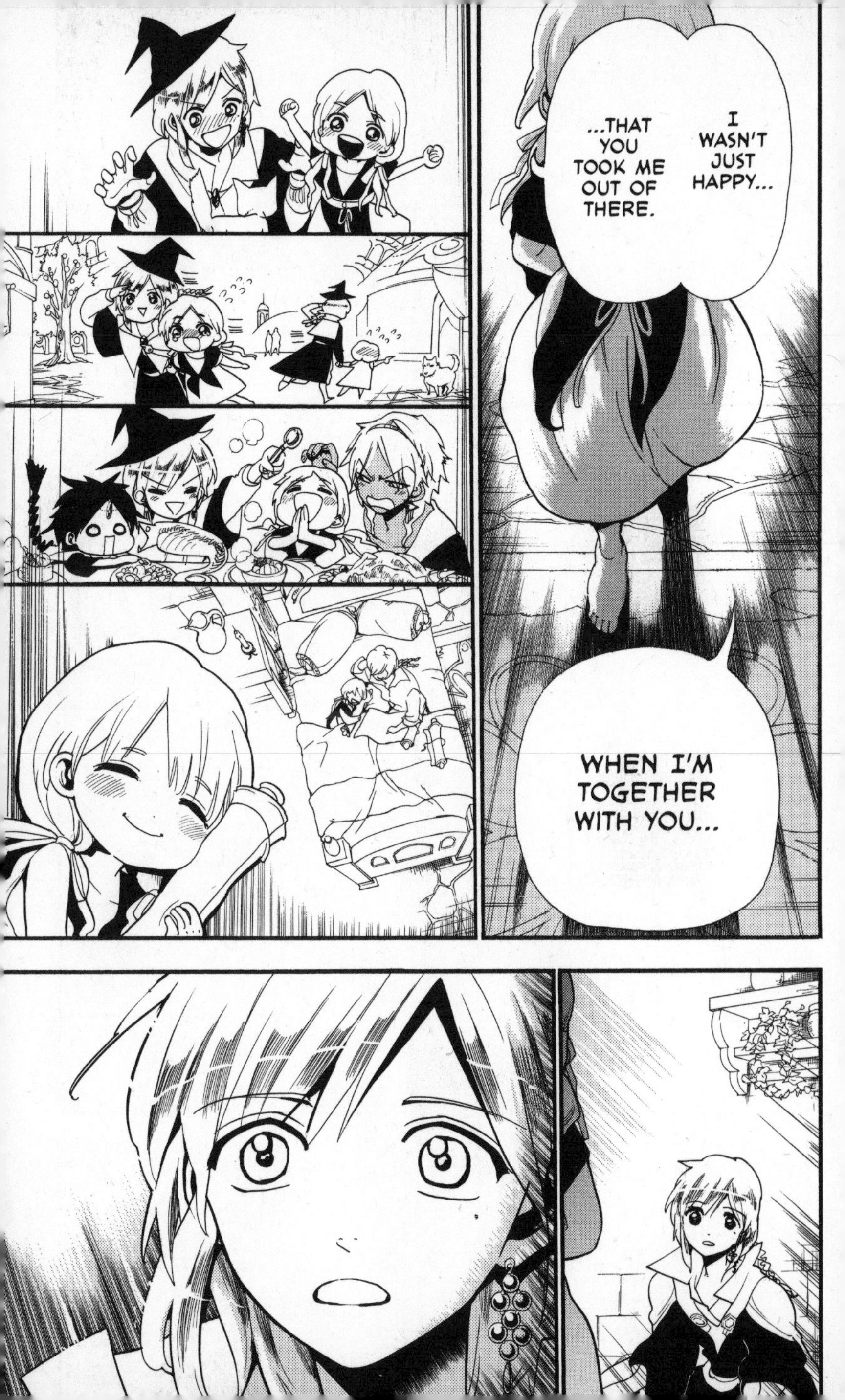
I WASN'T JUST HAPPY...
...THAT YOU TOOK ME OUT OF THERE.
WHEN I'M TOGETHER WITH YOU...

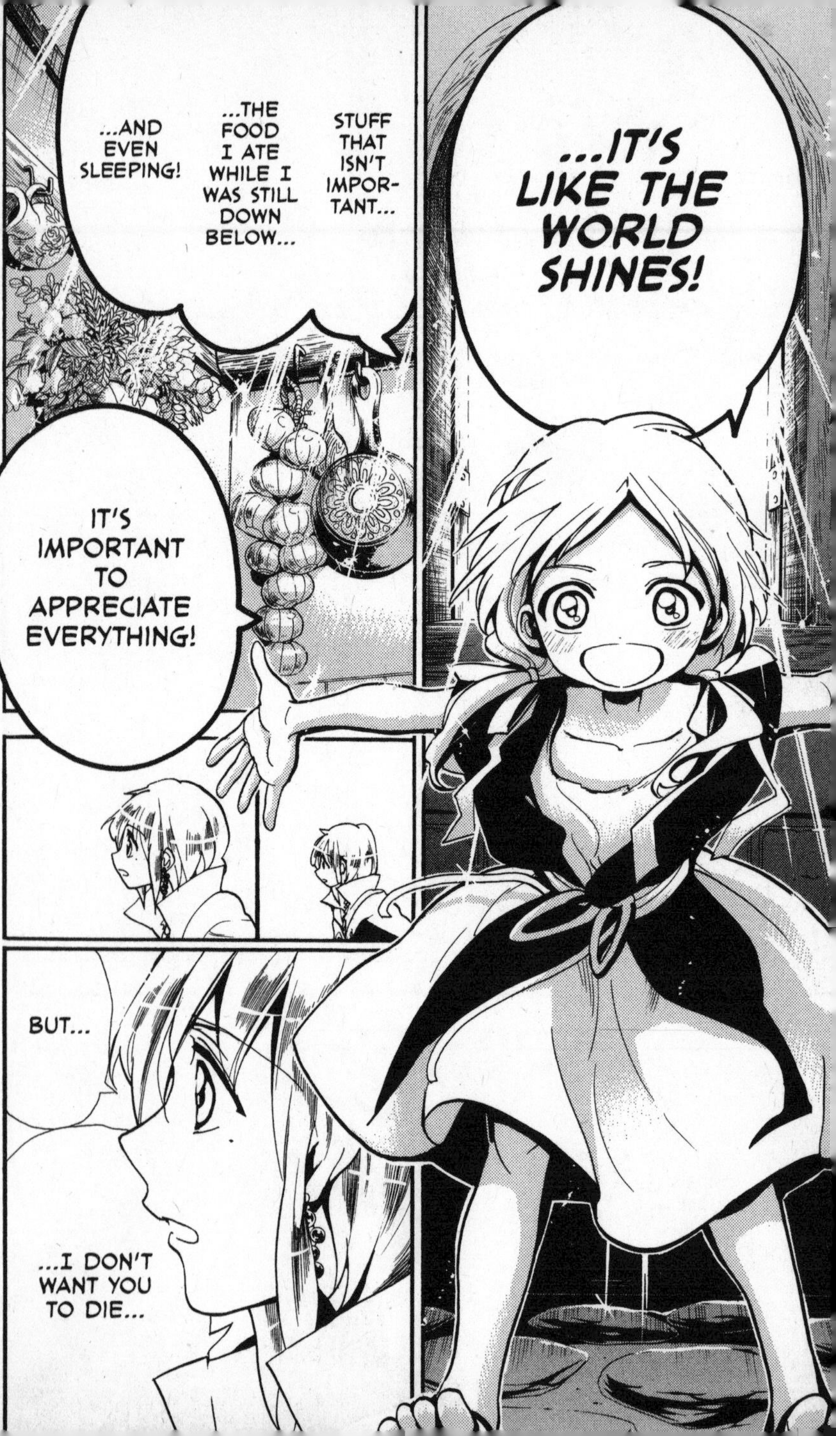
...IT'S LIKE THE WORLD SHINES!
STUFF THAT ISN'T IMPOR-TANT...
...THE FOOD I ATE WHILE I WAS STILL DOWN BELOW...
...AND EVEN SLEEPING!
IT'S IMPORTANT TO APPRECIATE EVERYTHING!
BUT...
...I DON'T WANT YOU TO DIE...

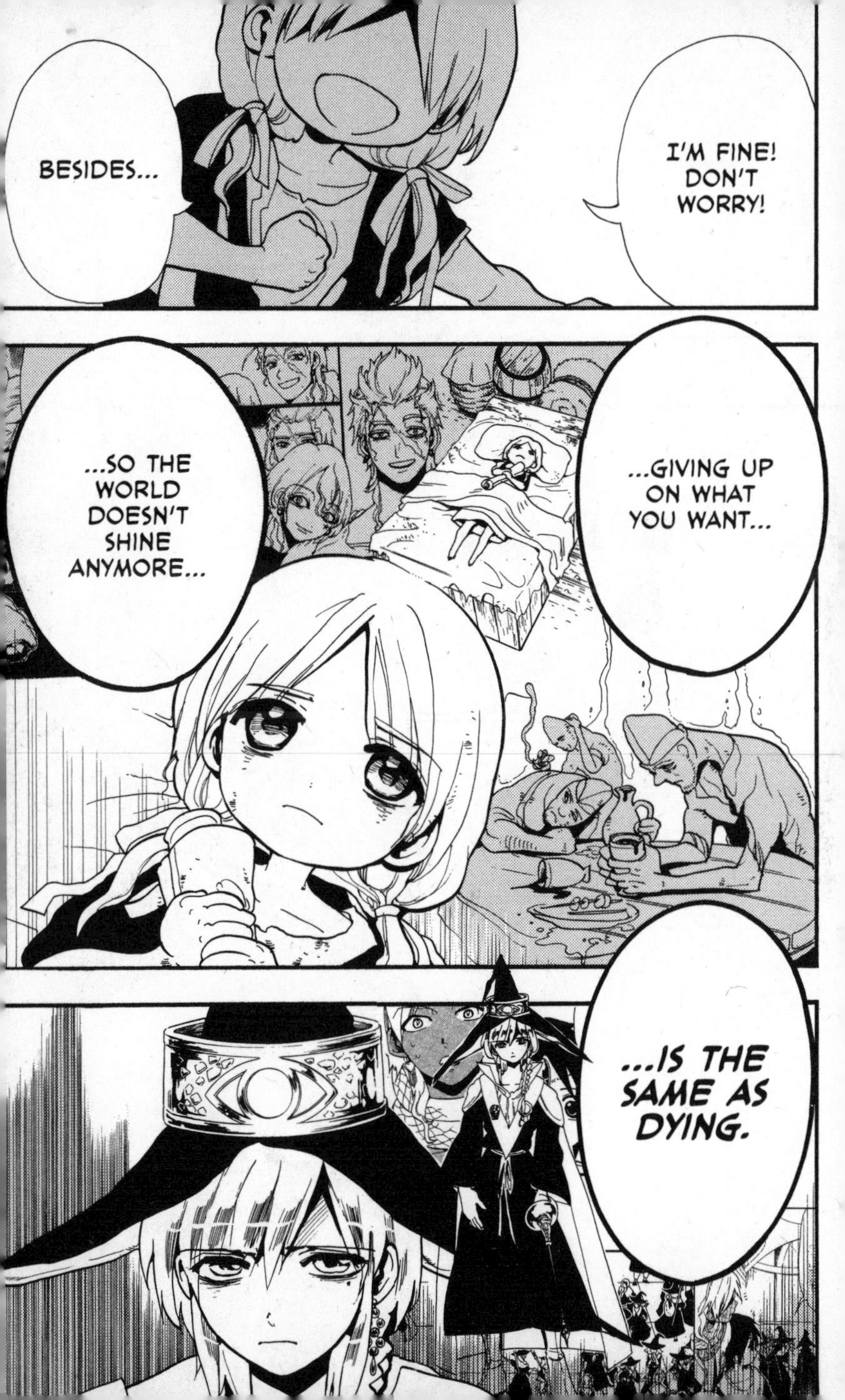
I'M FINE! DON'T WORRY!
BESIDES...
...GIVING UP ON WHAT YOU WANT...
...SO THE WORLD DOESN'T SHINE ANYMORE...
...IS THE SAME AS DYING.

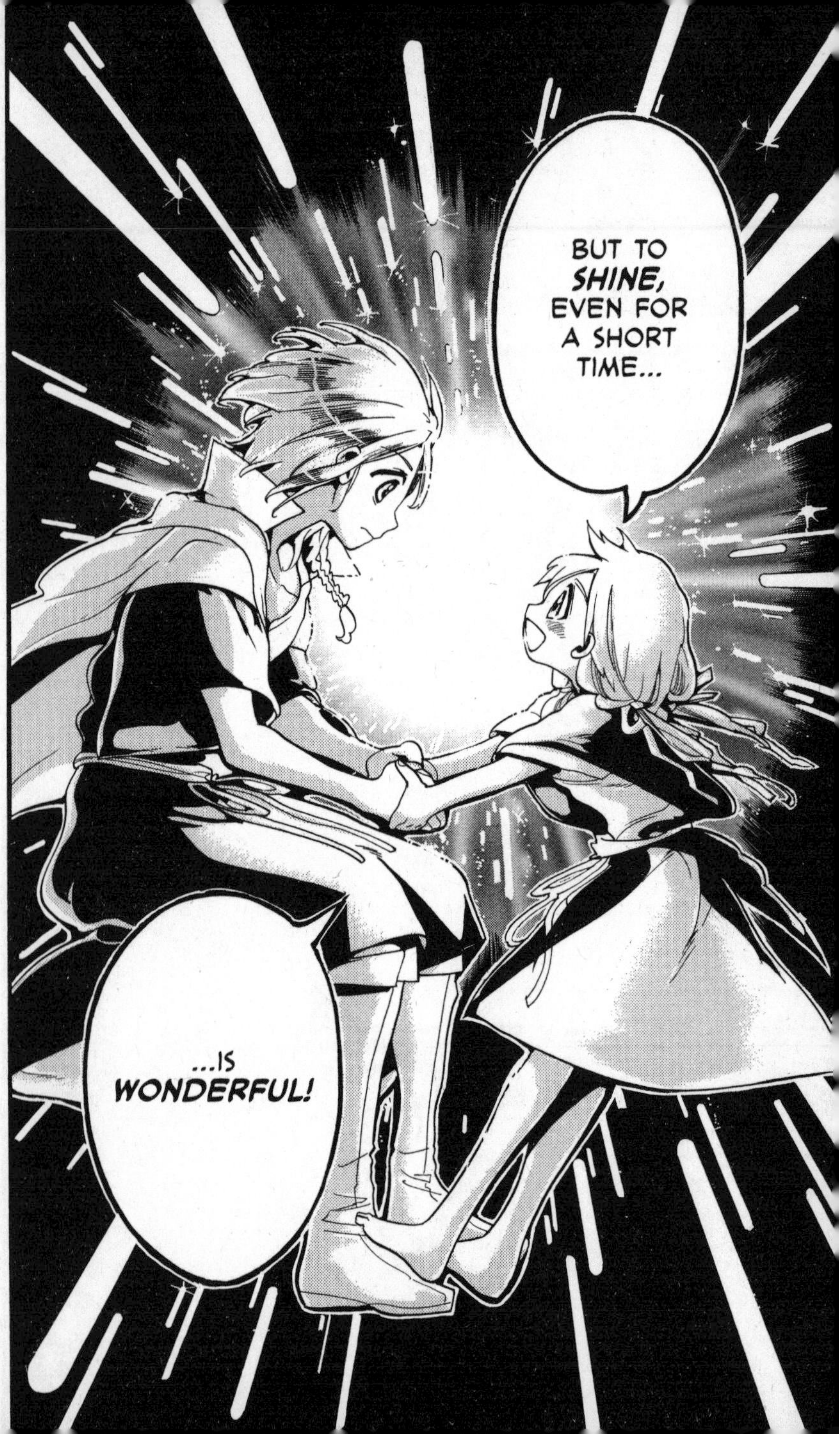
BUT TO SHINE, EVEN FOR A SHORT TIME...
...IS WONDERFUL!

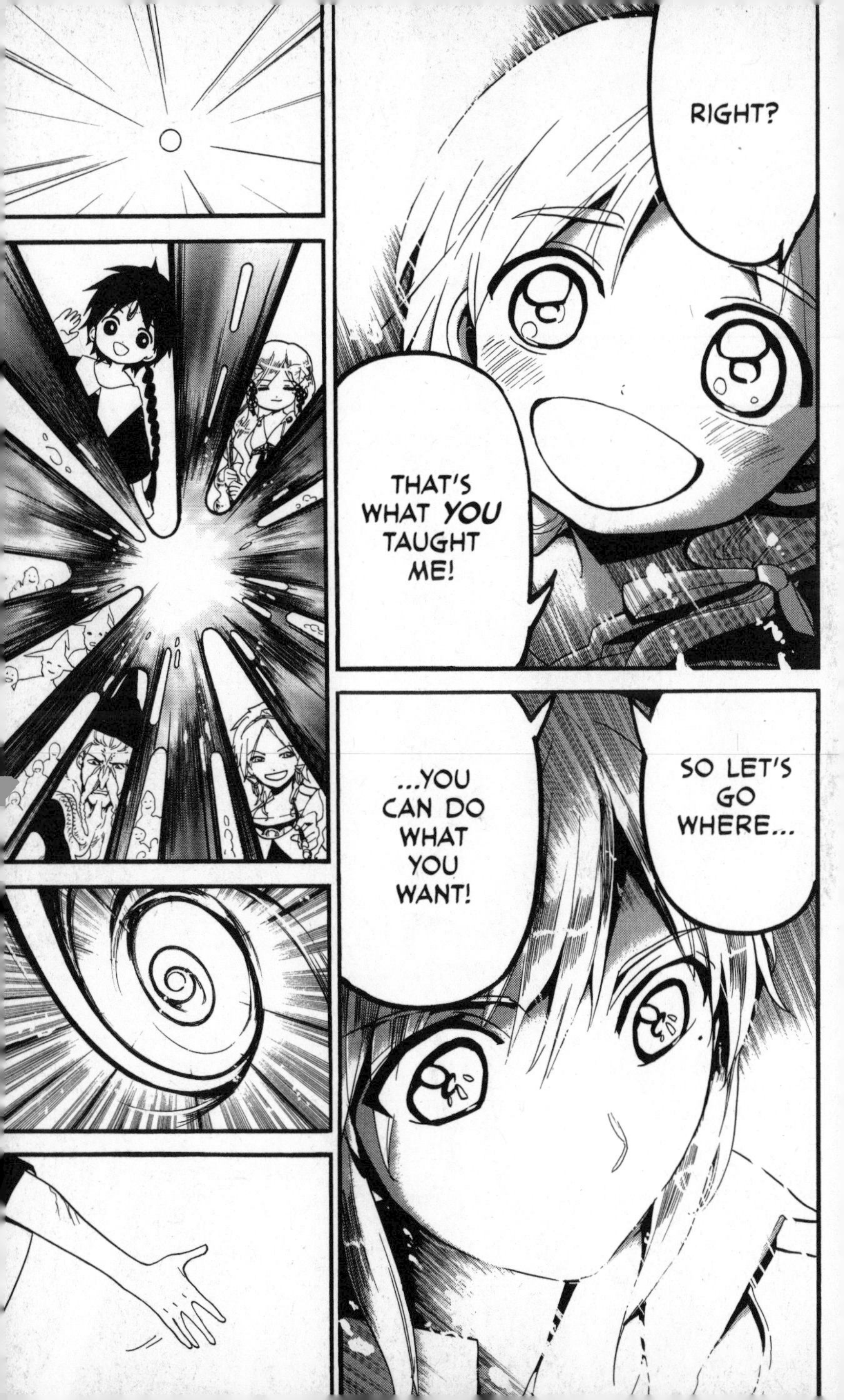
RIGHT?
THAT'S WHAT *YOU* TAUGHT ME!
SO LET'S GO WHERE...
...YOU CAN DO WHAT YOU WANT!

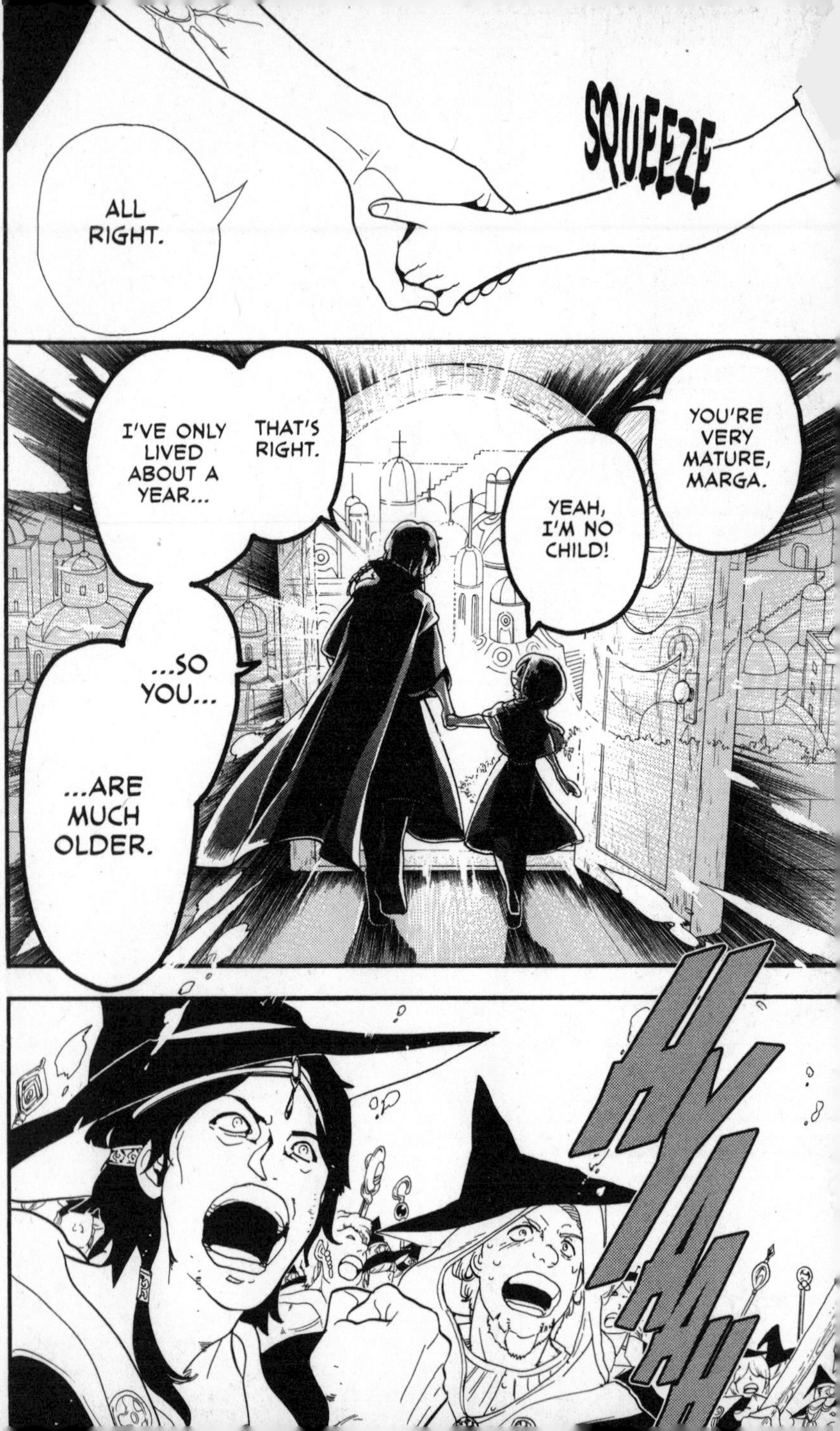
SQUEEZE
ALL RIGHT.
YOU'RE VERY MATURE, MARGA.
YEAH, I'M NO CHILD!
THAT'S RIGHT.
I'VE ONLY LIVED ABOUT A YEAR...
...SO YOU...
...ARE MUCH OLDER.

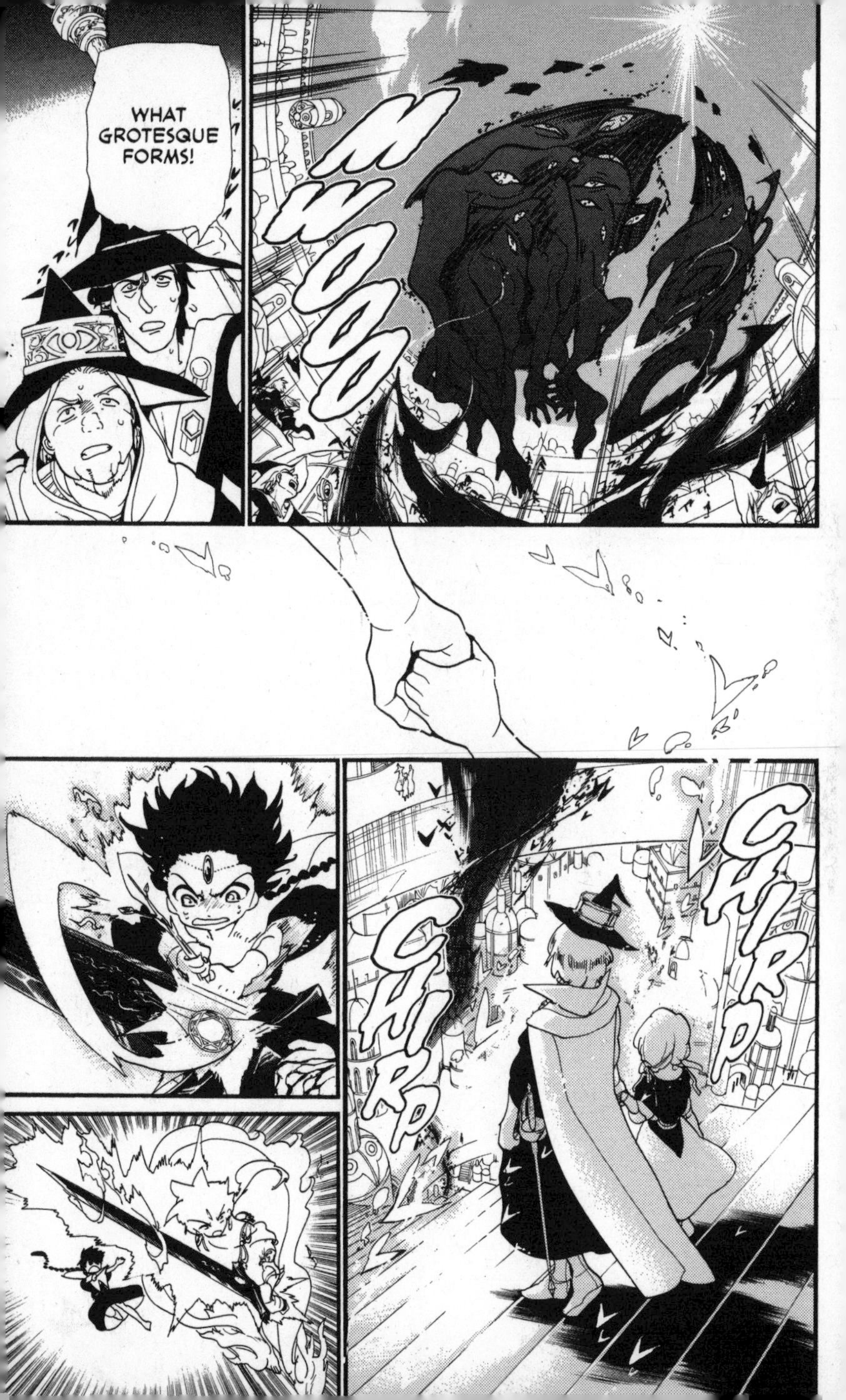
WHAT GROTESQUE FORMS!
CHIRP
CHIRP

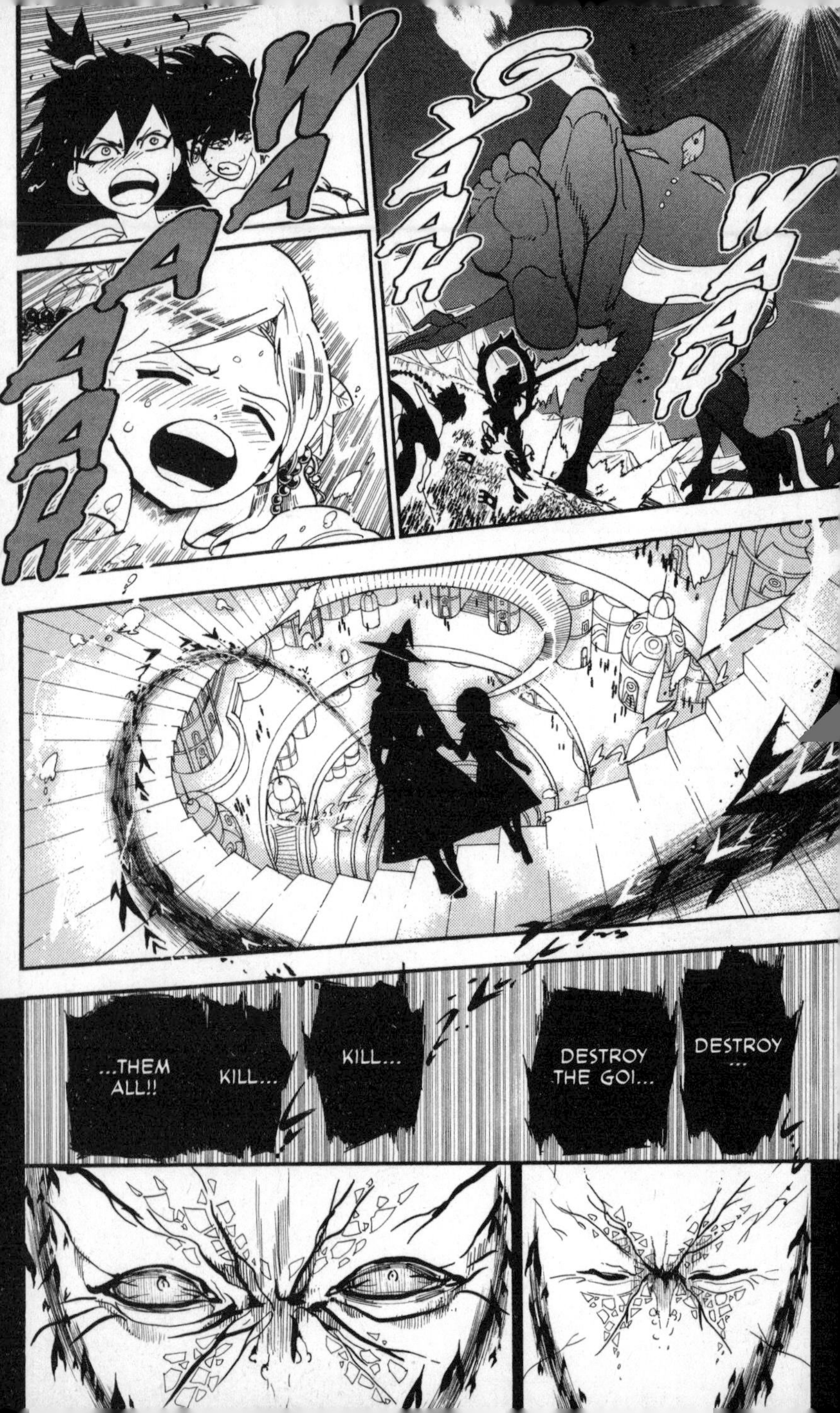

WAAAH
GYAAH
WAAAAAH
DESTROY ...
DESTROY THE GOI...
KILL...
KILL...
...THEM ALL!!

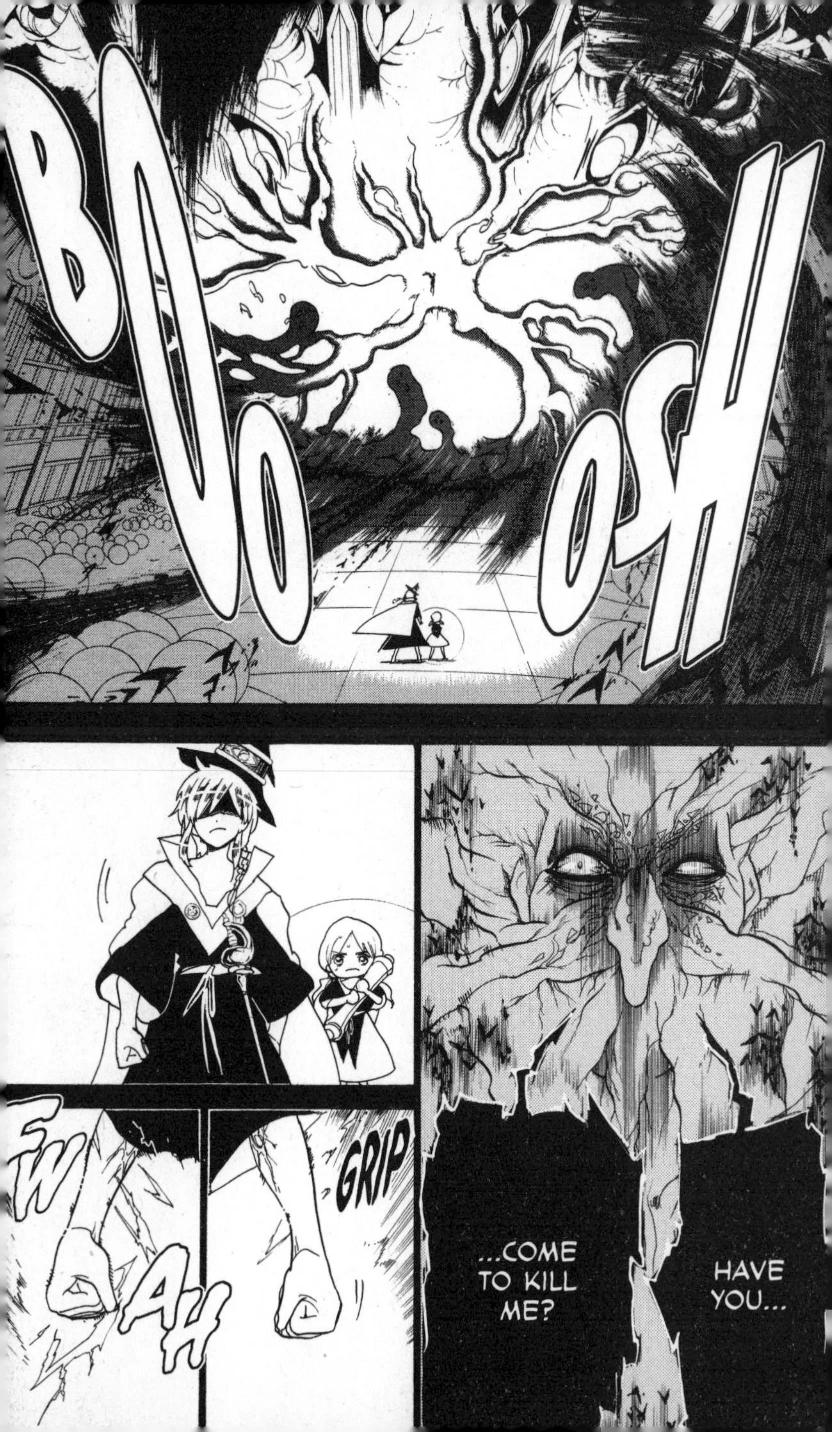
BOOOSH
HAVE YOU...
...COME TO KILL ME?
GRIP
FWAH

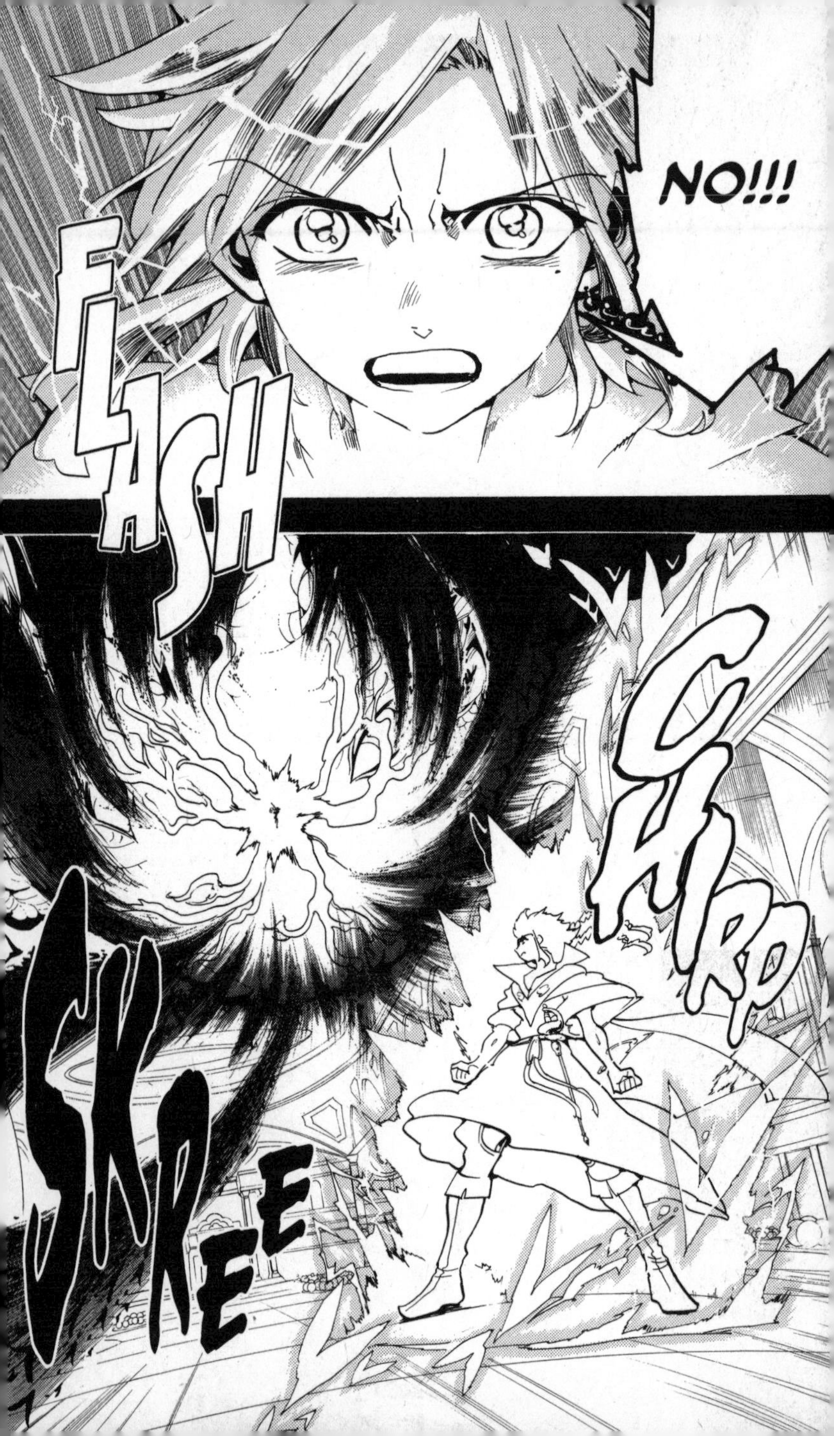
NO!!!
FLASH
CHIRP
SKREEE

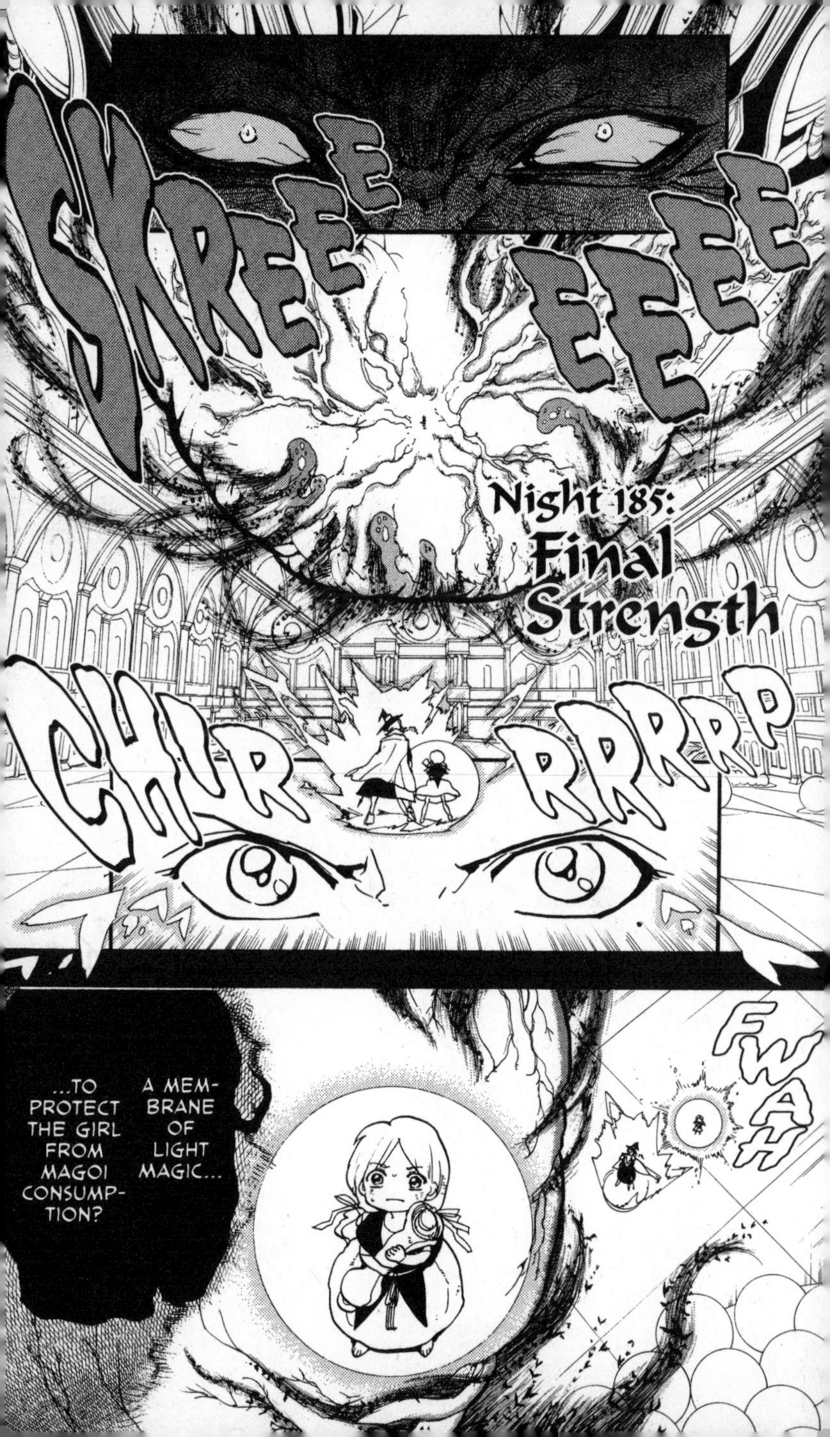
SKREEEEEEEE
Night 185:
Final Strength
CHIRRRRRP
FWAH
A MEM-BRANE OF LIGHT MAGIC...
...TO PROTECT THE GIRL FROM MAGOI CONSUMP-TION?

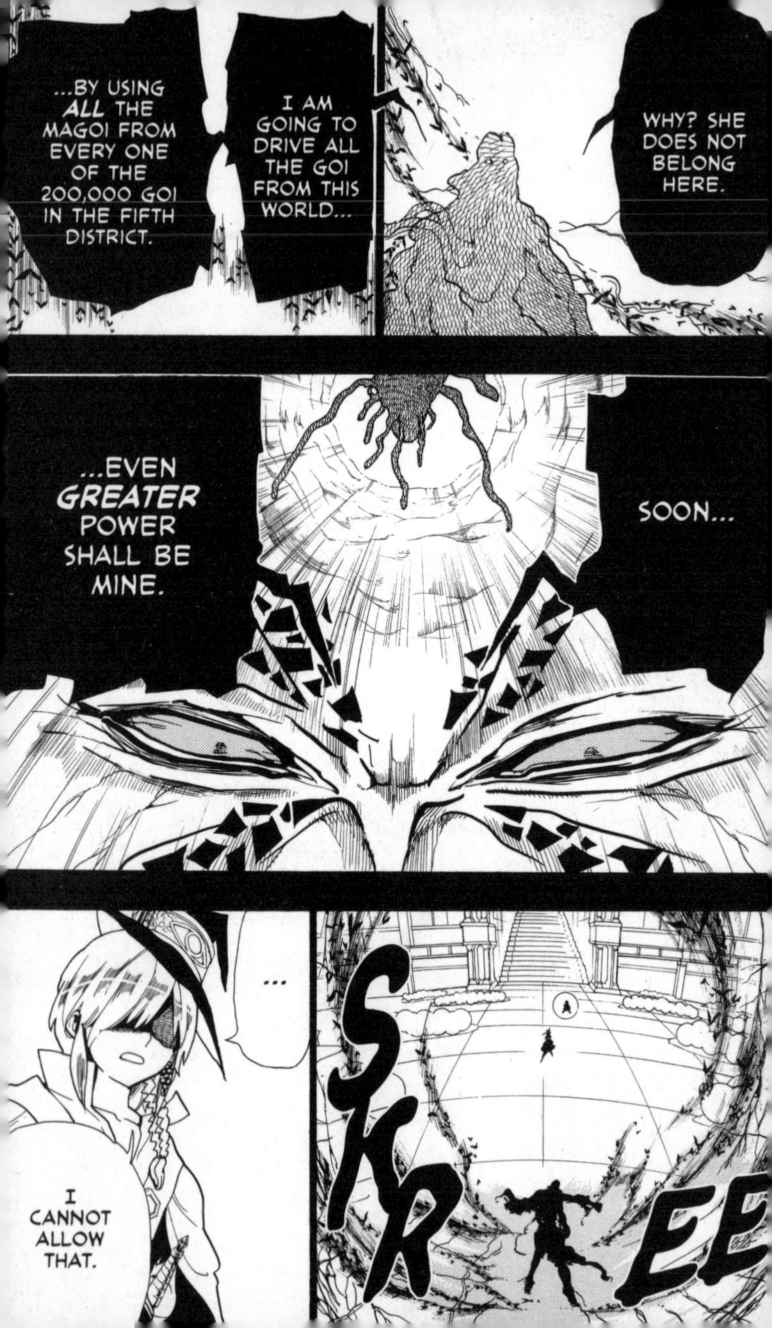
WHY? SHE DOES NOT BELONG HERE.
I AM GOING TO DRIVE ALL THE GOI FROM THIS WORLD...
...BY USING ALL THE MAGOI FROM EVERY ONE OF THE 200,000 GOI IN THE FIFTH DISTRICT.
SOON...
...EVEN GREATER POWER SHALL BE MINE.
SKREE
...
I CANNOT ALLOW THAT.

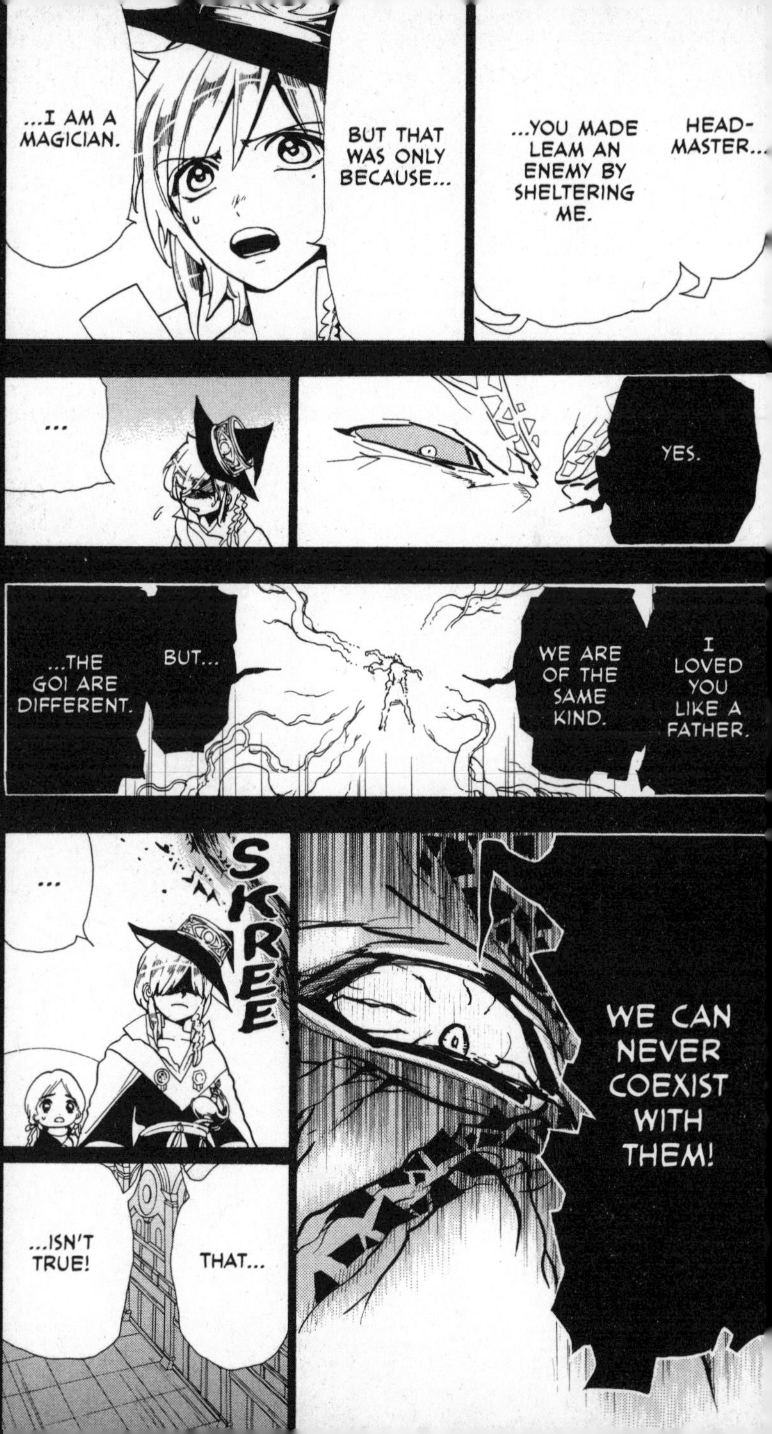
HEAD-MASTER...
...YOU MADE LEAM AN ENEMY BY SHELTERING ME.
BUT THAT WAS ONLY BECAUSE...
...I AM A MAGICIAN.
YES.
...
I LOVED YOU LIKE A FATHER.
WE ARE OF THE SAME KIND.
BUT...
...THE GOI ARE DIFFERENT.
WE CAN NEVER COEXIST WITH THEM!
SKREE
...
THAT...
...ISN'T TRUE!

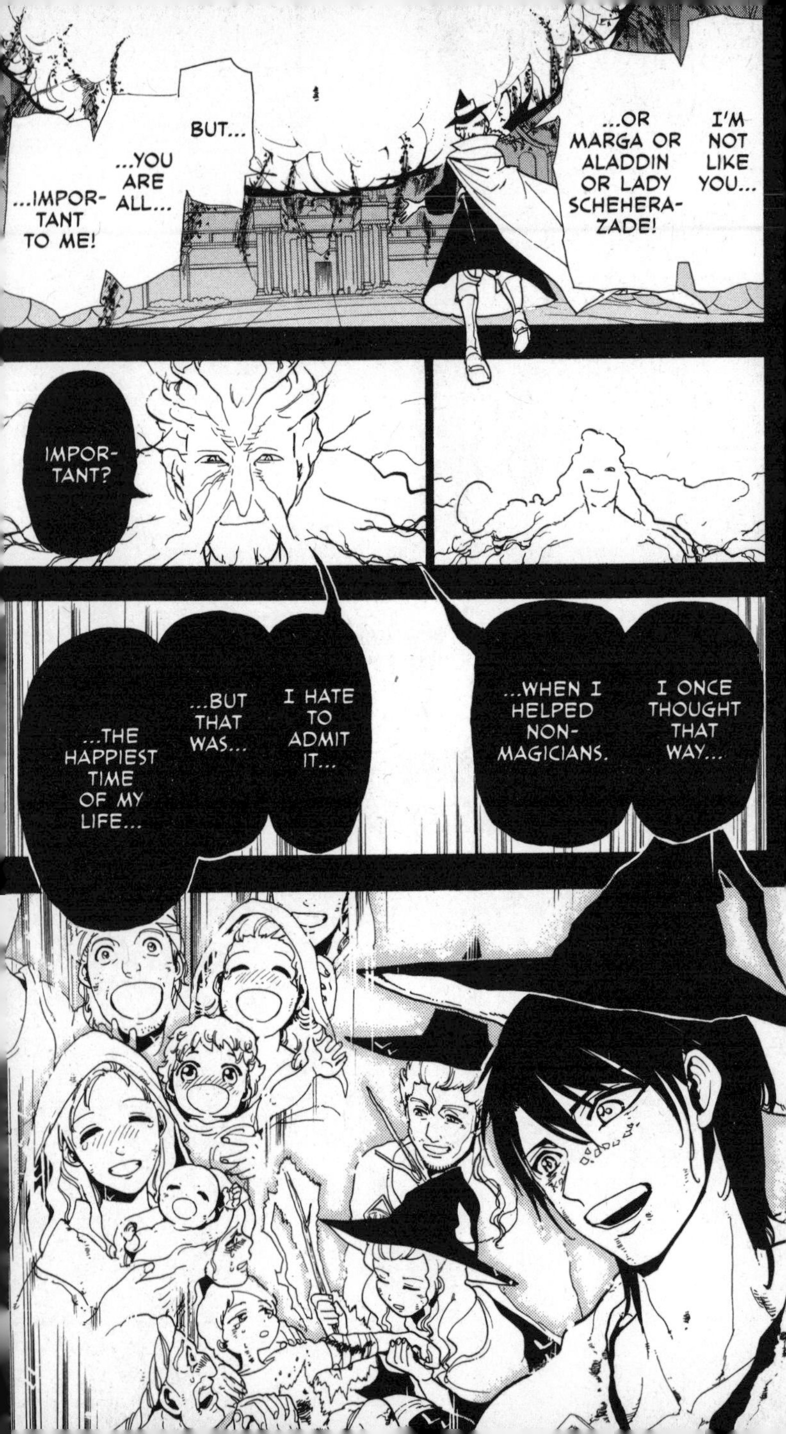
I'M NOT LIKE YOU...
...OR MARGA OR ALADDIN OR LADY SCHEHERAZADE!
BUT...
...YOU ARE ALL...
...IMPORTANT TO ME!
IMPORTANT?
I ONCE THOUGHT THAT WAY...
...WHEN I HELPED NON-MAGICIANS.
I HATE TO ADMIT IT...
...BUT THAT WAS...
...THE HAPPIEST TIME OF MY LIFE...

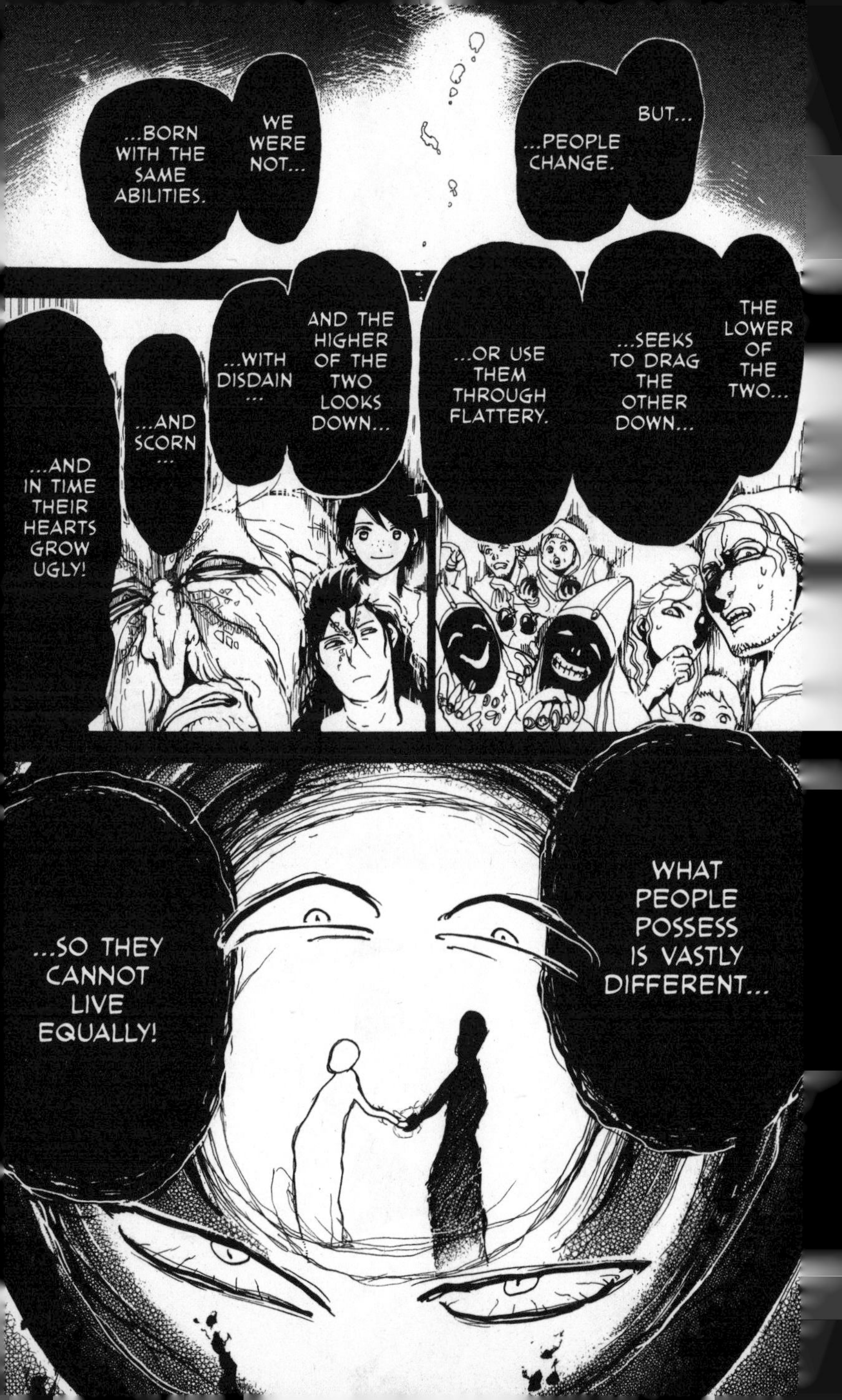

BUT...
...PEOPLE CHANGE.
WE WERE NOT...
...BORN WITH THE SAME ABILITIES.
THE LOWER OF THE TWO...
...SEEKS TO DRAG THE OTHER DOWN...
...OR USE THEM THROUGH FLATTERY.
AND THE HIGHER OF THE TWO LOOKS DOWN...
...WITH DISDAIN...
...AND SCORN...
...AND IN TIME THEIR HEARTS GROW UGLY!
WHAT PEOPLE POSSESS IS VASTLY DIFFERENT...
...SO THEY CANNOT LIVE EQUALLY!

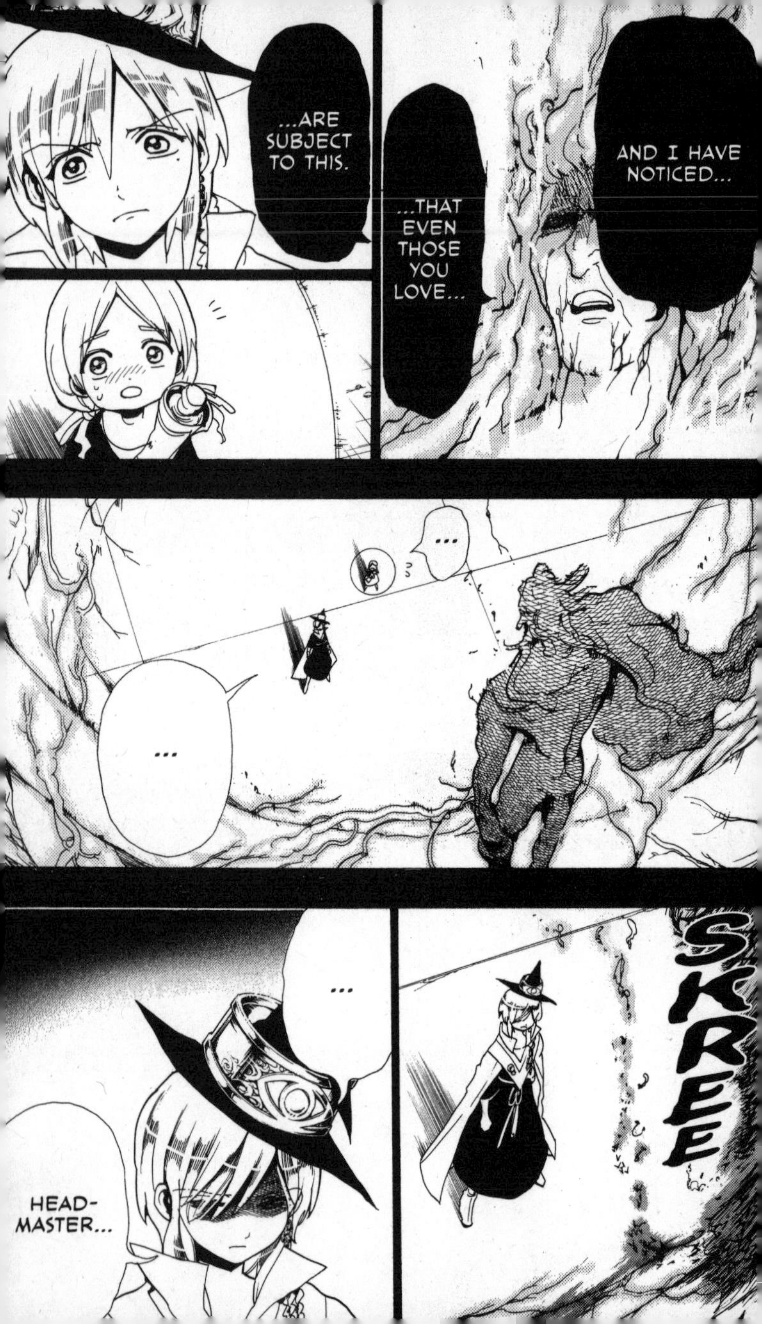
AND I HAVE NOTICED...
...THAT EVEN THOSE YOU LOVE...
...ARE SUBJECT TO THIS.
...
...
SKREE
...
HEAD-MASTER...

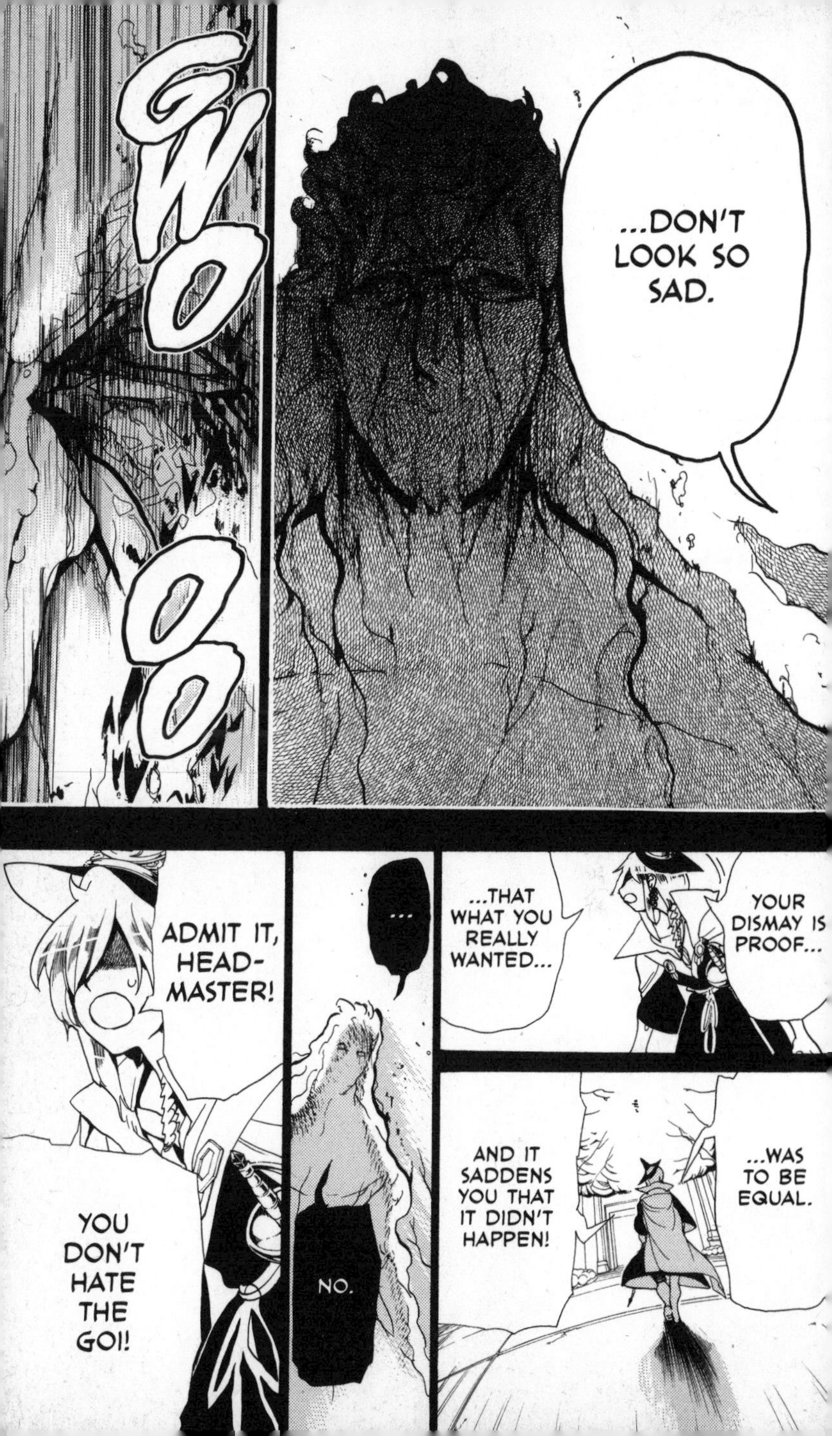
...DON'T LOOK SO SAD.
GWOOOO
YOUR DISMAY IS PROOF...
...THAT WHAT YOU REALLY WANTED...
...WAS TO BE EQUAL.
AND IT SADDENS YOU THAT IT DIDN'T HAPPEN!
...
NO.
ADMIT IT, HEAD-MASTER!
YOU DON'T HATE THE GOI!

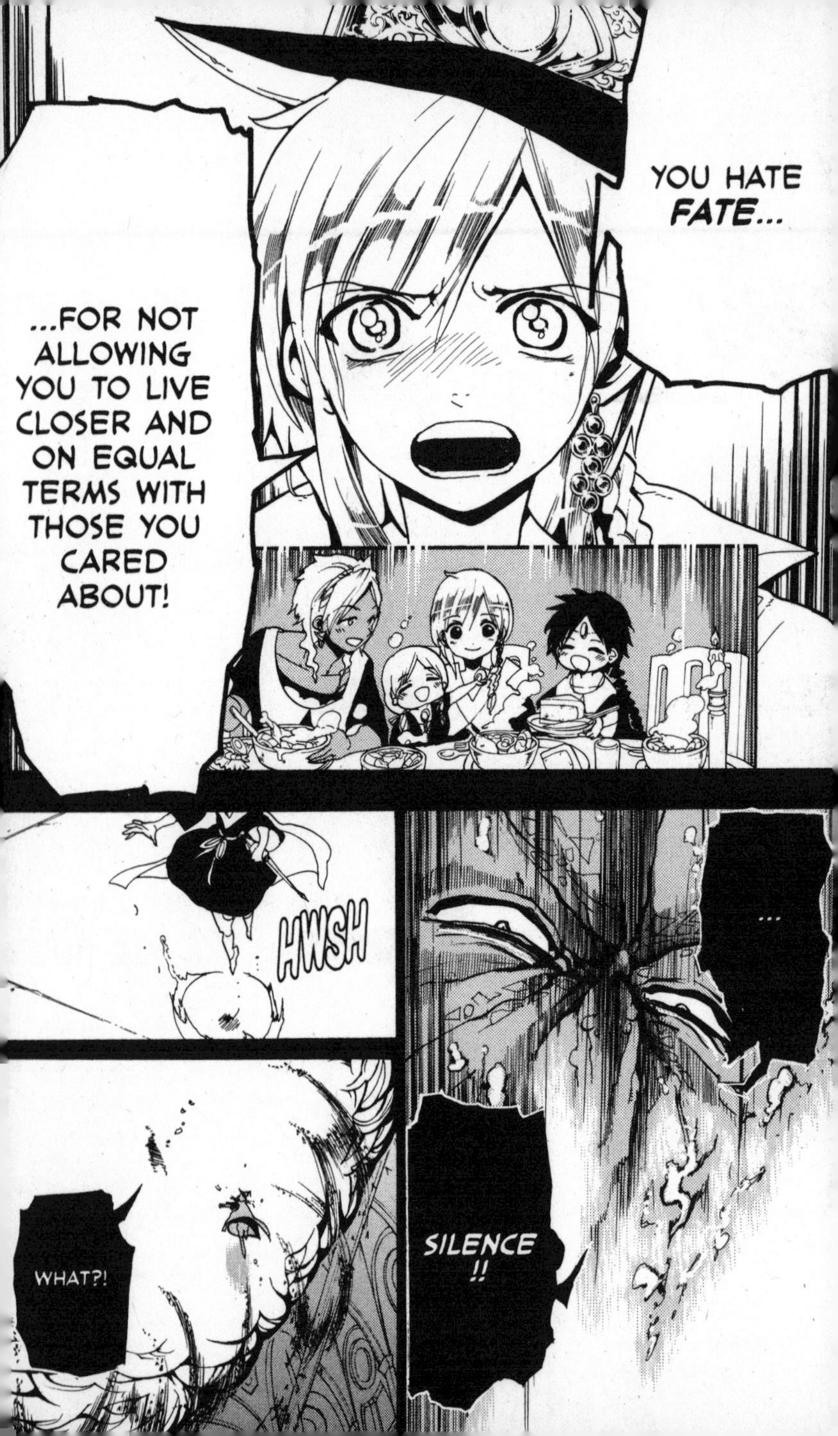
YOU HATE FATE...
...FOR NOT ALLOWING YOU TO LIVE CLOSER AND ON EQUAL TERMS WITH THOSE YOU CARED ABOUT!
...
HWSH
SILENCE !!
WHAT?!

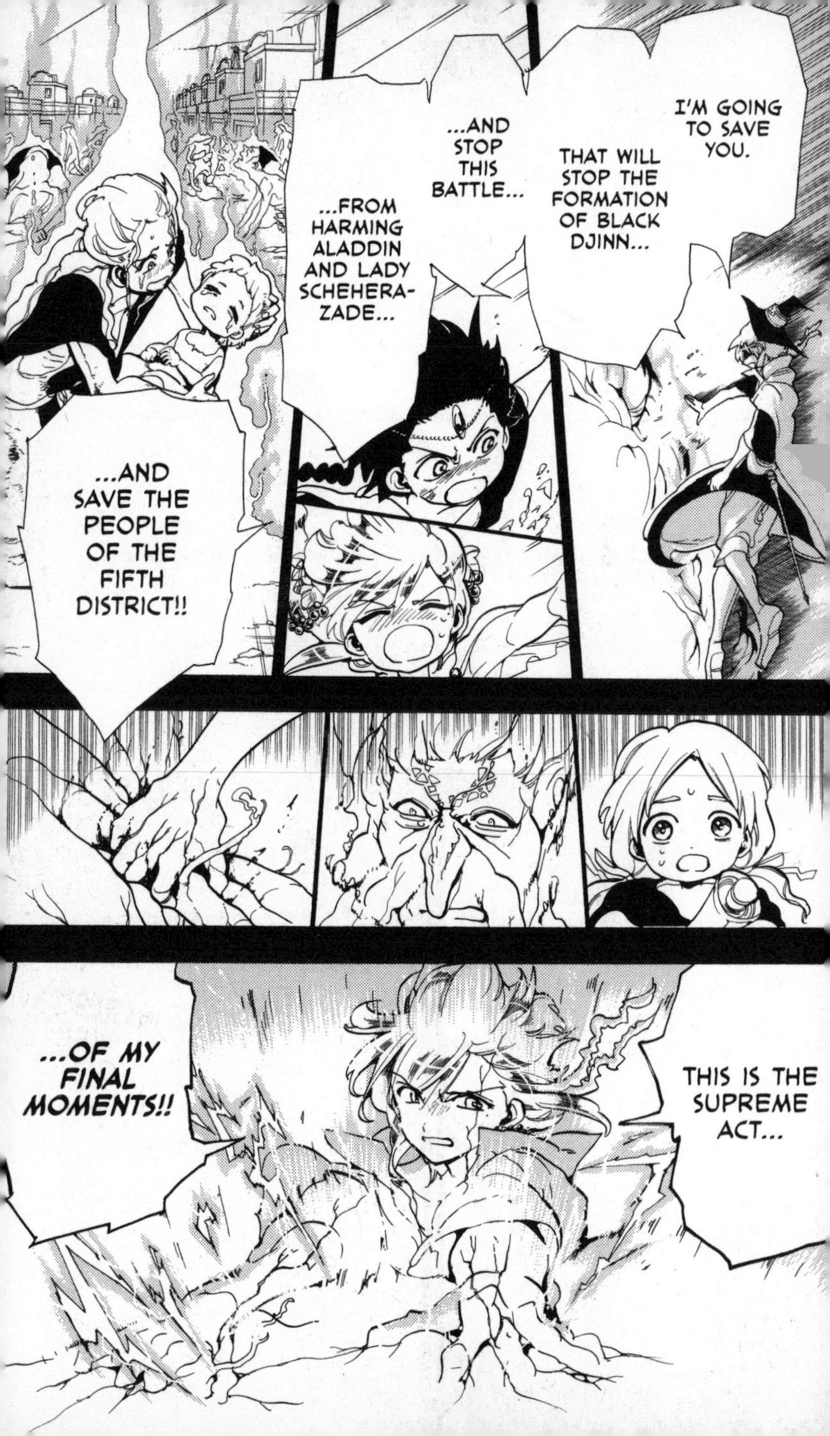
I'M GOING TO SAVE YOU.
THAT WILL STOP THE FORMATION OF BLACK DJINN...
...AND STOP THIS BATTLE...
...FROM HARMING ALADDIN AND LADY SCHEHERA-ZADE...
...AND SAVE THE PEOPLE OF THE FIFTH DISTRICT!!
THIS IS THE SUPREME ACT...
...OF MY FINAL MOMENTS!!

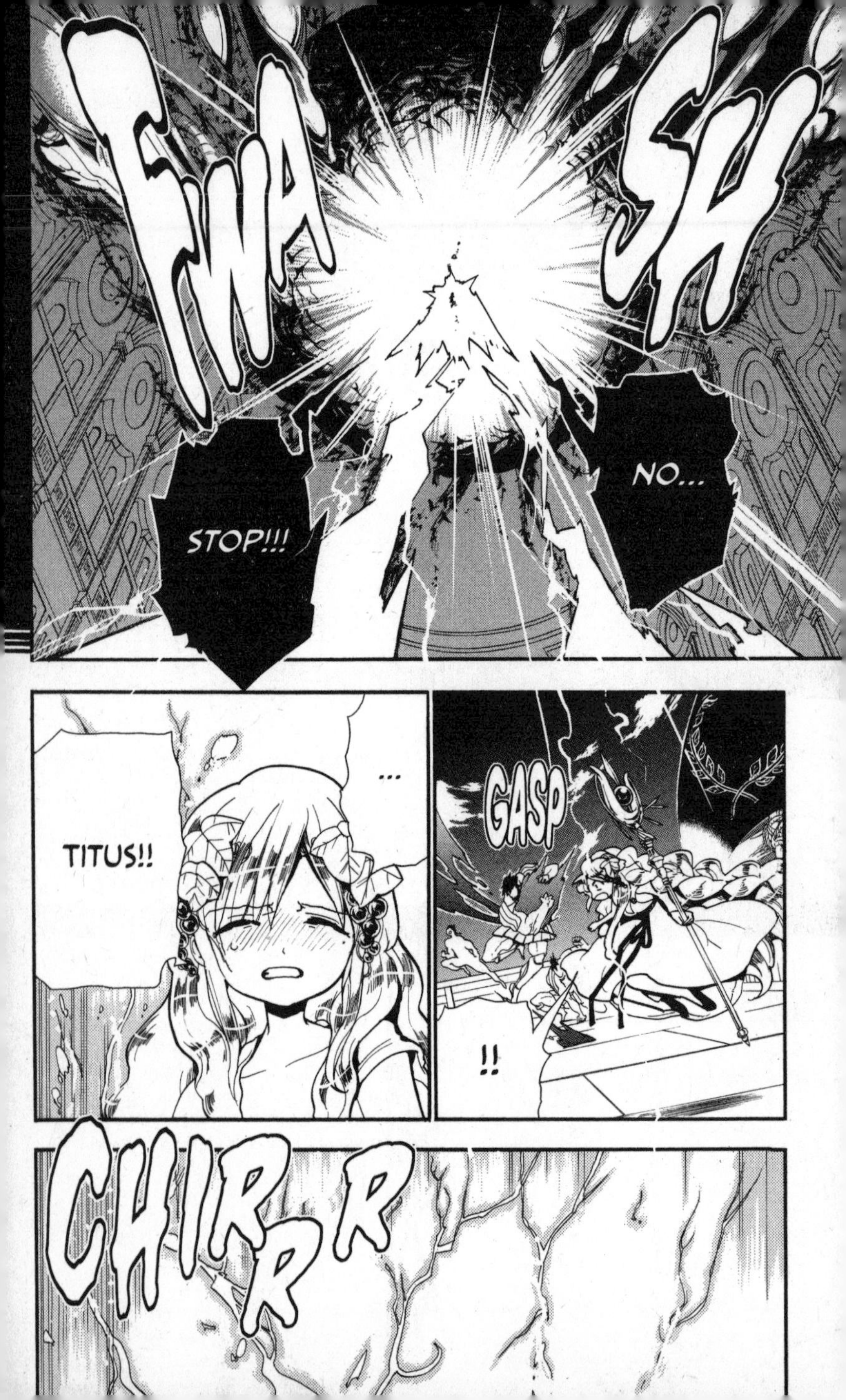
FWASH
NO...
STOP!!!
GASP
!!
...
TITUS!!
CHIRRR

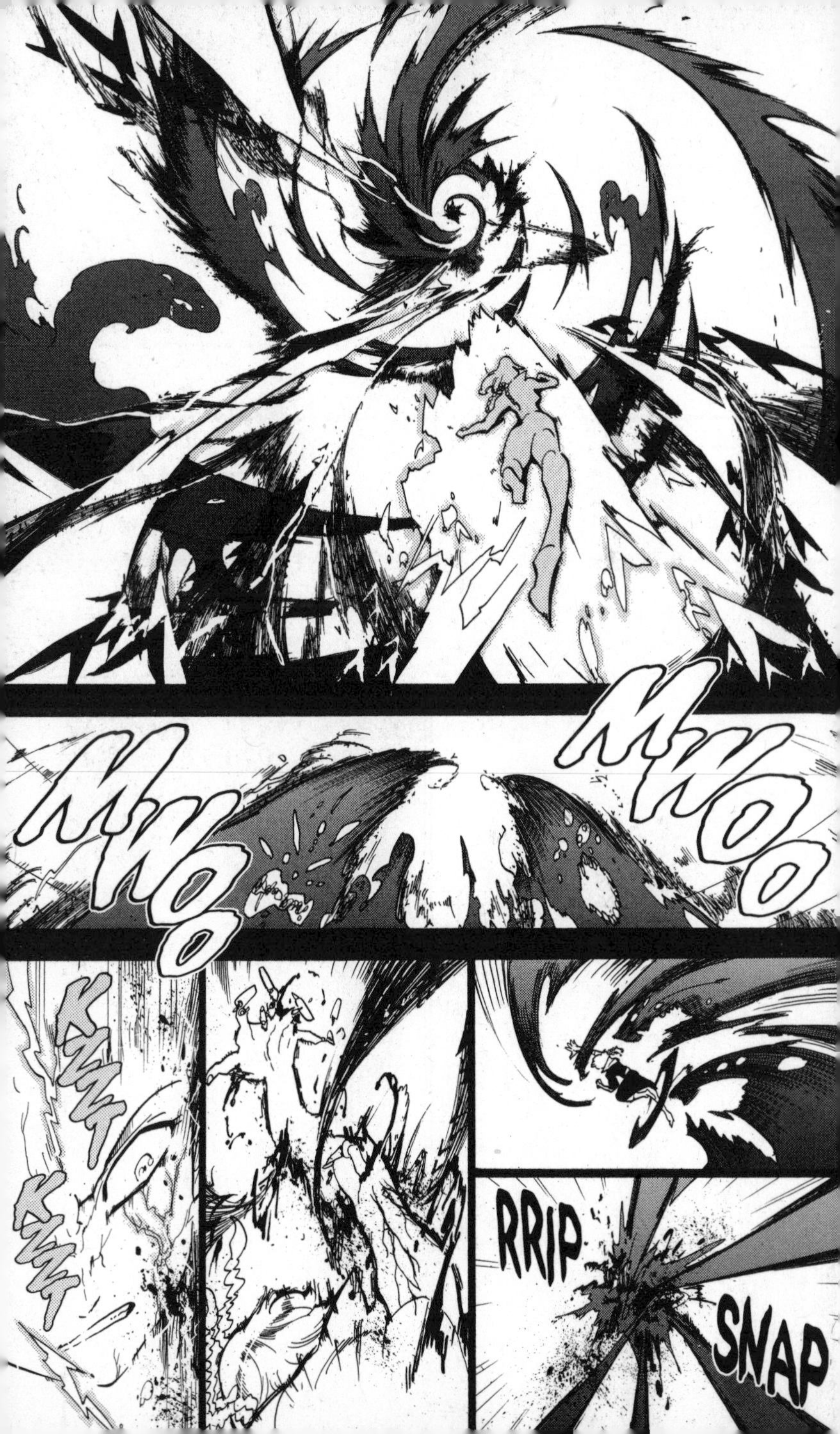
MWOO
MWOO
RRIP
SNAP
KWNK KWNK

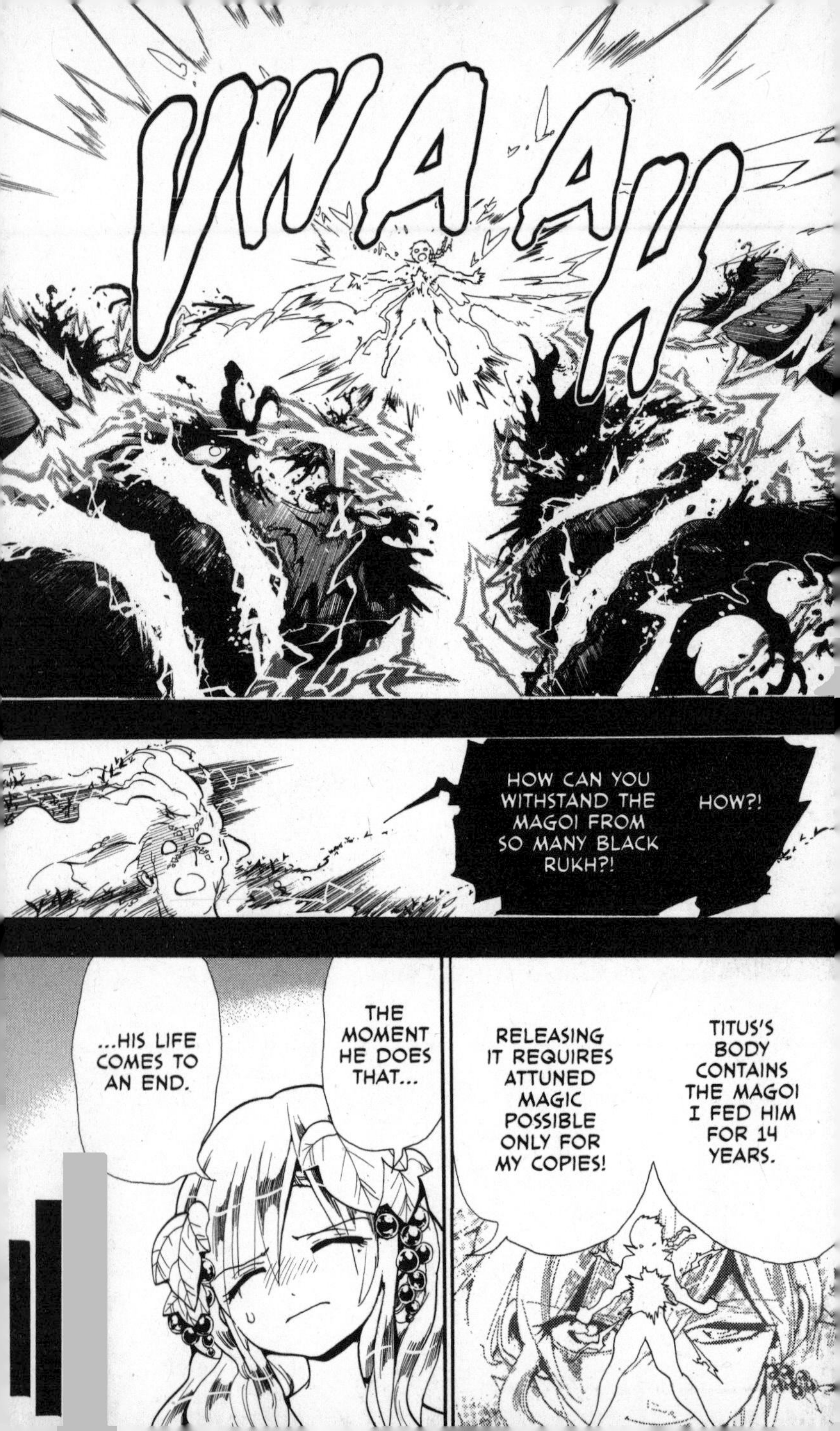
WAAH
HOW?!
HOW CAN YOU WITHSTAND THE MAGOI FROM SO MANY BLACK RUKH?!
TITUS'S BODY CONTAINS THE MAGOI I FED HIM FOR 14 YEARS.
RELEASING IT REQUIRES ATTUNED MAGIC POSSIBLE ONLY FOR MY COPIES!
THE MOMENT HE DOES THAT...
...HIS LIFE COMES TO AN END.

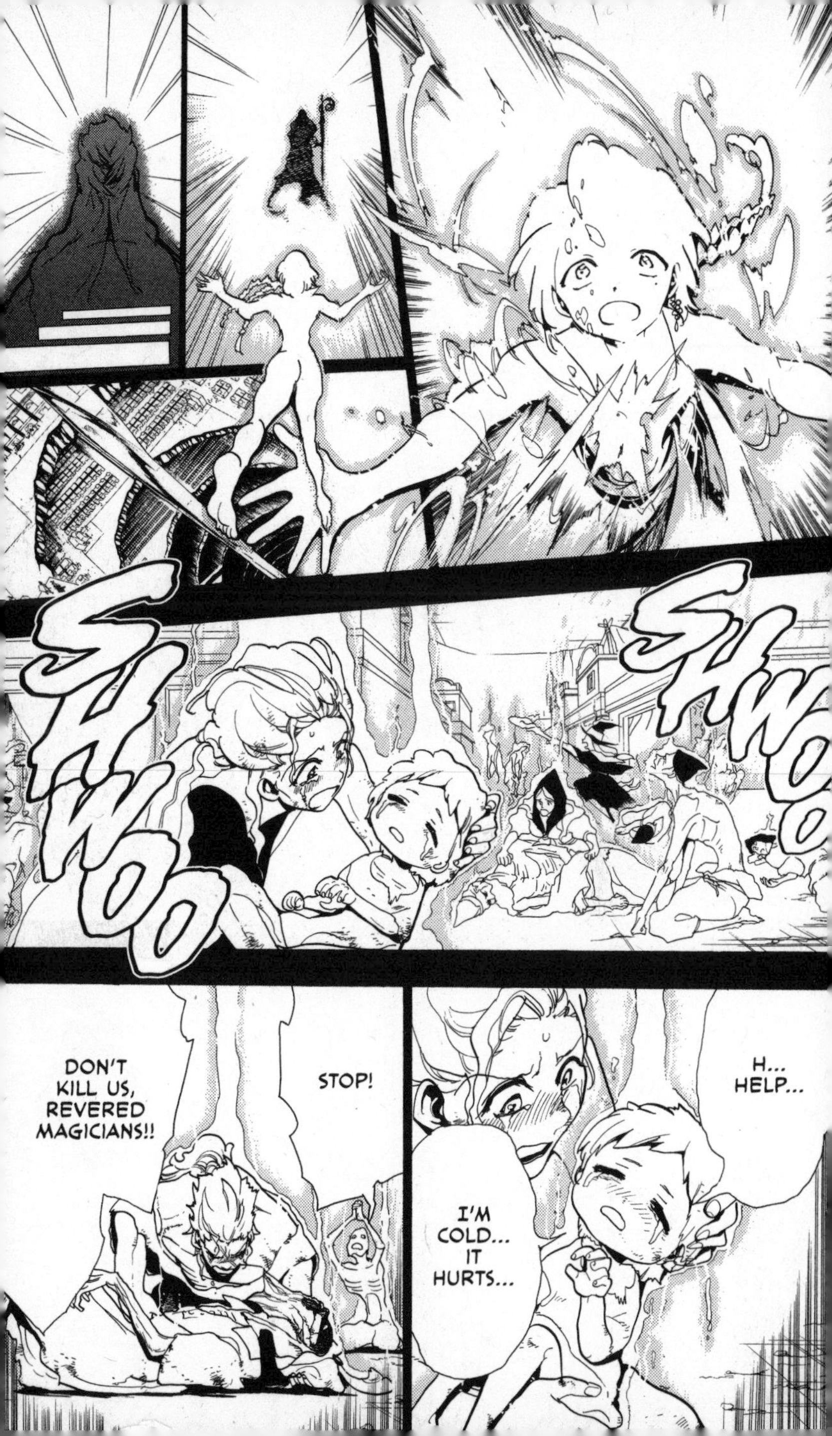
SHWO
SHWOO
H... HELP...
I'M COLD... IT HURTS...
STOP!
DON'T KILL US, REVERED MAGICIANS!!

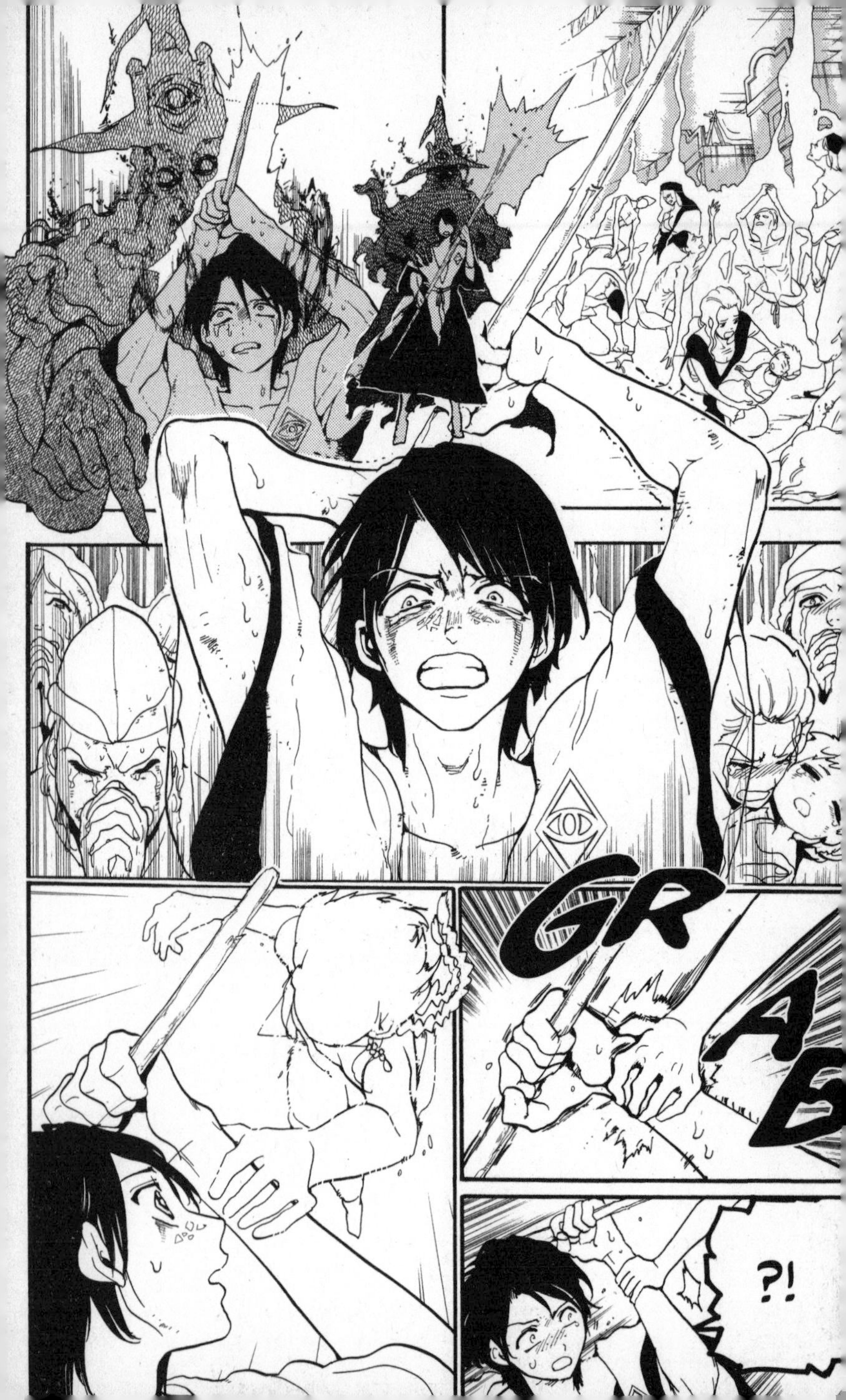
GRAB
?!

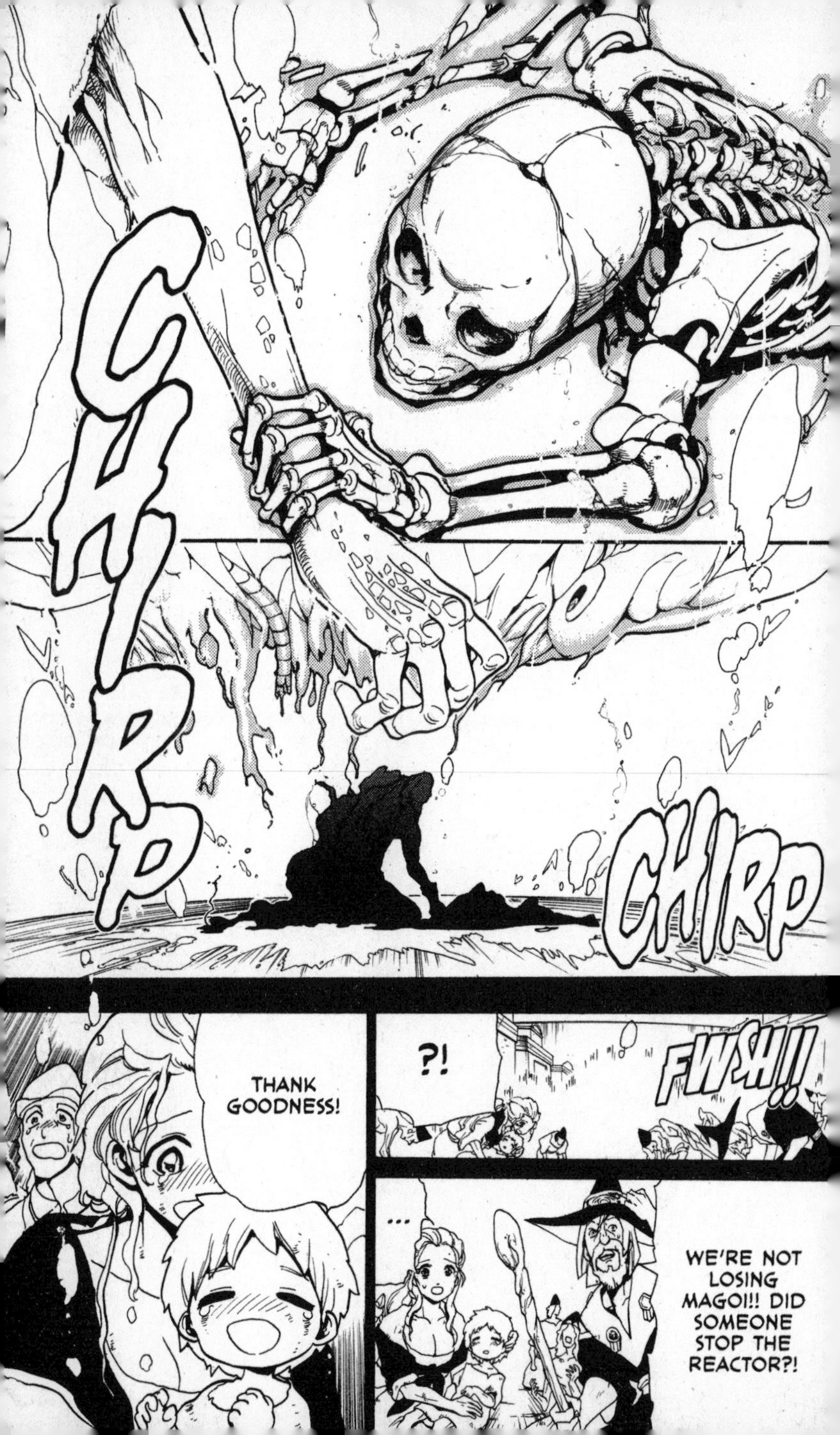
CHIRP
CHIRP
FWSH!!
?!
WE'RE NOT LOSING MAGOI!! DID SOMEONE STOP THE REACTOR?!
...
THANK GOODNESS!

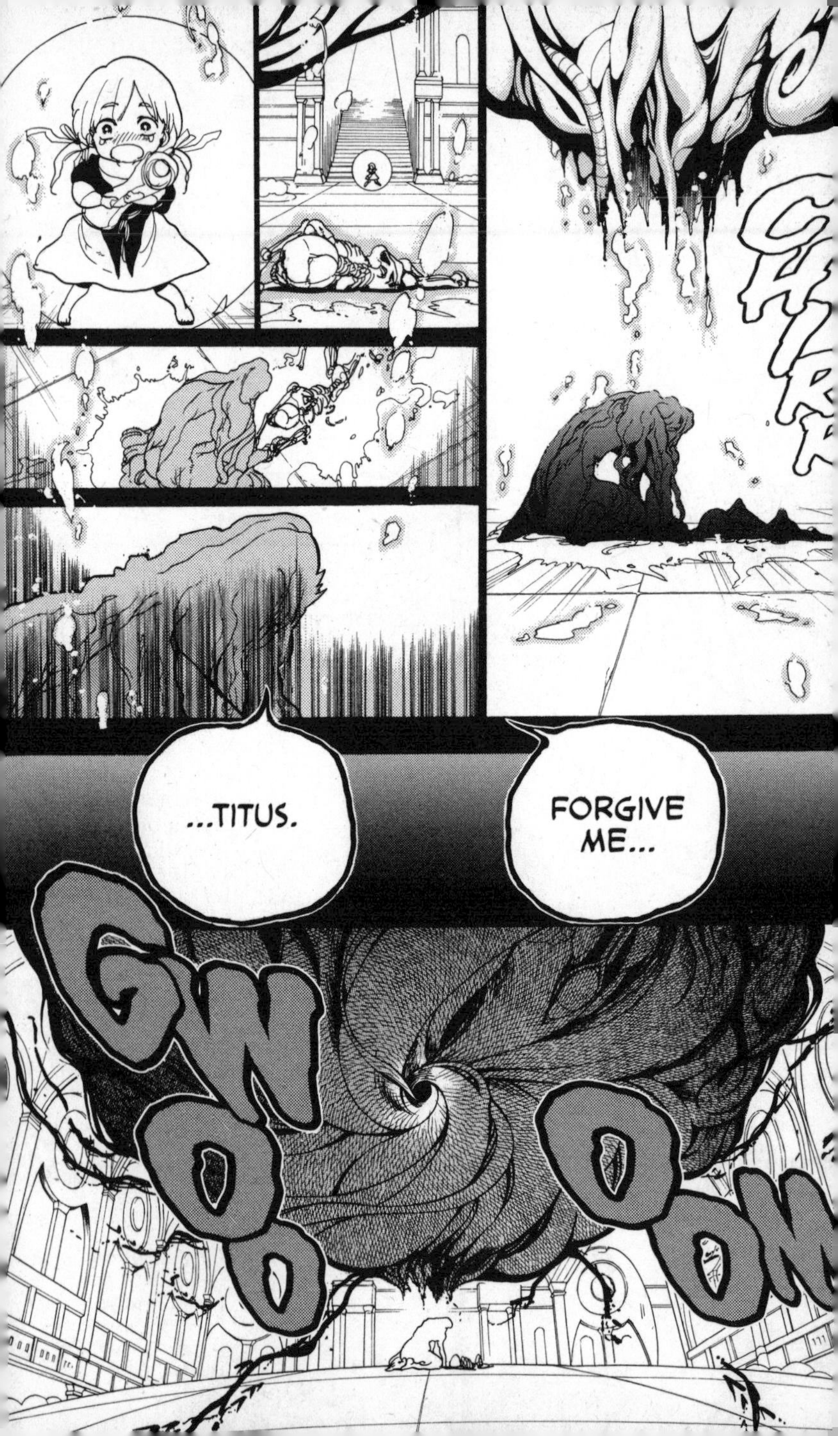
FORGIVE ME...
...TITUS.

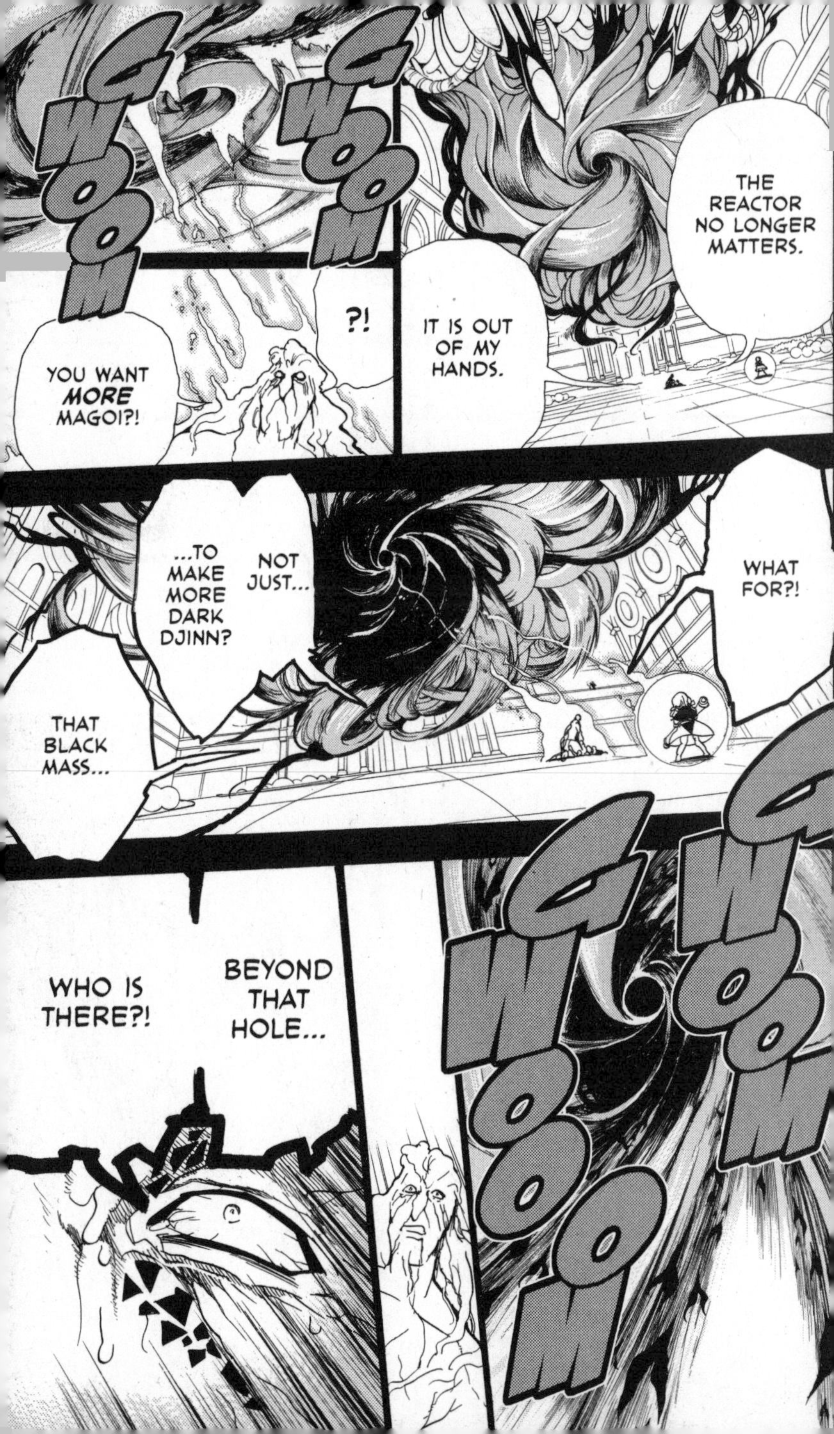
THE REACTOR NO LONGER MATTERS.
IT IS OUT OF MY HANDS.
GWOOOM
GWOOM
?!
YOU WANT *MORE* MAGOI?!
WHAT FOR?!
NOT JUST...
...TO MAKE MORE DARK DJINN?
THAT BLACK MASS...
GWOOOM
GWOOOOM
BEYOND THAT HOLE...
WHO IS THERE?!

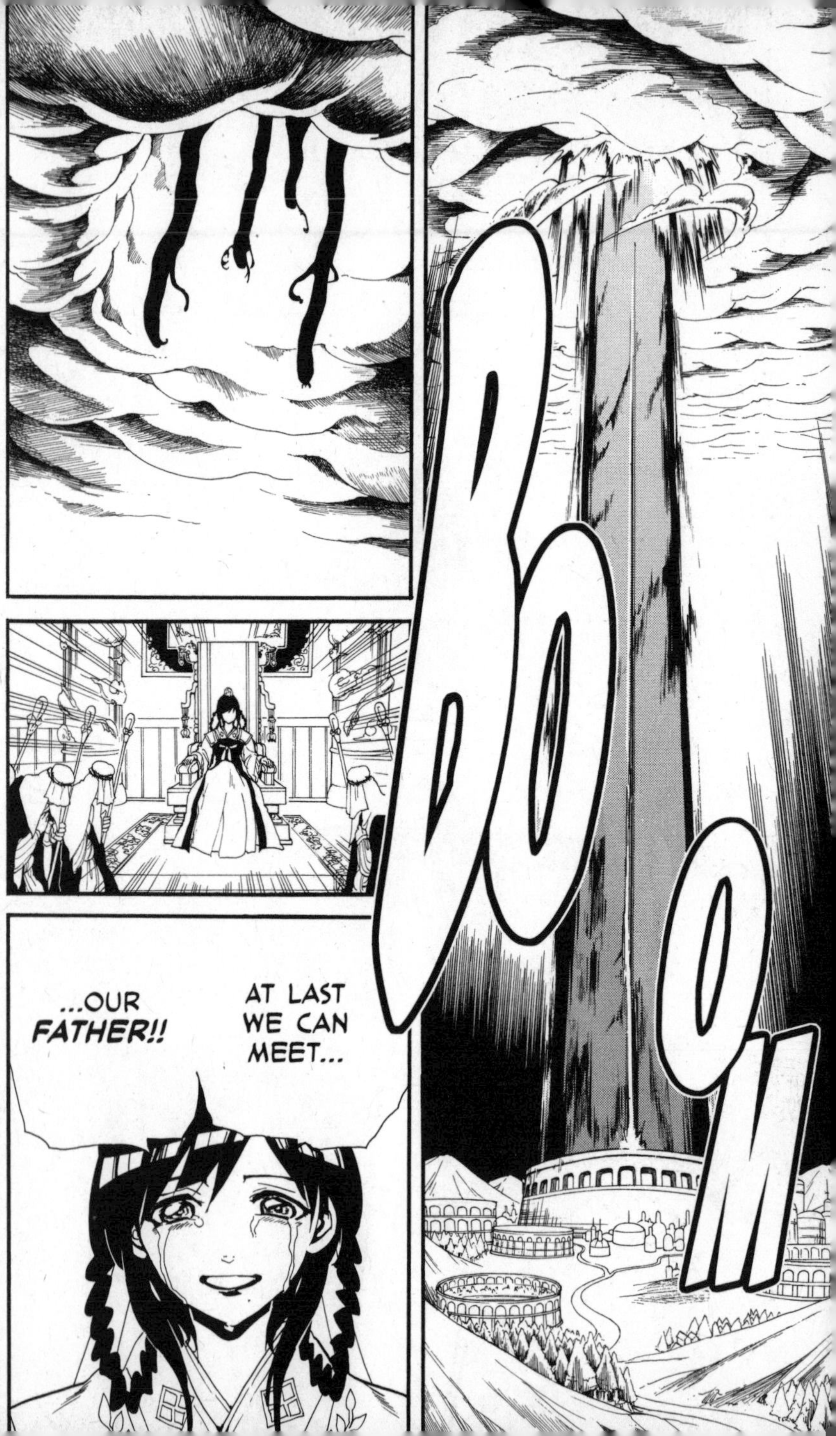
AT LAST WE CAN MEET...
...OUR FATHER!!

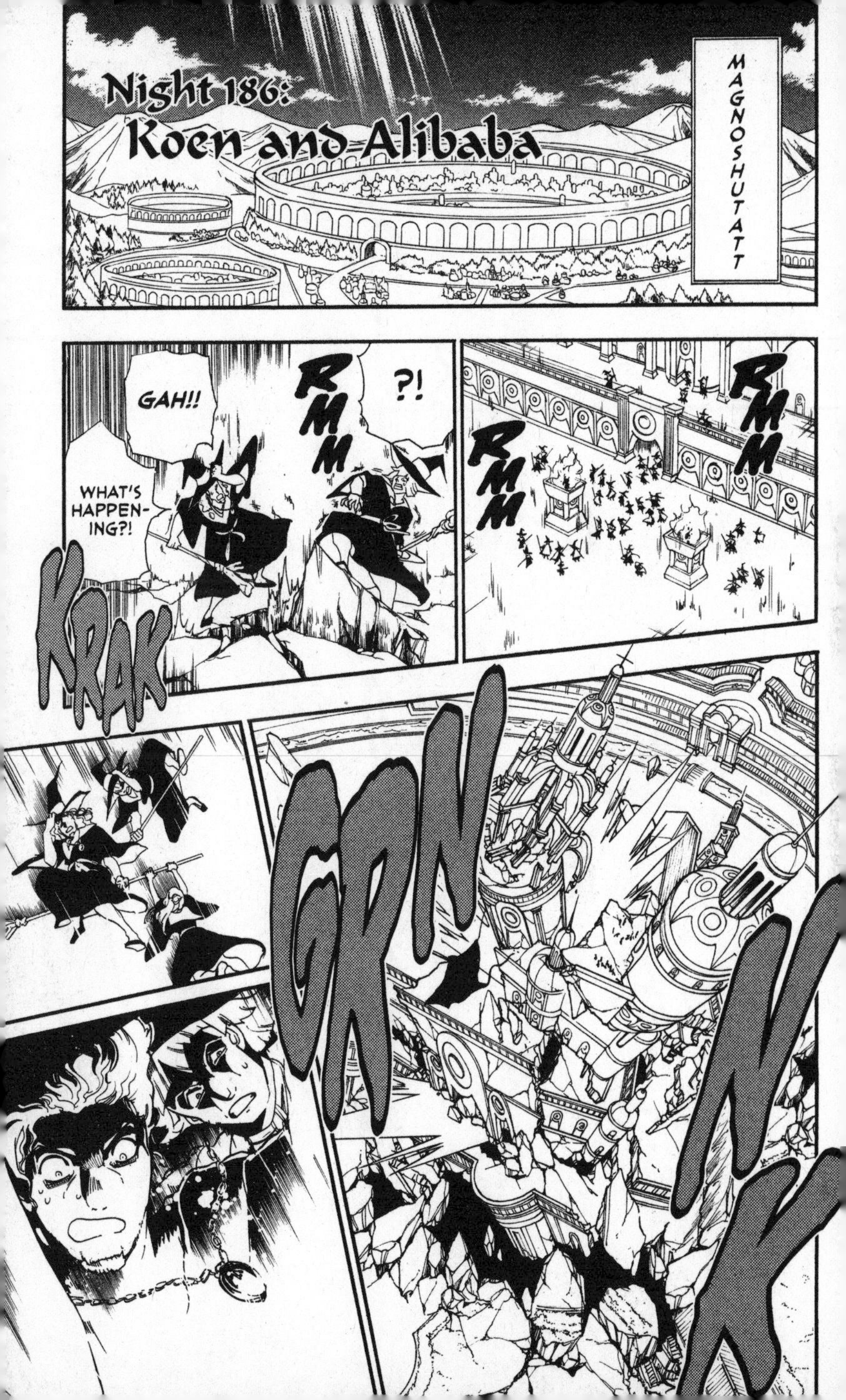
MAGNOSHUTATT
Night 186:
Koen and Alibaba
RMM
RMM
?!
RMM
GAH!!
WHAT'S HAPPENING?!
KRAK
GRNNK

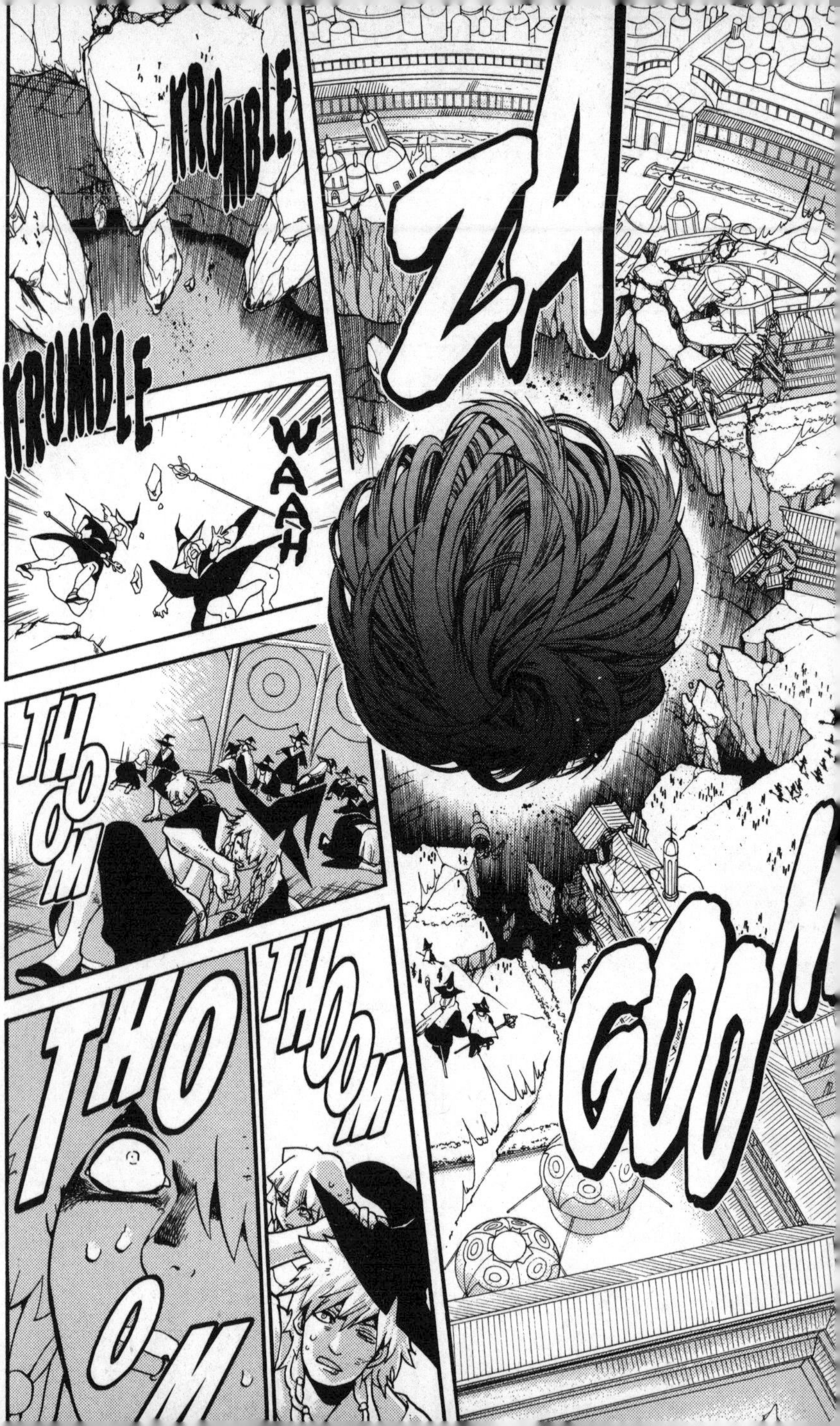
ZA
GOO
KRUMBLE
KRUMBLE
WAAAH
THOOM
THOOM
THO
OM

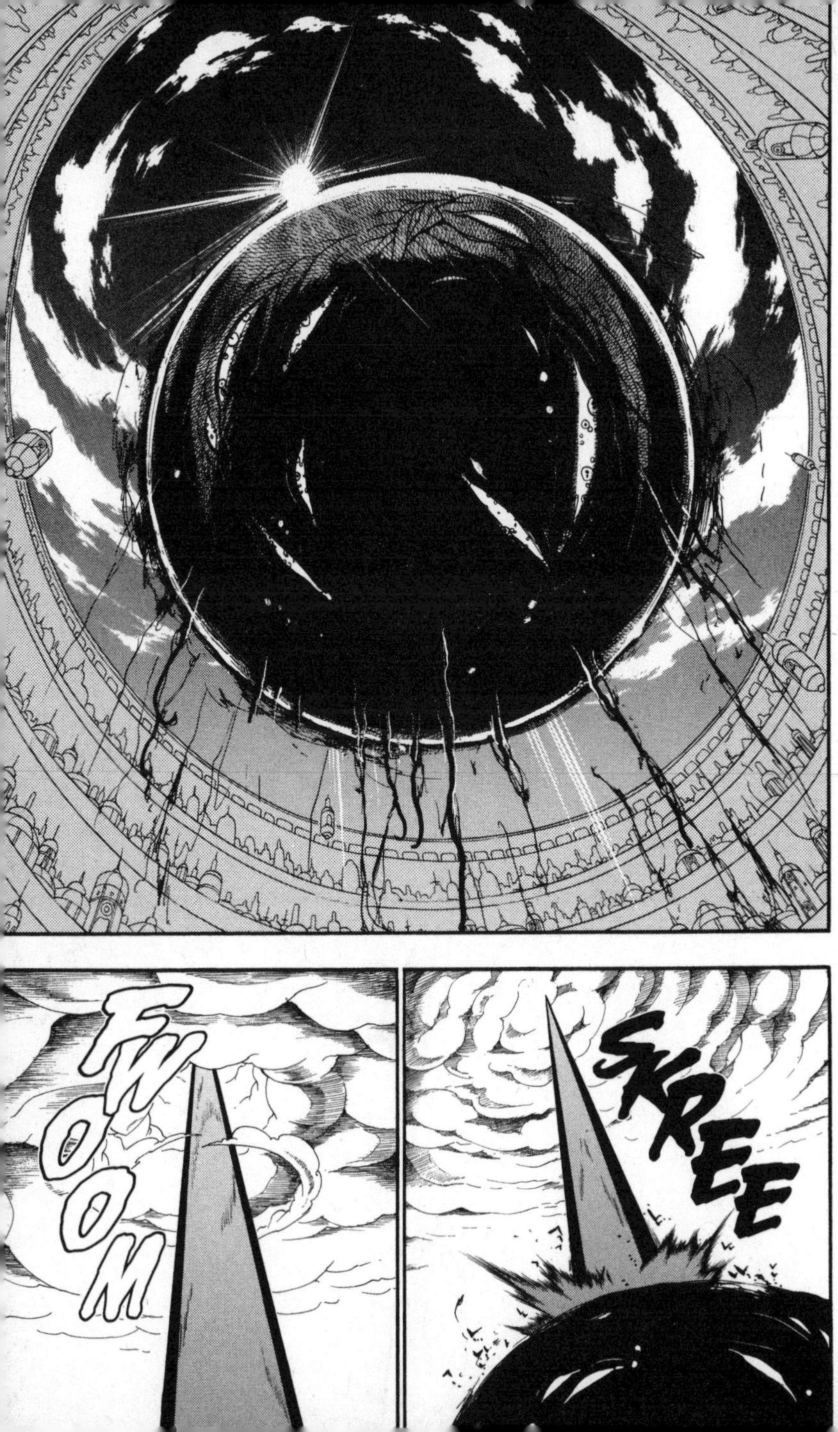
SKREE
FWOOM

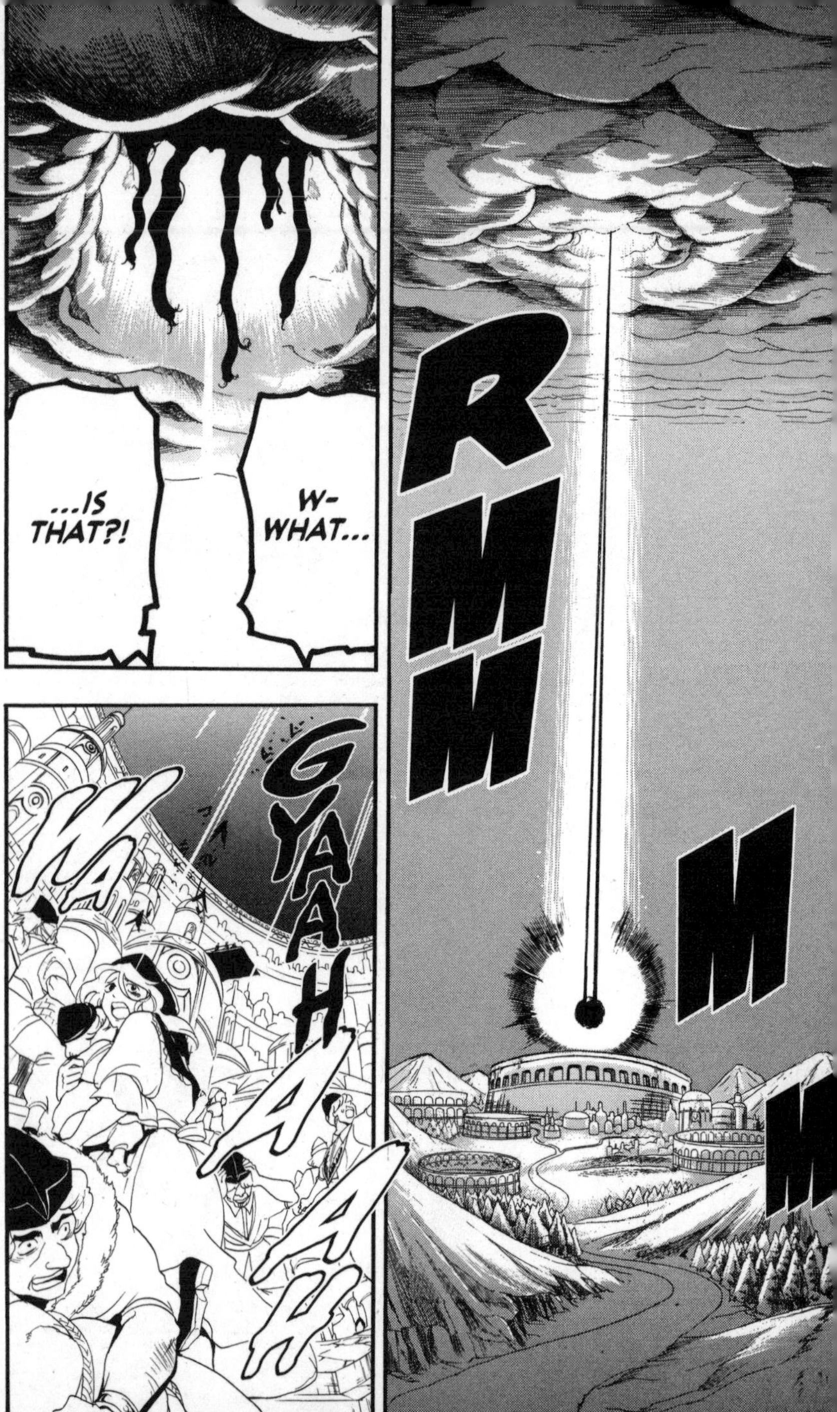
RMMMMM
W-WHAT...
...IS THAT?!
GYAAH
AAH
WA

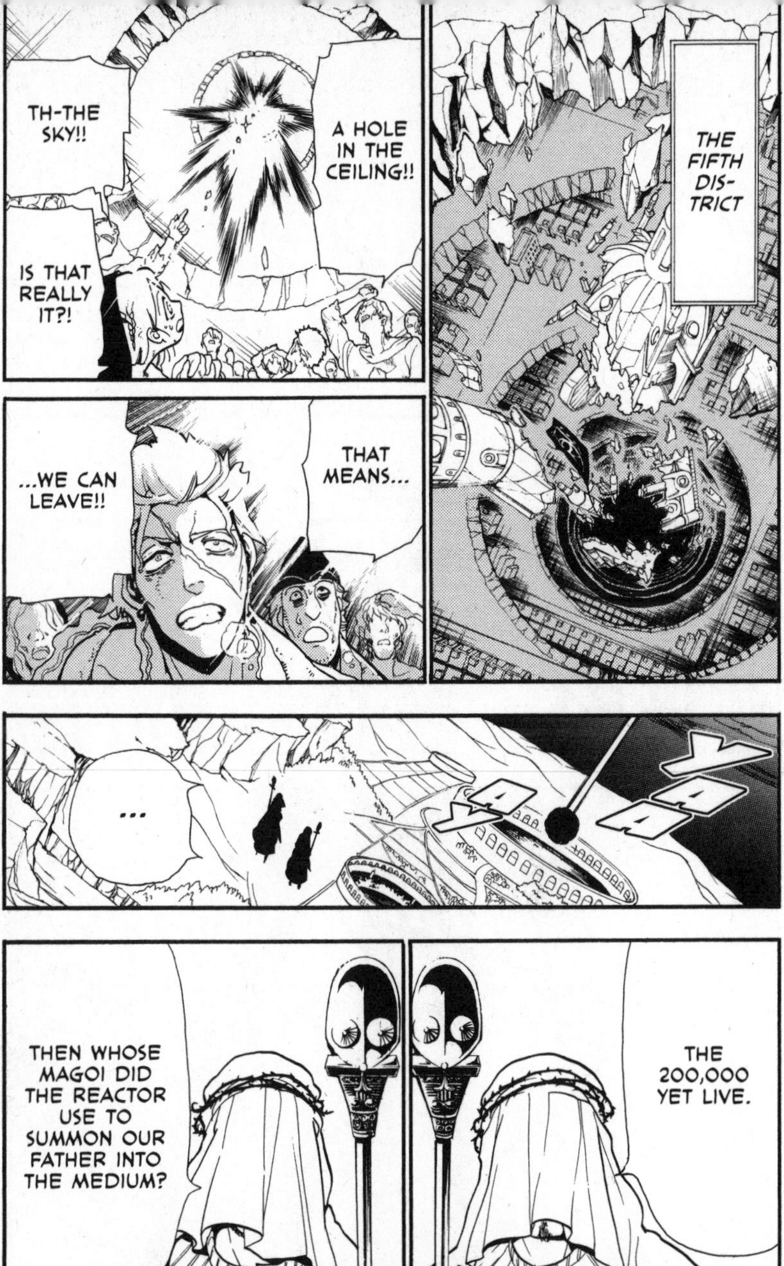
THE FIFTH DIS-TRICT
A HOLE IN THE CEILING!!
TH-THE SKY!!
IS THAT REALLY IT?!
THAT MEANS...
...WE CAN LEAVE!!
YAAAAY
...
THE 200,000 YET LIVE.
THEN WHOSE MAGOI DID THE REACTOR USE TO SUMMON OUR FATHER INTO THE MEDIUM?

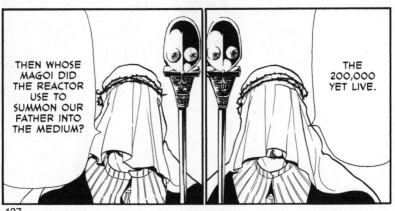

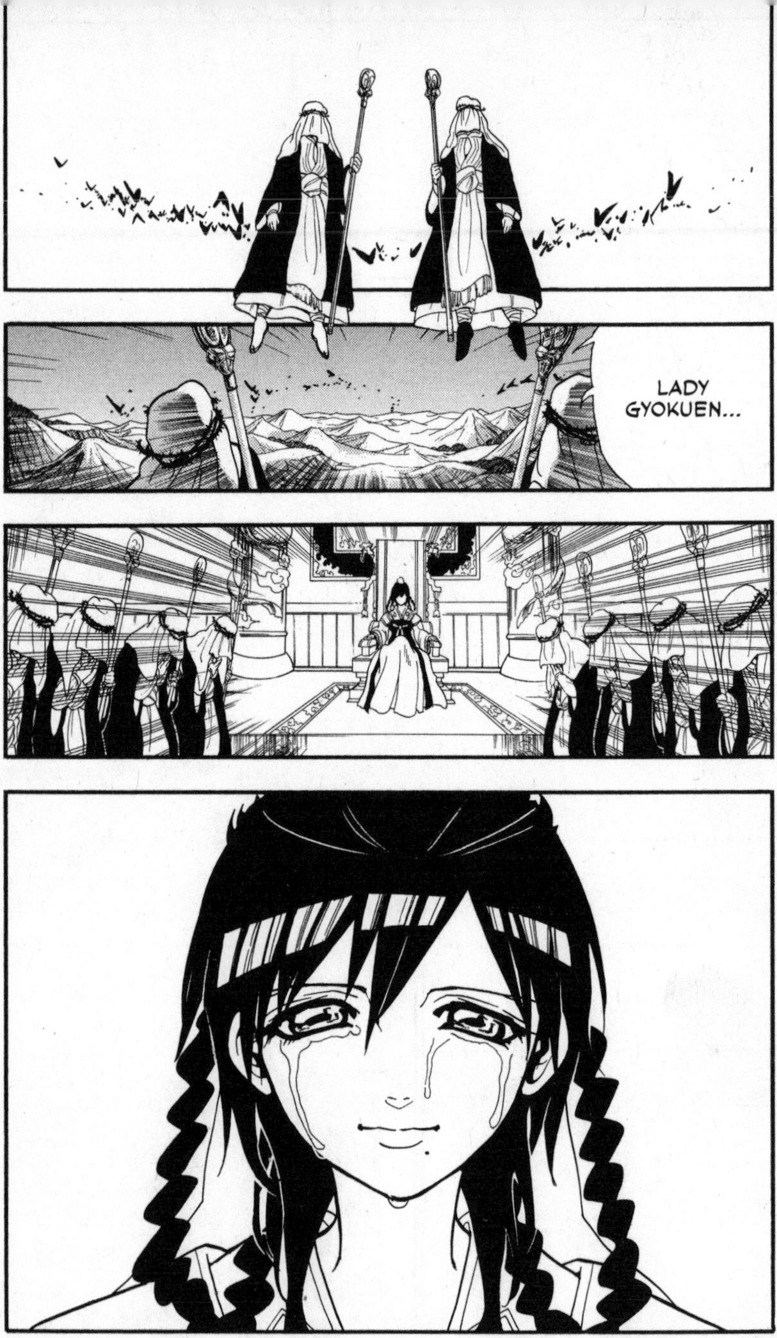
LADY GYOKUEN...

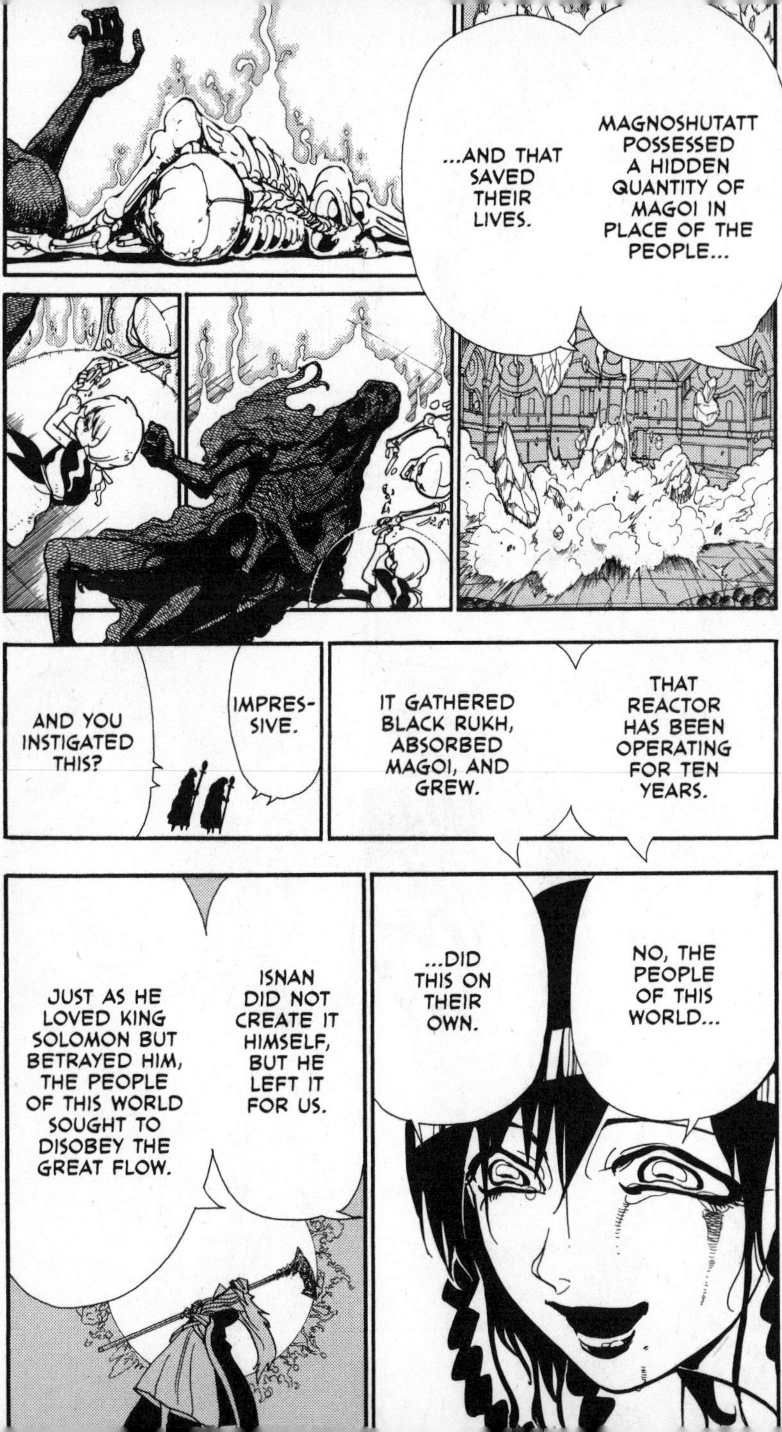
MAGNOSHUTATT POSSESSED A HIDDEN QUANTITY OF MAGOI IN PLACE OF THE PEOPLE...
...AND THAT SAVED THEIR LIVES.
THAT REACTOR HAS BEEN OPERATING FOR TEN YEARS.
IT GATHERED BLACK RUKH, ABSORBED MAGOI, AND GREW.
IMPRES-SIVE.
AND YOU INSTIGATED THIS?
NO, THE PEOPLE OF THIS WORLD...
...DID THIS ON THEIR OWN.
ISNAN DID NOT CREATE IT HIMSELF, BUT HE LEFT IT FOR US.
JUST AS HE LOVED KING SOLOMON BUT BETRAYED HIM, THE PEOPLE OF THIS WORLD SOUGHT TO DISOBEY THE GREAT FLOW.

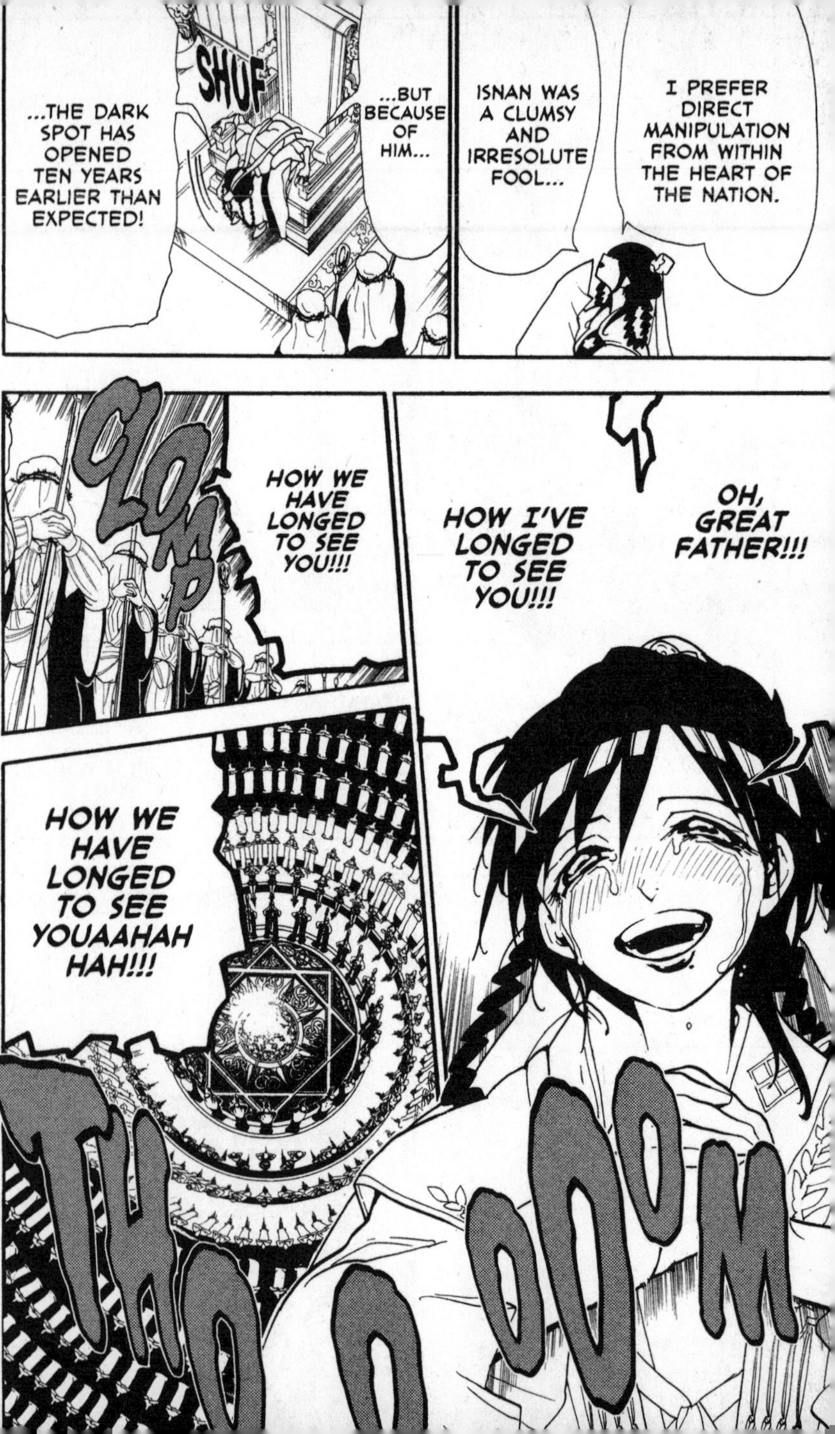
I PREFER DIRECT MANIPULATION FROM WITHIN THE HEART OF THE NATION.
ISNAN WAS A CLUMSY AND IRRESOLUTE FOOL...
SHUF
...BUT BECAUSE OF HIM...
...THE DARK SPOT HAS OPENED TEN YEARS EARLIER THAN EXPECTED!
OH, GREAT FATHER!!!
HOW I'VE LONGED TO SEE YOU!!!
CLOMP
HOW WE HAVE LONGED TO SEE YOU!!!
HOW WE HAVE LONGED TO SEE YOUAAHAH HAH!!!
THOOOOOOM

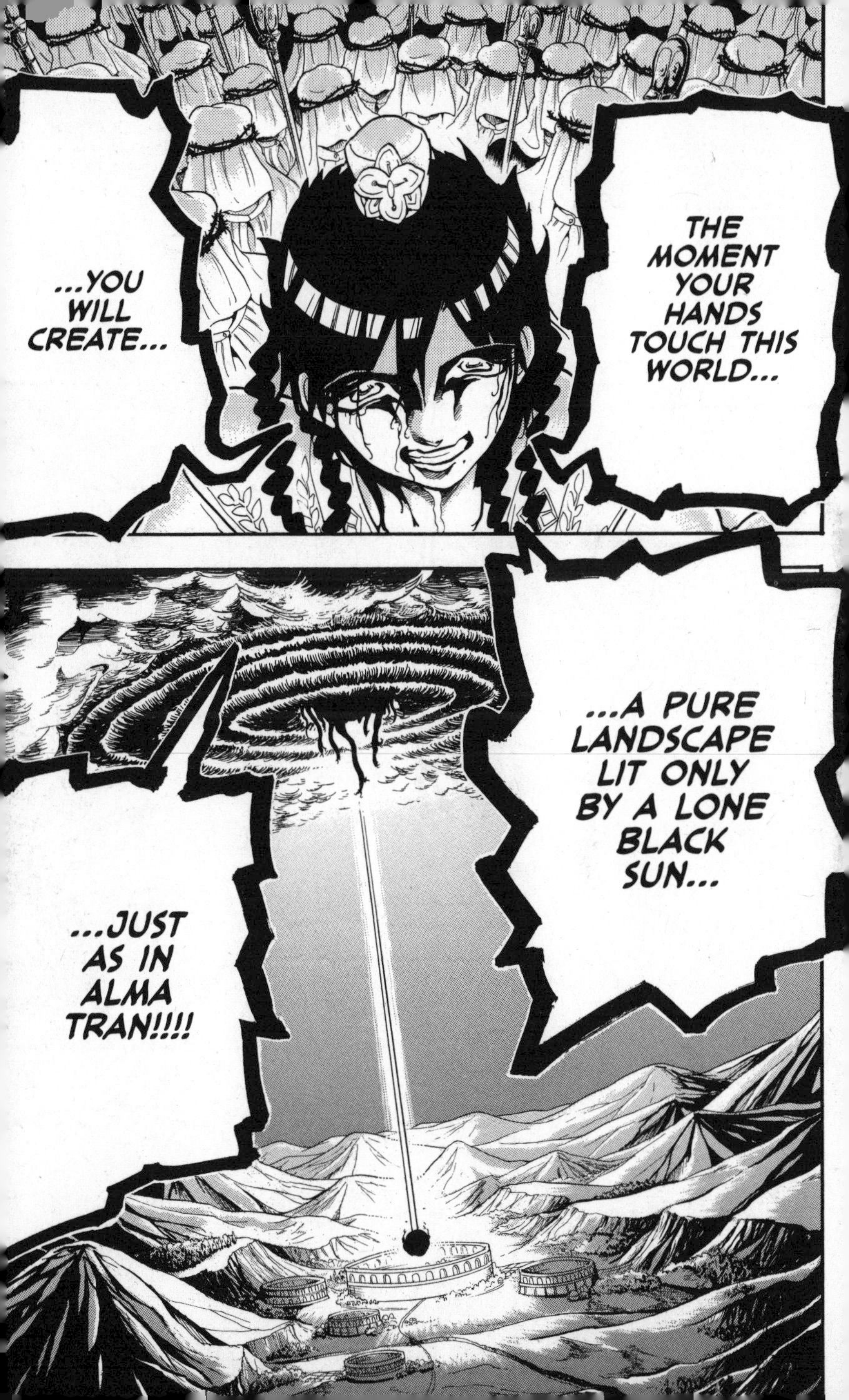
THE MOMENT YOUR HANDS TOUCH THIS WORLD...
...YOU WILL CREATE...
...A PURE LANDSCAPE LIT ONLY BY A LONE BLACK SUN...
...JUST AS IN ALMA TRAN!!!!

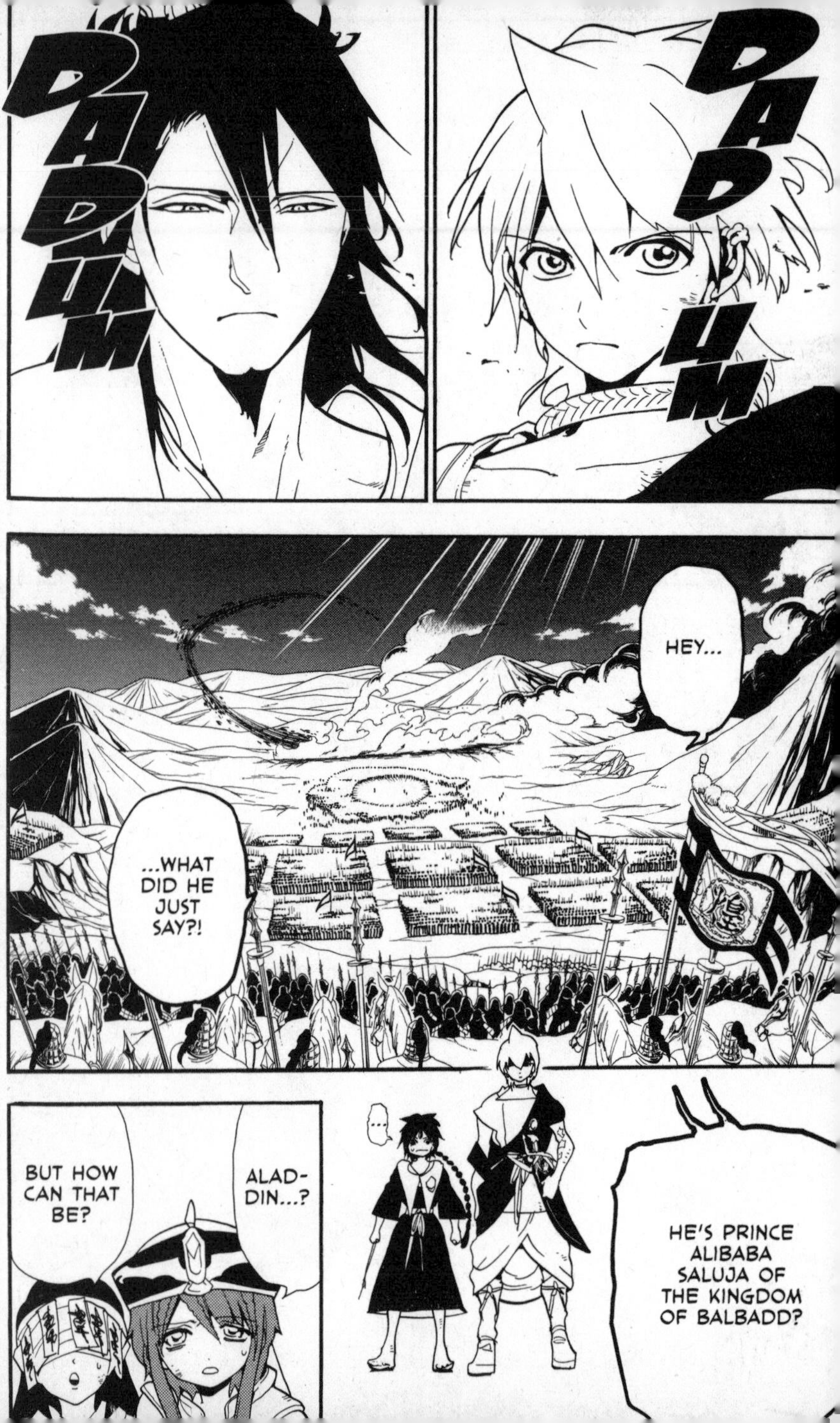
DADUM
DADUM
HEY...
...WHAT DID HE JUST SAY?!
HE'S PRINCE ALIBABA SALUJA OF THE KINGDOM OF BALBADD?
...
ALAD-DIN...?
BUT HOW CAN THAT BE?

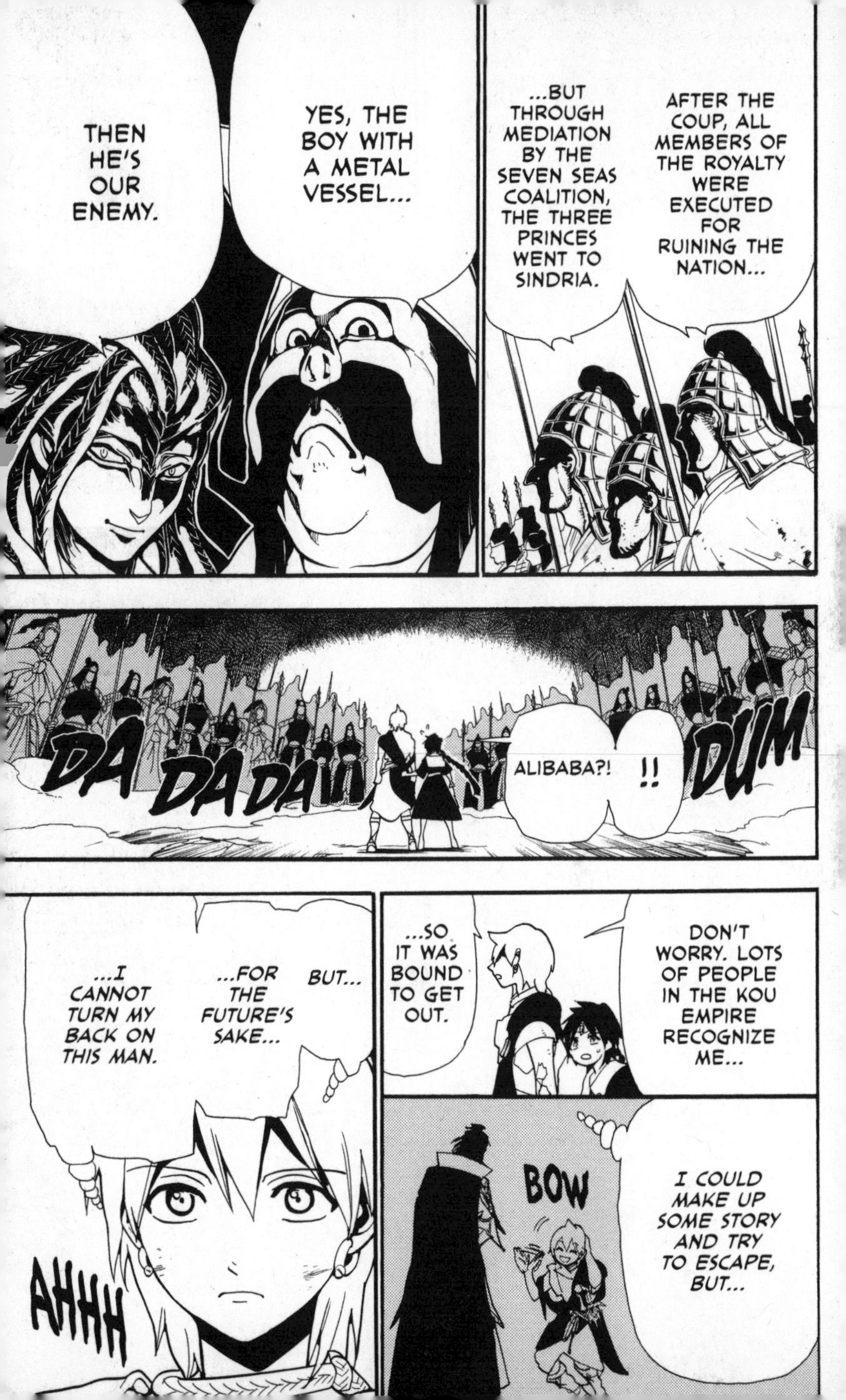
AFTER THE COUP, ALL MEMBERS OF THE ROYALTY WERE EXECUTED FOR RUINING THE NATION...
...BUT THROUGH MEDIATION BY THE SEVEN SEAS COALITION, THE THREE PRINCES WENT TO SINDRIA.
YES, THE BOY WITH A METAL VESSEL...
THEN HE'S OUR ENEMY.
DUM
!!
ALIBABA?!
DA DA DA
DON'T WORRY. LOTS OF PEOPLE IN THE KOU EMPIRE RECOGNIZE ME...
...SO IT WAS BOUND TO GET OUT.
I COULD MAKE UP SOME STORY AND TRY TO ESCAPE, BUT...
BOW
BUT...
...FOR THE FUTURE'S SAKE...
...I CANNOT TURN MY BACK ON THIS MAN.
AHHH

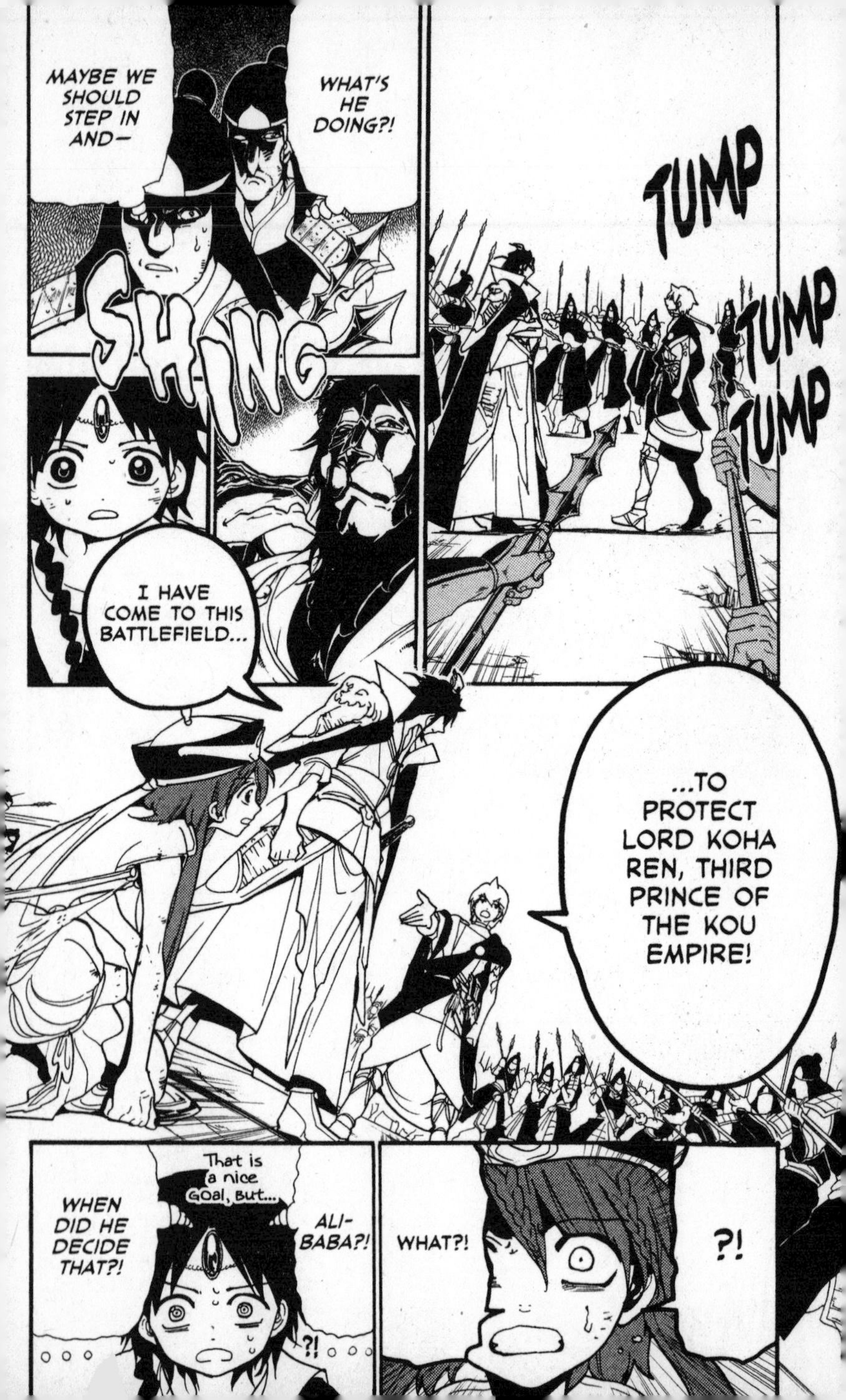
TUMP
TUMP
TUMP
WHAT'S HE DOING?!
MAYBE WE SHOULD STEP IN AND—
SHING
I HAVE COME TO THIS BATTLEFIELD...
...TO PROTECT LORD KOHA REN, THIRD PRINCE OF THE KOU EMPIRE!
?!
WHAT?!
ALI-BABA?!
That is a nice Goal, but...
WHEN DID HE DECIDE THAT?!
?!

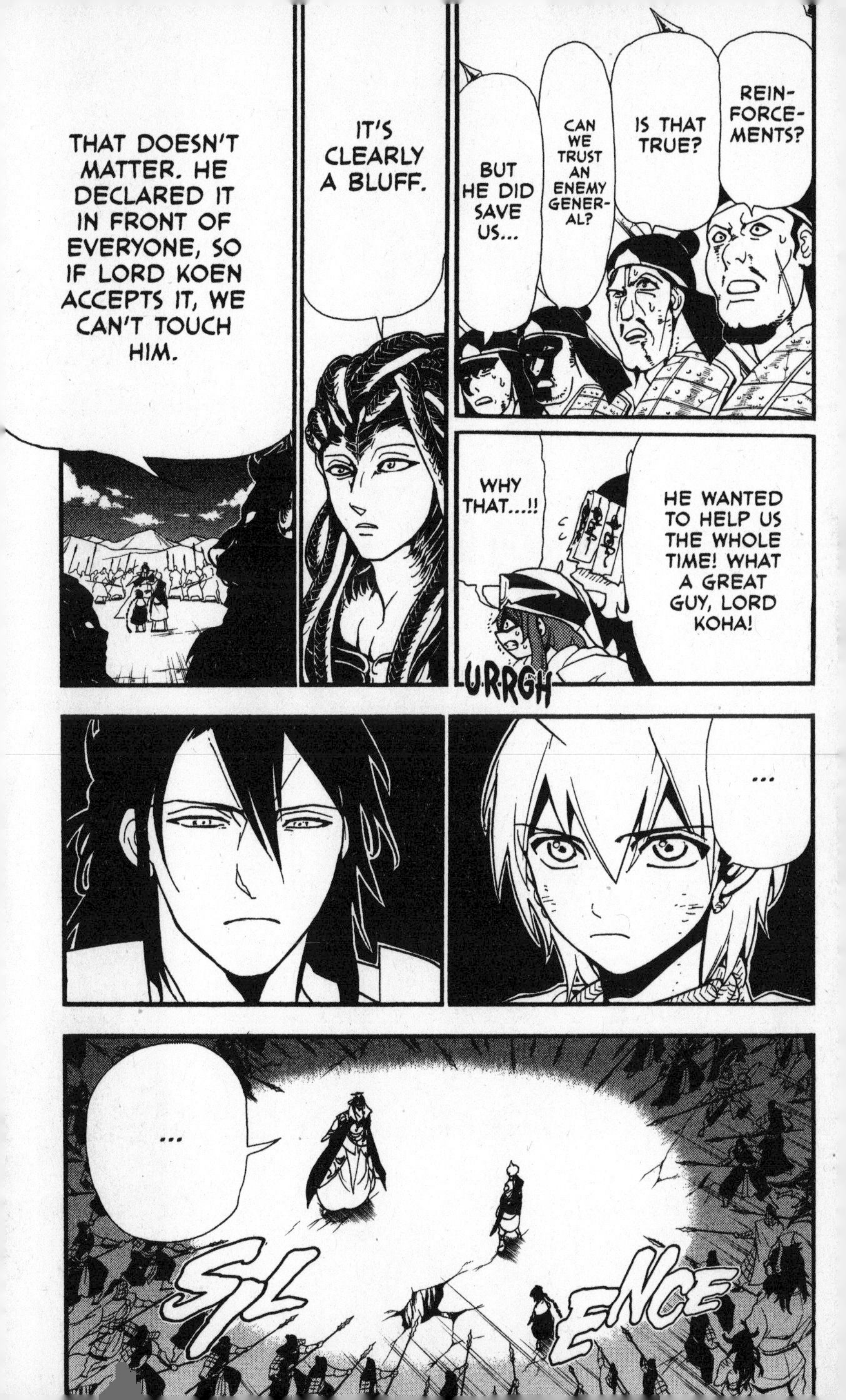
REIN-FORCE-MENTS?
IS THAT TRUE?
CAN WE TRUST AN ENEMY GENER-AL?
BUT HE DID SAVE US...
HE WANTED TO HELP US THE WHOLE TIME! WHAT A GREAT GUY, LORD KOHA!
WHY THAT...!!
URRGH
IT'S CLEARLY A BLUFF.
THAT DOESN'T MATTER. HE DECLARED IT IN FRONT OF EVERYONE, SO IF LORD KOEN ACCEPTS IT, WE CAN'T TOUCH HIM.
...
...
SIL ENCE

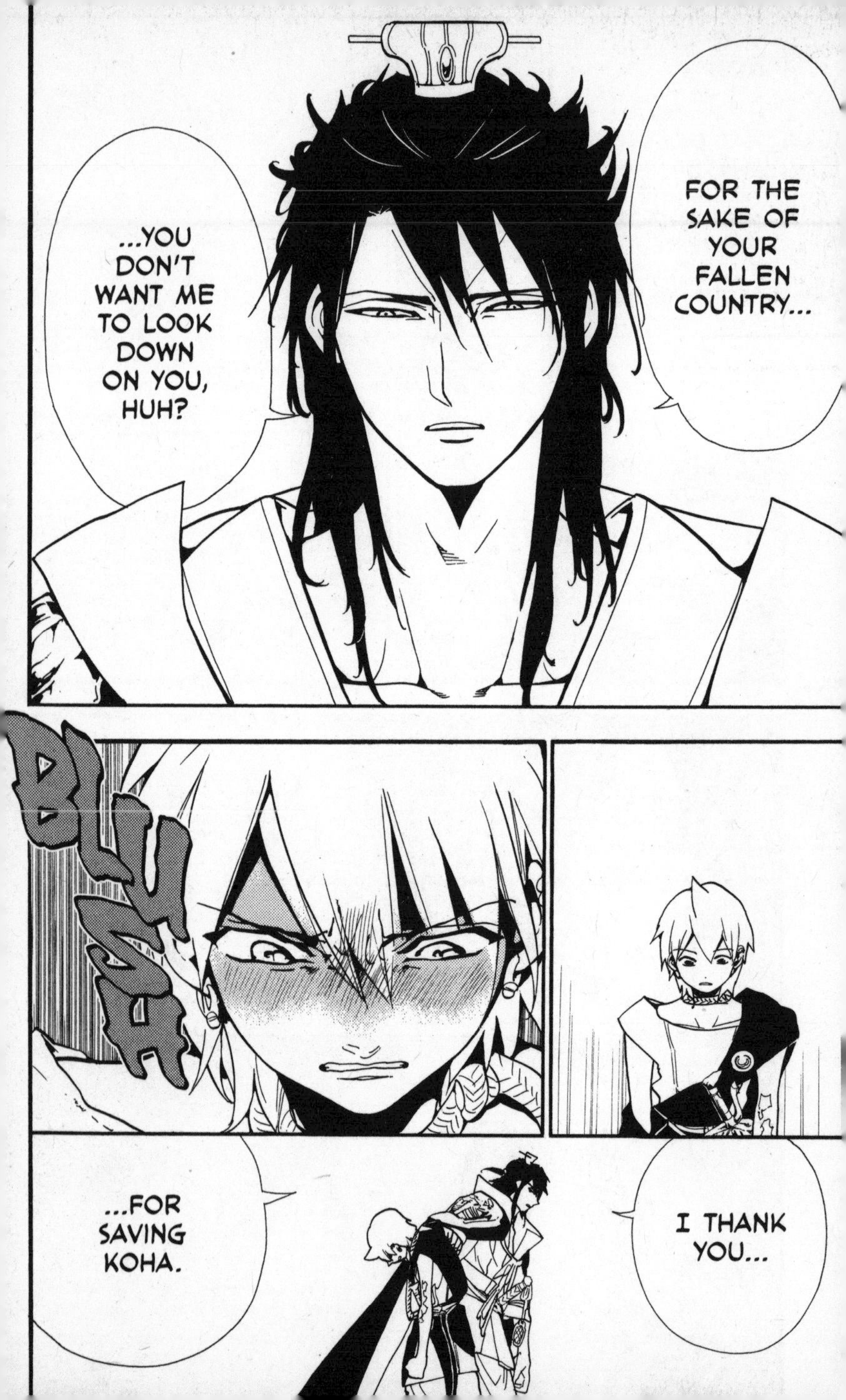
FOR THE SAKE OF YOUR FALLEN COUNTRY...
...YOU DON'T WANT ME TO LOOK DOWN ON YOU, HUH?
BLUSH
I THANK YOU...
...FOR SAVING KOHA.

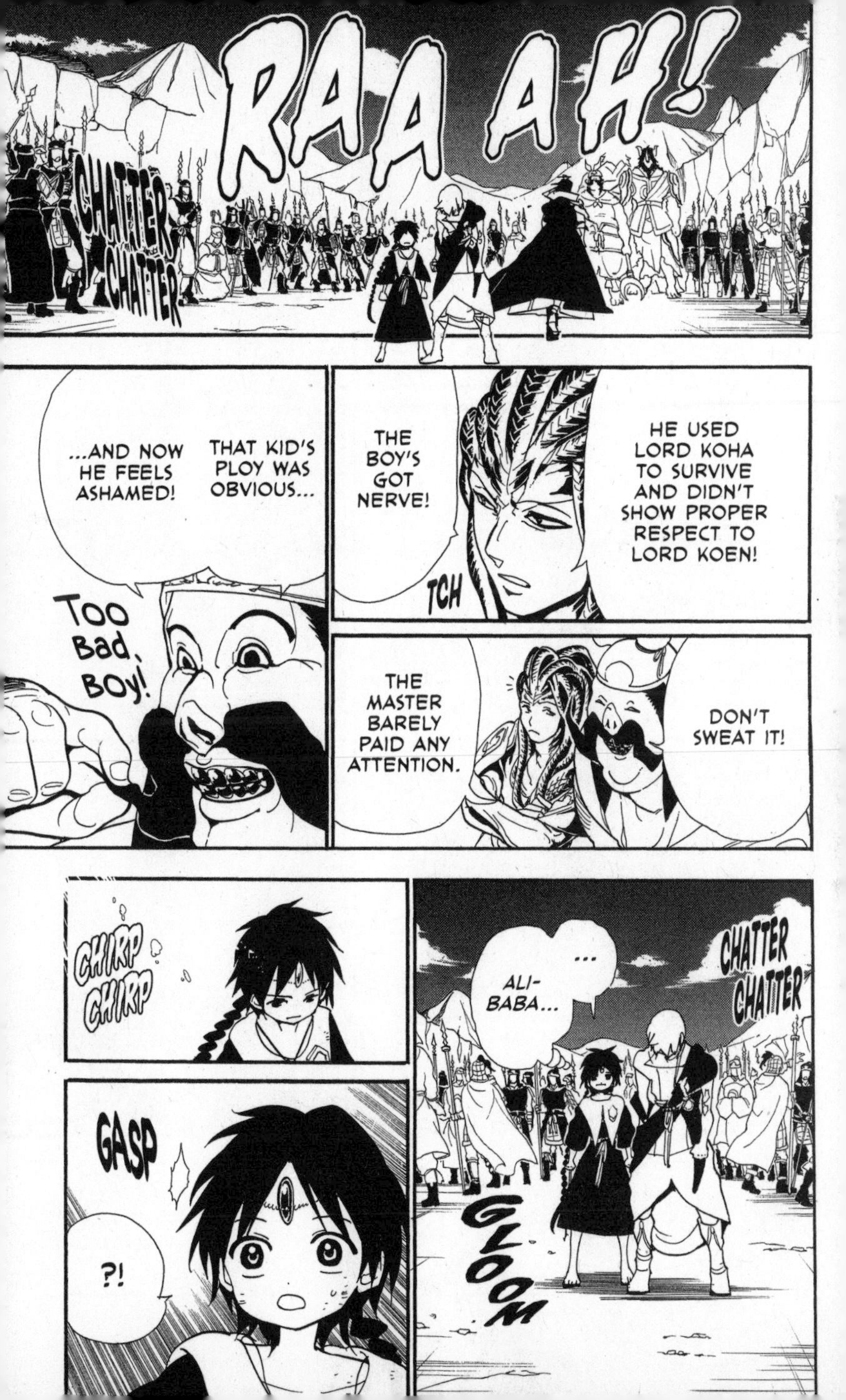
RAA AH!
CHATTER CHATTER
HE USED LORD KOHA TO SURVIVE AND DIDN'T SHOW PROPER RESPECT TO LORD KOEN!
THE BOY'S GOT NERVE!
TCH
DON'T SWEAT IT!
THE MASTER BARELY PAID ANY ATTENTION.
THAT KID'S PLOY WAS OBVIOUS...
...AND NOW HE FEELS ASHAMED!
Too Bad, Boy!
CHATTER CHATTER
...
ALI-BABA...
GLOOM
CHIRP CHIRP
GASP
?!

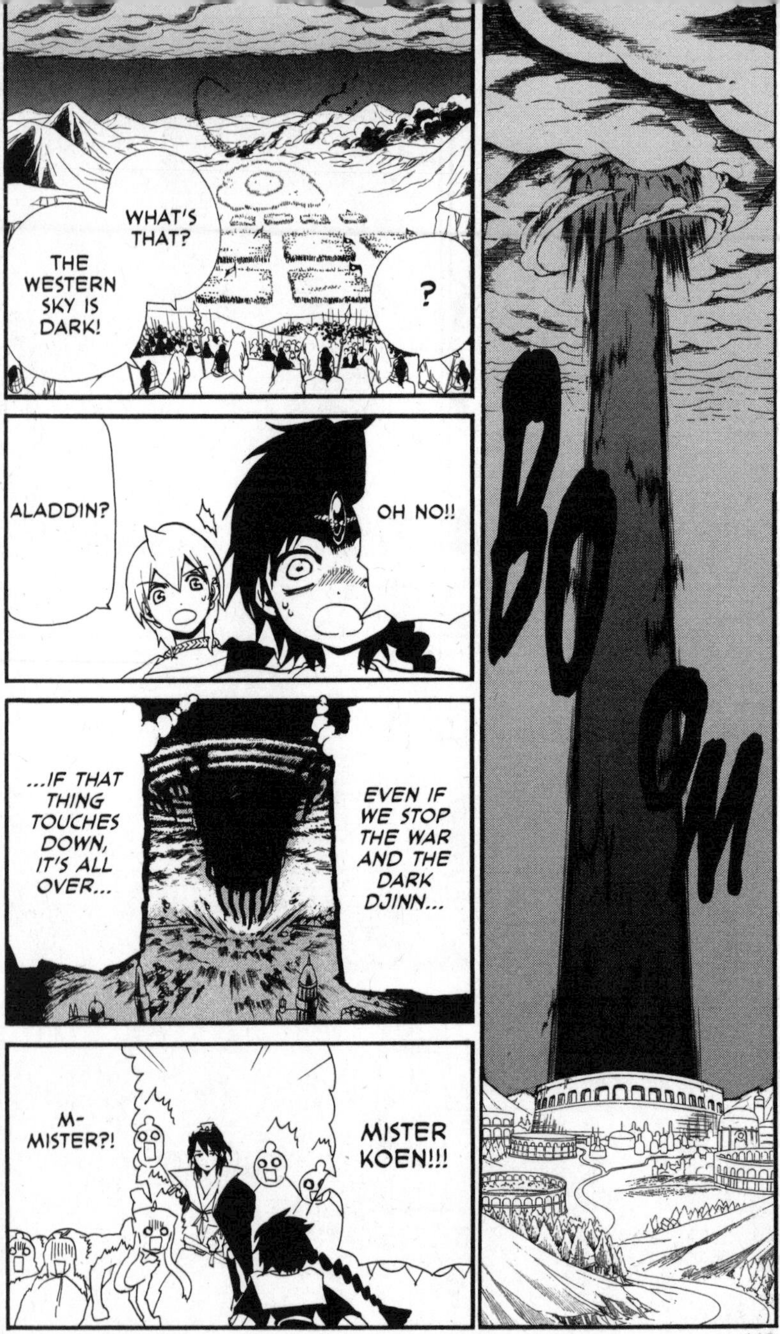
BOOM
WHAT'S THAT?
THE WESTERN SKY IS DARK!
?
OH NO!!
ALADDIN?
EVEN IF WE STOP THE WAR AND THE DARK DJINN...
...IF THAT THING TOUCHES DOWN, IT'S ALL OVER...
MISTER KOEN!!!
M-MISTER?!

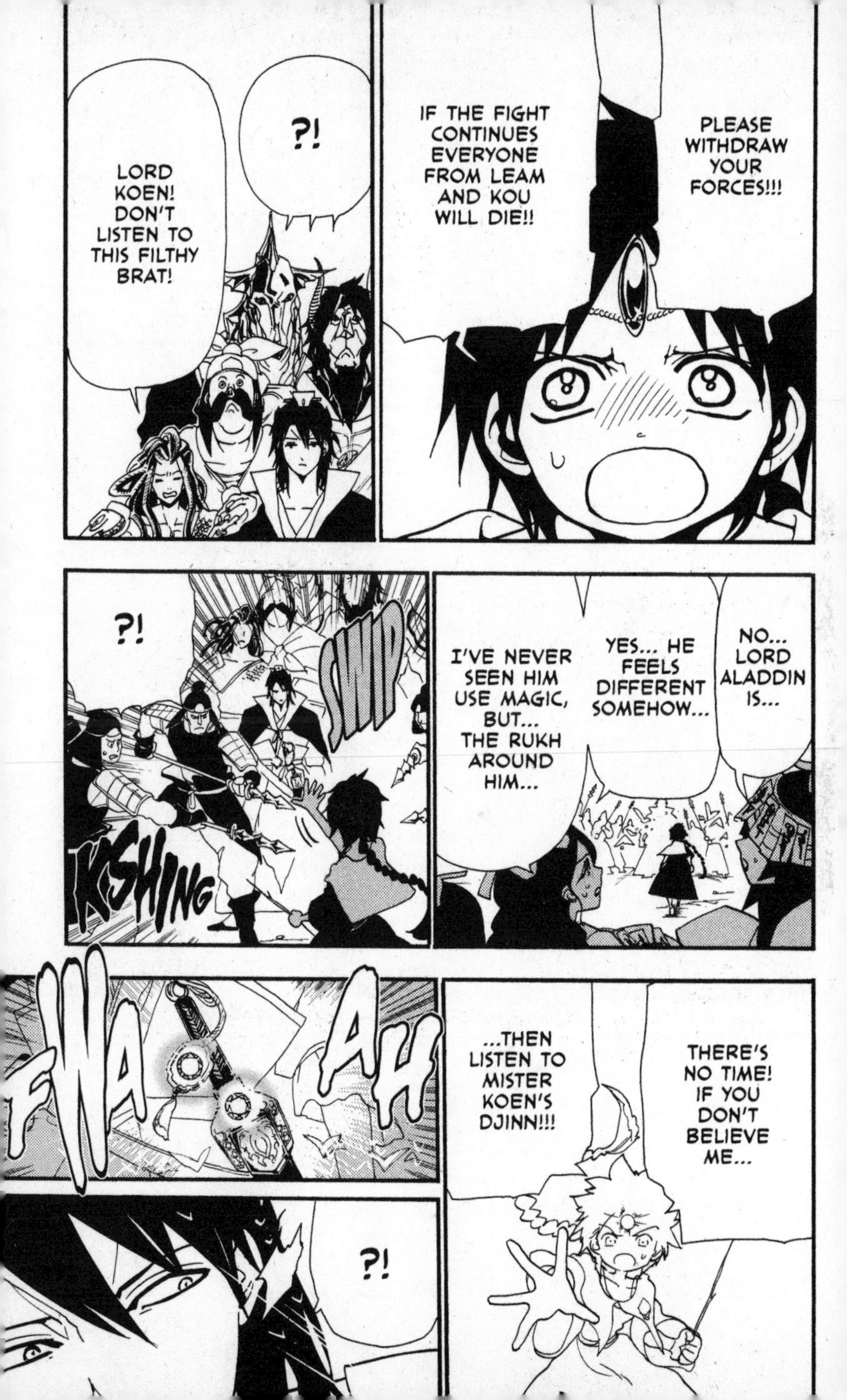
PLEASE WITHDRAW YOUR FORCES!!!
IF THE FIGHT CONTINUES EVERYONE FROM LEAM AND KOU WILL DIE!!
?!
LORD KOEN! DON'T LISTEN TO THIS FILTHY BRAT!
NO... LORD ALADDIN IS...
YES... HE FEELS DIFFERENT SOMEHOW...
I'VE NEVER SEEN HIM USE MAGIC, BUT... THE RUKH AROUND HIM...
SWIP
?!
KSHING
THERE'S NO TIME! IF YOU DON'T BELIEVE ME...
...THEN LISTEN TO MISTER KOEN'S DJINN!!!
FWAAH
?!

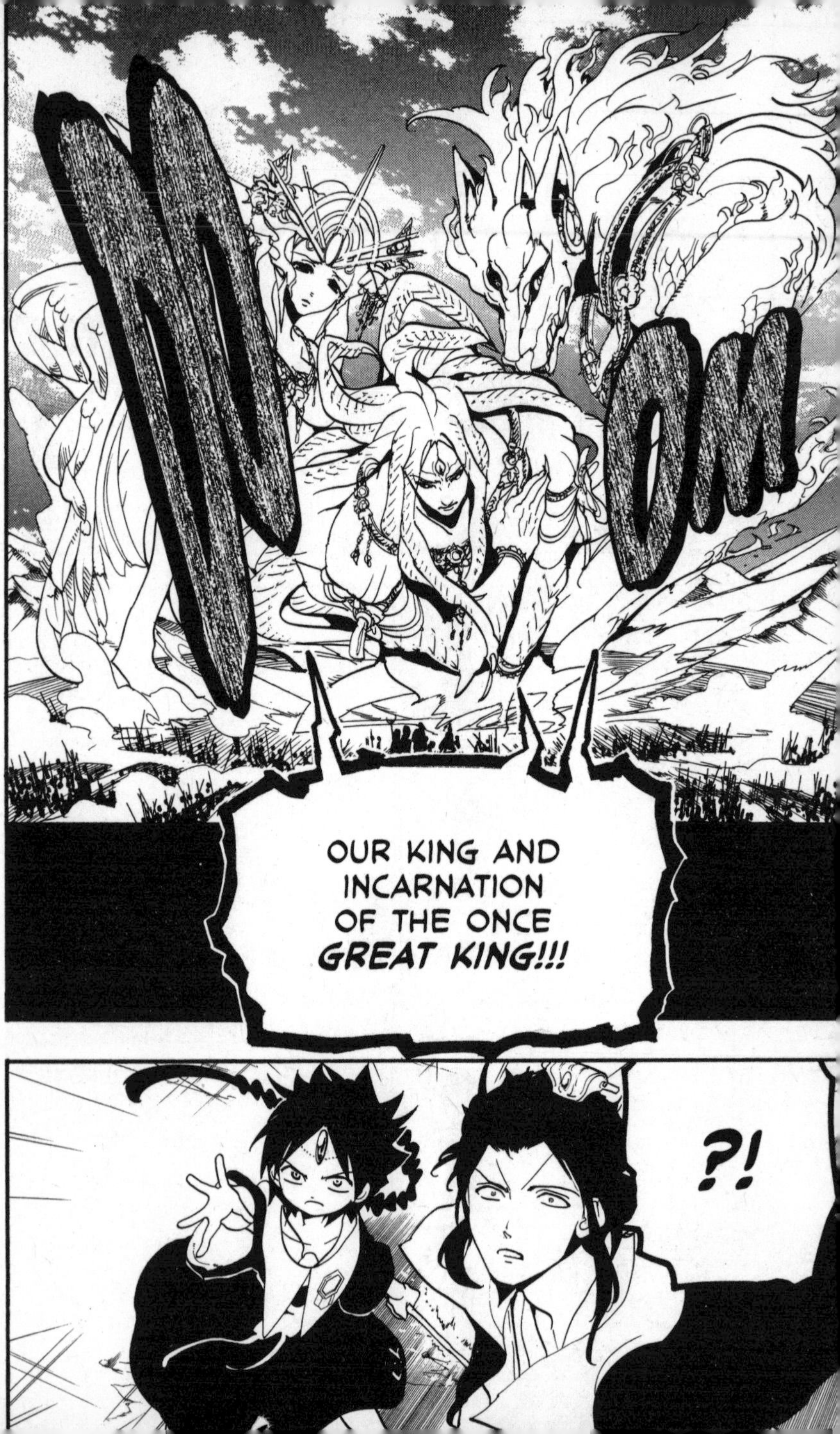
OUR KING AND INCARNATION OF THE ONCE GREAT KING!!!
?!

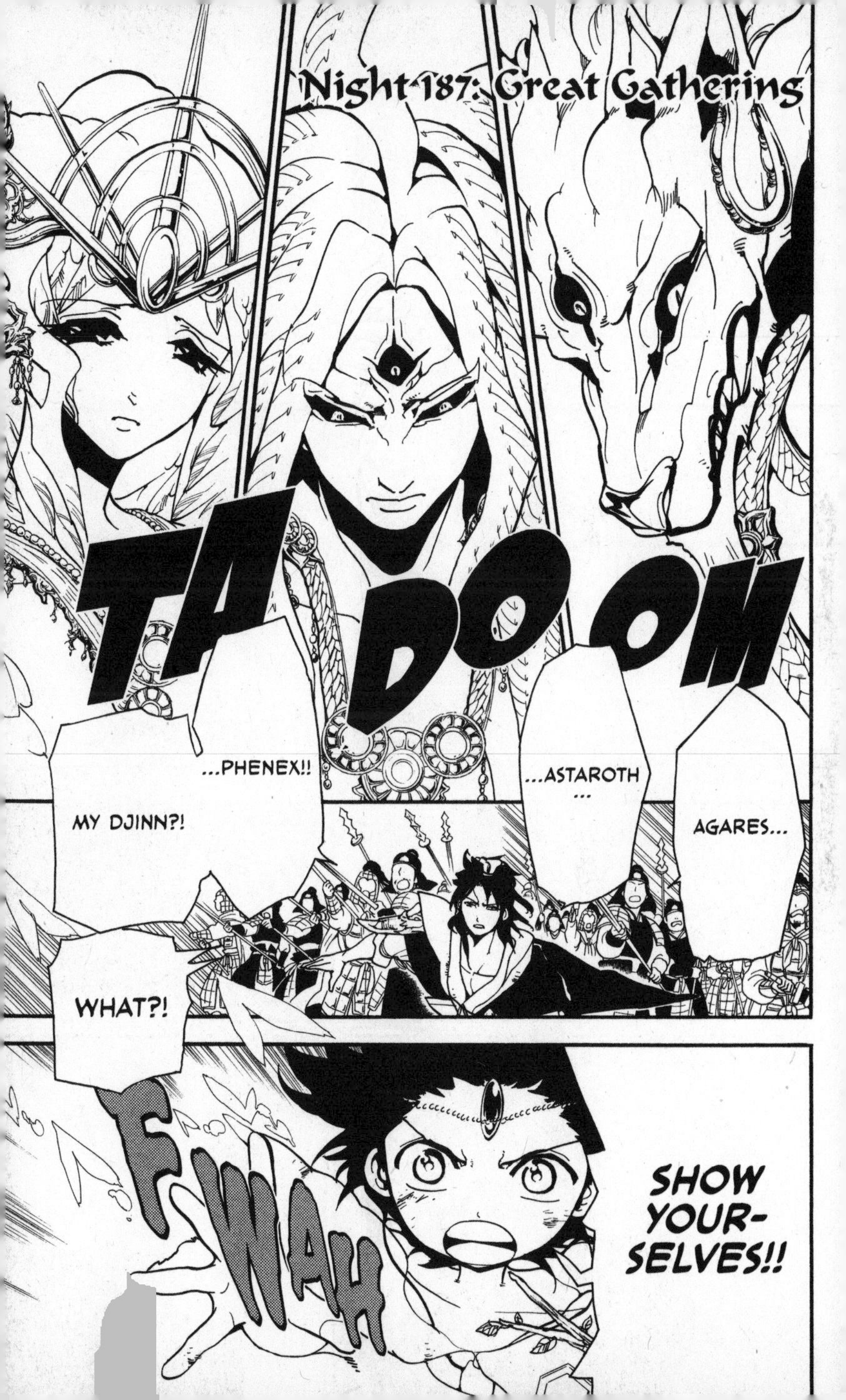
Night 187: Great Gathering
TA DO OM
AGARES...
...ASTAROTH ...
...PHENEX!!
MY DJINN?!
WHAT?!
SHOW YOURSELVES!!
FWAH

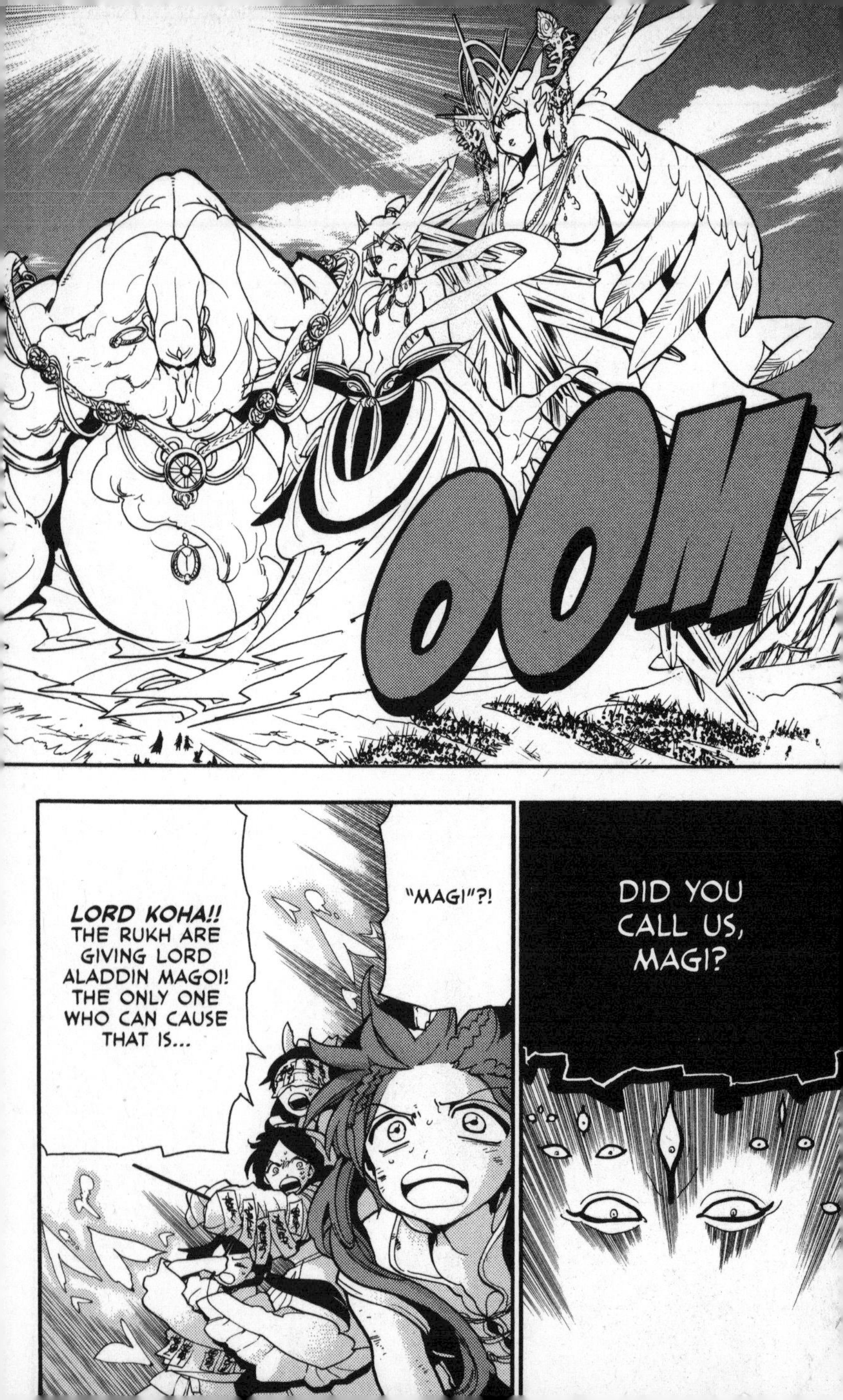
OOM
DID YOU CALL US, MAGI?
"MAGI"?!
LORD KOHA!! THE RUKH ARE GIVING LORD ALADDIN MAGOI! THE ONLY ONE WHO CAN CAUSE THAT IS...

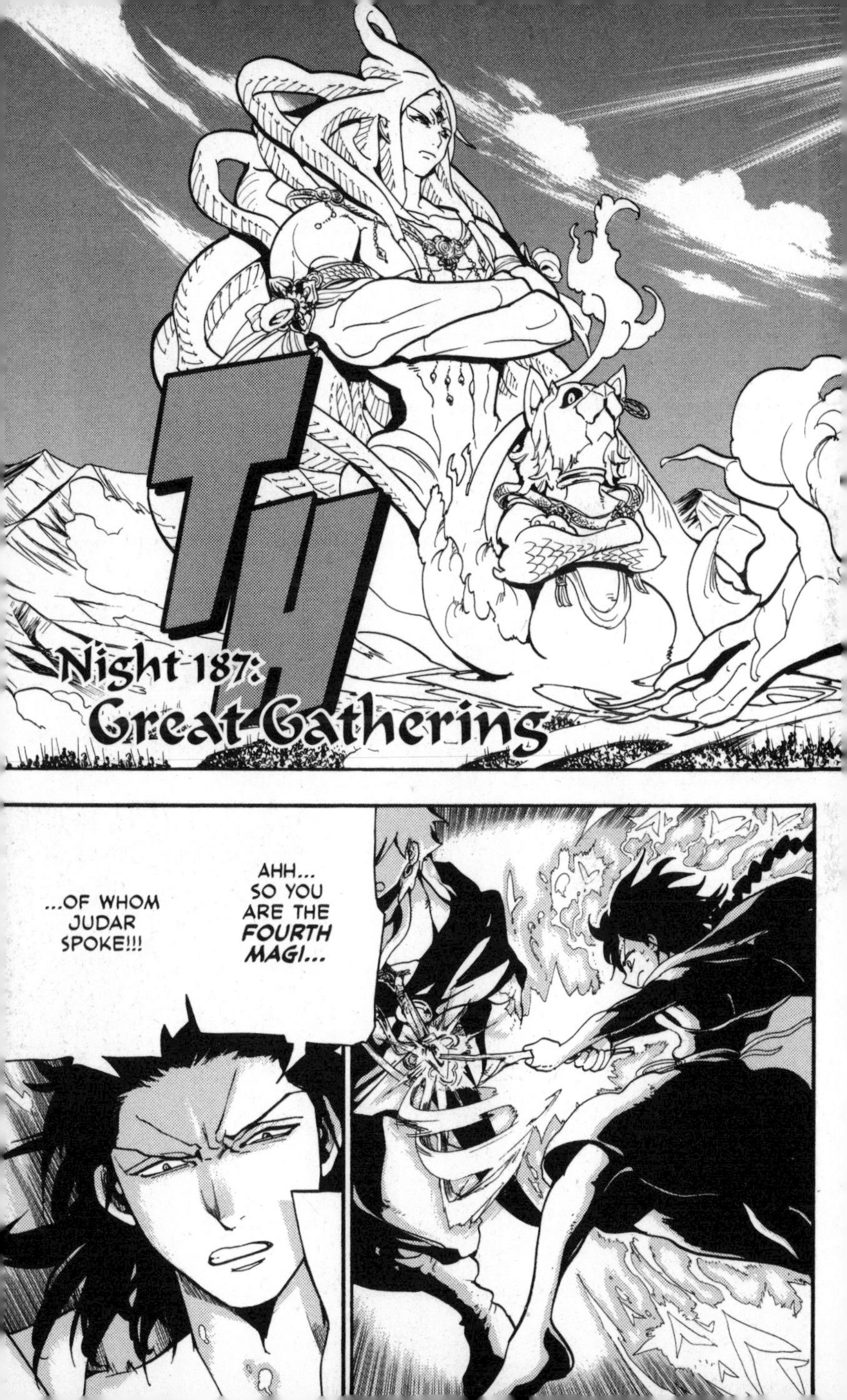
Night 187: Great Gathering
AHH... SO YOU ARE THE FOURTH MAGI...
...OF WHOM JUDAR SPOKE!!!

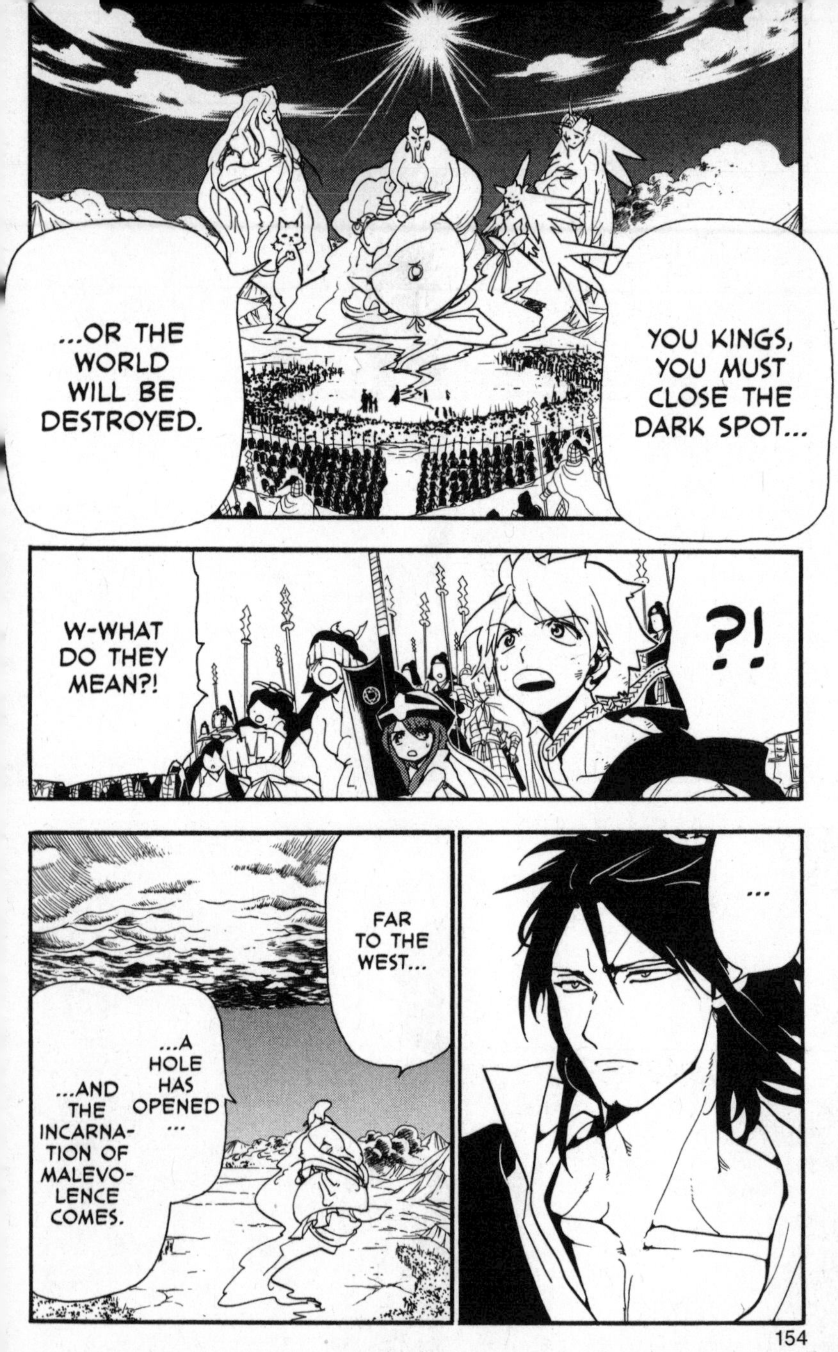
YOU KINGS, YOU MUST CLOSE THE DARK SPOT...
...OR THE WORLD WILL BE DESTROYED.
?!
W-WHAT DO THEY MEAN?!
...
FAR TO THE WEST...
...A HOLE HAS OPENED...
...AND THE INCARNATION OF MALEVOLENCE COMES.

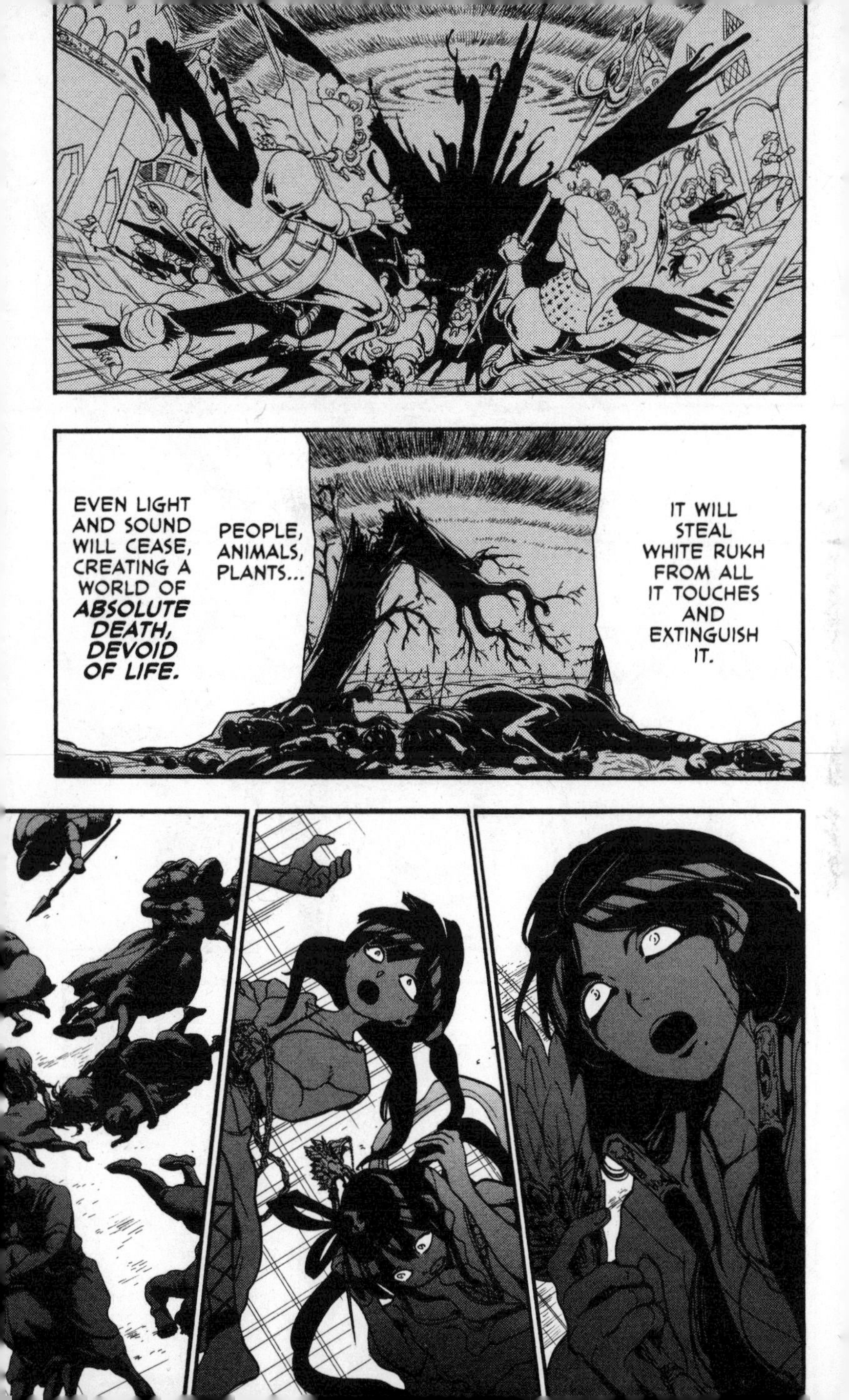
IT WILL STEAL WHITE RUKH FROM ALL IT TOUCHES AND EXTINGUISH IT.
PEOPLE, ANIMALS, PLANTS...
EVEN LIGHT AND SOUND WILL CEASE, CREATING A WORLD OF ***ABSOLUTE DEATH, DEVOID OF LIFE.***

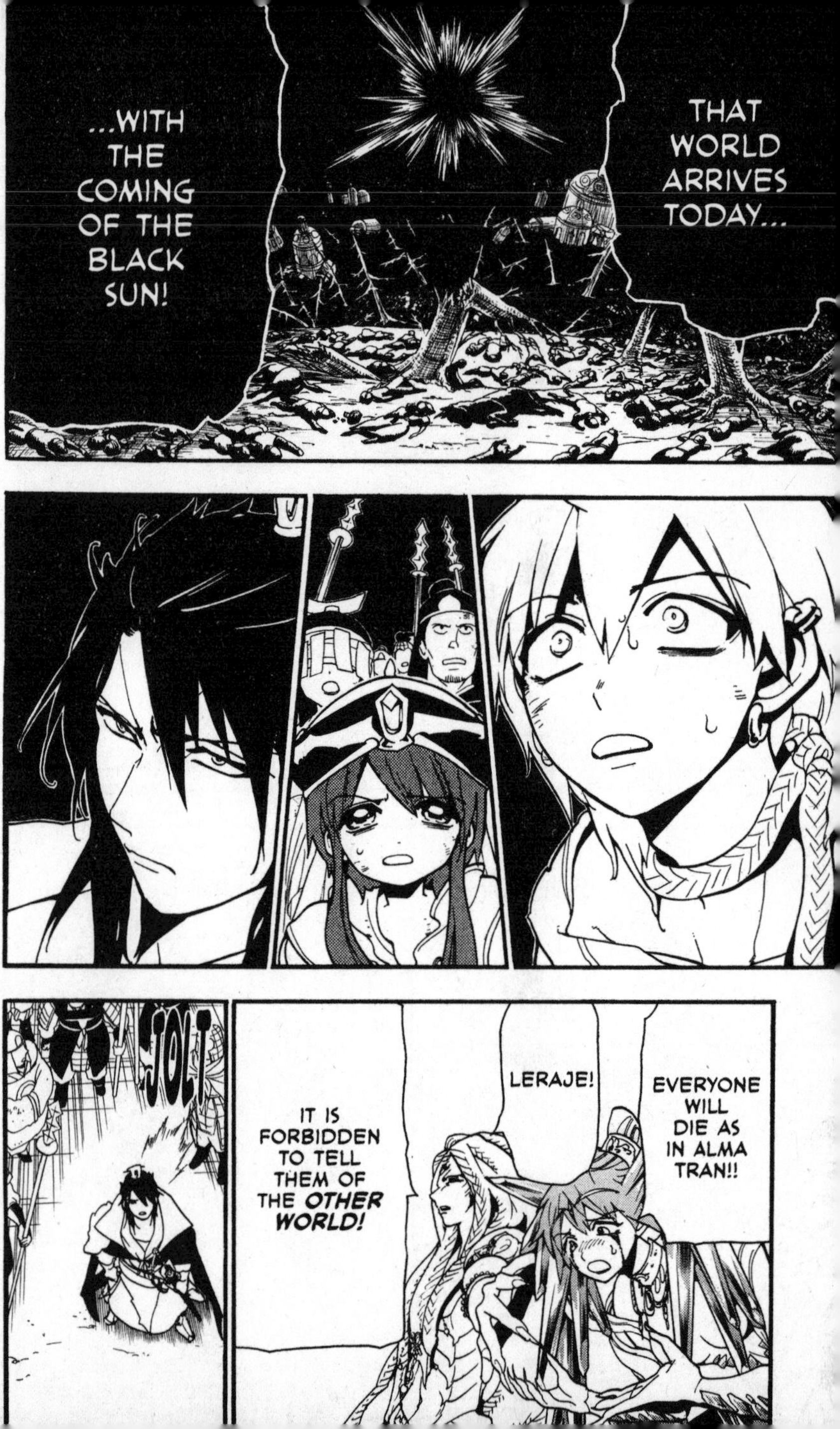
THAT WORLD ARRIVES TODAY...
...WITH THE COMING OF THE BLACK SUN!
EVERYONE WILL DIE AS IN ALMA TRAN!!
LERAJE!
IT IS FORBIDDEN TO TELL THEM OF THE *OTHER WORLD!*
JOLT

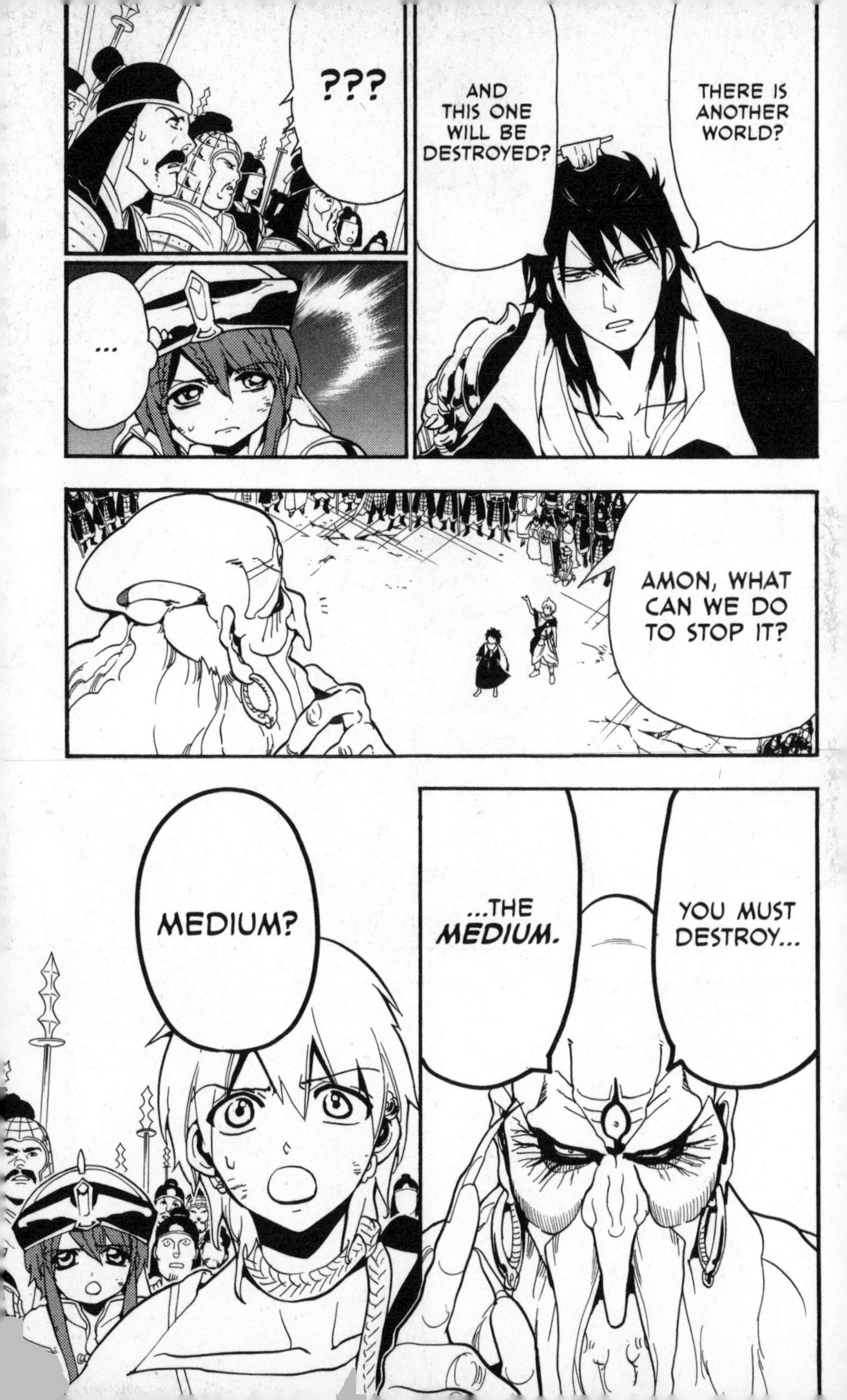
THERE IS ANOTHER WORLD?
AND THIS ONE WILL BE DESTROYED?
???
...
AMON, WHAT CAN WE DO TO STOP IT?
YOU MUST DESTROY...
...THE *MEDIUM.*
MEDIUM?

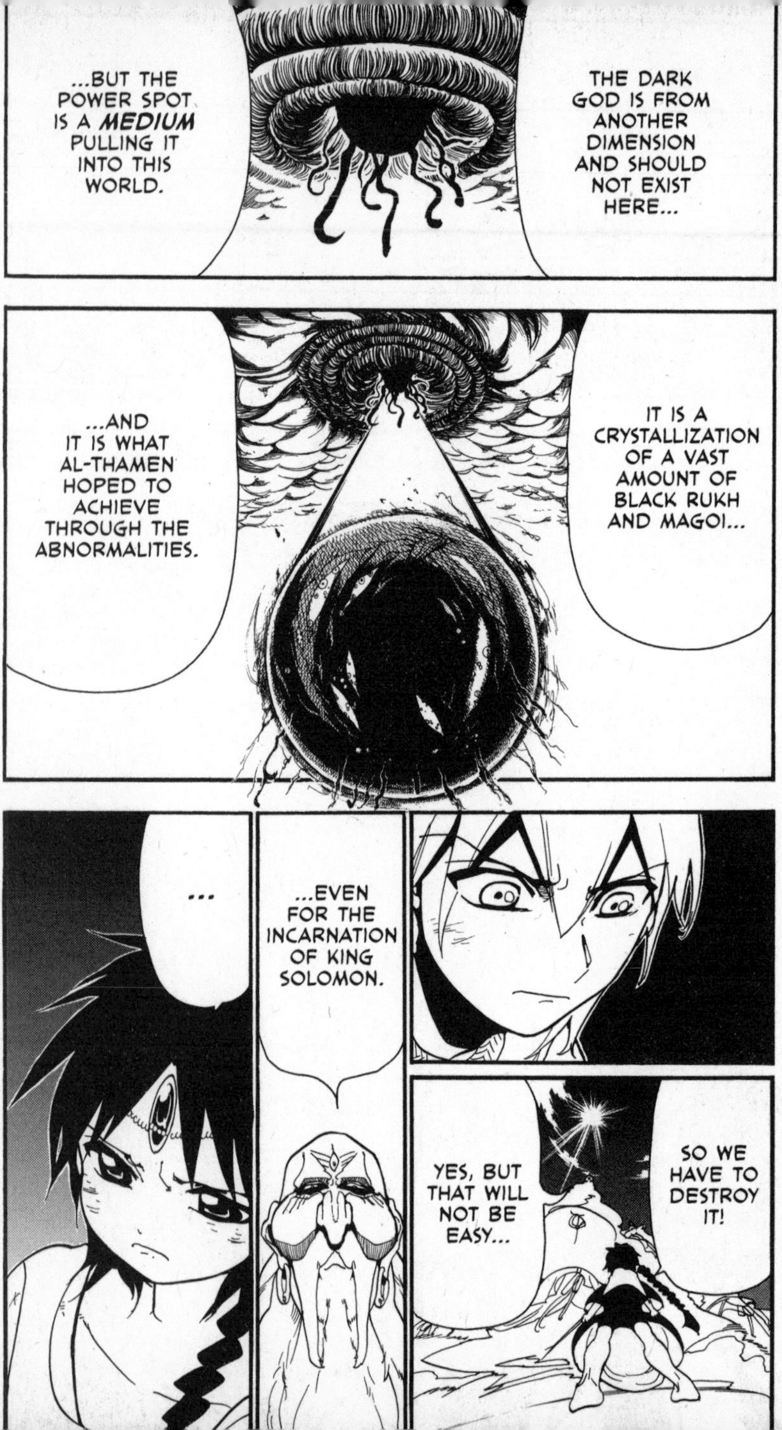
THE DARK GOD IS FROM ANOTHER DIMENSION AND SHOULD NOT EXIST HERE...
...BUT THE POWER SPOT IS A *MEDIUM* PULLING IT INTO THIS WORLD.
IT IS A CRYSTALLIZATION OF A VAST AMOUNT OF BLACK RUKH AND MAGOI...
...AND IT IS WHAT AL-THAMEN HOPED TO ACHIEVE THROUGH THE ABNORMALITIES.
SO WE HAVE TO DESTROY IT!
YES, BUT THAT WILL NOT BE EASY...
...EVEN FOR THE INCARNATION OF KING SOLOMON.
...

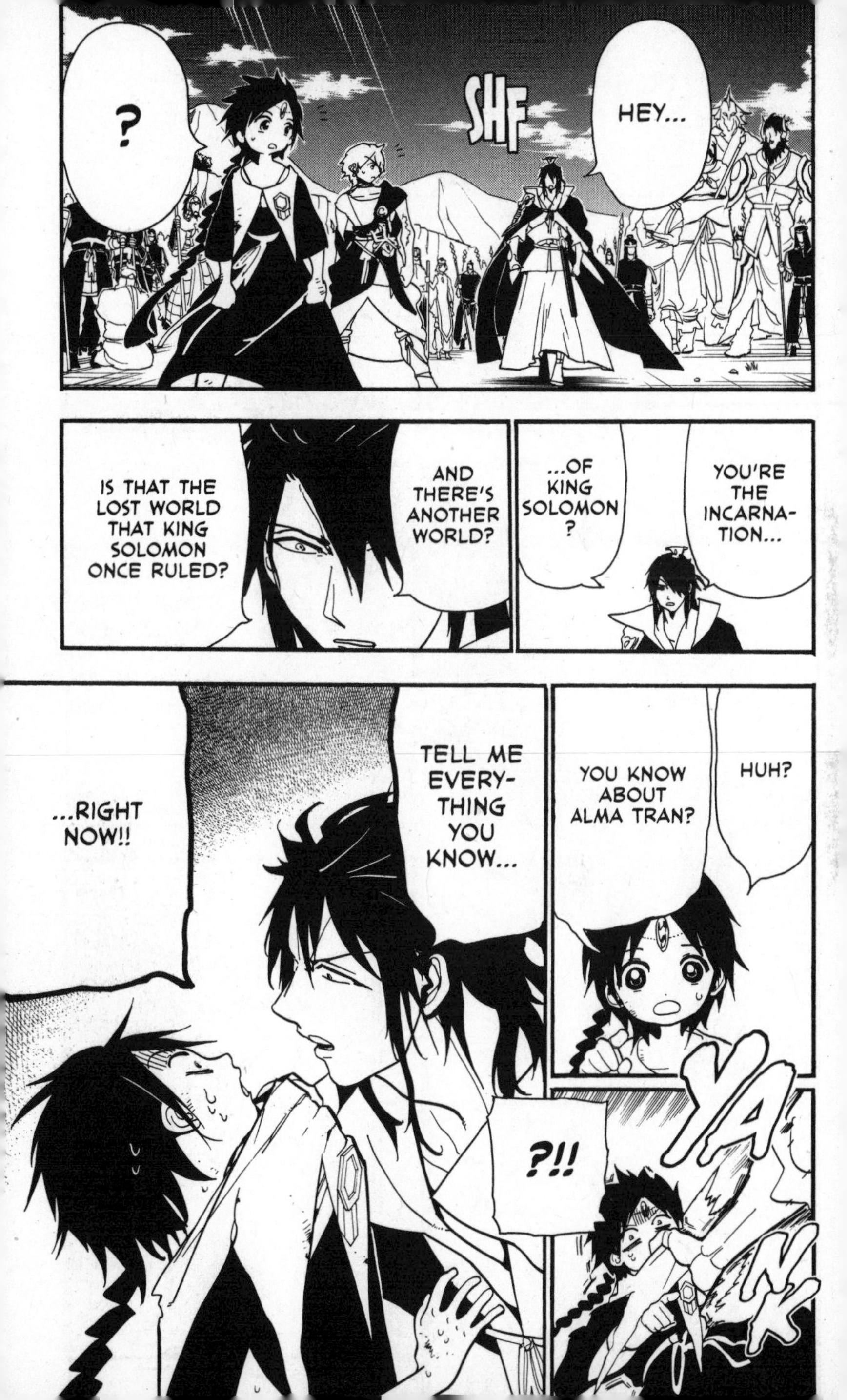
HEY...
SHF
?
YOU'RE THE INCARNATION...
...OF KING SOLOMON?
AND THERE'S ANOTHER WORLD?
IS THAT THE LOST WORLD THAT KING SOLOMON ONCE RULED?
HUH?
YOU KNOW ABOUT ALMA TRAN?
YANK
?!!
TELL ME EVERYTHING YOU KNOW...
...RIGHT NOW!!

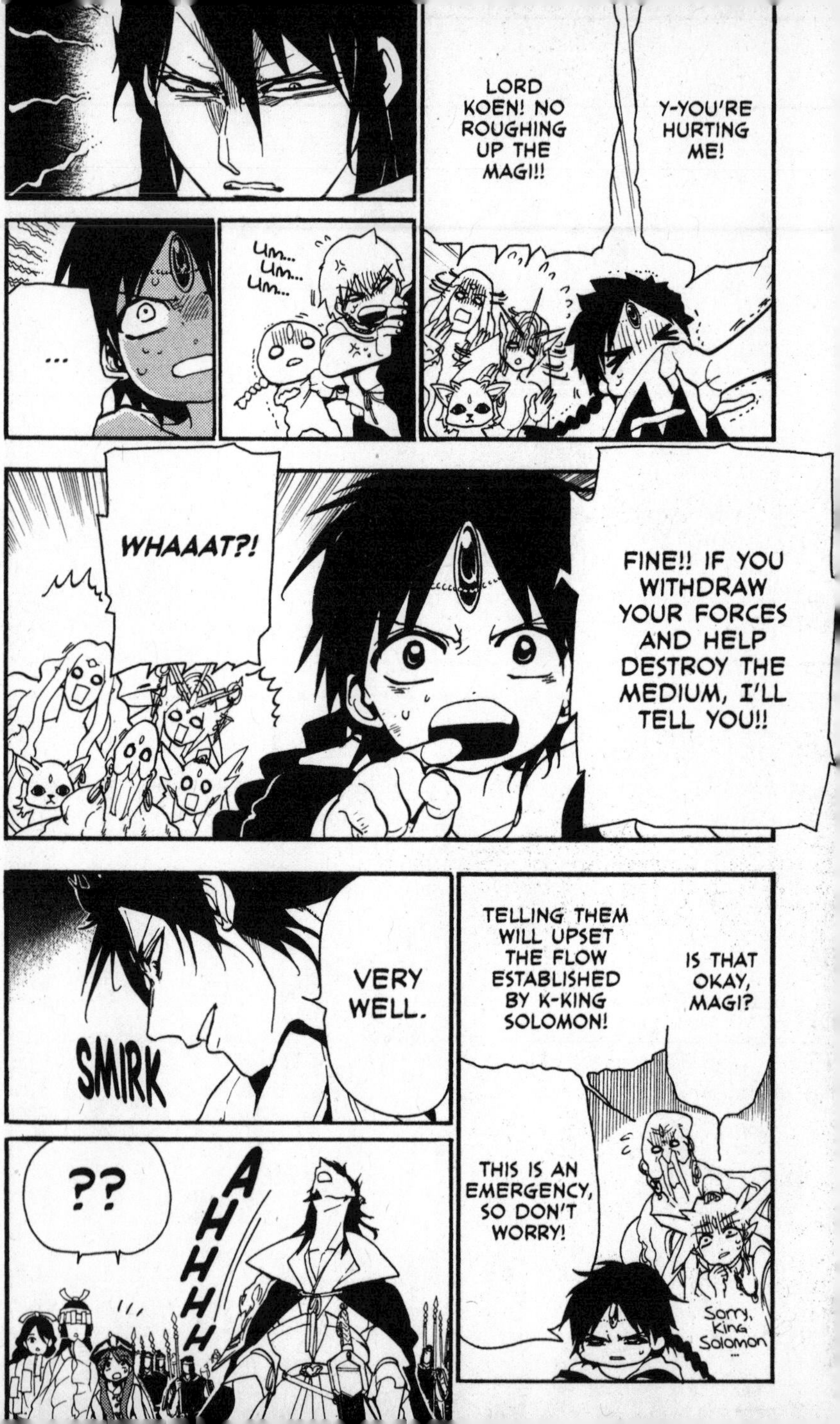
Y-YOU'RE HURTING ME!
LORD KOEN! NO ROUGHING UP THE MAGI!!
Um... Um... Um...
...
FINE!! IF YOU WITHDRAW YOUR FORCES AND HELP DESTROY THE MEDIUM, I'LL TELL YOU!!
WHAAAT?!
IS THAT OKAY, MAGI?
TELLING THEM WILL UPSET THE FLOW ESTABLISHED BY K-KING SOLOMON!
THIS IS AN EMERGENCY, SO DON'T WORRY!
Sorry, King Solomon...
VERY WELL.
SMIRK
AHHHH
??

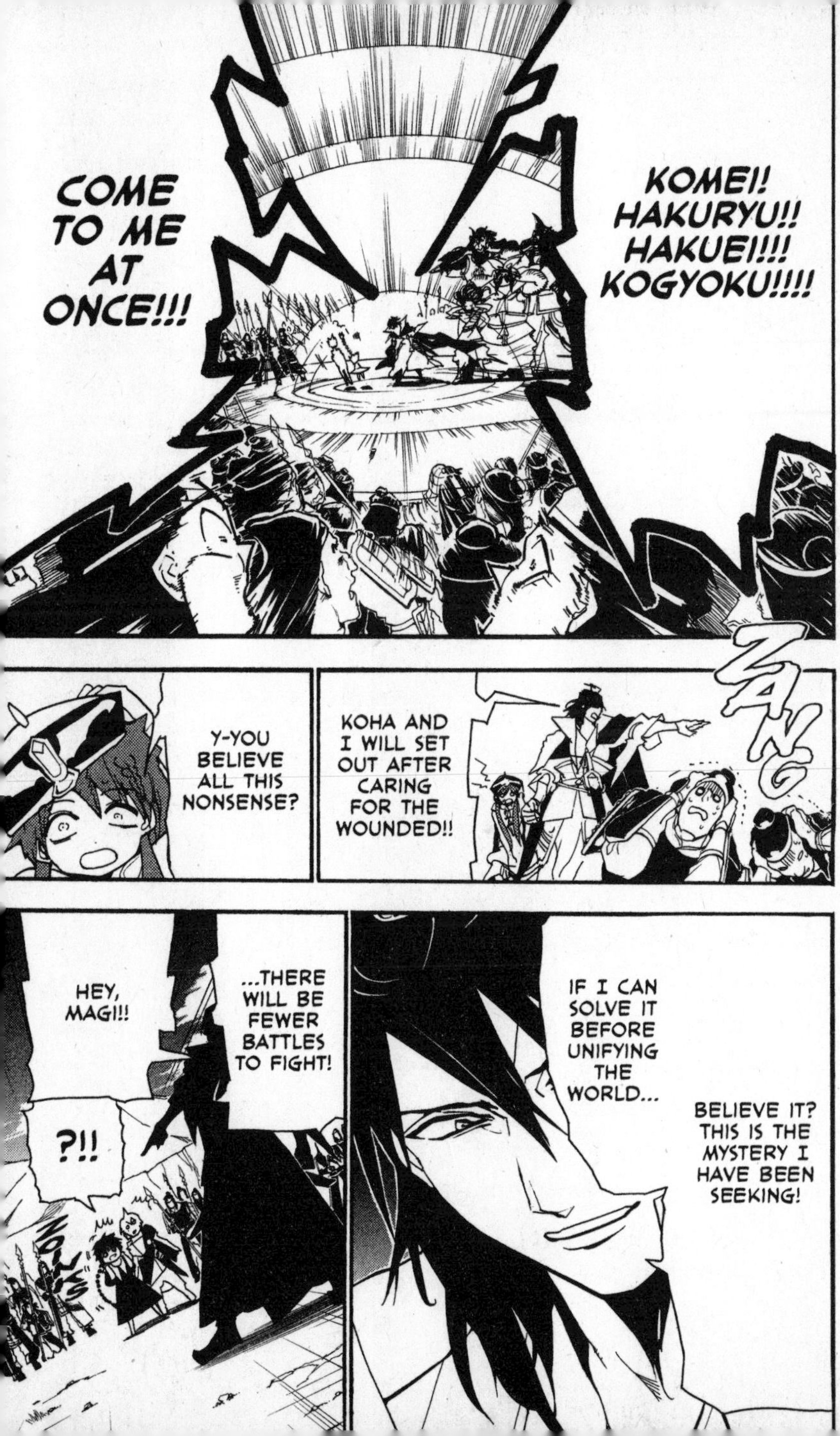
KOMEI! HAKURYU!! HAKUEI!!!! KOGYOKU!!!!
COME TO ME AT ONCE!!!
ZANG
KOHA AND I WILL SET OUT AFTER CARING FOR THE WOUNDED!!
Y-YOU BELIEVE ALL THIS NONSENSE?
BELIEVE IT? THIS IS THE MYSTERY I HAVE BEEN SEEKING!
IF I CAN SOLVE IT BEFORE UNIFYING THE WORLD...
...THERE WILL BE FEWER BATTLES TO FIGHT!
HEY, MAGI!!
?!!

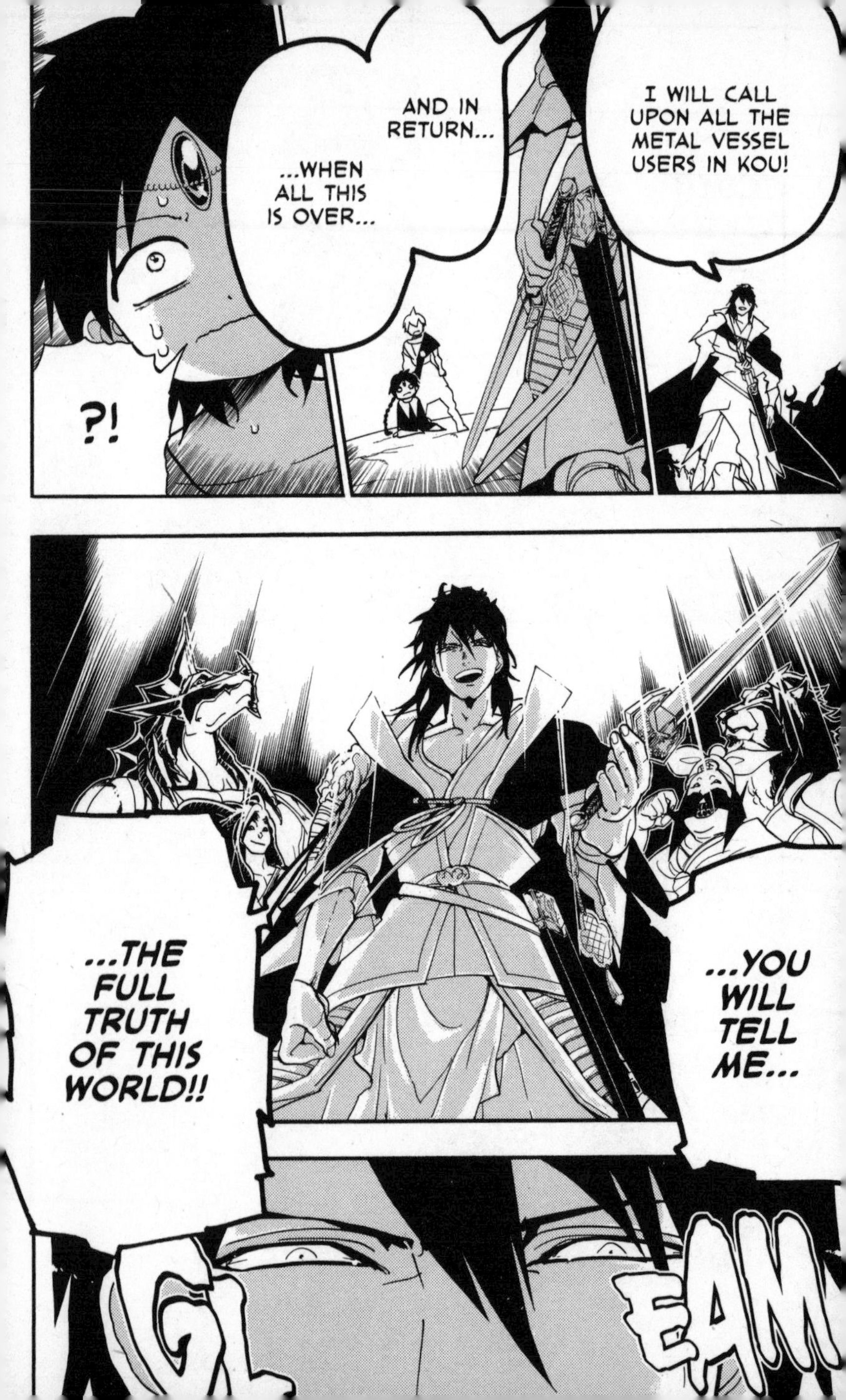
I WILL CALL UPON ALL THE METAL VESSEL USERS IN KOU!
AND IN RETURN...
...WHEN ALL THIS IS OVER...
?!
...YOU WILL TELL ME...
...THE FULL TRUTH OF THIS WORLD!!

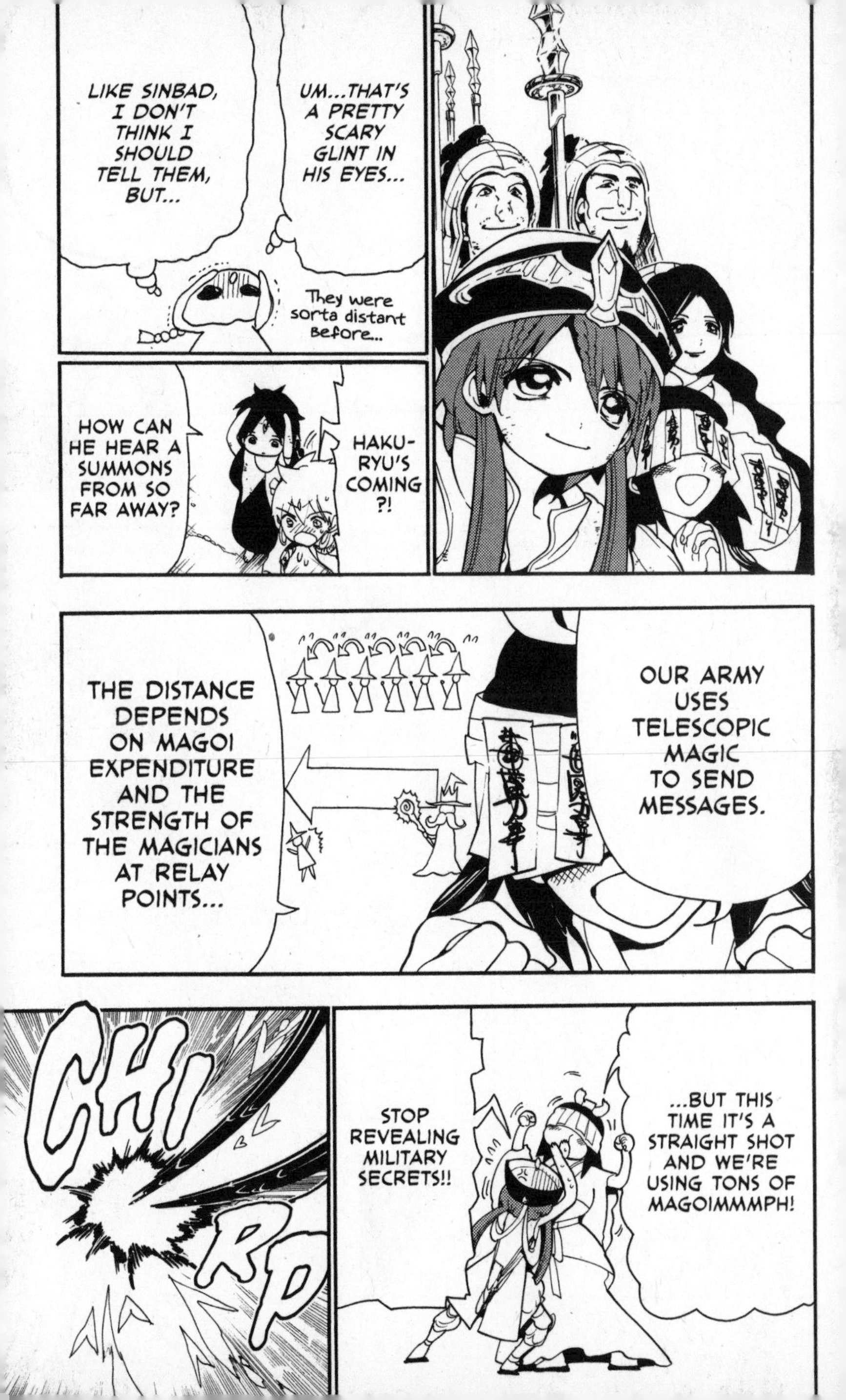
UM...THAT'S A PRETTY SCARY GLINT IN HIS EYES...
LIKE SINBAD, I DON'T THINK I SHOULD TELL THEM, BUT...
They were sorta distant before...
HAKU-RYU'S COMING?!
HOW CAN HE HEAR A SUMMONS FROM SO FAR AWAY?
OUR ARMY USES TELESCOPIC MAGIC TO SEND MESSAGES.
THE DISTANCE DEPENDS ON MAGOI EXPENDITURE AND THE STRENGTH OF THE MAGICIANS AT RELAY POINTS...
...BUT THIS TIME IT'S A STRAIGHT SHOT AND WE'RE USING TONS OF MAGOIMMMPH!
STOP REVEALING MILITARY SECRETS!!
CHIRP

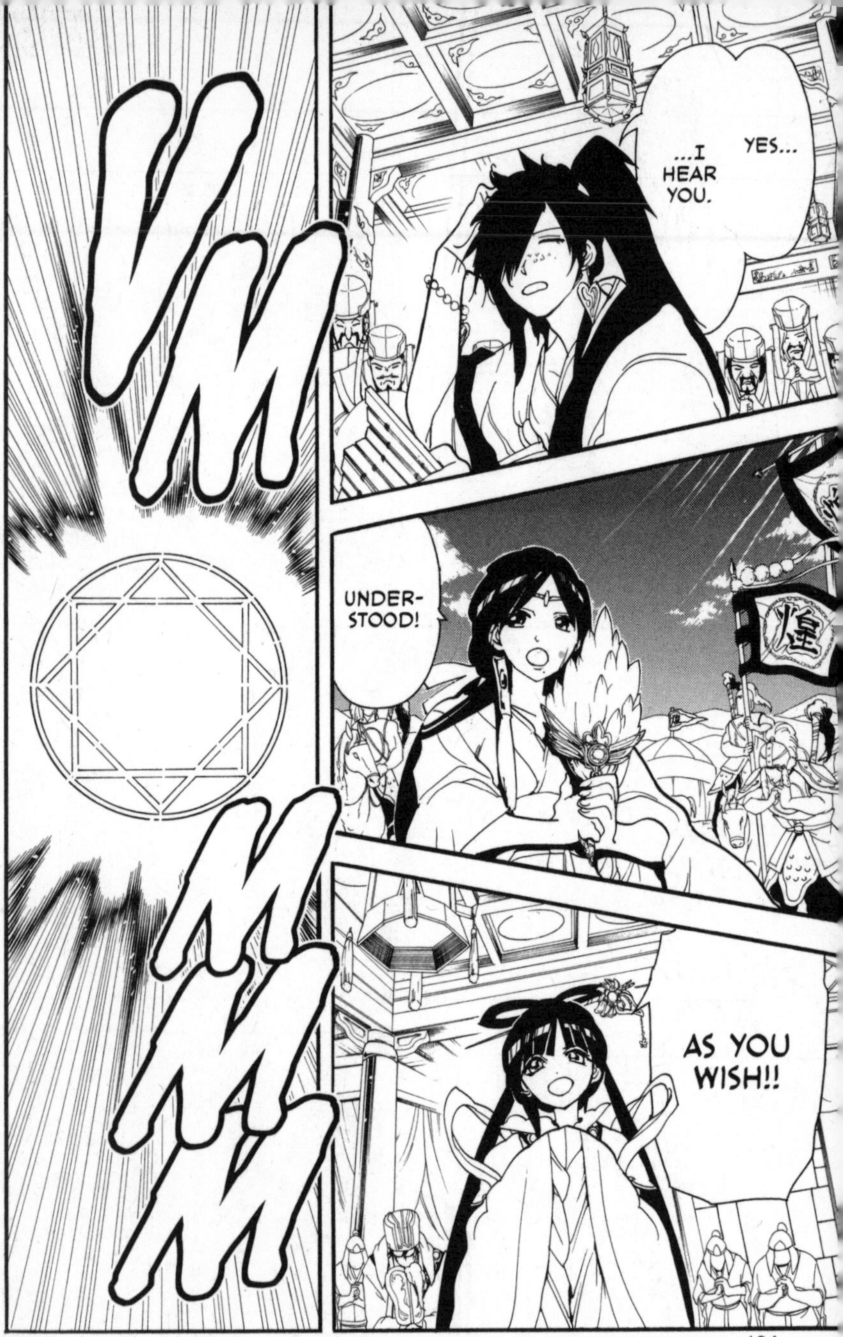
YES...
...I HEAR YOU.
UNDER-STOOD!
AS YOU WISH!!

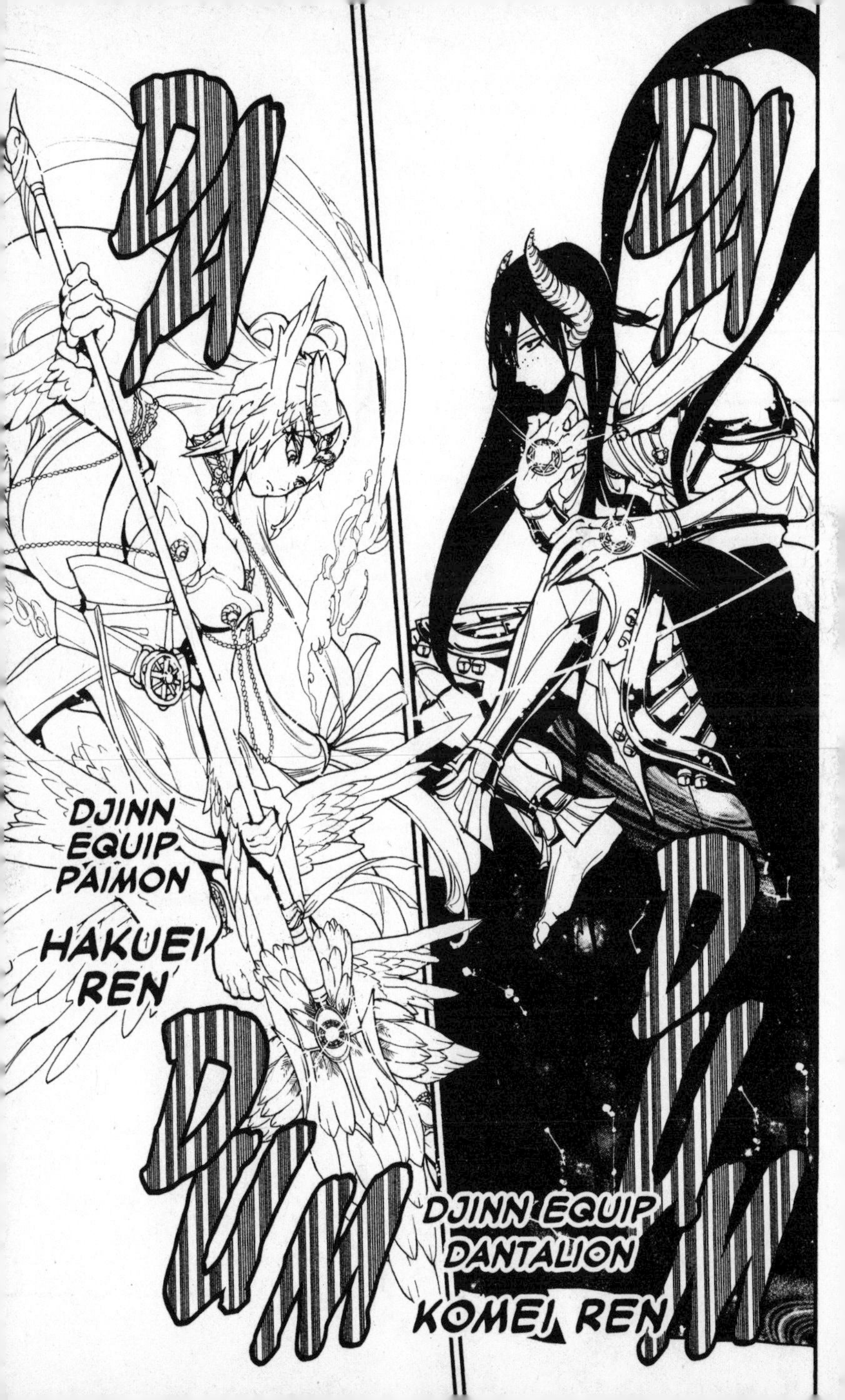
DJINN EQUIP DANTALION
KOMEI REN
DJINN EQUIP PAIMON
HAKUEI REN

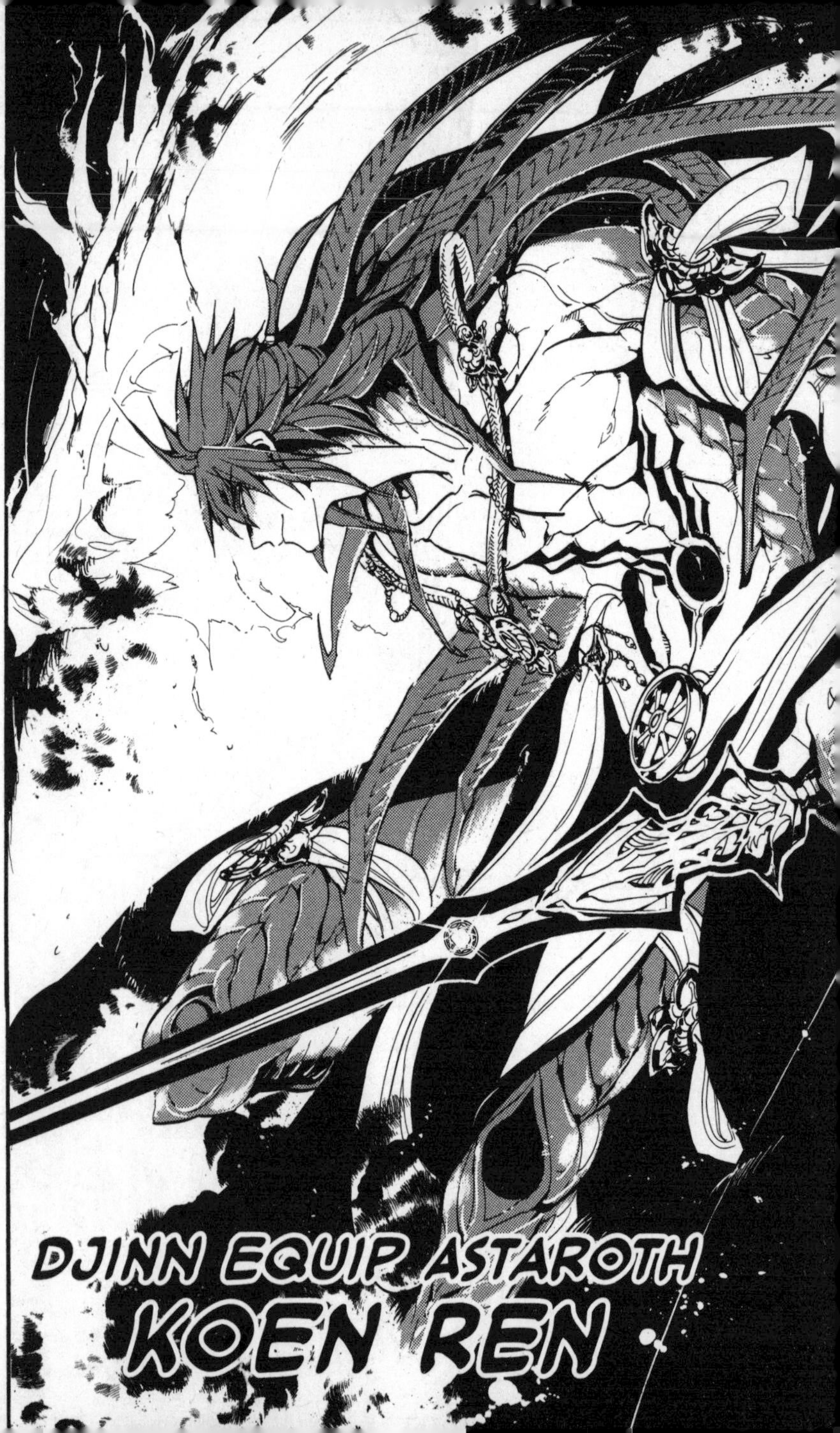
DJINN EQUIP ASTAROTH
KOEN REN

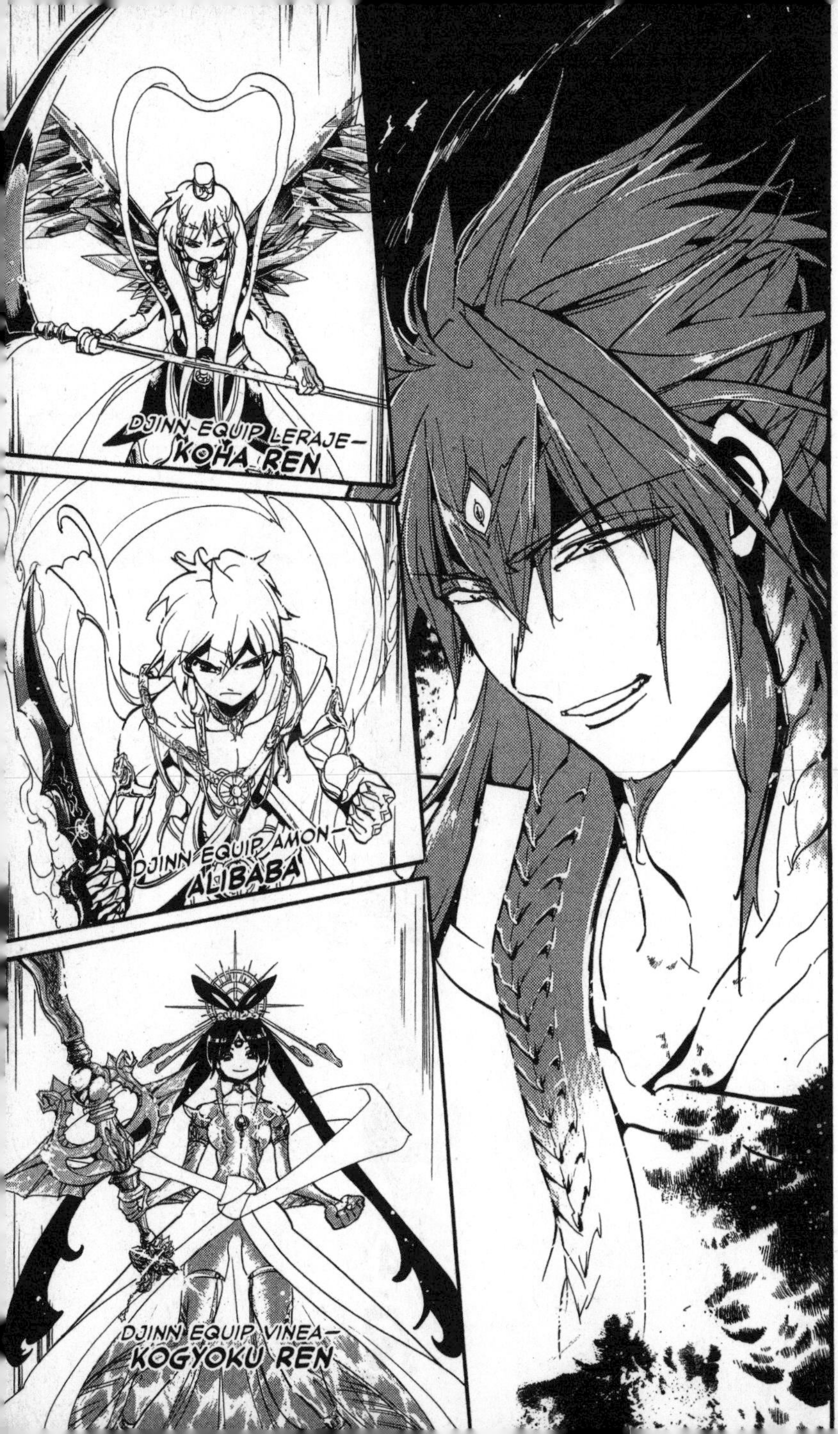
DJINN EQUIP LERAJE—
KOHA REN
DJINN EQUIP AMON—
ALIBABA
DJINN EQUIP VINEA—
KOGYOKU REN

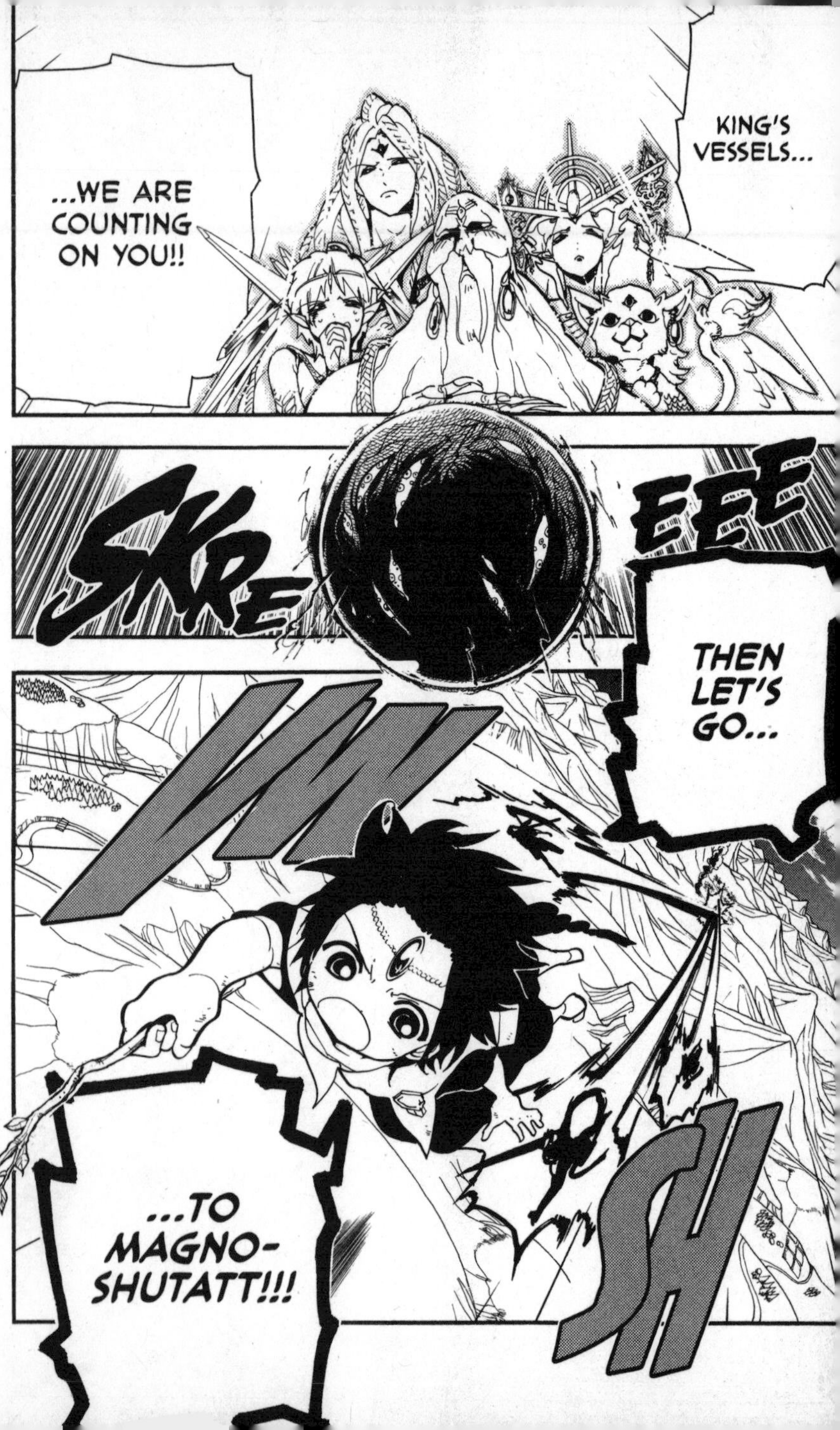
KING'S VESSELS...
...WE ARE COUNTING ON YOU!!
SKRE
EEE
THEN LET'S GO...
WH
...TO MAGNO-SHUTATT!!!
SH

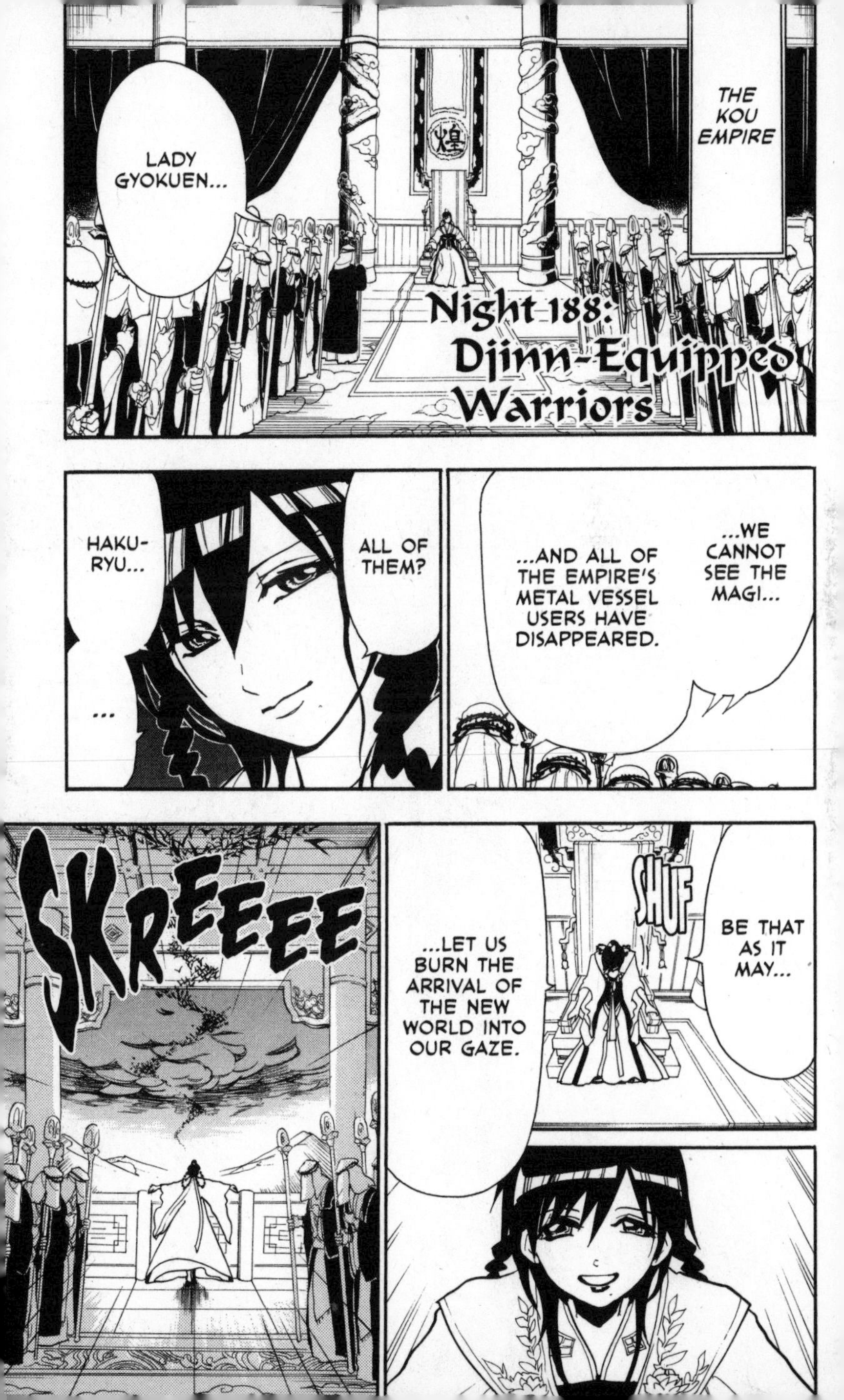
THE KOU EMPIRE
LADY GYOKUEN...
Night 188: Djinn-Equipped Warriors
...WE CANNOT SEE THE MAGI...
...AND ALL OF THE EMPIRE'S METAL VESSEL USERS HAVE DISAPPEARED.
ALL OF THEM?
HAKU-RYU...
...
SHUF
BE THAT AS IT MAY...
...LET US BURN THE ARRIVAL OF THE NEW WORLD INTO OUR GAZE.
SKREEEE

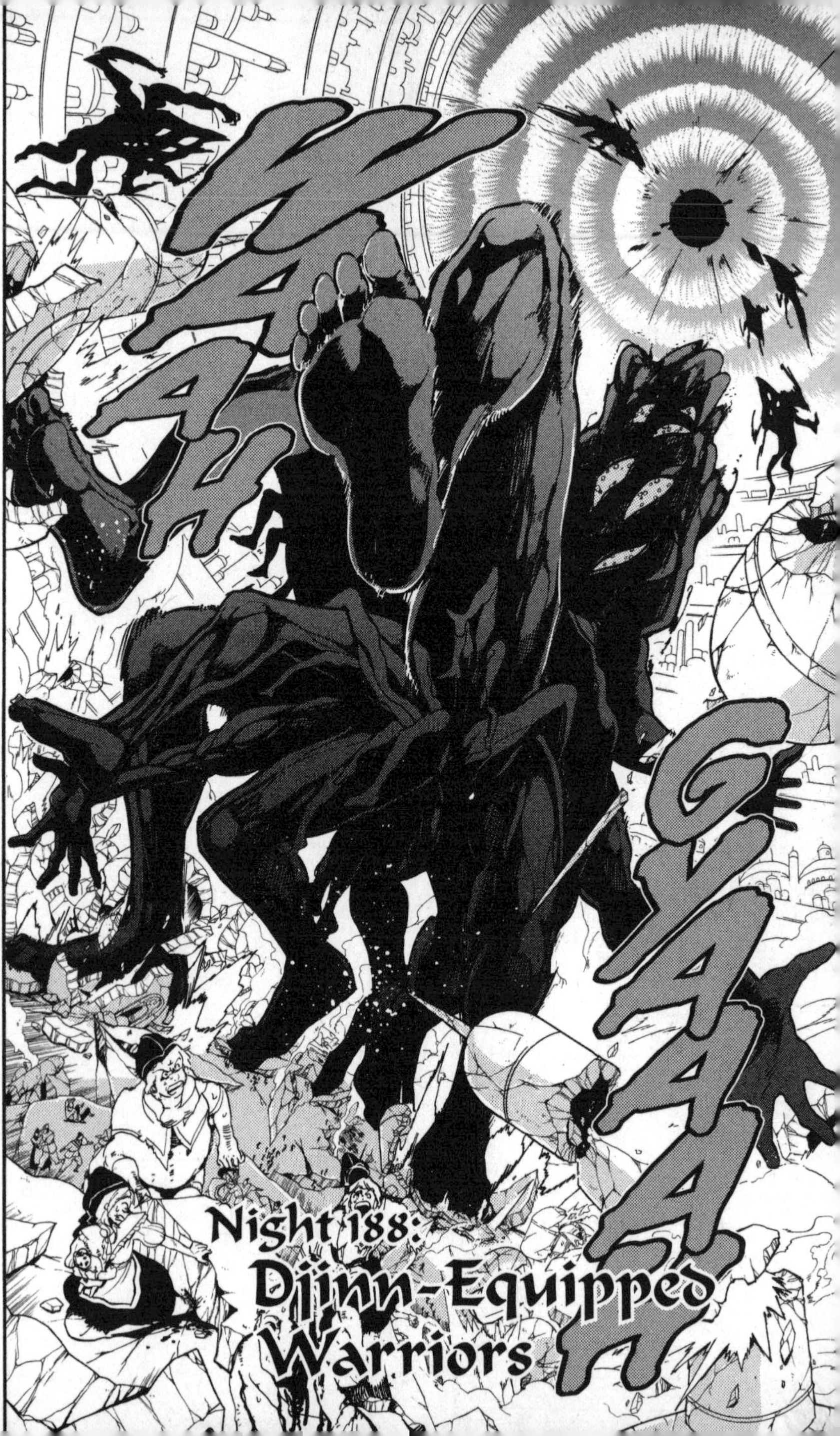
Night 188:
Djinn-Equipped
Warriors

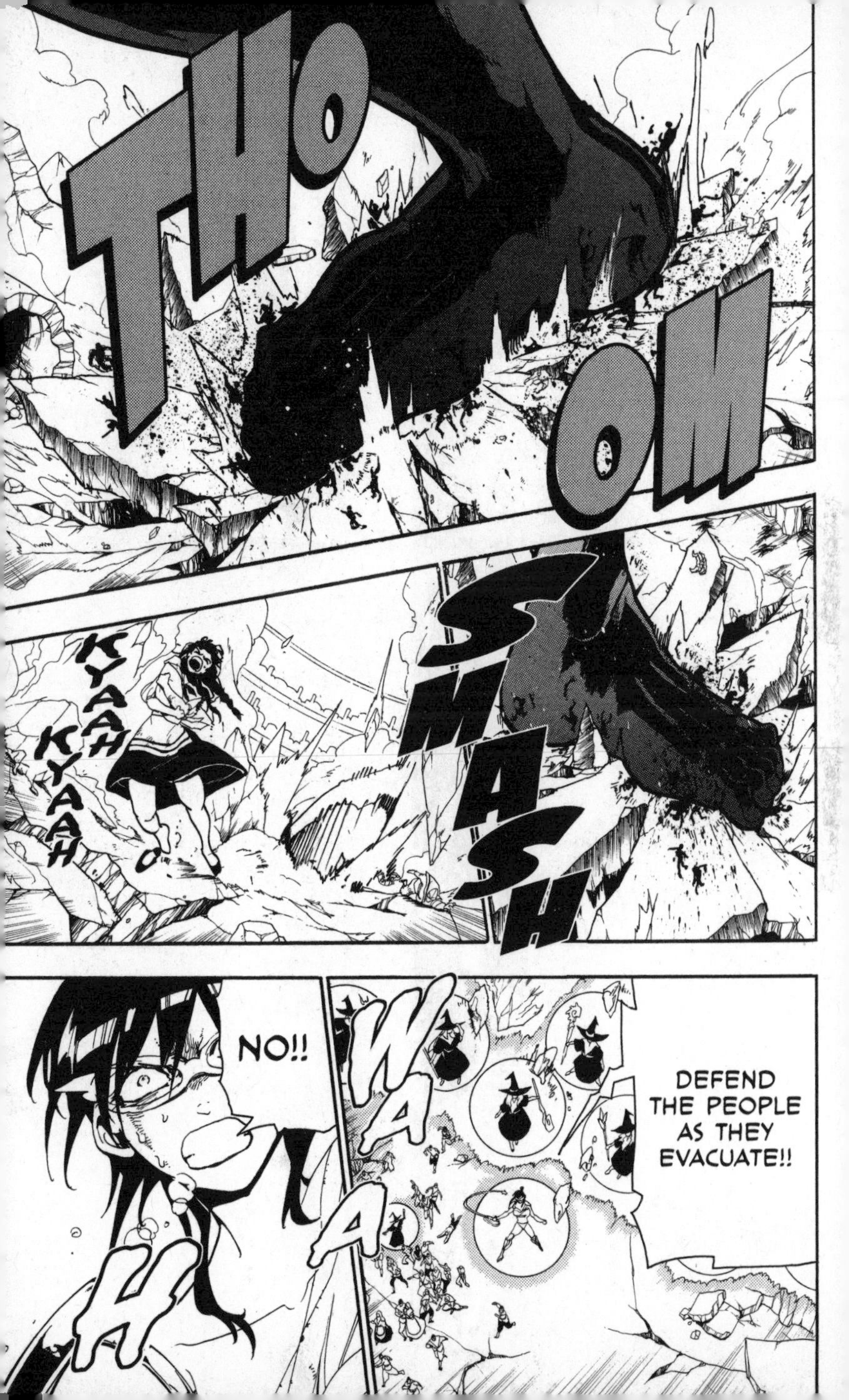
THOOM
SMASH
KYAAH KYAAH KYAAH
DEFEND THE PEOPLE AS THEY EVACUATE!!
WAA
NO!!
HA

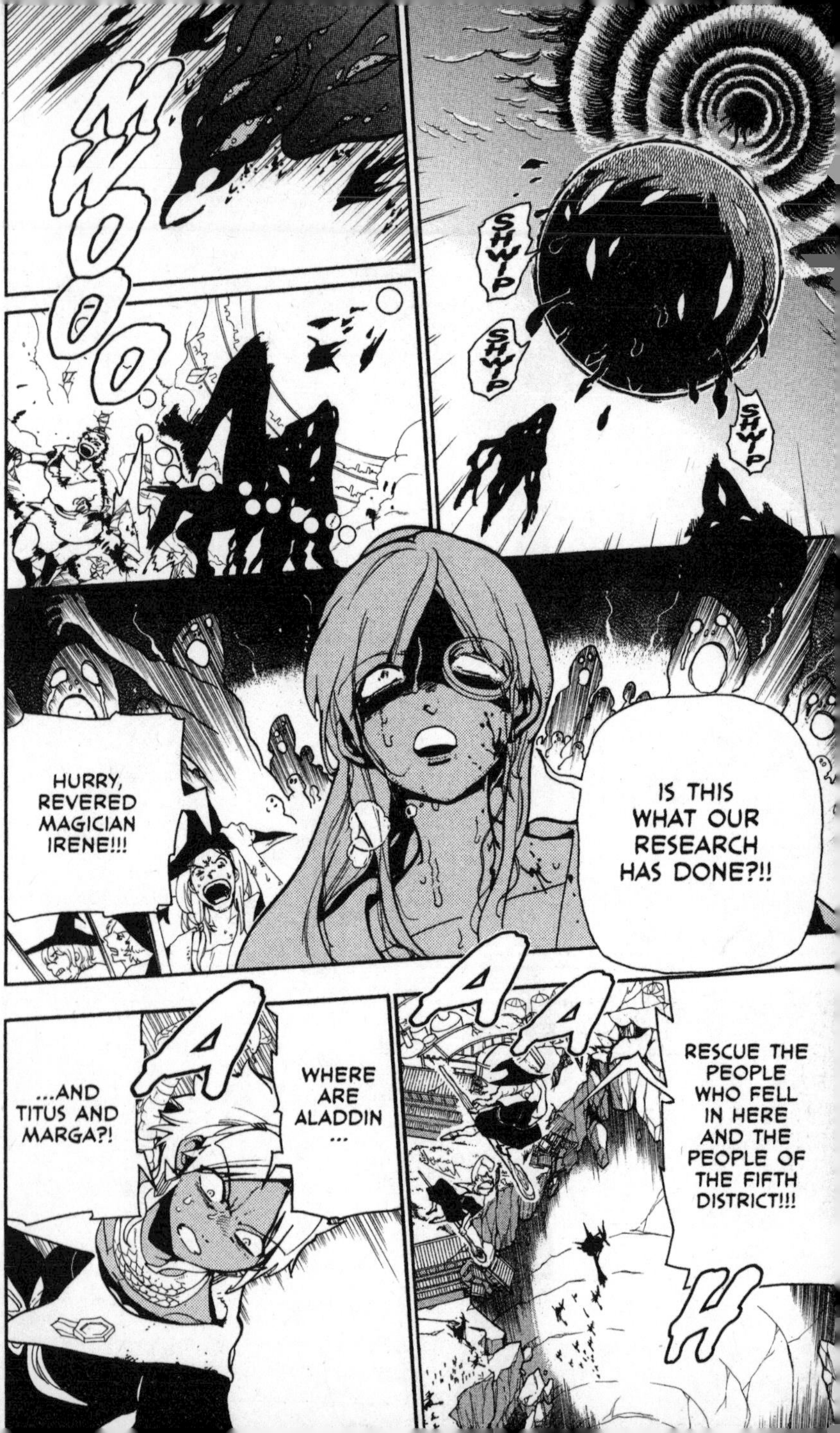

SHWIP
SHWIP
SHWIP
MWOOOO
IS THIS WHAT OUR RESEARCH HAS DONE?!!
HURRY, REVERED MAGICIAN IRENE!!!
AAAH
RESCUE THE PEOPLE WHO FELL IN HERE AND THE PEOPLE OF THE FIFTH DISTRICT!!!
WHERE ARE ALADDIN ...
...AND TITUS AND MARGA?!

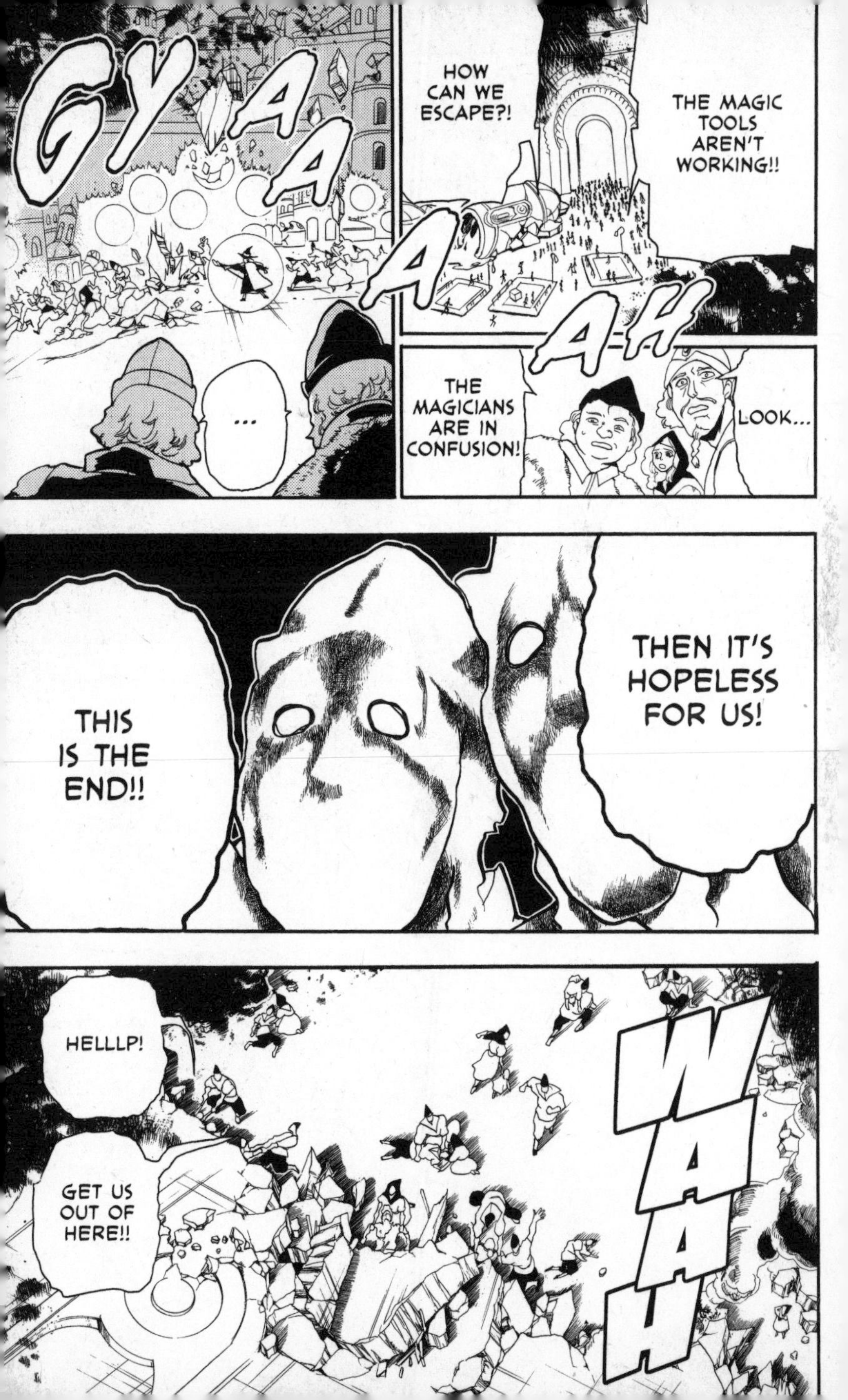
THE MAGIC TOOLS AREN'T WORKING!!
HOW CAN WE ESCAPE?!
LOOK...
THE MAGICIANS ARE IN CONFUSION!
GYAAAAAH
...
THEN IT'S HOPELESS FOR US!
THIS IS THE END!!
WAAAH
HELLLP!
GET US OUT OF HERE!!

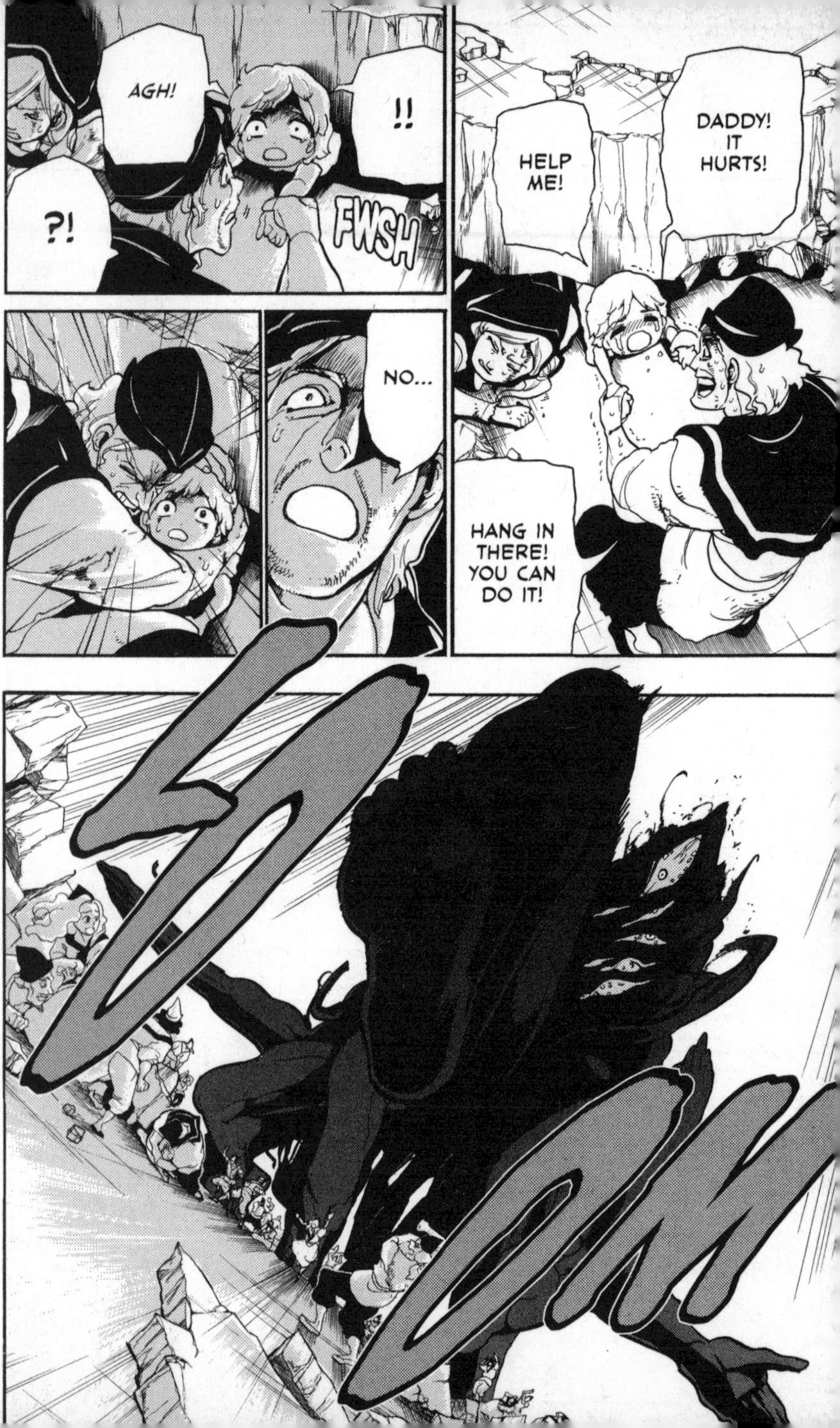
DADDY! IT HURTS!
HELP ME!
HANG IN THERE! YOU CAN DO IT!
!!
FWSH
AGH!
?!
NO...

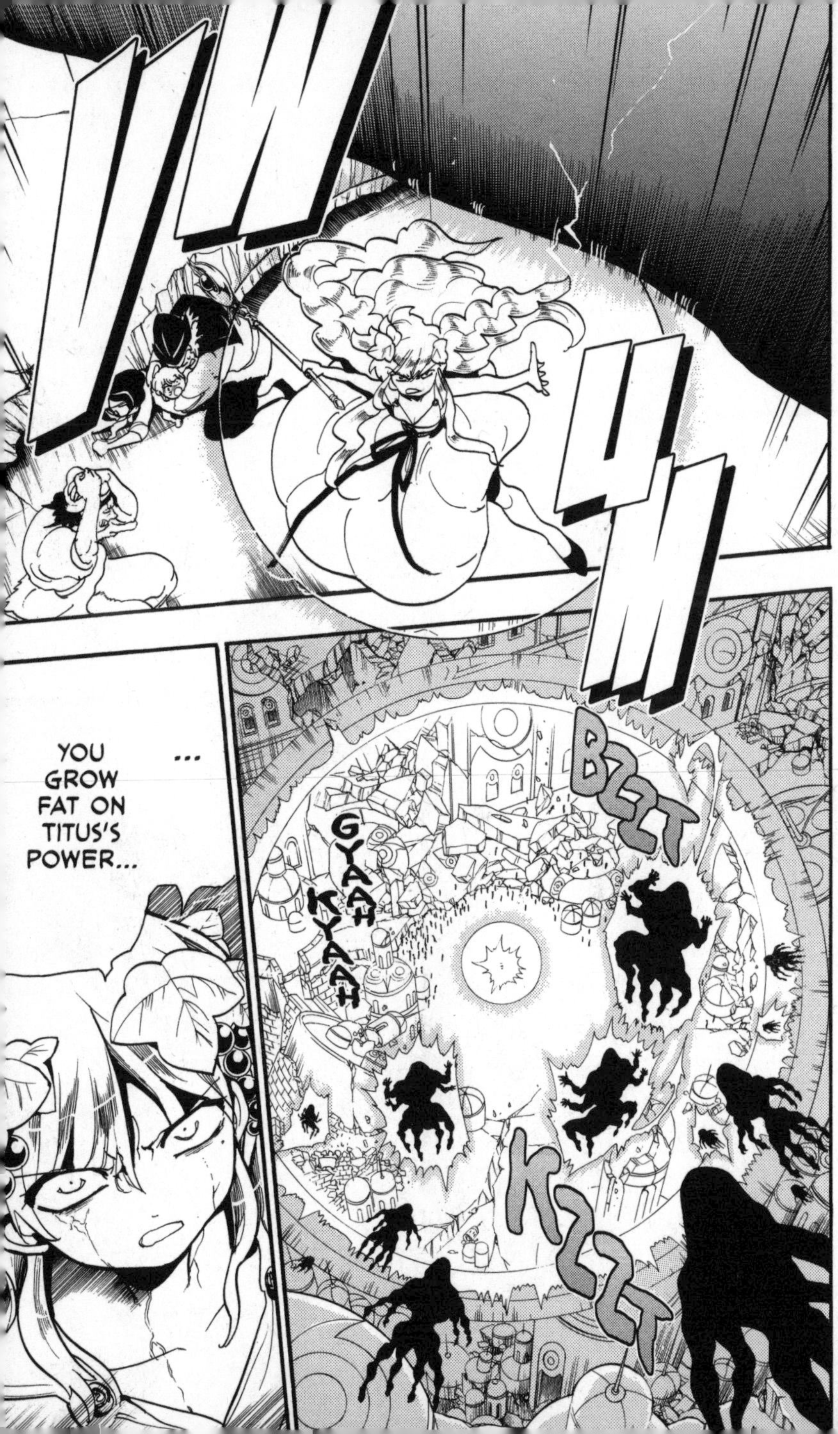
BZZT
GYAAH
KYAAH
KZZZT
...
YOU GROW FAT ON TITUS'S POWER...

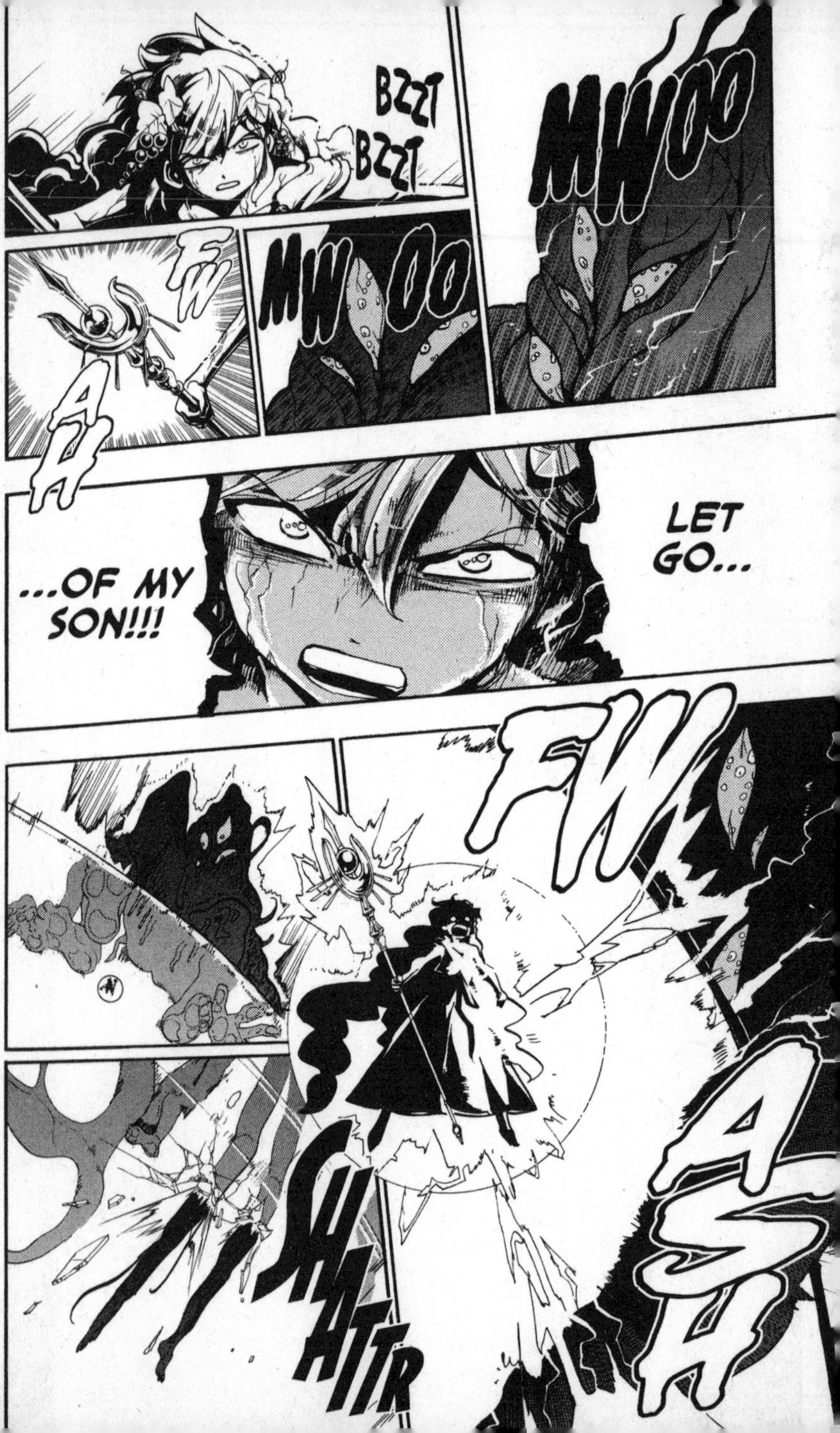
MWOO
BZZT
BZZT
MWOO
FWAH
LET GO...
...OF MY SON!!!
FWASH
SHATTR

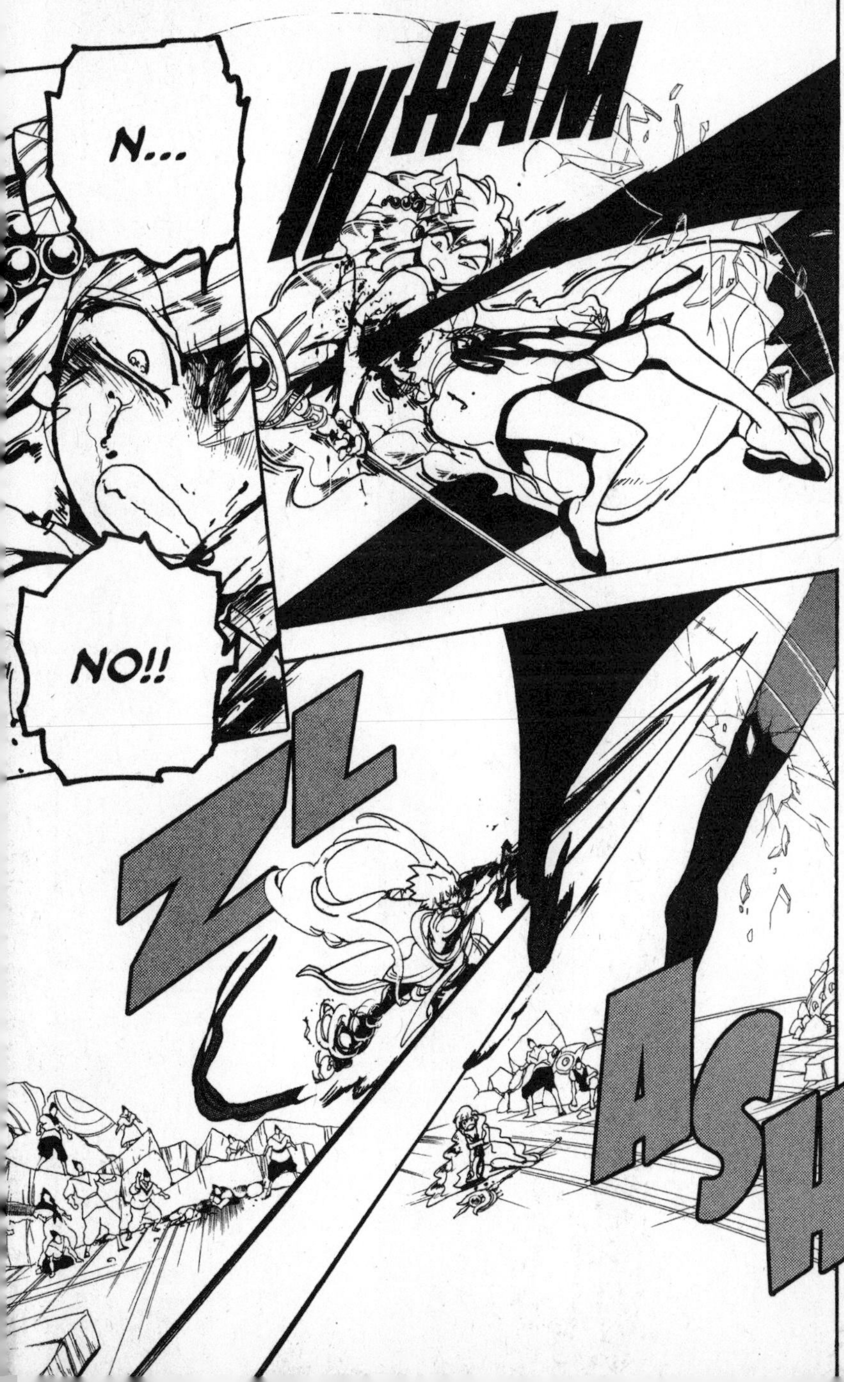
WHAM
N...
NO!!
ZLASH

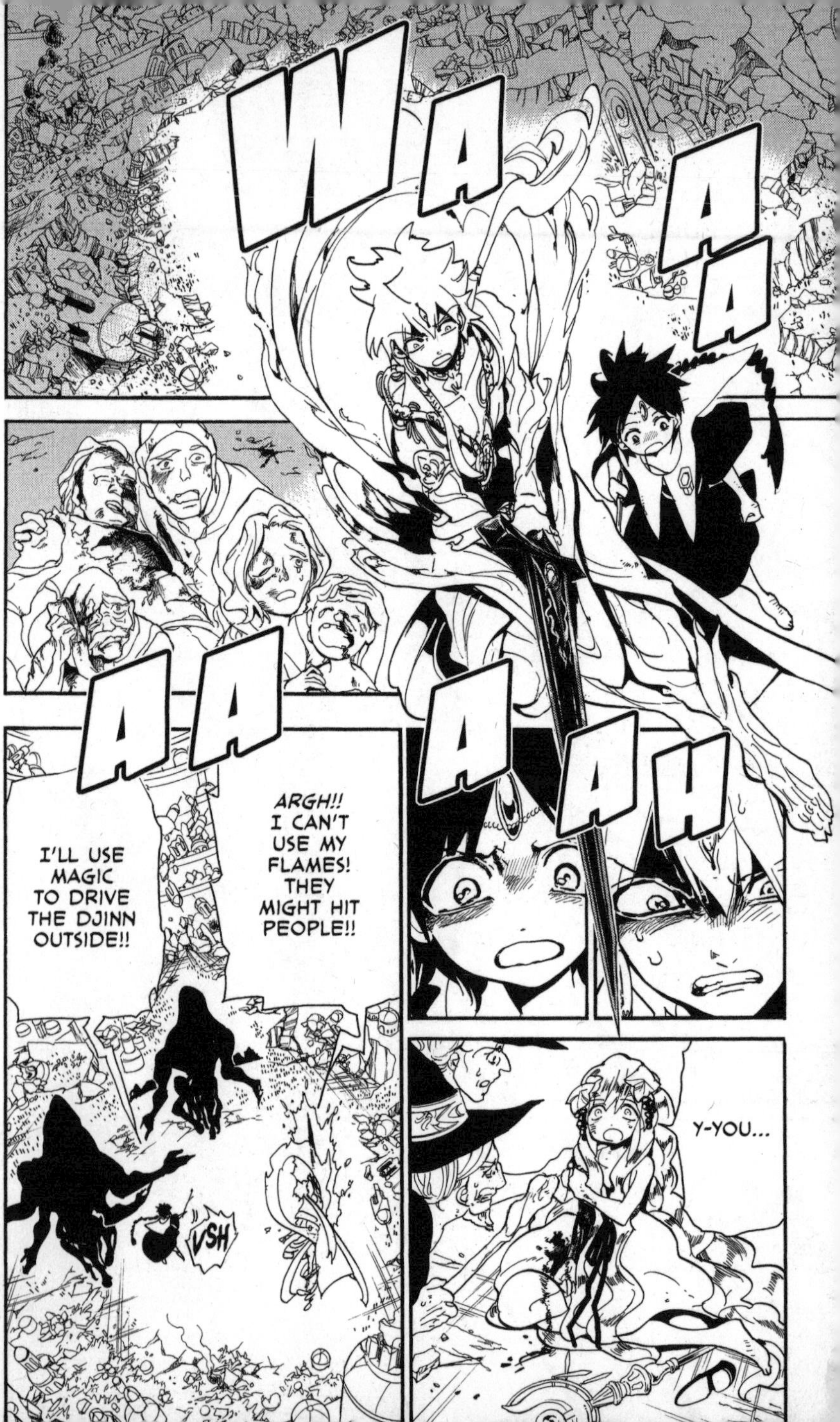
WAAAAAAAH
Y-YOU...
ARGH!! I CAN'T USE MY FLAMES! THEY MIGHT HIT PEOPLE!!
I'LL USE MAGIC TO DRIVE THE DJINN OUTSIDE!!
VSH

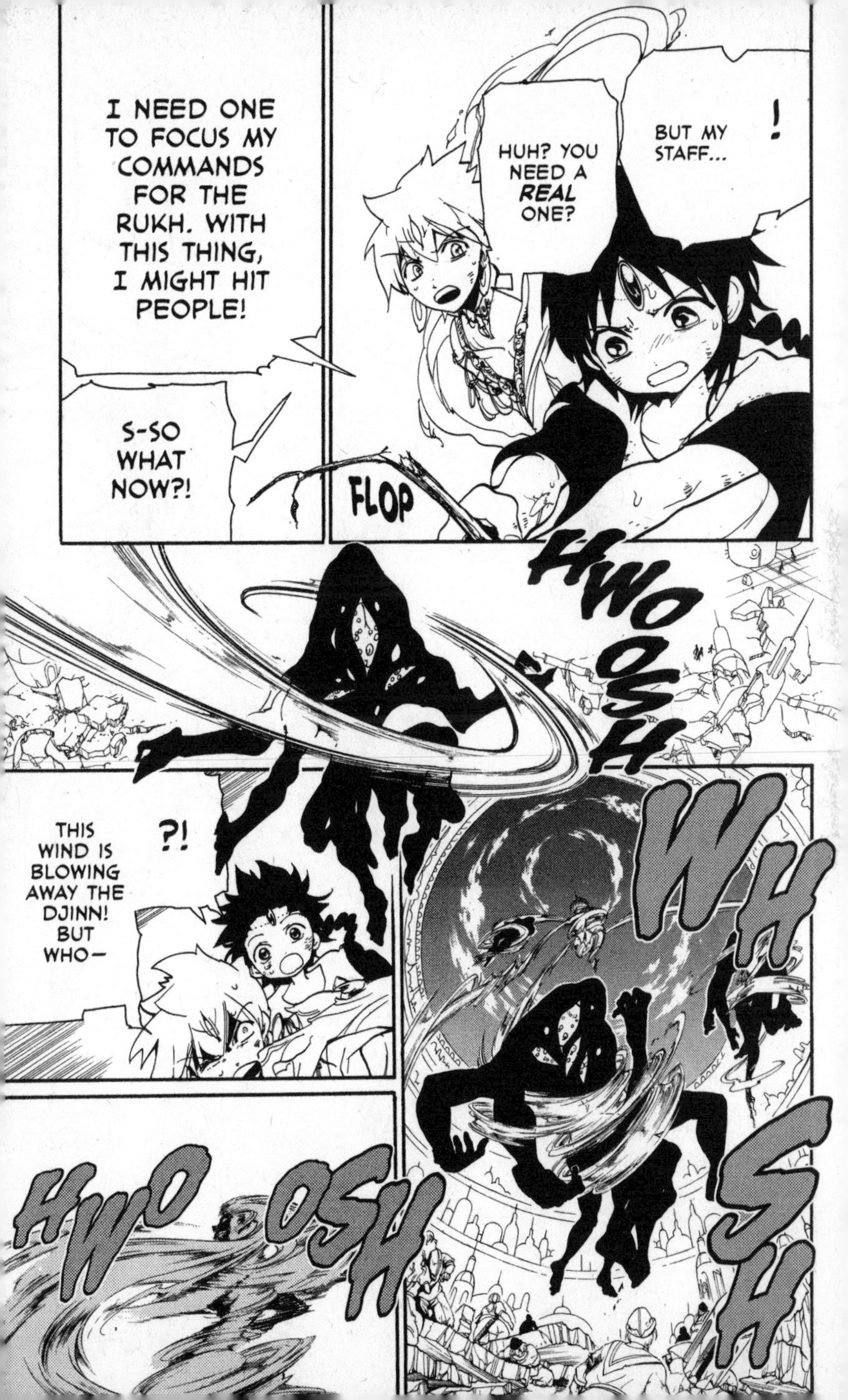
!
BUT MY STAFF...
HUH? YOU NEED A *REAL* ONE?
FLOP
I NEED ONE TO FOCUS MY COMMANDS FOR THE RUKH. WITH THIS THING, I MIGHT HIT PEOPLE!
S-SO WHAT NOW?!
HWOOSH
WH
SH
?!
THIS WIND IS BLOWING AWAY THE DJINN! BUT WHO—
HWOOSH

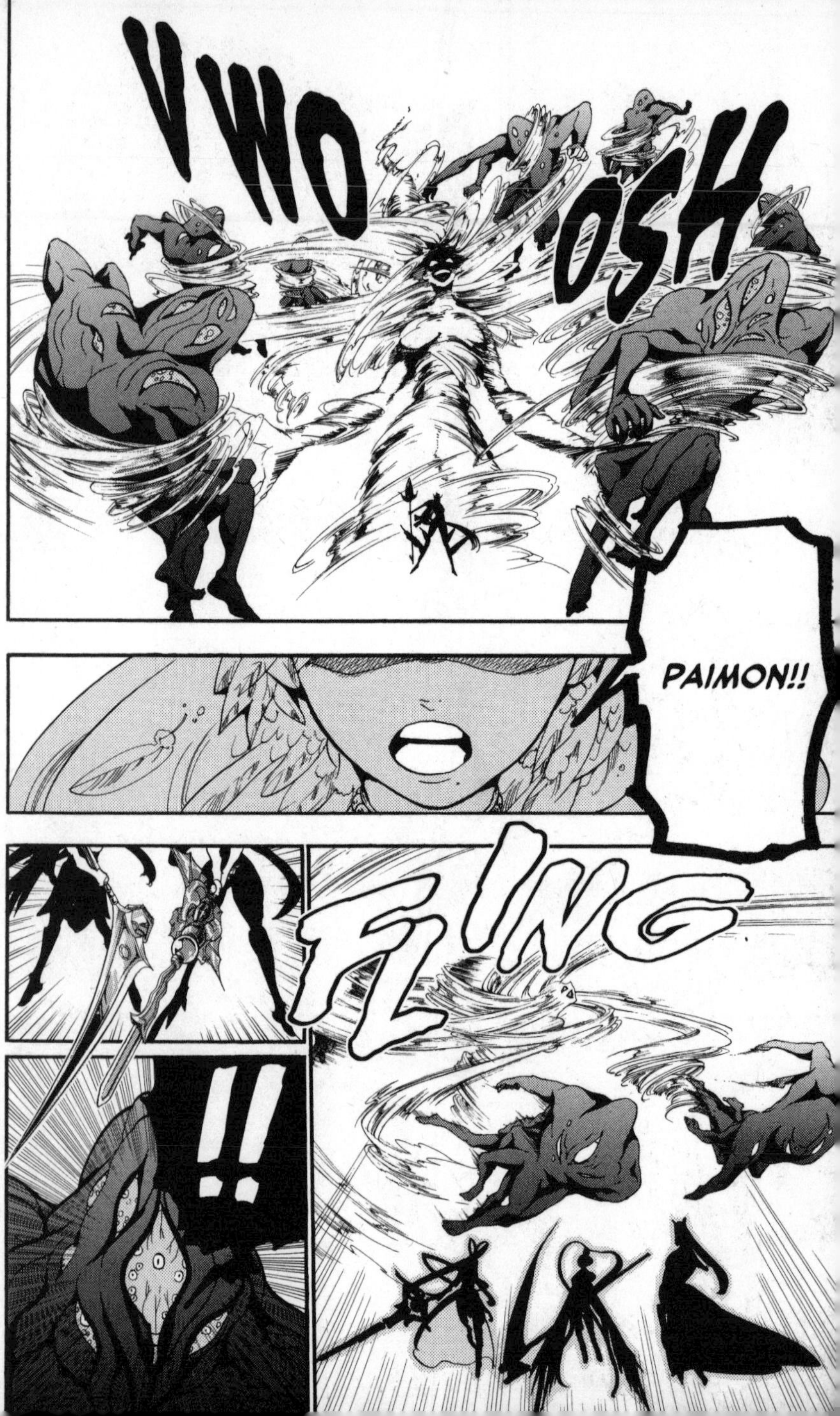
VWOOSH
PAIMON!!
FLING
!!

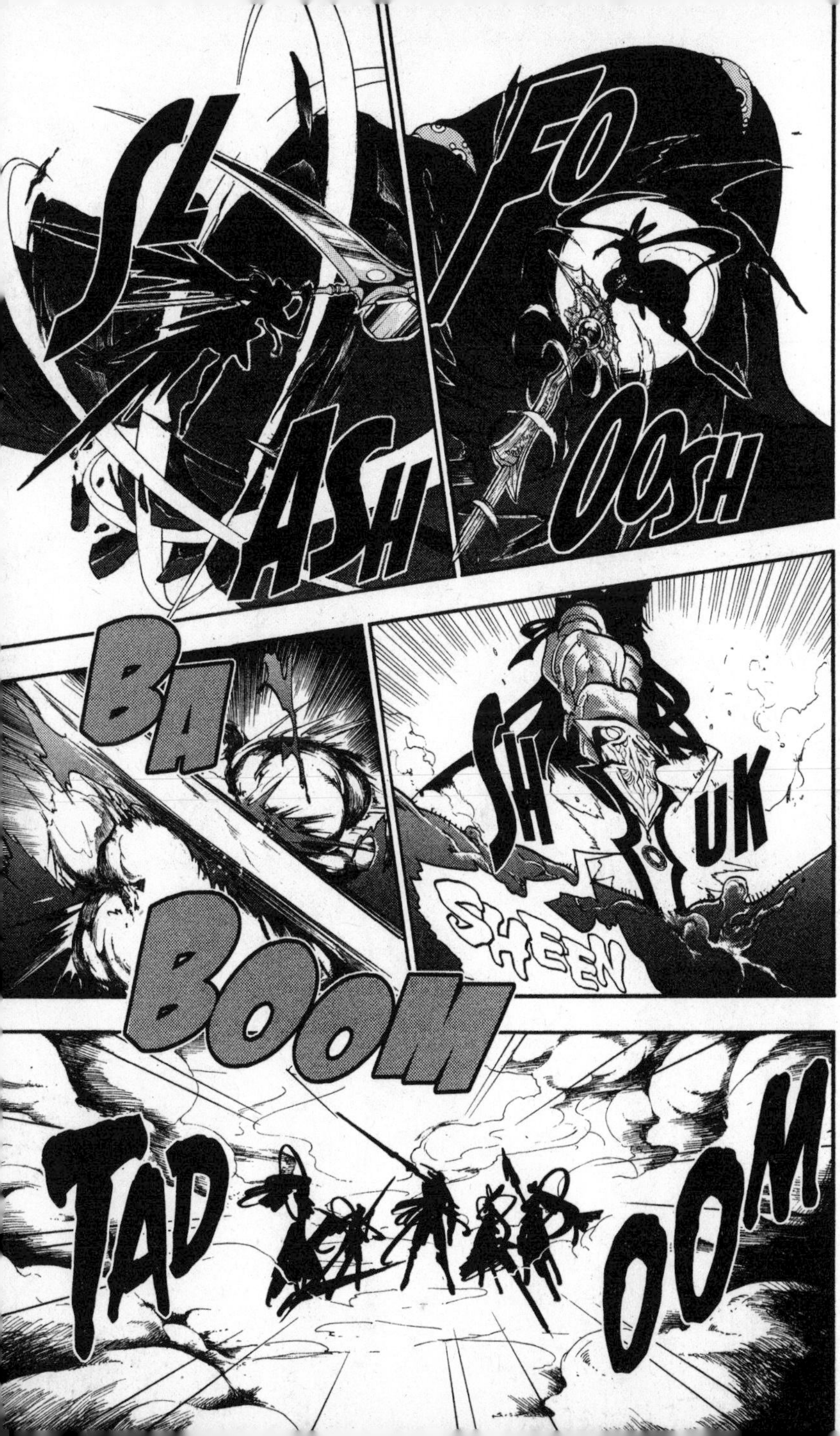
FOOOSH
SLASH
SHUK
SHEEN
BABOOM
TADOOOM

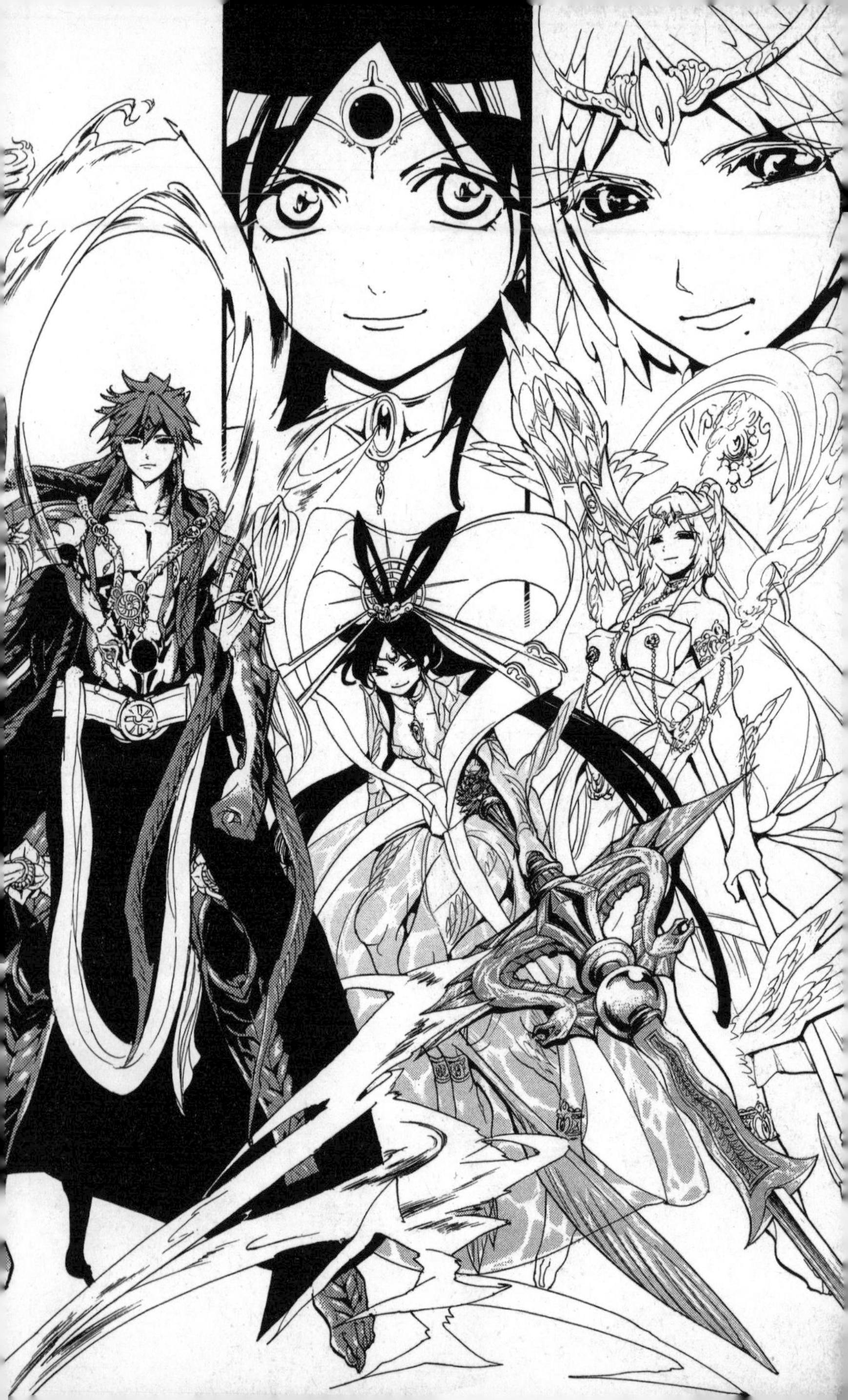

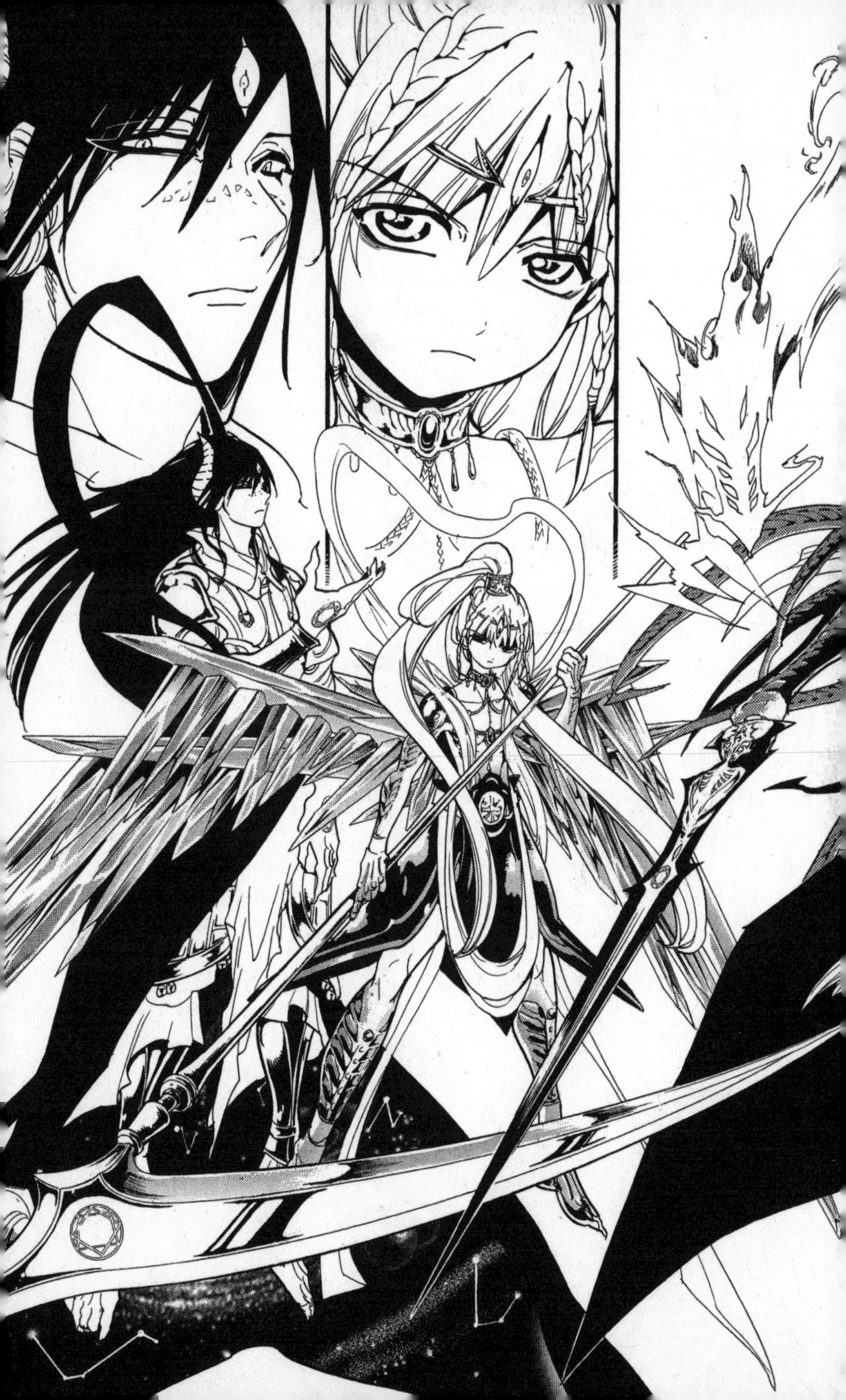

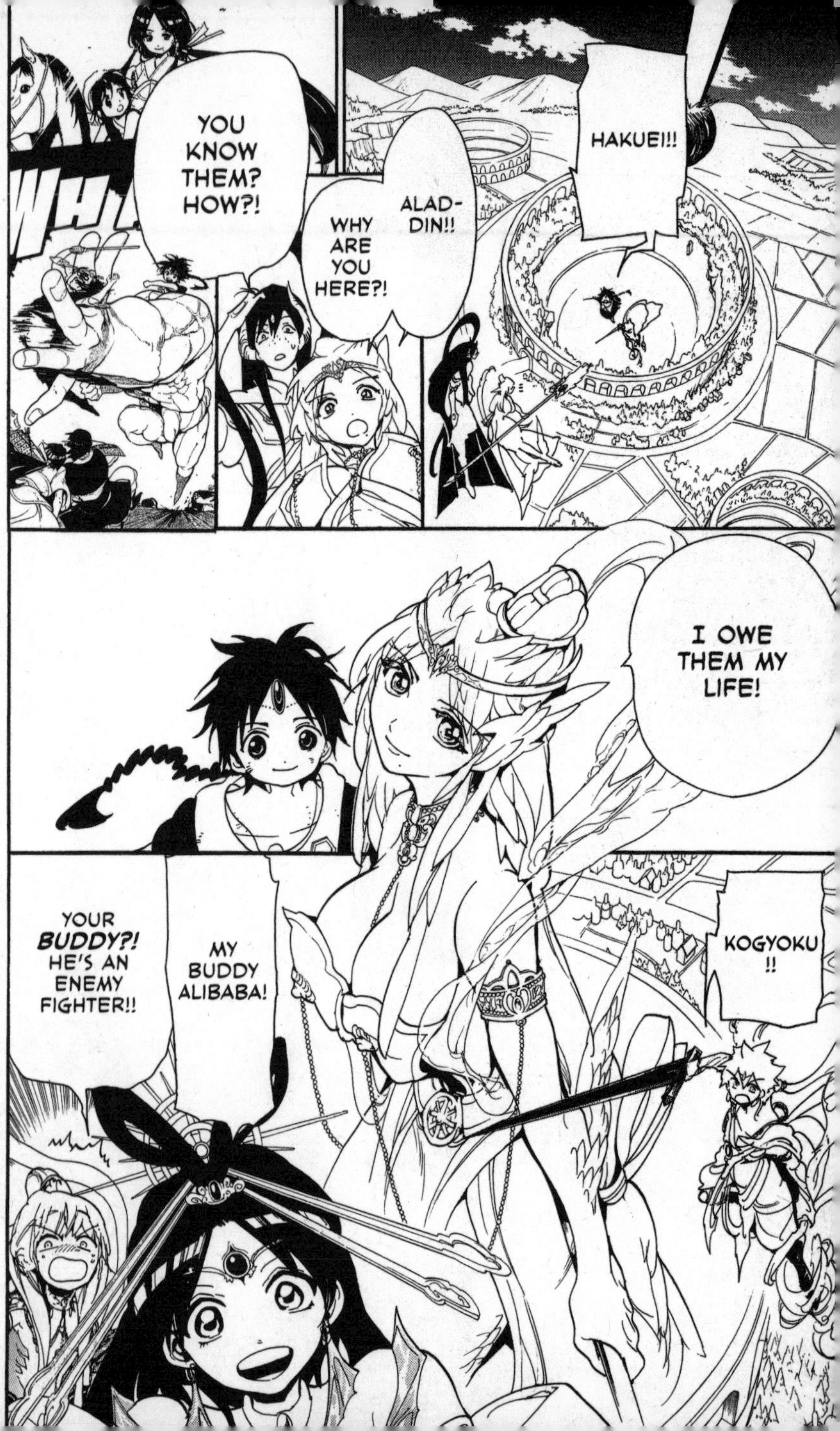
HAKUEI!!!
ALAD-DIN!!
WHY ARE YOU HERE?!
YOU KNOW THEM? HOW?!
I OWE THEM MY LIFE!
KOGYOKU!!
MY BUDDY ALIBABA!
YOUR BUDDY?! HE'S AN ENEMY FIGHTER!!

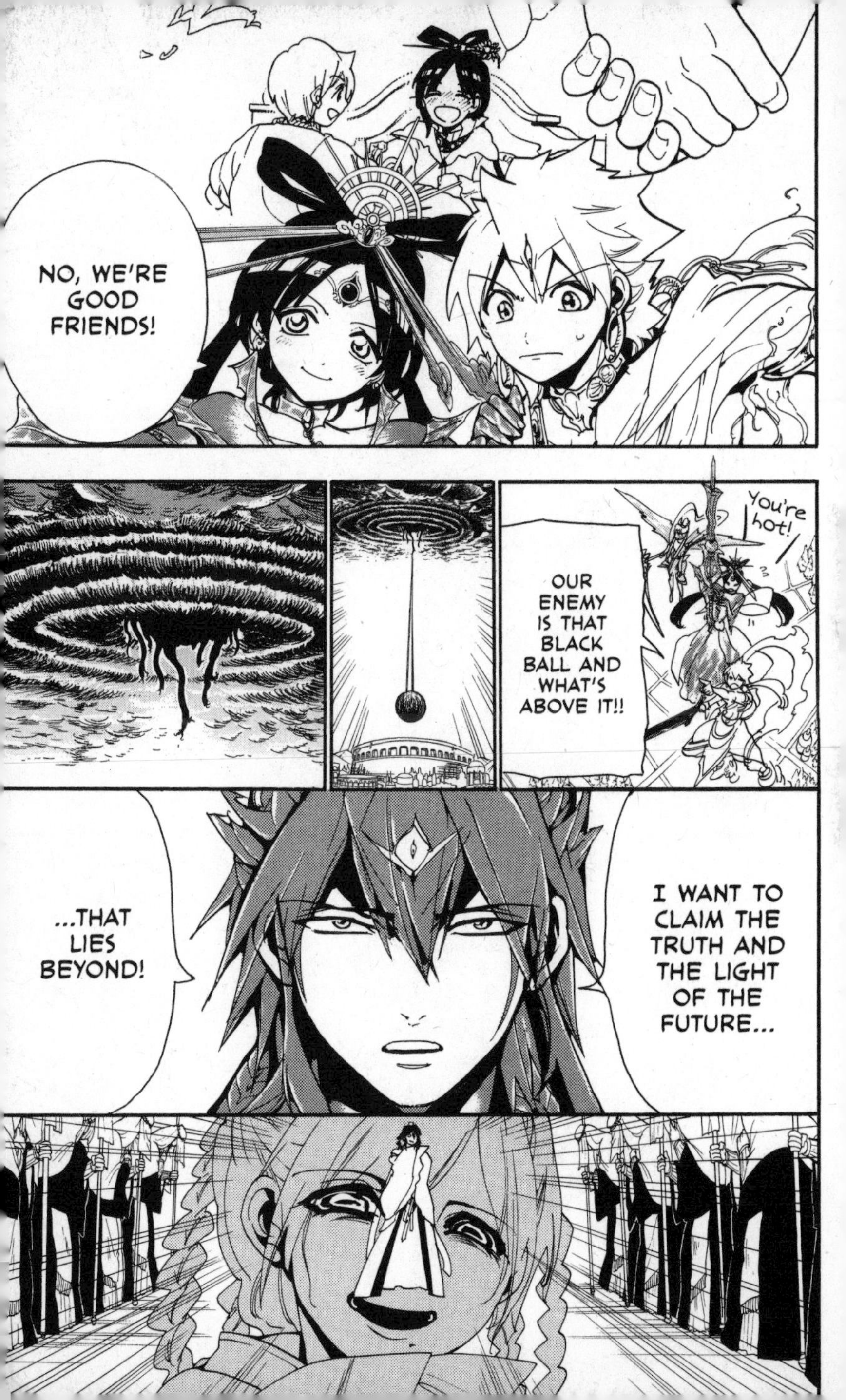
NO, WE'RE GOOD FRIENDS!
You're hot!
OUR ENEMY IS THAT BLACK BALL AND WHAT'S ABOVE IT!!
I WANT TO CLAIM THE TRUTH AND THE LIGHT OF THE FUTURE...
...THAT LIES BEYOND!

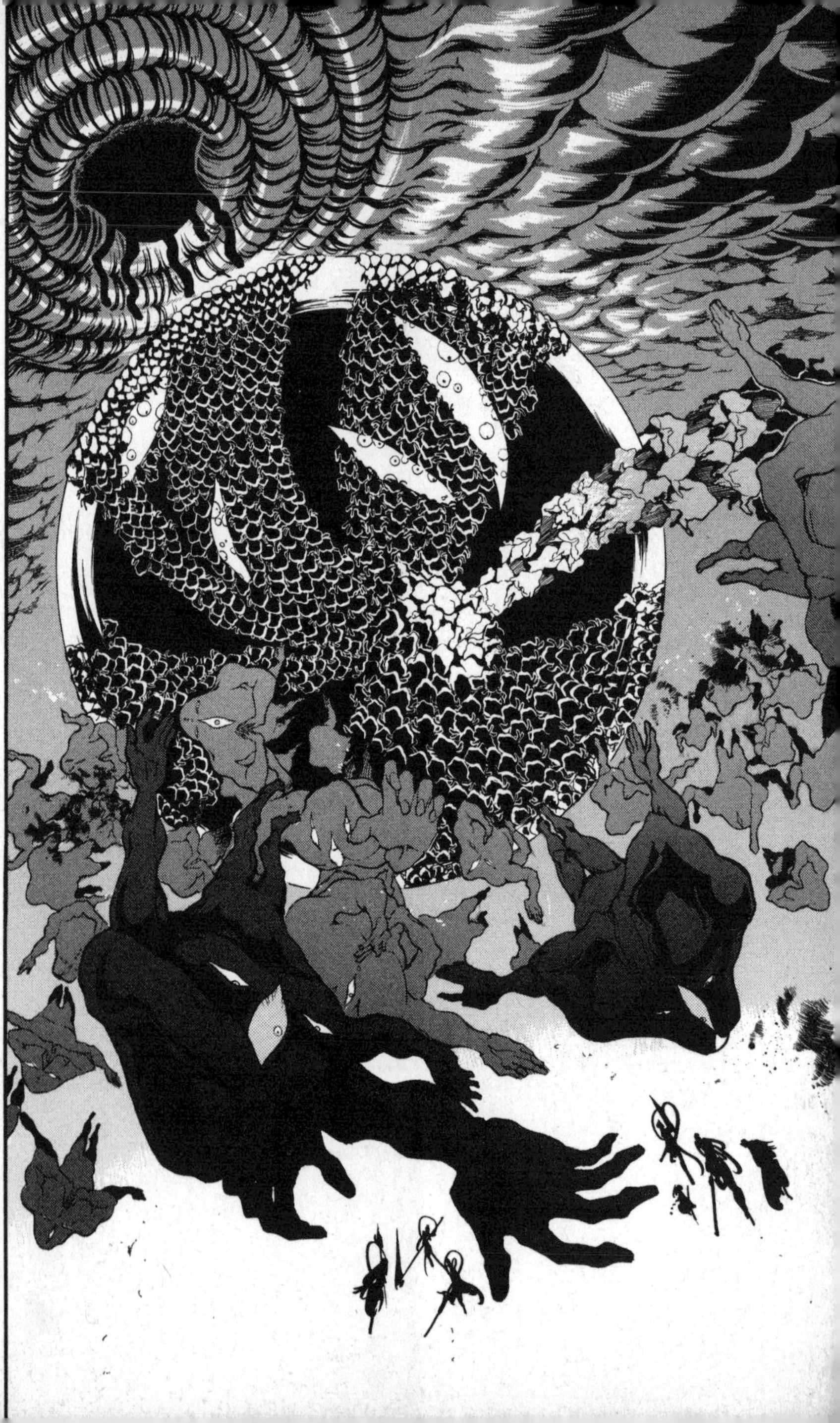

MAGI

The labyrinth of magic

19

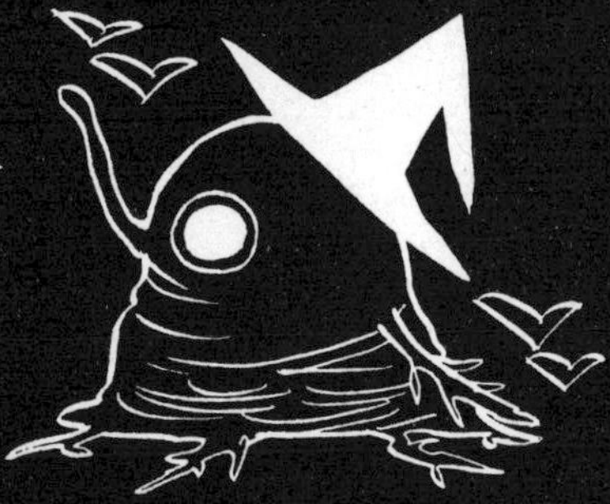

Staff

Story & Art

Shinobu Ohtaka

Regular Assistants

Hiro Maizima

Yurika Isozaki

Tomo Niiya

Yuiko Akiyama

Megi

Aya Umoto

Editor

Kazuaki Ishibashi

Sales & Promotion

Yuki Mizusawa

Atsushi Chiku

Designer

Yasuo Shimura + Bay Bridge Studio

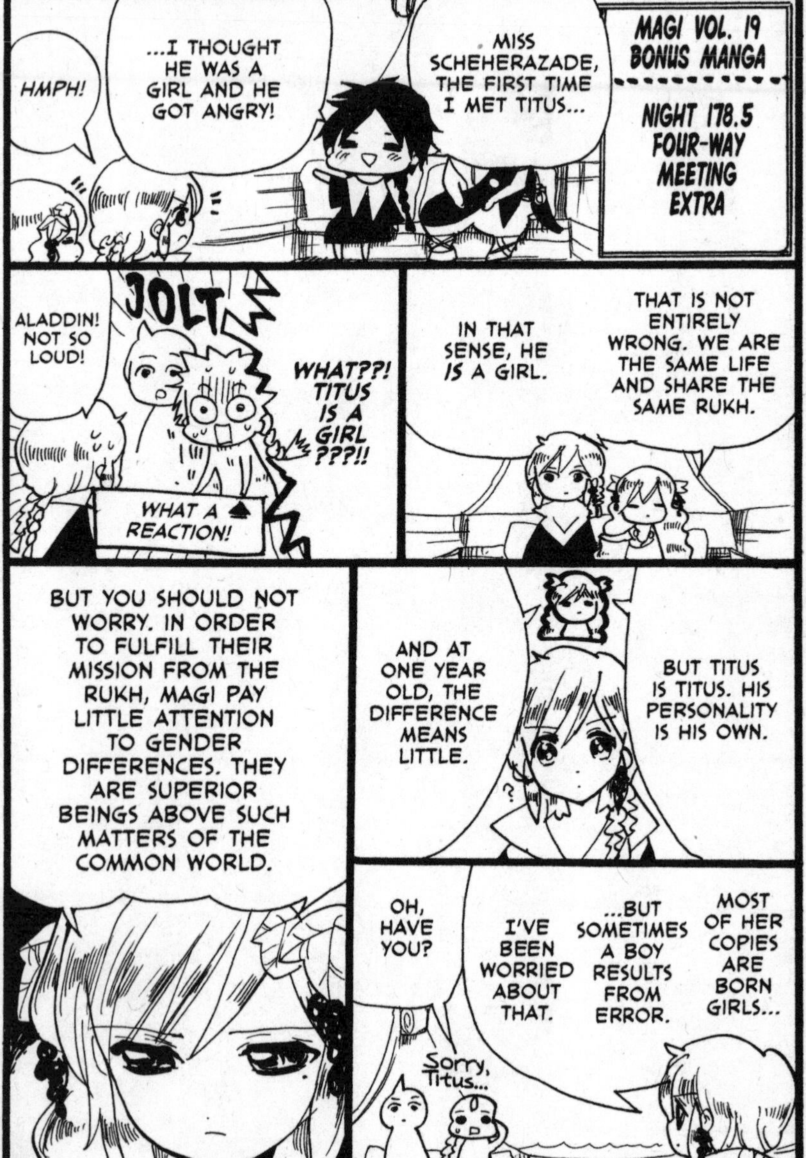
MAGI VOL. 19 BONUS MANGA
NIGHT 178.5 FOUR-WAY MEETING EXTRA
MISS SCHEHERAZADE, THE FIRST TIME I MET TITUS...
...I THOUGHT HE WAS A GIRL AND HE GOT ANGRY!
HMPH!
THAT IS NOT ENTIRELY WRONG. WE ARE THE SAME LIFE AND SHARE THE SAME RUKH.
IN THAT SENSE, HE *IS* A GIRL.
WHAT??! TITUS IS A GIRL???!!
JOLT
ALADDIN! NOT SO LOUD!
WHAT A REACTION!
BUT TITUS IS TITUS. HIS PERSONALITY IS HIS OWN.
AND AT ONE YEAR OLD, THE DIFFERENCE MEANS LITTLE.
MOST OF HER COPIES ARE BORN GIRLS...
...BUT SOMETIMES A BOY RESULTS FROM ERROR.
I'VE BEEN WORRIED ABOUT THAT.
OH, HAVE YOU?
Sorry, Titus...
BUT YOU SHOULD NOT WORRY. IN ORDER TO FULFILL THEIR MISSION FROM THE RUKH, MAGI PAY LITTLE ATTENTION TO GENDER DIFFERENCES. THEY ARE SUPERIOR BEINGS ABOVE SUCH MATTERS OF THE COMMON WORLD.

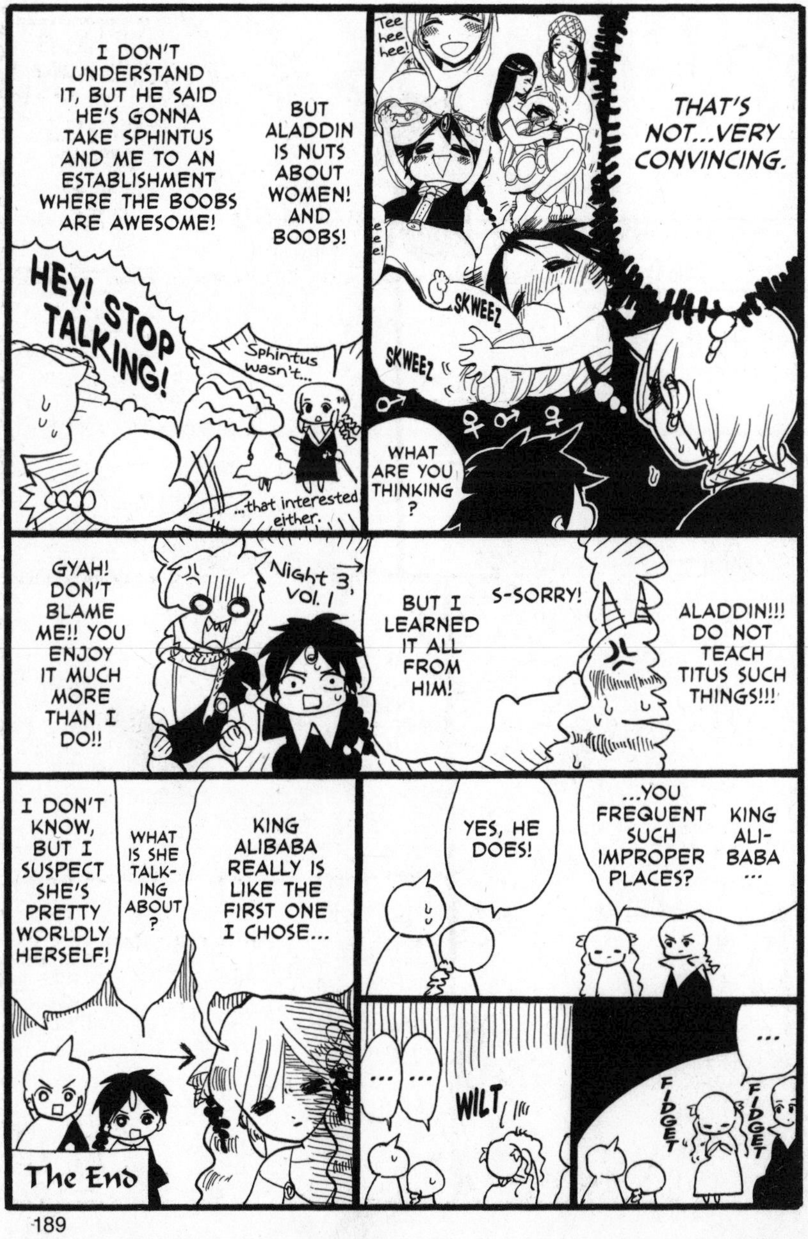
Tee hee hee!
THAT'S NOT...VERY CONVINCING.
SKWEEZ
SKWEEZ
WHAT ARE YOU THINKING?
BUT ALADDIN IS NUTS ABOUT WOMEN! AND BOOBS!
I DON'T UNDERSTAND IT, BUT HE SAID HE'S GONNA TAKE SPHINTUS AND ME TO AN ESTABLISHMENT WHERE THE BOOBS ARE AWESOME!
HEY! STOP TALKING!
Sphintus wasn't...
...that interested either.
ALADDIN!!! DO NOT TEACH TITUS SUCH THINGS!!!
S-SORRY!
BUT I LEARNED IT ALL FROM HIM!
Night 3, Vol. 1
GYAH! DON'T BLAME ME!! YOU ENJOY IT MUCH MORE THAN I DO!!
KING ALI-BABA...
...YOU FREQUENT SUCH IMPROPER PLACES?
YES, HE DOES!
...
FIDGET
FIDGET
WILT
...
...
KING ALIBABA REALLY IS LIKE THE FIRST ONE I CHOSE...
WHAT IS SHE TALKING ABOUT?
I DON'T KNOW, BUT I SUSPECT SHE'S PRETTY WORLDLY HERSELF!
The End

You're reading the
WRONG WAY

◇◇◇◇◇◇◇◇◇◇◇◇◇◇◇◇◇◇◇◇◇◇◇◇◇◇◇◇◇

MAGI reads from right to left, starting in
the upper-right corner. Japanese is read
from **right** to **left**, meaning that action,
sound effects, and word-balloon order are
completely reversed from English order.

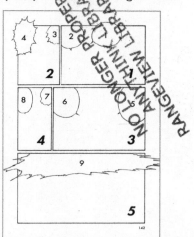